CAREER
OPPORTUNITIES

WORKING WITH ANIMALS

CAREER
OPPORTUNITIES

WORKING WITH ANIMALS

SHELLY FIELD

✓®Checkmark Books®
An Infobase Learning Company

Checkmark Books
An imprint of Infobase Learning
132 West 31st Street
New York NY 10001

Library of Congress Cataloging-in-Publication Data
Field, Shelly.
  Career opportunities working with animals / Shelly Field. — 1st ed.
      p. cm.
  Includes bibliographical references and index.
  ISBN-13: 978-0-8160-7782-3 (hardcover : alk. paper)
  ISBN-10: 0-8160-7782-7 (hardcover : alk. paper)
  ISBN-13: 978-0-8160-7783-0 (pbk. : alk. paper)
  ISBN-10: 0-8160-7783-5 (pbk. : alk. paper) 1. Veterinary medicine—Vocational guidance. 2. Veterinary medicine—
Vocational guidance—United States. I. Title.
  SF756.28.F54 2011
  636.089023—dc22
                                2011009180

Checkmark Books are available at special discounts when purchased in bulk quantities for businesses, associations, institutions, or sales promotions. Please call our Special Sales Department in New York at (212) 967-8800 or (800) 322-8755.

You can find Checkmark Books on the World Wide Web at http://www.infobaselearning.com

Text design by Kerry Casey
Composition by Julie Adams
Cover printed by Sheridan Printing, Ann Arbor, Mich.
Book printed and bound by Sheridan Printing, Ann Arbor, Mich.
Date printed: December 2011
Printed in the United States of America

10 9 8 7 6 5 4 3 2 1

CONTENTS

HOW TO USE THIS BOOK

Thousands of people work with animals in some capacity. There are many more who want to enter the industry but have no idea what opportunities are out there or how to go about getting a job. If you are thinking about a career related to animals in some manner, this book is for you!

According to the 2007 edition of the *U.S. Pet Ownership & Demographics Sourcebook,* in 2006 there were more than 72 million pet dogs in the United States and nearly 82 million pet cats. That same book indicates that nearly half of the pet owners considered their pets to be family members.

As of this writing, those numbers have in all likelihood increased. More than ever before, pets are considered to be part of the family. Thanks to this attitude toward pets, pet supplies, accessories, food, and other pet merchandise have grown into a multibillion-dollar industry. This attitude has also affected veterinary care. Years ago pet owners brought their pets to veterinarians for routine or acute veterinary care; today many people frequently use vets for preventive care as well.

Our love for pets has also spawned new businesses. There are doggie day-care centers, pet spas, and pet hotels. There are even bakeries that specialize exclusively in pet treats. For those seeking to have their own animal-related businesses, there is a plethora of possibilities, ranging from in-home doggie day care to dog training to grooming to creating pet fashions.

Pets are now big business, and this business can translate into a career that might be just right for you.

It is essential to know that working in the pet-care industry is only one option for those looking for a career working with animals. There are many others for you to choose from, depending on your specific career aspirations.

There are career opportunities working with large animals and wildlife; opportunities working in zoos, sanctuaries, refuges, and aquariums; and opportunities working with animals at racetracks, theme parks, and circuses. There are opportunities to work with animals in the entertainment industry and on television shows and movie sets. There are also magazines and Web sites geared toward animals, each of which offers an array of interesting opportunities.

Career opportunities to work with animals exist in the private sector and in the government, as well as in the for-profit and nonprofit arenas. Some careers are directly related to working hands-on with animals; others are more business-oriented. The choice is yours.

Career Opportunities Working with Animals is a comprehensive source for learning about job opportunities in this growing field. Reading this book will give you an edge over other applicants for jobs in the field. It will give you ideas about careers you might not have known about and will help you to turn your passion into a great career.

This book was written for everyone who aspires to work with animals but does not know all the career options, how to get a job, or how to succeed in this chosen profession. This book was written for you!

The jobs discussed in *Career Opportunities Working with Animals* include veterinarians and paraprofessionals, business-oriented careers in the industry, sales, and much, much more. It covers jobs in zoos, aquariums, shelters, racetracks, and jobs with animal advocacy groups.

The animal and pet industry offers an array of opportunities and requires people having a variety of skills and talents. The industry needs veterinarians, technicians, technologists, secretaries, receptionists, salespeople, publicists, trainers, educators, referees, judges, store managers, webmasters, marketing professionals, and more. It needs special-event coordinators, advertising directors, copywriters, Web content producers—the list goes on.

The trick to locating the job you want is developing your skills and using them to get you in the door. Once inside, you can climb the career ladder to success.

Read through this book and determine what careers you are qualified for or interested in. Learn what education, training, and skills are needed to enter the field you want to enter. You can then work toward having an interesting, exciting, and financially rewarding career working with animals.

Sources of Information

Information for this book was obtained through interviews, questionnaires, surveys, and a variety of books, magazines, newsletters, television and radio programs, and Web sites. Some information came through personal experience volunteering with dog rescue organizations as well as assisting with fund-raising, special events, public relations, and publicity for animal shelters and animal advocacy groups. Other data were obtained from business associates, colleagues, and friends who work for shelters, animal advocacy groups, the veterinary field, and various areas of the pet industry.

Among the people interviewed were men and women who have careers working with animals in a wide array of areas, including the pet industry, animal advocacy organizations, shelters, sanctuaries, zoos, and aquariums. Also interviewed were those who work in animal health and welfare and education, racing and entertainment, pet-oriented magazines, Web sites, and television shows. These individuals worked not only hands-on with animals, but also in business, administration, and support. Also interviewed were representatives from schools, colleges, personnel offices, and trade associations.

Organization of Material

Career Opportunities Working with Animals is divided into nine general employment sections. These sections are Veterinary Medicine; Veterinary Offices, Hospitals, and Clinics; Shelters, Sanctuaries, and Refuges; Animal Advocacy Organizations; Zoos and Aquariums; Pet Food, Pet Supply, and Pet Merchandise Stores; Pets; Horses; and Miscellaneous. Within each of these sections are descriptions of individual careers.

There are two components of each job classification. The first offers job information in abbreviated form. The second presents information in a narrative text. In addition to the basic career description, you will find information on unions and/or associations and tips for entry into the profession.

Seven appendixes are offered to help you locate the information you might want or need to begin looking for a job in the field or to climb the career ladder if you are already working in the industry.

Physical and e-mail addresses (when available) and Web sites are included so that you can send your résumé to the appropriate potential employer. You can also use these appendixes to assist you in locating internships or to obtain general information about a specific job.

These appendixes include veterinary colleges accredited by the American Veterinary Medical Association (AVMA); colleges with programs for training veterinary technicians and technologists that are accredited by the AVMA Committee on Veterinary Technicians Education and Activities (CVTEA); a directory of selected zoos, aquariums, and sanctuaries located in the United States; a selected listing of animal advocacy organizations in the United States; a listing of Thoroughbred racetracks in the United States; a listing of harness racing tracks in the United States; career and job Web sites; and trade associations and unions. A bibliography of books and periodicals related to animals is also included.

There is a wide variety of careers available for those who want to work with animals. These careers can be both exciting and fulfilling. With talent, training, the right opportunities, a few connections, and a little bit of luck, you can succeed.

A career involving animals is waiting for you. You just have to go after it. Persevere. I know if you do, you will make it.

Shelly Field
www.shellyfield.com

This book is dedicated to our favorite chocolate lab, Quincy,
and to the memory of
Honey, Samantha, Tiny, Chelsea, CousCous,
and all the other pets in our lives
who have been loved and are now missed

ACKNOWLEDGMENTS

I would like to thank every individual, company, zoo, animal advocacy group, corporation, agency, and association that provided information, assistance, and encouragement for this book.

I acknowledge with appreciation my editor, James Chambers, for his continuous help and encouragement. I would also like to express my sincere gratitude to Matthew Anderson, project editor for this book.

Others whose help was invaluable include: Ellen Ackerman; Harrison Allen; Julie Allen; Animals Alive; Dan Barrett; Ryan Barrett; Alan Barrish; Cindy Bennedum; Warren Bergstrom; Steve Blackman; Linda Bonsante; Bronx Zoo; Theresa Bull-Giglio; Sue Cabot; Earl "Speedo" Carroll; Catskill Regional Medical Center, Harris, N.Y.; Anthony Cellini, Town of Thompson Supervisor; Dr. Jessica L. Cohen; Norman Cohen; Community Employment Training Center, Las Vegas, Nev.; Jan Cornelius; Crawford Memorial Library Staff; Meike Cryan; Dewit Community Library; Mark DiRaffaele; Direct Mail/Marketing Association, Inc.; Direct Marketing Educational Foundation, Inc.; Scott Edwards; Michelle Edwards; Ernest Evans; Deborah K. Field, Esq.; Gregg Field; Lillian (Cookie) Field; Mike Field; Robert Field; Finkelstein Memorial Library Staff; Friends of Animals; Carman Garufi; John Gatto; Shelia Gatto; Alex Goldman; Sam Goldych; Greyhound Rescue Inc.; Gail Haberle; Lillian Hendrickson; Tom Hendrickson; Herman Memorial Library Staff; Joan Howard; Humane Association of CNY, Inc.; Humane Society of the United States; International Society of Animal Rights; Christine Jackson; Jimmy "Handyman" Jones; Katterskill Animal League; Bruce Kohl; Dennis Lessard; Karen Leever; LaMae Little; John Manzi; Tony Marsallo; Robert Masters, Esq.; Richard Mayfield; Phillip Mestman; Rima Mestman; Beverly Michaels, Esq.; Middletown Humane Society; Larry Miller; Monticello Central High School Guidance Department; Monticello Central School High School Library Staff; Monticello Central School Middle School Library Staff; Monticello Raceway; Mike Moore; Sharon Morris; Ellis Norman; North American Judges and Stewards Association; Ivy Pass; PETA; Barbara Pietrangelo; Public Relations Society of America; Doug Puppel; Harvey Rachlin; Ramapo Catskill Library System; Rosamond Gifford Zoo; Bob Rosen; Donna Salyers; Bob Saludares; Jefferey Serrette; Eva Shain; Frank Shain; Marjorie Snyder; John Sohigian, Orange County Choppers; Laura Solomon; Bob Sparks; Ron Scott Stevens; Matthew E. Strong; Sullivan County SPCA; Thrall Library Staff; Trevor Zoo; United States Department of Labor; United States Trotting Association; Brian Vargas; Brian Anthony Vargas; Sarah Ann Vargas; Amy Vasquez; Pat Vasquez; Kaytee Warren; Weimaraner Club of Greater St. Louis; Weimaraner Club of America; Rebecca J. Weimer; Marc Weiswasser; Cindy Whitcomb; Carol Williams; Chet Williams; and John Williams.

My thanks also to the many people, companies, and organizations who provided information and material for this book who wish to remain anonymous.

INTRODUCTION

If you have a love for animals and want to translate that love into a career, you have picked the right book. Career opportunities working with animals are huge and far-reaching. There is a wide array of career options in a variety of fields. One of them might be the career of your dreams.

When most people think of working with animals, they frequently picture some of the more well-known jobs such as veterinarian, veterinary technician, dog groomer, or jockey. While these are a number of the more traditional careers working with animals, they are just the tip of the iceberg. There are many more possibilities.

Depending on career aspirations, talents, skills, and education, the sky is the limit. Many choose careers involving direct contact with animals; others select careers in which they can help animals in some manner yet do not have direct contact with them.

There are some individuals who choose to work with domesticated animals, while others aspire to work with wildlife, fish, marine mammals, and other sea life.

Some choose to work in veterinary offices, animal hospitals, or shelters. The career path of others might lead them to zoos, aquariums, sanctuaries, refuges, or even the circus. There are a large number of individuals interested in working with animals who find rewarding careers in animal advocacy and animal rights organizations helping to assure that animals that cannot speak for themselves are protected. Others fulfill their passion by working in the conservation or rehabilitation of animals.

Many also work in businesses related to animals in some capacity. Some find careers working in an array of retail and wholesale areas of the animal and/or pet-care industry.

There are those who train animals, care for animals, and breed animals. There are others who find careers working with animals in various areas of the entertainment industry, and even in police work. Some have found ways to use their entrepreneurial spirit and create businesses working with animals.

Thousands and thousands of people work with animals in various capacities. One of them can be you! If you have a love of animals and wish you could turn that passion into a profession, no matter what you want to do, this book is for you.

It is an interesting concept to many that they can actually have a job doing something that they enjoy or work in an industry that they love. It's difficult for many to believe that they can be that lucky.

This book was written for everyone who has a passion for animals and wishes they could find a way to have a great career working with them in some capacity. This book can help make that dream a reality!

It is important to know that almost any talent you have can be applied to obtaining a job working with animals. The possibilities are endless. You can be anything from a veterinarian to the executive director of a zoo; you might become an animal trainer at an aquarium or a humane educator, a groom at a racetrack, or a veterinary assistant.

You might become a receptionist at an animal hospital or an adoption counselor at a shelter. Perhaps you want a career in which you can assure animals are treated humanely on television or movie sets. If you prefer, your job working with animals might be that of a pet sitter, pet groomer, dog trainer, or doggie day-care worker. You might even design clothes and accessories for pets. Maybe you want to become a professional dog handler.

You might want to work in some aspect of the animal advocacy movement. Perhaps you want to use your skills to handle public relations for an animal advocacy group or a zoo or aquarium. Maybe you want to use your skills to put together special events that benefit an animal advocacy organization. You might want to become the webmaster, Web Site Marketing Director, or content producer for an animal advocacy organization, zoo, or aquarium. The choice is yours.

As you read the various sections in this book searching for the perfect job, keep in mind that every job can be a learning experience and a stepping-stone to the next level. This book provides the guidelines. You have to do the rest.

Within each section of this book, you will find all of the information necessary to acquaint you with most of the important jobs in the industry. Following is a key to the organization of each entry.

Alternate Titles

Many jobs are known by alternate titles. The duties of these jobs are the same; only the name is different. Titles vary from company to company, organization to organization, and facility to facility.

Career Ladder

The career ladder illustrates a normal job progression. Remember that in many organizations, there are no hard-and-fast rules to climbing the career ladder. Job progression may not necessarily follow a precise order. Depending on your skills, talents, education, drive, determination, and the specific organization for which you work, you may be able to skip a rung on the ladder.

Position Description

Every effort has been made to give well-rounded job descriptions. Keep in mind that no two companies or organizations are structured exactly the same. Therefore, no two jobs will be identical.

Salaries

Salary ranges for the job titles in this book are as accurate as possible. Salaries for jobs working with animals reflect many variables. These include the individual's experience, responsibilities, and position. Earnings are also dependent on the specific company or organization for which an individual works, as well as its prestige, popularity, and budget.

It should be noted that earnings for those working in the nonprofit sector often are lower than those performing similar jobs in the for-profit world.

Employment Prospects

If you choose a job that has an EXCELLENT, GOOD, or FAIR rating, you are lucky. You will have an easier time finding a job. If, however, you would like to work at a job that has a POOR rating, don't despair. The rating only means that it may be difficult to obtain a job, not that finding one is totally impossible.

Advancement Prospects

Try to be as cooperative and helpful as possible in the workplace. Don't attempt to see how little work you can do. Be enthusiastic, energetic, and outgoing. Go that extra step that no one expects. Learn as much as you can. When a job advancement possibility opens up, make sure that you're prepared to take advantage of it.

A variety of options for career advancement are included. However, as noted previously, you should be aware that there are no hard-and-fast rules for climbing the career ladder. While work performance is important, advancement in many jobs is based on experience, education, training, employee attitude, talent, and individual career aspirations.

Many companies promote from within. The best way to advance your career is to get in the door at any level and then climb the career ladder.

Education and Training

This section presents the minimum educational and training requirements for each job area. This does not mean that you should limit yourself. Try to get the best training and education possible.

A college degree or background does not guarantee a job in any industry, but it might help prepare a person for life in the workplace. Education and training also encompass courses, seminars, programs, on-the-job training, and learning from others. Volunteer work, internships, and even helping out in family businesses can look good on your résumé.

Experience, Skills, and Personality Traits

This section indicates experience requirements as well as specific skills and personality traits necessary for each job. These will differ from job to job. No matter what type of career you want, having an outgoing personality helps. Networking is essential to success in every industry. Contacts are always important in both obtaining a job and advancing your career, so make as many as you can.

Special Requirements

This section covers any special licensing and credentials that may be required for a specific job.

Unions and Associations

This section offers other sources for career information and assistance. Unions and trade associations offer valuable help in obtaining career guidance, support, and contacts. They may also offer training, continuing education, scholarships, fellowships, seminars, and other beneficial programs.

Tips for Entry

Use this section to gather ideas on how to prepare for a job, secure a job, or gain entry into an area of interest.

When applying for any job, always be as professional as possible. Dress neatly and conservatively. Do not wear sneakers. Do not chew gum. Do not smoke. Do not wear heavy perfume or cologne.

Always have a few copies of your résumé with you. These, too, should look neat and professional. Have them typed and presented well, checked and rechecked for grammar, spelling, and content.

If asked to fill in an application, fill in the entire application even if you have a résumé with you. Print your information neatly.

Be prepared when applying for jobs and filling in applications. Make sure you know your Social Security number. Ask people in advance whether you can use them as references. Make sure you know their full names, addresses, e-mail addresses, and phone numbers. Try to secure at least three personal references as well as three professional references.

The ability to go online, whether from your home computer or one in a school or public library, puts you at a great advantage. No matter which aspect of the industry piques your interest, you need to be computer-literate.

Many animal advocacy organizations, zoos, aquariums, shelters, and other companies and other animal-oriented organizations today have Web sites that may be helpful in your quest for that perfect job. You can obtain information about them and their current job opportunities. You can also read up on industry news or even check the classifieds from newspapers in different geographical locations via their Web sites.

No matter what your career aspirations, get the best training possible. Refine your skills. Talk to people who are successful in the line of work you are trying to enter and ask for help. Most people are glad to provide it.

Use every contact you have. Don't get hung up on the idea that you want to get a job on your own. If you are lucky enough to know someone who can help you obtain a job you want, take him or her up on it. You'll have to prove yourself at the interview and on the job. Nobody can do that for you. (Remember to send a thank-you note to the person who helped you as well as to the interviewer after the interview.)

Once you get your foot in the door, learn as much as you can. As noted previously, doing a little bit more than is expected will be helpful in your career. Be cooperative. Be a team player. Don't burn bridges; it can hurt your career. Ask for help. Network. Find a mentor.

The last piece of advice in this section is to be on time for everything. This includes job interviews, phone calls, work, and meetings. People will remember when you are habitually late, and it will work against you in advancing your career.

Do not be afraid to pursue your dream job. You can have a career that will enable you to get up each morning happy that you are going to work. Do not get discouraged during your job-hunting period. Not everyone lands the first job they apply for.

You may have to pay your dues before you get the job you want. You may have to knock on a lot of doors, send out a lot of résumés, and apply for a lot of jobs you don't get, but eventually you can find the job of your dreams.

Have faith and confidence in yourself. You will make it to where you are headed eventually, but you must persevere. In many instances the individual who did not make it in the career he or she wanted is the one who gave up too soon and did not wait that extra day.

What you need to remember is that if you want to follow your passion and reach for your dreams, you can attain them if you work hard and prepare.

You have already taken the first step by picking up this book. Have fun reading it. Use it. It will help you find a career that you will truly love. When you do get the job of your dreams, do someone else a favor and pass along the benefit of your knowledge.

We love to hear success stories about your career and how this book helped you. If you have a story and want to share it, go to www.shellyfield.com. I hope to hear from you!

Good luck.

—Shelly Field

VETERINARY MEDICINE

SMALL ANIMAL VETERINARIAN

CAREER PROFILE

Duties: Perform examinations; give vaccinations; diagnose diseases; diagnose injuries; perform surgeries

Alternate Title(s): Vet; Small Animal Practitioner; Animal Shelter Specialist

Salary Range: $38,000 to $140,000+

Employment Prospects: Excellent

Advancement Prospects: Good

Best Geographical Locations for Position: Positions located throughout the country

Prerequisites:

Education or Training—Doctor of veterinary medicine degree from an accredited school of veterinary medicine; continuing education required

Experience and Qualifications—Experience working in veterinary office, shelters, humane societies, etc.

Special Skills and Personality Traits—Excellent judgment; quick thinking; compassion; people skills; communication skills; strong stomach

CAREER LADDER

Small Animal Veterinarian in Private Practice with Large Roster of Patients; Small Animal Veterinarian in Larger, More Exclusive Practice; or Small Animal Veterinarian in Specialty Field

Small Animal Veterinarian

Veterinary Student; Veterinary Intern; Veterinary Resident

Special Requirements—State licensing required

Position Description

Veterinarians work with animals of various sizes and breeds, preventing, diagnosing, and treating illnesses, diseases, and injuries. The mission of most veterinarians is to help animals have healthier, happier, and more comfortable lives.

Veterinarians care for the health of a variety of types of animals. Some take care of pets. Others take care of livestock. Still others care for animals in zoos, racetracks, aquariums, laboratories, shelters, or other locations. There are large animal veterinarians, research veterinarians, wildlife veterinarians, and Small Animal Veterinarians, among others. This entry will cover Small Animal Veterinarians.

Small Animal Veterinarians primarily care for companion animals such as dogs and cats. They may, however, also care for other animals that people keep as pets such as birds, rabbits, ferrets, and reptiles.

Small Animal Veterinarians have a number of responsibilities depending on their specific employment situation. Individuals may work in private practice, in clinics, shelters, or animal hospitals, among other locations. For many, the job of a Small Animal Veterinarian is similar to a family practitioner in that the individual provides general veterinary care. Some specialize in certain fields such as oncology, surgery, orthopedics, dentistry, chiropractic, or alternative medicine.

As part of the job, veterinarians (or vets as they are often called) are expected to keep animals as healthy as possible. Many people bring their pets to the veterinarian for preventive care. Vets may schedule well-care visits to be sure the animal's health is optimum. They may, for example, vaccinate pets against disease such as rabies, distemper, parvovirus, Lyme disease, feline AIDS, feline leukemia, and more.

In addition to vaccinations, vets may give animals general checkups, perform physical examinations, and administer various tests, including blood work, urinalysis, and specialized tests if warranted.

Small Animal Veterinarians frequently provide advice on exercise or diets to owners for their pets. They may additionally consult on the best foods and nutritional supplements to give animals.

Many pet owners bring their pets to the vet when their pets are experiencing behavioral issues. Sometimes these concerns are minor. In other situations behavioral problems may be major issues. Vets are expected to advise owners about how to best deal with their pet's behavior issues.

Small Animal Veterinarians are responsible for diagnosing animal health problems. When an animal is sick, the veterinarian must determine what specific infection or illness it has and then prescribe treatment. When animals are very ill or in pain and cannot be helped, the veterinarian may recommend putting the animal to sleep or honor their owner's wishes to euthanize them. For some, this is the most difficult part of the job.

Some Small Animal Veterinarians perform surgery to correct health problems or to spay or neuter animals. They also treat and dress wounds and set fractures.

Vets working in shelters, sanctuaries, or humane societies may have additional responsibilities. For example, they are often responsible for counseling people on the compassionate treatment of animals. They care for animals that have been abused, abandoned, and neglected, helping them to regain their health and find homes. Individuals often do a great deal of spaying and neutering of animals in order to help control the population of abandoned animals.

As in private practice, Small Animal Veterinarians working in shelters and humane societies set a lot of bones and treat a lot of injuries. This is especially common in shelters where animals are brought in after being in hit by vehicles. Vets in these situations may help determine the temperament of animals and assist in behavioral care. This is useful in finding new homes for abandoned and abused animals.

Pets in shelter situations are frequently stressed and scared. Many have not been cared for properly and are either ill or at risk of becoming ill. Vets working in shelters must deal with the transmission and control of diseases that sometimes affect large groups of animals kept in proximity to one another, including things like ringworm, kennel cough, parvo, fleas, and other infectious diseases.

No matter what the employment setting of Small Animal Veterinarians, they may work extended and weekend hours in response to emergencies. Whether keeping pets healthy, treating them for injuries or illness, or even having to euthanize them, most Small Animal Veterinarians feel their job is a calling.

Salaries

Earnings for Small Animal Veterinarians can vary greatly depending on their specific employment situation. Earnings are also dependent on the experience, education, and specialty of the vet as well as the geographic area. Some of these veterinarians have earnings starting at approximately $38,000, while others have earnings of $140,000 or more. Those at the higher end of the scale are generally specialists addressing issues such as cardiology, dentistry, surgery, oncology, or orthopedics.

Veterinarians working in a pet store or clinic may be paid by the hour or the week. For vets working in their own private practice, the sky is the limit in terms of earnings depending on the size of their practice. According to the Bureau of Labor Statistics, the median salary for veterinarians at this writing is close to $90,000.

Employment Prospects

Employment prospects are excellent for qualified individuals who have fulfilled the requirements to become Small Animal Veterinarians. Individuals may work in a number of settings. These may include working as employees in the private practice of other veterinarians and working for clinics, shelters, humane societies, pet stores, or emergency rooms. Many Small Animal Veterinarians open up their own practice.

Advancement Prospects

Advancement prospects are good for Small Animal Veterinarians. Individuals may climb the career ladder in a number of ways depending on their aspirations. Those working in clinics or shelters may find employment in larger shelters or clinics. Those working in pet stores may find employment in larger pet stores or in the private practice of other veterinarians.

Individuals working as employees in the private practice of other veterinarians may find employment at larger or more prestigious veterinary offices. They might also become partners or might even open their own veterinary practice. Veterinarians with their own practice climb the career ladder by doing more business and obtaining more clients.

Education and Training

In order to become a veterinarian, an individual must graduate with a doctor of veterinary medicine degree from an accredited college of veterinary medicine. At this time there are 28 colleges in 26 states that are accredited by the Council on Education of the American Veterinary Medical Association (AVMA) offering this four-year program. Once an individual has graduated, he or she receives either the designation D.V.M. or V.M.D.

While prerequisites for admission to this program vary by school, each at least requires between 45 and 90 semester hours of undergraduate work. With that being said, most individuals entering these programs hold a bachelor's degree. With only 28 programs in the United States, competition is fierce.

Those interested in pursuing a career in this field should take classes in the sciences, such as organic and inorganic chemistry, physics, biochemistry, biology, animal biology, animal nutrition, zoology, etc.

In order to be accepted into a veterinary program, individuals must also take a number of exams, such as the Graduate Record Examination (GRE), the Veterinary College Admission Test (VCAT), or the Medical College Admission Test (MCAT), depending on the requirements of the school.

While those who graduate with a doctorate in veterinary medicine may practice once they become licensed, some enter a one- or two-year internship. Those who want to be board certified in a specific area must also complete a three- to four-year residency program that provides training in one of the 38 AVMA specialties.

Individuals are expected to take continuing education classes in order to maintain their license.

Experience, Skills, and Personality Traits

Most Small Animal Veterinarians obtain experience by working in veterinary offices, clinics, or shelters before graduating from veterinary programs. In order to be successful in this line of work, Small Animal Veterinarians need to be compassionate, patient, kindhearted individuals with a strong love for animals. A scientific aptitude is needed as well as manual dexterity.

Excellent judgment is necessary as veterinarians must think quickly and make effective decisions. Verbal communication skills are essential, as are people skills.

Special Requirements

Veterinarians in every state are required to be licensed before they can practice. Licensing is governed by each state. Therefore, requirements for licensure are not standardized. Generally, in order to become licensed, individuals must have graduated from an accredited veterinary program with a D.V.M. degree as well as passed a national board examination called the North American Veterinary Licensing Exam. This test is an eight-hour exam composed of 360 multiple-choice questions that cover veterinary medicine in addition to a section covering diagnostic skills.

As mentioned previously, there are continuing education requirements for licensed veterinarians, which are necessary to demonstrate knowledge of medical and veterinary advancements.

Unions and Associations

Small Animal Veterinarians generally belong to the AVMA.

Tips for Entry

1. If you are still in school and considering becoming a veterinarian, make sure you take classes in the sciences.
2. Try to get a job with a veterinarian before you go to veterinary school. You will gain valuable experience and make sure this is the right career choice for you. The vet you work with might also be a good reference when you apply to veterinary school.
3. Send your résumé and a short cover letter to veterinarians, animal emergency hospitals, shelters, and humane societies to see if they have openings. Remember to ask that your résumé be kept on file if there are no current openings.
4. Check out openings online. Start with some of the more traditional job sites such as Monster.com. Then look on the Web sites of humane societies, societies for the prevention of cruelty to animals, and shelters.

LARGE ANIMAL VETERINARIAN

Position Description

Veterinarians work with animals of various sizes and breeds, preventing, diagnosing and treating illnesses, disease, and injuries. The mission of most vets is to help animals have healthier, happier, and more comfortable lives.

Veterinarians care for the health of a variety of types of animals. Some take care of pets. Some care for animals in zoos, racetracks, aquariums, laboratories, shelters, or more. Others take care of livestock and other large animals.

Veterinarians often have some sort of specialty. There are small animal veterinarians, research veterinarians, wildlife veterinarians, and Large Animal Veterinarians, among others. This entry will cover Large Animal Veterinarians.

Large Animal Veterinarians primarily care for horses, cows, goats, sheep, pigs, horses, and so on. They must be aware of the special physiology of large animals. Instead of primarily working in an office or clinical setting, Large Animal Veterinarians often drive to see their patients, visiting ranches or farms when

veterinary services are needed. As part of the job, veterinarians (or vets as they are often called) are expected to keep animals as healthy as possible. Much of this involves preventive care to maintain the health of the animals. While Large Animal Veterinarians may care for individual animals, they are frequently called upon to provide services for full herds of cattle or stables of animals.

Large Animal Veterinarians have varied responsibilities. While visiting farms or ranches to help farmers keep their livestock healthy, they may test for and vaccinate animals against diseases. During these visits they may also consult with farm or ranch owners and managers regarding animal production, feeding, and housing issues. In addition to vaccinations, vets may give animals general checkups and physical examinations and administer various tests, including blood work, urinalysis, and specialized tests if warranted.

Large animals frequently get puncture wounds or fracture limbs. Vets are expected to treat and dress wounds and set fractures. A major responsibility of Large Animal Veterinarians is assisting animals with difficult births. In some situations, this may mean that the vet may need to perform surgery such as a C-section. Because farm animals are often too large to transport, the vet may need to perform surgery at the farm or ranch. Another responsibility of Large Animal Veterinarians is assisting the farmer in assuring that his or her livestock is getting the correct nutrition.

Large Animals Veterinarians are expected to diagnose animal health problems. When an animal is sick, the individual is responsible for determining what specific infection or illness it has and then prescribing the treatment. In situations where a vet is caring for livestock in which products such as milk are used for human consumption, this is especially important.

Large Animal Veterinarians generally have to travel a great deal more than small animal veterinarians do. As farm animals are large and not domesticated, vets in this line of work stand the chance of being kicked or bitten. Additionally, these vets have to be able to physically handle the size and weight of many of the animals they care for.

Some Large Animal Veterinarians don't work with animals on farms or ranches. Instead, they work at racetracks handling the veterinary needs of racehorses. Other Large Animal Veterinarians oversee the health of large animals in zoos. Still others work for the federal government assuring that the animals and by-products used for human consumption are healthy and treated humanely.

It should be noted that there are some Large Animal Veterinarians who perform research instead of actually caring for animals. These individuals assist other medical professionals in learning more about both human and animal health.

Large Animal Veterinarians may work long hours when handling emergencies or attending to animals in need of care. Most Large Animal Veterinarians, however, enjoy their work and are very dedicated to their career, knowing that they make an impact on the health and safety of farm animals and the community at large.

Salaries

Earnings for Large Animal Veterinarians can vary greatly depending on a number of factors, including the specific employment situation of the individual, his or her experience, education, specialty, and geographic area. Veterinarians who work exclusively with large animals generally earn more than their counterparts who work with small animals.

Veterinarians' earnings start at approximately $42,000, while others have earnings of $150,000 or more. Those at the higher end of the scale are generally specialists addressing issues such as cardiology, dentistry, surgery, oncology, or orthopedics among others, or those working in research.

For vets with their own private practice, the sky is the limit in terms of earnings, depending on the size of their practice. According to the Bureau of Labor Statistics, the median salary for veterinarians at this writing is close to $80,000.

Employment Prospects

As there is a shortage of veterinarians specializing in the care of large farm animals, employment prospects are excellent for qualified individuals.

Individuals may work in a number of different settings. These settings may include the private practice of other veterinarians, clinics, or their own practice. Still others work at zoos, sanctuaries, racetracks, or for the federal government.

Advancement Prospects

Advancement prospects are good for Large Animal Veterinarians. Individuals may climb the career ladder in a number of ways depending on their aspirations. Those working for other veterinarians may advance their careers by becoming partners or opening their own practice. Large Animal Veterinarians with their own practice climb the career ladder by increasing their business and obtaining more patients.

Those working for zoos, sanctuaries, or the federal government may advance their careers by landing jobs with larger, more prestigious facilities.

Education and Training

In order to become any type of veterinarian, an individual must graduate with a doctor of veterinary medicine degree from an accredited college of veterinary medicine. At this time there are 28 colleges in 26 states that are accredited by the Council on Education of the American Veterinary Medical Association (AVMA) offering this four-year program. Once an individual has graduated, he or she receives either the designation D.V.M. or V.M.D.

While prerequisites for admission to this program vary by school, each at least requires between 45 and 90 semester hours of undergraduate work. With that being said, most individuals entering these programs hold a bachelor's degree. With only 28 programs in the United States, competition is fierce.

Those interested in pursuing a career in this field should take classes in the sciences, such as organic and inorganic chemistry, physics, biochemistry, biology, animal biology, animal nutrition, zoology, etc.

In order to be accepted into one of these programs, individuals must also take a number of exams, such as the Graduate Record Examination (GRE), the Veterinary College Admission Test (VCAT), or the Medical College Admission Test (MCAT), depending on the requirements of the school.

While those who graduate with a doctor of veterinary medicine degree may practice once they become licensed, some enter a one-year internship. Those who want to be board certified in a specific area must also complete a three- to four-year residency.

Individuals are expected to take continuing education classes in order to maintain their license.

Experience, Skills, and Personality Traits

Veterinarians initially obtain experience by working in veterinary offices, clinics, or shelters before graduating from veterinary programs. After graduation, many go through a one-year internship. Those seeking to be board certified go through two-year residency programs in their specialty.

Large Animal Veterinarians should be compassionate, patient, kindhearted individuals with a strong love for animals. Excellent judgment is necessary. The ability to think quickly and make effective decisions is critical. Verbal communication skills are essential. People skills are also a must. As the animals they treat are generally larger than companion animals, it is especially important for Large Animal Veterinarians to have physical strength and stamina.

Special Requirements

Veterinarians in every state are required to be licensed before they can practice. Licensing is governed by each state, so requirements for licensure are not standardized. Generally, in order to become licensed, individuals must have graduated from an accredited veterinary program with a D.V.M. degree as well as passed a national board examination called the North American

Veterinary Licensing Exam. This test is an eight-hour exam composed of 360 multiple-choice questions that cover veterinary medicine in addition to a section covering diagnostic skills.

As mentioned previously, there are continuing education requirements for licensed veterinarians that are necessary to demonstrate knowledge of medical and veterinary advancements.

Unions and Associations

Large Animal Veterinarians generally belong to the AVMA. Individuals can find additional information on education by contacting the Association of American Veterinary Medical Colleges.

Tips for Entry

1. If you are still in school and considering becoming a veterinarian, make sure you take classes in the sciences.
2. Try to get a job with a veterinarian before you go to veterinary school. You will gain valuable experience and can make sure this is the right career choice for you. If you can land a job with a Large Animal Veterinarian, that's great. If not, a job with any type of veterinarian will be useful experience. The vet you work with might also be a good reference when you apply for veterinary school.
3. Once you are licensed (or close to being licensed), send your résumé and a short cover letter to veterinarians with whom you are interested in working. Remember to ask that your résumé be kept on file if there are no current openings.
4. Check out openings online. Start with some of the more traditional job sites such as Monster.com. Then check out career Web sites specific to the veterinary field. (Be sure to look in the appendix for some ideas.)
5. Keep in contact with your college career placement office. They often know of job opportunities.

HOLISTIC VETERINARIAN

CAREER PROFILE

Duties: Perform examinations; diagnose diseases; diagnose injuries; treat animals on a holistic level

Alternate Title(s): Vet; Alternative Medicine Veterinarian; Complementary Medicine Veterinarian

Salary Range: $38,000 to $175,000+

Employment Prospects: Excellent

Advancement Prospects: Good

Best Geographical Locations for Position: Positions located throughout the country

Prerequisites:

Education or Training—Doctor of veterinary medicine degree from an accredited school of veterinary medicine; continuing education required; continuing education classes in various areas of holistic, complementary, and integrative medicine

Experience and Qualifications—Experience working in veterinary office, shelters, humane societies, etc.; experience with various modalities of complementary medicine

CAREER LADDER

```
Holistic Veterinarian in Private Practice
with Large Roster of Patients; Holistic
Veterinarian in Specialty Field

            ↑

Holistic Veterinarian

            ↑

Veterinary Student; Veterinary Intern;
Veterinary Resident
```

Special Skills and Personality Traits—Caring of animals; understanding of complementary and holistic medicines and treatments; excellent judgment; quick thinking; compassion; people skills; communication skills

Special Requirements—State licensing required; voluntary certification available

Position Description

Veterinarians work with animals of various sizes and breeds, preventing, diagnosing, and treating illnesses, disease, and injuries. The mission of vets is to help animals have healthier, happier, and more comfortable lives. Most veterinarians today use traditional medicines and treatments when caring for animals.

As alternative medicine has become more popular, many veterinarians are now looking at treating animals in a holistic manner. Holistic Veterinarians use a variety of alternative or complementary medicines in approaching veterinary health care. Holistic treatments may be used alone or in conjunction with traditional treatments.

Like other holistic practitioners, Holistic Veterinarians focus on wellness as well as illness. They are licensed veterinarians who have chosen to obtain further and specialized training in various modalities. These might include, for example, acupuncture, acupressure, massage, aromatherapy, nutritional therapy, kinesiology, Reiki, western herbal therapy, magnetic therapy, homeopathy, and natural medicines, among others. Holistic Veterinarians may utilize one or more modality or may specialize in a specific modality.

Veterinarians care for the health of a variety of types of animals. Some take care of pets. Others take care of livestock. Still others care for animals in zoos, racetracks, shelters, or other locations.

The popularity and acceptance of holistic treatment for animals mirrors its popularity with humans. Holistic Veterinarians, like all other vets, work to keep animals as healthy as possible. Many individuals today seek out Holistic Veterinarians because of their own personal beliefs that the "natural" way may be safer and more effective than traditional medicine. Many people also turn to a holistic approach when traditional veterinary medicines or treatments don't work. Holistic Veterinarians may focus more on animal lifestyles such as diet, vitamins and minerals, exercise programs, and emotional well-being than traditional vets do.

People often bring their pets to Holistic Veterinarians for preventive care. These well-care visits can be vital to keeping an animal's health optimum. Instead of routinely giving immunizations, some Holistic Veterinarians may use alternatives to vaccinations such as homeopathic nosodes (a remedy prepared from a pathological specimen, such as blood or tissue) or titer tests (a laboratory test that measures the presence and amount of antibodies in the blood) to determine animals' immunity to specific diseases.

Holistic Veterinarians, like traditional vets, often give animals general checkups, perform physical examinations, and administer various tests, including blood work, urinalysis, and specialized tests if warranted. They also may provide advice on exercise and often some supervised training as well. Holistic vets often offer advice on diet, nutrition, and nutritional supplements that they feel can make the animal healthier.

Holistic Veterinarians frequently work with pet owners dealing with any behavioral issues the pet may have. They may, for example, offer advice on separation anxiety, chewing, integrating new pets and family members, aggression, and everything in between. Holistic vets may use behavior modification, music therapy, aromatherapy, herbal therapy, massage, and natural medicines in the course of treatment.

Holistic Veterinarians are responsible for diagnosing animal health problems. When an animal is sick, the veterinarian is responsible for determining what specific infection or illness it has and then prescribing the treatment. While the holistic vet may prescribe traditional medication at times, he or she may also utilize things like herbs, homeopathic medicines, and vitamins.

When animals are very ill or in pain and cannot be helped, the veterinarian may also honor their owners' wishes to euthanize their pets. For some, this is the most difficult part of the job. There are some Holistic Veterinarians who focus on end-of-life choices for animals, including hospice care.

Holistic Veterinarians may treat and dress wounds and set fractures. Some may also perform surgery to correct health problems or to spay or neuter animals. Others may refer patients to other vets for these services.

Holistic vets may work in a traditional office setting or may do home visits. Many holistic vets also do phone consultations. No matter what the employment setting, individuals may work extended and weekend hours in response to emergencies.

A career as a Holistic Veterinarian is the perfect choice for an individual who is dedicated to holistic medicine and healing animals.

Salaries

Earnings for Holistic Veterinarians can vary greatly depending on a number of factors. These include the specific employment situation of the individual and his or her experience, education, professional reputation, and geographic location. According to the Bureau of Labor Statistics, the median salary for all veterinarians at the time of this writing is close to $90,000.

With that being said, there are some Holistic Veterinarians who have earnings starting out at approximately $38,000, while others earn $175,000 or more. Those at the higher end of the scale are generally individuals in upscale markets who have their own practice and have built a good reputation for dealing with pets on a holistic level.

Employment Prospects

Employment prospects are excellent for qualified individuals who have fulfilled the requirements to first become veterinarians and then specialize in holistic veterinary medicine. The popularity and acceptance of holistic treatment for animals mirrors its acceptance in the health system for people. Today more people than ever are looking for a more natural and holistic way to stay healthy.

Individuals may work in a number of different settings, including as employees in the private practice of other veterinarians and working for clinics, shelters, humane societies, or in emergency rooms. The majority of Holistic Veterinarians, however, open their own practice.

Advancement Prospects

Advancement prospects are good for Holistic Veterinarians. As noted previously, the popularity and acceptance of holistic treatment for animals is on the rise. As more people look for natural and holistic ways to stay healthy, Holistic Veterinarians will become more and more popular and in demand.

Individuals may climb the career ladder in a number of ways depending on their aspirations. Individuals working as employees in the private practice of other veterinarians may find employment at larger or more prestigious veterinary offices. They might also become partners or might even open their own holistic veterinary practice. Holistic Veterinarians with their own practice can climb the career ladder by increasing their business and obtaining more clients.

Education and Training

In order to become any type of veterinarian, an individual must graduate with a doctor of veterinary medicine degree from an accredited college of veterinary medicine. At this time there are 28 colleges in 26 states that are accredited by the Council on Education of the American Veterinary Medical Association (AVMA) offering this four-year program. Once an individual has graduated, he or she receives either the designation D.V.M. or V.M.D.

While prerequisites for admission to this program vary by school, each at least requires between 45 and 90 semester hours of undergraduate work. With that being said, most individuals entering these programs hold a bachelor's degree. With only 28 programs in the United States, competition is fierce.

Those interested in pursuing a career in this field should take classes in the sciences, such as organic and inorganic chemistry, physics, biochemistry, biology, animal biology, animal nutrition, zoology, etc.

In order to be accepted into one of these programs, individuals must also take a number of exams, such as the Graduate Record Examination (GRE), the Veterinary College Admission Test (VCAT), or the Medical College Admission Test (MCAT), depending on the requirements of the school.

While those who graduate with a doctor of veterinary medicine degree may practice once they become licensed, some enter a one- or two-year internship. Those who want to be board certified in a specific area must also complete a three- to four-year residency program that provides training in one of the 38 AVMA specialties. Individuals are expected to take continuing education classes in order to maintain their license.

Holistic Veterinarians must also take additional training in the modalities in which they want to treat patients. This training might encompass classes, courses, and workshops in herbal therapy, homeopathy, acupuncture, acupressure, and massage therapy. This training may be located through various associations and organizations as well as educational institutions.

Experience, Skills, and Personality Traits

Most Holistic Veterinarians obtain experience by first working in veterinary offices, clinics, or shelters before graduating from veterinary programs. They then often seek an established Holistic Veterinarian to work under.

In order to be successful in this line of work, veterinarians need to be compassionate, patient, kindhearted individuals with a strong love for animals. An interest and belief in holistic and complementary therapies are mandatory.

Excellent judgment is necessary, as the ability to think quickly and make effective decisions is critical. Verbal communication skills are essential, as are people skills.

Special Requirements

Veterinarians in every state are required to be licensed before they can practice. Licensing is governed by each specific state, so requirements for licensure are not standardized nationally. Generally, in order to become licensed, individuals must have graduated from an accredited veterinary program with a D.V.M. degree as well as passed a national board examination called the North American Veterinary Licensing Exam. This test is an eight-hour exam composed of 360 multiple-choice questions that cover veterinary medicine in addition to a section covering diagnostic skills.

As mentioned previously, there are continuing education requirements for licensed veterinarians, which are necessary to demonstrate the individual's knowledge of medical and veterinary advancements.

Voluntary certification is also available through organizations such as the Academy of Veterinary Homeopathy (AVH).

Unions and Associations

Holistic Veterinarians may belong to a number of organizations that provide professional support and educational opportunities. Depending on the individual's interests, these may include the AVMA, the American Holistic Veterinary Medical Association, and the AVH, among others.

Tips for Entry

1. If you are still in school and considering becoming a veterinarian, make sure you take classes in the sciences.
2. Look for courses and workshops in various areas of complementary medicine. Some will be people-oriented. Others may be geared toward animals. Both will be useful.
3. Seek out the advice of a Holistic Veterinarian. Tell him or her about your aspirations and ask for advice. You might even be able to shadow him or her.
4. Consider calling a Holistic Veterinarian and asking about an internship. The experience will be well worth it.
5. Send your résumé and a cover letter to Holistic Veterinarians. Remember to ask that your résumé be kept on file if there are no current openings.
6. Check out openings online. Start with some of the more traditional job sites such as Monster.com, and go from there.

HOMEOPATHIC VETERINARIAN

Duties: Take case histories; perform examinations; diagnose diseases; diagnose injuries; treat animals with homeopathic medicines

Alternate Title(s): Vet; Alternative Medicine Veterinarian

Salary Range: $40,000 to $175,000+

Employment Prospects: Excellent

Advancement Prospects: Good

Best Geographical Locations for Position: Positions located throughout the country

Prerequisites:

Education or Training—Graduate with a doctor of veterinary medicine degree from an accredited school of veterinary medicine; continuing education required; courses, workshops, symposiums, and seminars in homeopathy and homeopathic veterinary medicine

Experience and Qualifications—Experience working in veterinary offices, shelters, humane societies, etc.; experience taking case histories and prescribing homeopathic remedies

---

CAREER LADDER

Homeopathic Veterinarian in Private Practice with Large Roster of Patients; Homeopathic Veterinarian in Specialty Field
Homeopathic Veterinarian
Veterinary Student; Veterinary Intern; Veterinary Resident

Special Skills and Personality Traits—Love of animals; understanding of homeopathy; excellent judgment; quick thinking; compassion; people skills; communication skills; listening skills; detail orientation; good memory

Special Requirements—State licensing required; voluntary certification available

Position Description

Veterinarians work with animals of various sizes and breeds, preventing, diagnosing, and treating illnesses, disease, and injuries. The mission of vets is to help animals have healthier, happier, and more comfortable lives. Most veterinarians today use traditional medicines and treatments when caring for animals.

As alternative medicine becomes more mainstream, many veterinarians are now looking at treating animals in a holistic manner using various modalities. One of these modalities is homeopathy. Homeopathy is a type of medicine based on the principles developed by Samuel Hahnemann in the late 1700s. Popular in the 1800s and early 1900s, homeopathy is once again becoming accepted as many are looking for a more natural approach to medicine and healing.

As there are homeopathic physicians who care for people, there are Homeopathic Veterinarians who care for animals. Homeopathic Veterinarians, like homeopathic physicians, treat the patient as a whole rather than treating one specific symptom. In order to do this, individuals select homeopathic remedies or medicines

that most closely match the broad range of symptoms unique to the particular patient. Homeopathic Veterinarians may care for the health of a variety of types of animals, including small animals, livestock, horses, wildlife, and more.

In addition to giving physical examinations, the Homeopathic Veterinarian, like the homeopathic physician, must take extensive case histories from the patient. As animals can't talk, the animal's owner often is of assistance in giving the veterinarian the animal's physical, mental, and emotional symptoms. The veterinarian, too, must closely observe the animal. For example, does the animal just sit quietly or is he or she excitable? Does the animal whimper? Do the animal's eyes look clear? Is his or her coat glossy or dull? Does the animal like to stay alone or does it crave attention? The answers to these questions are all helpful in making a proper diagnosis so the correct remedy can be prescribed.

Homeopathic medicine and remedies are based on the principles of a minimum dosage and like cures. Whether they are for humans or animals, they are prepared in a special manner by homeopathic pharmacists. There are literally thousands of different remedies, each prepared with different potencies, that the Homeopathic Veterinarian can prescribe.

Homeopathic Veterinarians, like traditional vets, give animals general checkups and administer various tests, including blood work, urinalysis, and physical examinations, and also specialized tests, if warranted, such as titer tests (a laboratory test that measures the presence and amount of antibodies in the blood), to determine an animal's immunity. Rather than giving routine immunizations, most Homeopathic Verterinarians may use homeopathic nosodes, remedies prepared from a pathological specimen, such as blood or tissue.

Pet owners may bring their pets to a Homeopathic Veterinarian for an acute illness, a chronic illness, or for preventive health care. Vets often offer pet owners advice on how the animal can live a healthier life, including diet and exercise recommendations.

Homeopathic Veterinarians, like all other vets, work to keep animals as healthy as possible. Many individuals today seek out Homeopathic Veterinarians because of their own personal beliefs in homeopathy. Others turn to homeopathy when traditional veterinary medicines or treatments don't work.

Many Homeopathic Veterinarians work with pet owners dealing with behavioral issues. They may, for example, treat separation anxiety, chewing, integrating new pets and family members into the house, aggression, and everything in between with homeopathic remedies.

Homeopathic Veterinarians are responsible for diagnosing animal health problems. When an animal is sick, the veterinarian is responsible for determining what specific infection or illness it has and then prescribing the treatment.

Homeopathic Veterinarians, like traditional vets, may treat and dress wounds and set fractures. Some may also perform surgery to correct health problems or to spay or neuter animals. Others may refer patients to other vets for these services.

Homeopathic vets may work in a traditional office setting or may do home visits. Many also do phone consultations. No matter what the employment setting, individuals may work extended and weekend hours in response to emergencies.

Salaries

Earnings for Homeopathic Veterinarians can vary greatly depending on a number of factors. These include the specific employment situation of the individual and his or her experience, education, professional reputation, and geographic location. According to the Bureau of Labor Statistics, the median salary for all veterinarians at the time of this writing is around $90,000.

With that being said, there are some Homeopathic Veterinarians who have earnings starting out at approximately $38,000, and others have earnings of $175,000 or more. Those at the higher end are generally individuals in upscale markets who not only have their own practice, but also have built a good reputation for dealing with pets on a homeopathic level.

Employment Prospects

Employment prospects are excellent for qualified individuals who have fulfilled the requirements to first become veterinarians and then specialize in homeopathic veterinary medicine. The popularity and acceptance of homeopathy for animals mirrors its acceptance in treating people. Today more people than ever are looking for more natural ways to stay healthy.

Individuals may work in a number of different settings. These may include working as employees in the private practice of other veterinarians and working for clinics, shelters, humane societies, or in emergency rooms. The majority of Homeopathic Veterinarians have their own practice.

Advancement Prospects

Advancement prospects are good for Homeopathic Veterinarians. As noted previously, the popularity and acceptance of holistic treatment, including homeopathy, for animals is on the rise. As more people look for natural and holistic ways to keep their pets healthy, Homeopathic Veterinarians will become more and more popular and in demand.

Individuals may climb the career ladder in a number of ways depending on their aspirations. Individuals working as employees in the private practice of other veterinarians may find employment at larger or more prestigious homeopathic veterinary offices. They might also become partners or even open their own homeopathic veterinary practice. Homeopathic Veterinarians with their own practice can climb the career ladder by increasing their business and obtaining more clients.

Education and Training

In order to become any type of veterinarian, an individual must graduate with a doctor of veterinary medicine degree from an accredited college of veterinary medicine. At this time there are 28 colleges in 26 states that are accredited by the Council on Education of the American Veterinary Medical Association (AVMA) offering this four-year program. Once an individual has graduated, he or she receives either the designation D.V.M. or V.M.D.

While prerequisites for admission to this program vary by school, each at least requires between 45 and 90 semester hours of undergraduate work. With that being said, most individuals enrolled in these programs hold a bachelor's degree. With only 28 colleges offering these programs in the United States, competition is fierce.

Those interested in pursuing a career in this field should take classes in the sciences, such as organic and inorganic chemistry, physics, biochemistry, biology, animal biology, animal nutrition, zoology, etc.

In order to be accepted into one of these programs, individuals must also take a number of exams, such as the Graduate Record Examination (GRE), the Veterinary College Admission Test (VCAT), or the Medical College Admission Test (MCAT), depending on the requirements of the school.

While those who graduate with a doctor of veterinary medicine degree may practice once they become licensed, some enter a one- or two-year internship. Those who want to be board certified in a specific area must also complete a three- to four-year residency program that provides training in one of the 38 AVMA specialties. Individuals are expected to take continuing education classes in order to maintain their license.

Homeopathic Veterinarians must also take specialized training in homeopathy focusing on its unique methods of diagnosis and treatment. Individuals often do this by working and studying under experienced Homeopathic Veterinarians. Most Homeopathic Veterinarians also continue their education in homeopathy through lectures, seminars, and/or correspondence courses. The Academy of Veterinary Homeopathy (AVH) offers classes as well as complete courses in all levels of homeopathy as it relates to veterinary medicine.

In addition, certain veterinary colleges may also offer classes or seminars on homeopathy.

Experience, Skills, and Personality Traits

Many Homeopathic Veterinarians obtain experience by working with other established Homeopathic Veterinarians. Most have also worked in veterinary offices, clinics, or shelters before graduating from veterinary programs.

In order to be successful in this line of work, Homeopathic Veterinarians need to have good diagnostic skills. As animals can't talk, the vet needs to be very perceptive in how the animal is acting. He or she needs to be a good listener, as the animal's owner often can provide information about important symptoms. All this information is necessary when selecting an appropriate remedy.

Scientific aptitude is essential. Homeopathic Veterinarians also need to be organized, detail-oriented individuals with excellent memory. Communication skills are vital. Homeopathic Veterinarians, like all vets, should be compassionate, patient, kindhearted individuals with a strong love for animals. An interest and belief in homeopathy is mandatory.

Excellent judgment is necessary, as the ability to think quickly and make effective decisions is critical.

Special Requirements

Veterinarians in every state are required to be licensed before they can practice, and Homeopathic Veterinarians are no exception. Licensing is governed by each specific state, so requirements for licensure are not federally standardized. Generally, in order to become licensed, individuals must have graduated from an accredited veterinary program with a D.V.M. degree as well as passed a national board examination called the North American Veterinary Licensing Exam. This test is an eight-hour exam composed of 360 multiple-choice questions that cover veterinary medicine in addition to a section covering diagnostic skills.

As mentioned previously, there are continuing education requirements for licensed veterinarians that are necessary to demonstrate the individual's knowledge of medical and veterinary advancements and developments.

Voluntary certification is also available through organizations such as the AVH.

Unions and Associations

Homeopathic Veterinarians may belong to a number of organizations that provide professional support and educational opportunities. Depending on the individual's interests, these may include the AVMA, the AVH, and the American Holistic Veterinary Medical Association, among others.

Tips for Entry

1. If you are still in school and considering becoming a veterinarian, make sure you take classes in the sciences.
2. Look for courses and workshops in various areas of homeopathy. Sometimes they may be geared specifically toward animals and veterinary medicine.

Other times they might be geared toward homeopathy for people. Both will be useful.

3. Find a Homeopathic Veterinarian and, if you are still in school, you might be able to shadow him or her. If you are out of school and licensed, you might be able to work with him or her as an intern.

4. Send your résumé and a cover letter to Homeopathic Veterinarians. Remember to ask that your résumé be kept on file if there are no current openings.

5. Check out openings online. Start with some of the more traditional job sites such as Monster.com, and expand your search from there.

6. Join the AVH. In addition to educational opportunities and professional support, you will make a lot of helpful contacts.

EQUINE VETERINARIAN

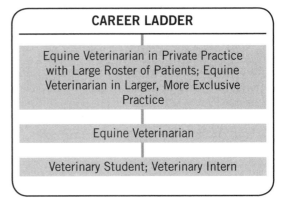

Position Description

Veterinarians care for the health of a variety of animals. Some take care of small animals such as pets. Others take care of livestock and other large animals. Veterinarians often have some sort of specialty. There are small animal veterinarians, research veterinarians, wildlife veterinarians, and large animal veterinarians, among others. There are also some veterinarians who specialize in caring for specific animals, such as Equine Veterinarians, who provide medical care for horses.

Equine Veterinarians prevent, diagnose, and treat illnesses, disease, and injuries in horses. They may work with horses in conducting research to protect humans against various diseases. Equine Veterinarians frequently also specialize in areas such as surgery.

There are a number of differences between Equine Veterinarians and small animal vets. To begin with, individuals must be aware of the special physiology of horses, which differs from that of small animals. Another difference is that instead of primarily working in an office setting, Equine Veterinarians generally have to go to their patients. Depending on the specific job, Equine Veterinarians may drive to see the horses at ranches, farms, or racetracks. They may provide medical services for one horse or for an entire stable.

Specific duties of Equine Veterinarians may vary depending on the work situation. Equine Veterinarians (or vets, as they are often called) working directly with horses are expected to keep the horses as healthy as possible. Much of this involves preventive care to maintain the health of the horse or horses.

Equine vets are expected to test for and vaccinate horses against diseases. As part of the job, individuals also perform general checkups on horses. They may additionally administer various tests, including blood work, urinalysis, physical examinations, and specialized tests if necessary.

Equine Veterinarians often must "patch up" a horse. They may, for example, need to fuse joints or repair broken bones in a horse's leg. They may dress wounds. They might additionally need to perform surgery.

Equine Veterinarians frequently are called upon to assist with the birth of foals. While some births may be easy, others are difficult. The Equine Veterinarian may need to perform surgery such as C-sections. As horses may be too large to transport at times, the vet may need to perform surgery at a farm or ranch.

Equine vets are expected to diagnose health problems. When a horse is sick, the individual is responsible for determining what specific infection or illness it has and then prescribing the treatment.

Equine Veterinarians working at racetracks need to handle the veterinary needs of racehorses. For example, the individual may be responsible for determining why a horse is lame and then trying to rectify the situation.

As horses are large and not domesticated, vets in this line of work stand the chance of being kicked or bitten. Individuals have to be physically able to handle the size and weight of the horses for which they are caring.

There are Equine Veterinarians who perform research instead of actually caring for horses. These individuals assist other medical professionals in learning more about both human and horse health.

Salaries

Earnings for Equine Veterinarians can vary greatly depending on their specific employment situation. Earnings are also dependent on the experience, education, and specialty of the vet as well as the geographic area in which he or she practices. Some veterinarians have earnings starting at approximately $45,000 while others have earnings of $140,000 or more. Those at the higher end of the scale are generally specialists, such as Equine Veterinarian surgeons, or those working in research or for pharmaceutical companies.

Employment Prospects

Employment prospects are excellent for Equine Veterinarians. As the majority of vets graduating from veterinary school go into small animal veterinary medicine, this field is wide open for qualified individuals.

Individuals may work in a number of different settings. These may include among others working in private practice, as employees in the private practice of other Equine Veterinarians, and working for clinics, farms, stables, and racetracks. Some Equine Veterinarians also work for the government at the federal or state level. Others may work for pharmaceutical companies.

Advancement Prospects

Advancement prospects are good for Equine Veterinarians. Individuals may climb the career ladder in a number of ways depending on their aspirations. Those working as employees in the private practice of other veterinarians may advance their careers by opening up their own practice. Those already in private practice may advance their careers by building a larger roster of clients.

Equine Veterinarians working at racetracks, stables, or ranches may find similar positions in larger or more prestigious facilities, resulting in increased responsibilities and earnings.

Education and Training

In order to become a veterinarian of any type, an individual must graduate with a doctor of veterinary medicine degree from an accredited college of veterinary medicine. At this time there are 28 colleges in 26 states that are accredited by the Council on Education of the American Veterinary Medical Association (AVMA) offering this four-year program. Once an individual has graduated, he or she receives either the designation D.V.M. or V.M.D.

While prerequisites for admission to this program vary by school, each at least requires between 45 and 90 semester hours of undergraduate work. With that being said, most individuals entering these programs hold a bachelor's degree. With only 28 programs in the United States, competition is fierce.

Those interested in pursuing a career in this field should take classes in the sciences, such as organic and inorganic chemistry, physics, biochemistry, biology, animal biology, animal nutrition, zoology, etc.

In order to be accepted into one of these programs, individuals must also take a number of exams, such as the Graduate Record Examination (GRE), the Veterinary College Admission Test (VCAT), or the Medical College Admission Test (MCAT), depending on the requirement of the school.

While those who graduate with a doctorate in veterinary medicine may practice once they become licensed, those who want to work in a specialty must enter a one- or two-year internship. Those who want to be board certified in a specific area must also complete a three- to four-year residency program that provides training in one of the 38 AVMA specialties.

The American Association of Equine Practitioners (AAEP) provides internships for individuals who aspire to become Equine Veterinarians. These internships are available to equine veterinary students who have gone through an equine large animal clinical rotation. They must graduate before the internship begins.

Individuals are expected to take continuing education classes in order to maintain their license.

Experience, Skills, and Personality Traits

Equine Veterinarians generally obtain experience during their internships. Many also have worked in veterinary offices, clinics, or shelters before graduating from veterinary programs.

Equine Veterinarians should love horses. They should be compassionate, patient, kindhearted individuals. The ability to think quickly and make effective decisions is crucial, as is excellent judgment.

Verbal communication skills are essential. People skills are also a must. As horses are large animals, it is especially important for Equine Veterinarians to have physical strength and stamina.

Special Requirements

Veterinarians in every state are required to be licensed before they can practice. Licensing is governed by each specific state. Therefore requirements for licensure are not federally standardized. Generally, in order to become licensed, individuals must have graduated from an accredited veterinary program with a D.V.M. degree as well as passed a national board examination called the North American Veterinary Licensing Exam. This test is an eight-hour exam composed of 360 multiple-choice questions that cover veterinary medicine in addition to a section covering diagnostic skills.

As mentioned previously, there are continuing education requirements for licensed veterinarians that are necessary to demonstrate the individual's knowledge of medical and veterinary advancements.

Unions and Associations

Equine Veterinarians generally belong to the AAEP and the AVMA. Individuals can find additional information on education by contacting the Association of American Veterinary Medical Colleges.

Tips for Entry

1. If you are still in school and considering becoming an Equine Veterinarian, make sure you take classes in the sciences.
2. Try to either volunteer or get a job with a veterinarian before you go to veterinary school. Working with an Equine Veterinarian would be ideal. However, if that is not an option, working with any vet will both give you valuable experience and help you be sure this is the right career choice for you. The vet with whom you work might also be a good reference when you apply to veterinary school.
3. Send your résumé and a short cover letter to equine veterinarian practices, private Equine Veterinarians, racetracks, and other potential employers to see if they have openings. Remember to ask that your résumé be kept on file if there are no current openings.
4. Check out openings online. Start with some of the more traditional job sites such as Monster. com and expand your search from there.

WILDLIFE VETERINARIAN

CAREER PROFILE

Duties: Research how wild animals become sick; study how diseases are transmitted to animals; provide veterinary care to wild animals who are injured; study health of the wildlife population; determine the cause of death of birds and other wildlife; investigate parasites and unusual tissue found in harvested game animals; help save animals from extinction

Alternate Title(s): Vet

Salary Range: $45,000 to $120,000+

Employment Prospects: Excellent

Advancement Prospects: Good

Best Geographical Locations for Position: Positions located throughout the country

Prerequisites:

Education or Training—Graduate with a doctor of veterinary medicine degree from an accredited school of veterinary medicine; continuing education required; internship and/or residency generally required

Experience and Qualifications—Experience working with other Wildlife Veterinarians; experience working with wildlife

CAREER LADDER

Wildlife Veterinarian Supervisor; Wildlife Veterinarian for Larger, More Prestigious Facility; Wildlife Veterinarian Assigned to Larger, More Prestigious Project

↑

Wildlife Veterinarian

↑

Veterinary Student; Veterinary Intern; Veterinary Resident

Special Skills and Personality Traits—Inquisitive mind; excellent judgment; quick thinking; compassion; communication skills; scientific aptitude; physical strength; stamina

Special Requirements—State licensing required; certification available

Position Description

Zoological medicine integrates ecology, conservation, and veterinary medicine. It then applies these principles to wild animals that live in both natural and artificial environments. Wildlife Veterinarians are veterinarians who work with wildlife. They may work with a variety of wild animals, including lions, tigers, deer, bears, foxes, moose, elephants, elk, giraffe, antelopes, and birds, among many others. Duties of Wildlife Veterinarians in general are vastly different from vets who care for domestic animals and livestock. Their responsibilities can also vary tremendously depending on their specific employment situation.

Wildlife Veterinarians may work in a variety of environments. Some work in zoos caring for captive animals. These vets are also called zoo vets and will be covered in another article. Some Wildlife Veterinarians provide veterinary care to wild animals that are injured. These individuals may work in wildlife rehabilitation clinics or sanctuaries.

Some work with wild animals that roam free. These animals are also known as free-ranging wildlife. While Wildlife Veterinarians who work in zoos, rehabilitation clinics, or sanctuaries may provide veterinary services to sick or injured animals, those that work with free-ranging wildlife generally have other duties. These individuals study the health of the wildlife population to learn things like how wild animals become sick or how diseases are transmitted to animals.

Some Wildlife Veterinarians may be responsible for chemically immobilizing animals with drugs and then reviving them. This may be done for a number of reasons. Animals may, for example, need to be captured so they can be relocated to a different area. This might be necessary if animals are being reintroduced to a specific area or to help save animals from extinction.

Wildlife vets may be expected to do a great deal of research. They may, for example, be responsible for gathering information on the best way to relocate animals. They may need to do research on the best ways to chemically immobilize and anesthetize animals and the best way to revive them. Wildlife vets must know how long the drugs will keep the animal asleep and the amount of time it takes for an antidote to work. If wildlife is moved from one area to another, there may be other concerns. The wildlife vet must do research to determine what diseases are prevalent in the area and what might make the animals sick if they were moved.

When animals are anesthetized, the Wildlife Veterinarian may examine the animal and check for injuries. The individual may also perform tests such as taking the animal's temperature and pulse rate and measuring respiration to be sure that it is responding safely to the anesthesia.

As noted previously, Wildlife Veterinarians are very interested in studying the health of the wildlife population to learn things like how wild animals become sick. They may take blood samples to test for disease, take body measurements, and look at the animal's teeth to tell their approximate age. In some cases, Wildlife Veterinarians vaccinate animals as well as give them medication to eliminate parasites.

Wildlife Veterinarians study how diseases affect the population of specific groups of animals as well as how diseases move through populations of animals and are transmitted. They may gather information and perform research.

Wildlife Veterinarians may capture and release animals for research, to provide veterinary services, or to relocate animals that may be on the brink of extinction.

Some Wildlife Veterinarians do investigative work. They may have duties that resemble those of a medical examiner. For example, Wildlife Veterinarians may be expected to determine the cause of death of an animal or group of animals. In doing so, they may explore the types of parasites found in dead animals.

Many Wildlife Veterinarians perform necropsies, which are similar to autopsies performed on people. These may be done to determine not only why animals may have died, but also to find out if they had any medical conditions. This is important because wildlife illnesses can wipe out a large portion of a wildlife population.

Wildlife Veterinarians may work with wildlife biologists or wildlife rehabilitators, among other professionals. They may surgically implant tracking devices or put tracking collars on animals.

Wildlife Veterinarians may be responsible for monitoring the health of animals, handling disease surveillance and diagnostic pathology. While performing their duties, wildlife vets must address animal welfare issues,

assuring that research and management done in the field is conducted in a humane manner.

While the veterinarian is not always the one who actually administers drugs when animals are being anesthetized in any given project, there always needs to be a vet supervising the process. The vet is expected to approve the dosage and administration of the drug as well as ensure that the individuals who actually are administering the drugs are fully trained.

In addition to teaching biologists how to administer drugs to wildlife, Wildlife Veterinarians often teach biologists, rehabilitators, and other researchers how to handle wildlife, as well as how to take tissue samples and preserve them.

Wildlife Veterinarians not only have the opportunity to keep entire groups of animals healthy, but often save them from extinction as well. For individuals interested in an exciting life where no two days are the same, this may be the perfect career.

Salaries

Earnings for Wildlife Veterinarians can vary greatly depending on a number of factors. These include the specific employment situation and experience, education, professional reputation, and geographic area.

There are some Wildlife Veterinarians who have earnings starting at approximately $45,000, while others have earnings of $120,000 or more.

Employment Prospects

Employment prospects for Wildlife Veterinarians are excellent. Individuals may work in a number of different employment settings. These may include wildlife preserves, zoos, wildlife rehabilitation clinics, and captive wildlife facilities, among others. Individuals may work for private groups, foundations, and for local, state, and federal governmental agencies. Depending on an individual's interests, he or she might also be self-employed, working on a contract basis. Wildlife Veterinarians may find employment throughout the United States and around the world depending on their interests and expertise.

Advancement Prospects

Advancement prospects for Wildlife Veterinarians are good. Individuals may climb the career ladder in a number of ways depending on their career aspirations. Some may find similar positions in larger agencies or facilities, while others are given more prestigious assignments. Some advance their career by teaching. Others climb the career ladder by being promoted to supervisory positions. Some individuals end up teaching part of the time. Still others freelance and take consulting projects of interest to them.

Education and Training

In order to become any type of veterinarian, an individual must graduate with a doctor of veterinary medicine (D.V.M.) degree from an accredited college of veterinary medicine. At this time there are 28 colleges in 26 states that are accredited by the Council on Education of the American Veterinary Medical Association (AVMA) offering this four-year program. Once an individual has graduated, he or she receives either the designation D.V.M. or V.M.D.

While prerequisites for admission to this program vary by school, each at least requires between 45 and 90 semester hours of undergraduate work. With that being said, most individuals in these programs hold a bachelor's degree. With only 28 programs available in the United States, competition is fierce.

Those interested in pursuing a career in this field should take classes in the sciences, such as organic and inorganic chemistry, physics, biochemistry, biology, animal biology, animal nutrition, zoology, etc.

In order to be accepted into one of these programs, individuals must also take a number of exams, such as the Graduate Record Examination (GRE), the Veterinary College Admission Test (VCAT), or the Medical College Admission Test (MCAT), depending on the specific school.

While those who graduate with a doctor of veterinary medicine degree may practice once they become licensed, some enter a one-year internship. Those who want to be board certified in a specific area must also complete a three- to four-year residency.

Individuals are expected to take continuing education classes in order to maintain their license.

Wildlife Veterinarians must undergo additional training in order to prepare for their job. Many individuals find experienced Wildlife Veterinarians to serve as mentors. Those who want to be certified will need to go through an approved training program. Information on these educational programs is available from the American College of Zoological Medicine (ACZM).

Experience, Skills, and Personality Traits

Wildlife Veterinarians may obtain experience in a number of ways. Some may work in veterinary offices, clinics, or shelters before graduating from veterinary programs. Some get experience working or volunteering in wildlife rehabilitation clinics, captive wildlife facilities, and zoos.

After graduation, Wildlife Veterinarians may have a one-year internship. Those seeking to be board certified in zoological medicine must go through a two-year residency program.

Wildlife Veterinarians should be compassionate, kindhearted individuals with an inquisitive mind and scientific aptitude. As Wildlife Veterinarians may need to perform necropsies as well as take tissue samples and conduct other testing, they cannot have a queasy stomach.

A strong love of wildlife is necessary. An interest in conservation is also helpful. Excellent judgment is mandatory, as is the ability to think quickly and make effective decisions. Verbal communication skills are essential. Physical strength and stamina are also helpful.

As a great deal of the work of Wildlife Veterinarians is done outdoors, and in less than pristine conditions, individuals need the ability to work effectively in extreme environments or inclement weather.

Special Requirements

Veterinarians in every state are required to be licensed before they can practice. Licensing is governed by each specific state. Therefore requirements for licensure are not federally standardized. Generally, in order to become licensed, individuals must have graduated from an accredited veterinary program with a D.V.M. degree as well as passed a national board examination called the North American Veterinary Licensing Exam. This test is an eight-hour exam composed of 360 multiple-choice questions that cover veterinary medicine in addition to a section covering diagnostic skills.

As mentioned previously, there are continuing education requirements for licensed veterinarians that are necessary to demonstrate the individual's knowledge of medical and veterinary advancements.

Certification is available from the ACZM for veterinarians with expertise in zoological medicine, including Wildlife Veterinarians. The ACZM is an international specialty organization recognized by the AVMA. In order to become certified, individuals must go through an approved training program and then pass an examination.

Unions and Associations

Wildlife Veterinarians may belong to a number of organizations that provide professional support and educational opportunities. These might include the AVMA and the American Association of Wildlife Veterinarians

(AAWV). Individuals might also contact the Association of American Veterinary Medical Colleges and the ACZM to obtain additional information on education.

Tips for Entry

1. If you are still in school and considering becoming a veterinarian, make sure you take classes in the sciences.
2. Get experience by volunteering at a wildlife rehabilitation clinic or center or a captive wildlife facility.
3. Consider working as a field research assistant to gain additional experience.
4. Send your résumé and a short cover letter to wildlife rehabilitation clinics, captive wildlife facilities, and zoos. You might also consider relevant governmental agencies. Remember to ask that your résumé be kept on file if there are no current openings.
5. Check out openings online. Start with some of the more traditional job sites such as Monster.com. Then check out career Web sites specific to the wildlife veterinary field. (Be sure to look in the appendix for some ideas.)
6. Join the AAWV. This organization provides educational opportunities and professional support.

VETERINARY OFFICES, HOSPITALS, AND CLINICS

VETERINARY TECHNOLOGIST

Duties: Assist veterinarians in caring for animals; supervise technicians; collect specimens; assist in surgery; monitor animals after surgery; change dressings; perform medical and laboratory tests; train new staff

Alternate Title(s): Animal Health Technologist; Technologist

Salary Range: $9.50 to $25.00+ per hour

Employment Prospects: Excellent

Advancement Prospects: Good

Best Geographical Locations for Position: Positions located throughout the country

Prerequisites:

Education or Training—Bachelor's degree in veterinary technology

Experience and Qualifications—Experience requirements vary; see text

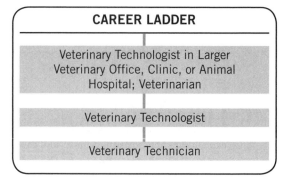

CAREER LADDER

Veterinary Technologist in Larger Veterinary Office, Clinic, or Animal Hospital; Veterinarian

Veterinary Technologist

Veterinary Technician

Special Skills and Personality Traits—Ability to take care of animals; good judgment; supervisory skills; ability to follow directions; strong stomach; compassion; communication skills

Special Requirements—State licensing, registration, or credentialing required; see text

Position Description

Veterinary Technologists work closely with animals, assisting veterinarians in much the same way registered nurses help physicians. Duties and responsibilities vary with each job. Individuals may work in a variety of settings, including veterinary offices, clinics, animal hospitals, kennels, and shelters, among others.

While the job titles Veterinary Technologist and veterinary technician are often used interchangeably and a great many of the duties are the same, Veterinary Technologists are required to have more education. This prepares them for supervisory and management duties, responsibilities, and advanced positions.

Veterinary Technologists working in veterinary offices, animal clinics, and animal hospitals work under the supervision of veterinarians. They may perform many of the functions of veterinarians with the exception of diagnosing medical problems, performing surgery, and prescribing medication. They do, however, assist veterinarians in these situations.

Technologists are responsible for assisting in the treatment of animals. This may include cleaning them, changing dressings, or holding them while the veterinarian performs procedures. They may perform various medical and laboratory tests, draw blood, prepare

tissue samples, and collect specimens to check for diseases and parasites.

Individuals may also administer other tests as well as exposing and developing X-rays. They often are responsible for checking for fleas and ticks on animals. Some technologists assist with dental prophylaxis (teeth cleaning and scaling) and other dental procedures.

Depending on the situation, Veterinary Technologists may be responsible for supervising veterinary technicians and veterinary assistants in the veterinary office, clinic, or animal hospital. They may also be expected to train these individuals in performing procedures.

Veterinary Technologists help prepare animals for surgery. They may, for example, help calm an animal, get him or her up on the table, and assist in administering anesthesia. Technologists may prepare the operating room for surgery and often assist the veterinarian during surgeries by handing him or her instruments.

Veterinary Technologists are responsible for monitoring animals under the care of the veterinarian. They are expected to check on animals coming out of anesthesia and be sure that the animal is recovering according to schedule. They may also administer medications under the direction of the veterinarian.

While watching animals under care, Veterinary Technologists are expected to report any problems or issues to the veterinarian. This might includes an animal's physical symptoms and well-being, as well as its psychological attitude.

Veterinary Technologists have a lot of interaction with animals whether they are working in a veterinary office, clinic, or animal hospital. They may play with them, give them special attention, or comfort them when they are in physical or emotional pain.

Technologists take case histories from pet owners. They may also speak to the owners regarding the pet's symptoms, explain pre- and postsurgical care, and clarify instructions for medication or care.

Technologists may be responsible for keeping surgical instruments clean and sterile and making sure they are in good working order. Individuals may be responsible for taking inventory of medications and other supplies. They may also be expected to order and store needed equipment and supplies.

Depending on the specific employment situation, the Veterinary Technologist may also handle management of the veterinary office, hospital, or clinic. He or she may, for example, schedule appointments, keep records, and handle billing. Some Veterinary Technologists work as clinical specialists, supervisors, or practice managers.

For individuals who have a true love for animals, yet are not prepared to commit to veterinary school, this type of position can be very fulfilling and rewarding.

Salaries

Veterinary Technologists working in veterinary offices, animal hospitals, and clinics are generally paid an hourly wage. This can range from approximately $9.50 to $25.00 per hour or more. Factors affecting earnings include experience, education, and specific job responsibilities. Other factors affecting earnings include the type, size, and prestige of the specific employer as well as geographic location.

Employment Prospects

Employment prospects for Veterinary Technologists are excellent. A growing number of people consider their pet to be part of the family and thus make their pet's health-care needs a top priority. With this growing need for veterinary care, more Veterinary Technologists will be needed as well.

Veterinary Technologists may find employment throughout the country in veterinary offices, animal hospitals, and clinics. Employment may also be found at shelters, humane societies, sanctuaries, zoos, and kennels.

Advancement Prospects

Advancement prospects for Veterinary Technologists are good. Individuals can climb the career ladder in a number of ways. Those working in veterinary offices, animal hospitals, and clinics may find similar positions in larger facilities. This generally results in increased earnings and responsibilities. Those who are working as clinical technologists may become practice managers, supervisors, or clinical specialists. These promotions also result in increased earnings and responsibilities.

Some decide that they want to advance and go back to school to become veterinarians.

Education and Training

Veterinary Technologists must complete a four-year program accredited by the American Veterinary Medical Association (AVMA). About 16 colleges offer veterinary technology programs that culminate in a four-year degree.

A period of clinical experience in a veterinary practice is required for all students in an AVMA-accredited veterinary technology program. This hands-on training is called a preceptorship, practicum, or externship.

Experience, Skills, and Personality Traits

As noted previously, Veterinary Technologists must undergo hands-on training with a veterinarian before they graduate. Experience requirements for Veterinary Technologists vary from job to job. Some positions may be entry level. Other employers may require or prefer experience in other veterinary offices, clinics, or animal hospitals.

In order to be successful in this line of work, individuals must have a true love for animals. Veterinary Technologists need to be compassionate, patient, and kindhearted.

The ability to follow instructions is essential. Supervisory and management skills are needed as well. Verbal communication skills are a must. Finally, a strong stomach is needed in order to perform certain tasks and duties.

Special Requirements

While each state regulates Veterinary Technologists in a different manner, all states require them to pass a credentialing examination. This exam includes oral, written, and practical components and is regulated by either the specific state's board of veterinary examiners or another state agency. Depending on the specific state, Veterinary Technologists may then become registered, licensed, or certified.

Most states use the National Veterinary Technician exam. As a result, individuals can transfer their scores from one state to another as long as both states use the exam.

Unions and Associations

Veterinary Technologists can obtain career information by contacting the AVMA. Individuals can also join the National Association of Veterinary Technicians in America. This organization offers professional support and educational opportunities to members.

Tips for Entry

1. Get experience by volunteering at a veterinary office, shelter, or humane society before you enter school.

2. Send your résumé and a short cover letter to veterinarians, animal hospitals, and clinics to see if they have openings. Remember to ask that your résumé be kept on file if there are no current openings.

3. Research openings online. Start with some of the more traditional job sites such as Monster.com, and expand your search from there.

4. Openings are often advertised in the classifieds section of the newspaper. Look under heading classifications such as "Veterinary Technologists," "Veterinary Technicians," "Animal Hospital," "Animal Clinic," or "Veterinary Office."

5. If you have a pet, ask your veterinarian for career advice. He or she might become a mentor, or, if you have graduated from college, a potential employer.

VETERINARY TECHNICIAN

Position Description

Veterinary Technicians work closely with animals, assisting veterinarians in much the same way nurses help physicians. Duties and responsibilities of Veterinary Technicians vary in accordance with the requirements of each individual job.

It should be noted that while the job titles Veterinary Technician and veterinary technologist are often used interchangeably, there is a difference. Although a great many of the duties are the same, Veterinary Technicians do not require as much education as veterinary technologists.

Veterinary Technicians working in veterinary offices, animal clinics, and animal hospitals work under the supervision of veterinarians. Individuals may perform many of the functions of veterinarians with the exception of diagnosing medical problems, performing surgery, and prescribing medication. They do, however, assist the veterinarian in these tasks.

Technicians are responsible for assisting in the treatment of animals. This may include cleaning them, changing dressings, or holding them while the veterinarian performs procedures. They may perform various medical and laboratory tests, draw blood, prepare tissue samples, and collect specimens to check for diseases and parasites.

Individuals may also administer other tests as well as expose and develop X-rays. They often are responsible for checking for fleas and ticks on animals, taking animals' temperatures, and giving injections. Some technicians assist with dental prophylaxis (teeth cleaning and scaling) and other dental procedures.

Veterinary Technicians often help prepare animals for surgery. They may, for example, help calm an animal, get him or her up on the examination table, and assist in administering anesthesia. The technician often assists the veterinarian during surgeries by handing him or her instruments.

Veterinary Technicians are responsible for monitoring animals under the care of the veterinarian. They are expected to check on animals coming out of anesthesia and be sure that the animal is recovering according to schedule. They may also administer medications under the direction of the veterinarian.

Animals cannot communicate verbally to tell anyone what is wrong. They cannot tell anyone when they are hurt or when they are suffering ill effects from medication. Veterinary Technicians are thus expected to watch animals under their care, reporting any problems to the veterinarian. They must not only keep tabs on an animal's physical symptoms and well-being, but monitor its psychological attitude as well.

Whether in a veterinary office, animal clinic, animal hospital, or any other setting, Veterinary Technicians have a lot of interaction with animals. They may play with them, give them special attention, or comfort them when they are in physical or emotional pain.

Depending on the specific office setting, Veterinary Technicians are often responsible for taking case histories from pet owners. They may be expected to speak to the owners regarding their pet's symptoms, pre- and postsurgical care, and instructions for medication or care.

Technicians are responsible for keeping the instruments the veterinarian uses clean and sterile. They are expected to keep an inventory of instruments, medications, and other supplies and either order required supplies or inform the veterinarian of what is needed.

For individuals who have a true love for animals, this type of position can be very fulfilling and rewarding.

Salaries

Veterinary Technicians working in veterinary offices, animal hospitals, and clinics are generally paid an hourly wage. This can range from approximately $8.50 to $20.00 an hour or more. Factors affecting earnings include experience, education, and specific job responsibilities. Other factors affecting earnings include the type, size, and prestige of the specific employer as well as geographic location.

Employment Prospects

Employment prospects are excellent for Veterinary Technicians and improving every day. More and more people consider their pet to be part of the family and thus make their pet's health-care needs a top priority. With this growing need for veterinary care, more Veterinary Technicians will be needed as well.

Veterinary Technicians may find employment throughout the country in veterinary offices, animal hospitals, and clinics. Employment may also be found in shelters, humane societies, sanctuaries, zoos, and kennels.

Advancement Prospects

Advancement prospects for Veterinary Technicians are fair. Individuals can climb the career ladder in a num-

ber of ways. Those working in veterinary offices, animal hospitals, and clinics may find similar positions in larger facilities. This generally results in increased earnings and responsibilities.

Some individuals obtain a four-year degree in veterinary technology and become veterinary technologists. Others go back to school and become full-fledged veterinarians.

Education and Training

Veterinary Technicians need a minimum of a two-year associate's degree from a program accredited by the American Veterinary Medical Association (AVMA). These programs are generally offered in community colleges and include work in both clinical and laboratory settings. There are also four-year programs for individuals who want to earn a bachelor's degree.

Experience, Skills, and Personality Traits

Experience requirements for Veterinary Technicians vary from job to job. Some positions are entry level. Others require or prefer experience in other veterinary offices, clinics, or animal hospitals. In order to be successful in this line of work, individuals must have a genuine love for animals. Veterinary Technicians need to be compassionate, patient, and kindhearted.

The ability to follow instructions is essential. Verbal communication skills are necessary as well. A strong stomach is needed in order to perform certain tasks and duties.

Special Requirements

While each state regulates Veterinary Technicians in a different manner, all states require them to pass a credentialing examination. This exam includes oral, written, and practical components and is regulated by either the specific state's board of veterinary examiners or another state agency. Depending on the specific state, Veterinary Technicians may then become registered, licensed, or certified.

Most states use the National Veterinary Technician exam. As a result, individuals can have their scores transferred from one state to another as long as both states use the exam.

Unions and Associations

Veterinary Technicians can obtain career information by contacting the AVMA. Individuals may also join the National Association of Veterinary Technicians in America. This organization offers its members professional support and educational opportunities.

Tips for Entry

1. Get experience by volunteering at a veterinary office, shelter, humane society, or other facility.

2. Send your résumé and a short cover letter to veterinarians, animal hospitals, and clinics to see if they have openings. Remember to ask that your résumé be kept on file if there are no current openings.

3. Explore openings online. Start with some of the more traditional job sites such as Monster.com. Expand your search from there.

4. Openings are often advertised in the classifieds section of newspapers. Look under heading such as "Veterinary Technologists," "Veterinary Technicians," "Animal Hospital," "Animal Clinic," or "Veterinary Office."

VETERINARY ASSISTANT

Duties: Assist and support veterinarians, veterinary technologists, and veterinary technicians in caring for animals; work in the front office; work in the back area; groom animals; clean cages, exam rooms, and holding areas; exercise animals

Alternate Title(s): Assistant; Vet Assistant

Salary Range: $7.25 to $8.50+ per hour

Employment Prospects: Good

Advancement Prospects: Fair

Best Geographical Locations for Position: Positions located throughout the country

Prerequisites:

Education or Training—High school diploma or equivalent; training programs available; see text

Experience and Qualifications—Entry level

CAREER LADDER

Veterinary Technician; Veterinary Technologist

Veterinary Assistant

Intern or Volunteer

Special Skills and Personality Traits—Animal-care abilities; good judgment; ability to follow directions; strong stomach; compassion; communication skills; time-management skills; organizational skills

Position Description

Veterinary Assistants are nonlicensed individuals who help veterinarians care for animals. They perform a wide spectrum of duties in veterinary offices, animal hospitals, and clinics, depending on the specific job. While they may help during procedures, they cannot perform any test or procedure on their own.

Individuals are generally responsible for making sure that areas within the veterinarian's office, clinic, and/or animal hospital are kept clean. They are expected to clean animal cages, examining rooms, surgical areas, and grooming areas. They may also be responsible for cleaning up any accidents animals may have in the waiting room area.

Veterinary Assistants are expected to feed and give water to animals under their care. They may prepare the food, measuring out the correct amounts, and place the food dishes in cages. If animals are on special diets, Veterinary Assistants are responsible for not only preparing the special meals, but also ensuring that each animal gets the correct food.

Depending on the employment situation, Veterinary Assistants may be responsible for assisting in the grooming and cleaning of animals under their care. They may help wash, deflea, and comb or brush them, among other tasks.

Veterinary Assistants may help veterinarians, veterinary technicians, and technologists in performing their duties. Individuals may, for example, help put animals on or off an examination table, surgical table, or scale. They may help restrain animals while the vet is conducting examinations or administering medication or shots. They may weigh animals or help comfort animals during procedures.

Veterinary Assistants often take animals from their owners in the waiting room of veterinary offices and accompany them to examination rooms, surgical suites, or cages. They may also bring animals from these locations back to the waiting room to their owners. Veterinary Assistants working in animal hospitals or clinics often bring pet owners from the waiting room to see pets that have either had surgery or are otherwise ill to visit.

In some veterinary offices, clinics, and animal hospitals, Veterinary Assistants work in the front office greeting pet owners, answering the phone, scheduling appointments, filling in charts, filing, and processing payments. In others, they may work in the back area where animals receive treatment. Many Veterinary Assistants work in both areas, filling in wherever needed.

Veterinary Assistants may take animals out for walks, help socialize them, or perform any additional duties veterinarians, vet technicians, vet technologists, or practice managers may require.

Salaries

Veterinary Assistants working in veterinary offices, animal hospitals, and clinics are generally paid an hourly wage. This can range from approximately $7.25 to $8.50 per hour or more. Factors affecting earnings include experience, training, and responsibilities of the job. Other factors affecting earnings include the type, size, and prestige of the specific employer as well as geographic location.

Employment Prospects

Employment prospects for Veterinary Assistants are good. Employment opportunities exist in veterinary offices, animal hospitals, clinics, and emergency centers throughout the country.

Employment may also be found at shelters, humane societies, sanctuaries, zoos, and kennels, among other places.

Advancement Prospects

Advancement prospects for Veterinary Assistants are fair. Individuals may climb the career ladder in a number of ways depending on their aspirations. After obtaining some experience, those working in veterinary offices, animal hospitals, and clinics may find similar positions in larger facilities. This generally results in increased earnings and responsibilities.

Some individuals go to college to obtain a two-year degree in veterinary technology and become veterinary technicians.

Education and Training

Most employers require or prefer their Veterinary Assistants to have a minimum of a high school diploma or its equivalent. Individuals generally receive on-the-job training. There are also some training programs at community colleges and vocational or technical schools that help prepare individuals for working as Veterinary Assistants. These programs run generally less than a year and offer a certificate upon completion.

Experience, Skills, and Personality Traits

While experience requirements vary for Veterinary Assistants, this is generally an entry-level position. Individuals should have a true love for animals as well as compassion, patience, and kindness.

The ability to follow instructions is essential. A strong stomach is needed in order to perform certain tasks and duties. Time-management skills are also needed.

Unions and Associations

Veterinary Assistants may obtain career information by contacting the American Veterinary Medical Association.

Tips for Entry

1. Acquire experience by volunteering at a veterinary office, animal shelter, humane society, or other facility.
2. Send your résumé and a short cover letter to veterinarians, animal hospitals, and clinics to see if they have openings. Remember to ask that your résumé be kept on file if there are no current openings.
3. Check out openings online. Start with some of the more traditional job sites such as Monster.com. Expand your search from there.
4. Openings are often advertised in the classifieds section of the newspaper. Look under headings such as "Veterinary Assistant," "Animal Hospital," "Animal Clinic," or "Veterinary Office."

RECEPTIONIST

CAREER PROFILE

Duties: Greet pet owners; answer phones; make appointments; deal with clients; send out e-mails; process payments

Alternate Title(s): None

Salary Range: $8.00 to $18.00+ per hour

Employment Prospects: Fair

Advancement Prospects: Fair

Best Geographical Locations for Position: Positions located throughout the country

Prerequisites:

Education or Training—High school diploma or equivalent

Experience and Qualifications—Experience requirements vary; see text

Special Skills and Personality Traits—Good judgment; attention to detail; personableness; commu-

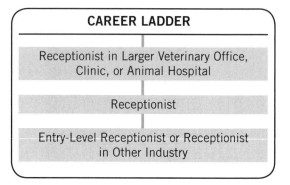

CAREER LADDER

Receptionist in Larger Veterinary Office, Clinic, or Animal Hospital

Receptionist

Entry-Level Receptionist or Receptionist in Other Industry

nication skills; computer skills; phone skills; ability to follow directions; compassion; time-management skills; organizational skills

Position Description

The impression made by a Receptionist at a veterinarian's office, animal clinic, or hospital is very important. He or she is the first person a visitor sees when walking into the office. He or she is also the last person a visitor may be in contact with before leaving.

Duties of Receptionists in these environments depend to a great extent on the structure of the specific employment setting. Receptionists may handle secretarial duties, clerical duties, and/or administrative duties. Some Receptionists in veterinary offices, animal hospitals, and clinics also assist with simple animal care.

Receptionists must greet visitors in a pleasant, cheerful, and enthusiastic manner. When people come in to the veterinary office, animal hospital, or clinic, receptionists likely will greet both the owners and the pets. It is the individual's responsibility to make pet owners feel as welcome and confident as possible about their visit from the moment they walk in the door.

When pet owners arrive with their pet, the Receptionist is responsible for getting their name, their pet's name, and inquiring about the reason for their visit. They may take preliminary information about the pet such as age, symptoms, past care, and history. In some situations, someone else performs this task.

The Receptionist is often responsible for pulling the pet's chart (if there is one) from the files to get it ready for the vet. If there is no chart, the Receptionist may create one. He or she directs pet owners to be seated, telling them approximately how long it will be until they will be going in to see the vet. In an effort to make pet owners comfortable, the Receptionist often talks to them while they are waiting.

Depending on the structure of the specific office, the Receptionist may either tell the veterinarian or vet technician that a patient has arrived or may bring the pet and its owner directly to an examination room.

The Receptionist is expected to answer phones and direct calls to the correct party in the office. When appropriate, he or she may answer questions from callers. Each call must be handled in a courteous and cordial manner. As some calls may be emergencies, the Receptionist must have good judgment and follow office policies in alerting the veterinarians.

Depending on the size and structure of the veterinary office, clinic, or hospital, the Receptionist may also handle secretarial and clerical duties. These might include typing correspondence, envelopes, reports, and other materials. It might also include copying documents, maintaining files and charts, sorting mail, and sending faxes.

Many veterinary offices and clinics now augment income by selling pet-related products, pet food, and nutritional supplements. In offices that do this, the Receptionist may be responsible for providing information regarding products as well as selling them and taking payment.

Receptionists are expected to make appointments. In certain offices this is done manually, while others use specialized computer software. In some offices, Receptionists may call pet owners a day ahead of time to remind them of an upcoming appointment.

Receptionists may handle e-mails as well as input information regarding a pet's condition, diagnosis, and medications into the computer. Individuals in most offices are also expected to process payments. They may print out bills and invoices for clients and handle accounts payable and receivable for the office.

Receptionists working in veterinary offices, clinics, and animal hospitals are expected to deal with clients, answering their questions and providing good customer service.

This is the perfect type of job for an individual who enjoys working around animals and people.

Salaries
Receptionists working in veterinary offices, animal hospitals, and clinics are generally paid an hourly wage. This can range from approximately $8.00 to $18.00 per hour or more. Factors affecting earnings include the experience of the Receptionist and the responsibilities of the position. Other factors affecting earnings include the type, size, and prestige of the specific employer as well as geographic location.

Employment Prospects
Employment prospects for Receptionists working in veterinary offices, animal hospitals, and clinics are fair. Employment opportunities exist in veterinary offices, animal hospitals, clinics, and emergency centers throughout the country.

Advancement Prospects
Advancement prospects for Receptionists working in veterinary offices, animal hospitals, and clinics are fair. The most common method of career advancement is for individuals to secure similar jobs in larger, more prestigious facilities. This generally results in increased earnings and responsibilities. Some individuals find similar positions outside of the veterinary industry.

Education and Training
Most employers require their Receptions to have a minimum of a high school diploma or its equivalent. Some may prefer a college background. Individuals generally receive on-the-job training.

Experience, Skills, and Personality Traits
Experience requirements vary for Receptionists working in veterinary offices, animal hospitals, and clinics. Some employers prefer prior experience as a Receptionist. For others, this is an entry-level position.

Individuals should be detail-oriented with the ability to multitask effectively. Good judgment is necessary. Successful Receptionists are personable, compassionate individuals who have good communication skills and excellent phone skills.

Computer skills are necessary. The ability to follow directions is essential. Time-management and organizational skills are mandatory. A love of animals is also helpful in this type of position.

Unions and Associations
There is no association specifically geared toward Receptionists working in veterinary offices, animal hospitals, and clinics. Individuals may obtain career information by contacting the American Veterinary Medical Association.

Tips for Entry
1. Send your résumé and a short cover letter to veterinarians, animal hospitals, and clinics to see if they have openings. Remember to ask that your résumé be kept on file if there are no current openings.
2. Check out openings online. Start with some of the more traditional job sites such as Monster.com. Expand your search from there.
3. Openings are often advertised in the classifieds section of newspapers. Look under heading classifications such as "Receptionist–Veterinary Office," "Receptionist," "Animal Hospital," "Animal Clinic," or "Veterinary Office."
4. Call your local vet and ask about openings. You might just get lucky.

SHELTERS, SANCTUARIES, AND REFUGES

SHELTER MANAGER

CAREER PROFILE

Duties: Oversee shelter operation; hire, supervise, and train staff; maintain the facility; oversee investigations; implement programs; develop budgets

Alternate Title(s): Shelter Director; Operations Manager

Salary Range: $24,000 to $47,000+

Employment Prospects: Fair

Advancement Prospects: Fair

Best Geographical Locations for Position: Positions located throughout the country

Prerequisites:

Education or Training—Educational requirements vary; most jobs prefer or require college degree or background; see text

Experience and Qualifications—Supervisory experience in animal shelters, rescues, animal-related nonprofit organizations or veterinary hospitals

Special Skills and Personality Traits—Animal-care skills; people skills; administrative skills; supervi-

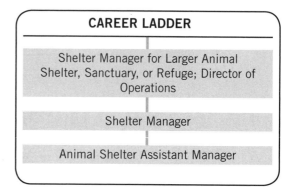

CAREER LADDER

Shelter Manager for Larger Animal Shelter, Sanctuary, or Refuge; Director of Operations

Shelter Manager

Animal Shelter Assistant Manager

sory skills; compassion; communication skills; time-management skills; business skills; organizational skills; management skills; grant-writing skills; fund-raising skills; creativity

Special Requirements—Certification or license as a veterinary technician may be required; state licensing may be required; see text

Position Description

Animal shelters and refuges are operated throughout the country. Some care for domesticated animals such as dogs and cats. Others care for a wide assortment of other animals including pet rabbits, chickens, birds, ferrets, guinea pigs, and horses. The main function of these shelters is to take animals that are in trouble and help them live better lives. Each has its own philosophy and its own rules and regulations governing the way animals are treated.

The person in charge of overseeing the shelter operation is called the Shelter Manager. Within the scope of the job, the individual has a great many responsibilities. One of the most important parts of the job of the Shelter Manager is making sure the shelter animals are properly cared for. It is the responsibility of the Shelter Manager to assure that animals are given proper medical care and food. The Shelter Manager must also ensure that the animals are kept clean and safe. The manager is further expected to assure to the best of his or her knowledge that animals will not be exposed to unsafe conditions.

The Shelter Manager is heavily involved in the budget and finances of the facility. Often a major responsi-

bility of the individual is the preparation of the annual budget. Depending on the size and structure of the organization, this may be difficult because many shelters work with limited funds.

In order to help increase the funds of the shelter, the manager may be responsible for fund-raising. The individual may develop, implement, and execute a number of special events during the year to raise needed money. These events may include dinners, membership drives, auctions, galas, golf tournaments, and more. If the shelter is large, there may be a fund-raising director, volunteers, or a board of directors who handle this function.

Grants are another source of funds that shelters often depend on to sustain themselves. The Shelter Manager may locate grants from federal, state, or local agencies as well as from private sources. He or she must then write and prepare the grant application. In some situations there may be a grant writer, a consultant, or a volunteer who handles this task.

A great deal of the job of the Shelter Manager involves paperwork. The Shelter Manager is responsible for completing reports and submitting them to the appropriate parties. He or she is expected to handle billings for services rendered such as veterinary care. The individual must also handle the accounting for adoption fees, supplies, medications, and other expenses. If the shelter does not have a bookkeeper, the Shelter Manager may be responsible for paying bills incurred by the facility. He or she may also be expected to handle payroll.

The Shelter Manager is expected to recruit, hire, supervise, and train the shelter staff. This may include, among others, assistant shelter managers, clerks, animal attendants, veterinary technicians and technologists, adoption counselors, humane educators, animal treatment investigators, and more.

The Shelter Manager may place ads in local papers or other local media or online to recruit staff members. He or she may also post signs in local stores or even in the shelter itself. The individual is responsible for reviewing applications, calling in applicants for interviews, and conducting the interview process. Before hiring any potential employee, the Shelter Manager will generally check references.

The Shelter Manager is responsible for scheduling employees so that all shifts are covered. He or she must also train employees in following the shelter's procedures. In some cases, the individual will assign these tasks to an assistant shelter manager.

The Shelter Manager is expected to make sure that the shelter adheres to all operational policies, safety rules, regulations, and procedures. The individual must stay updated on all local, state, and national regulations regarding sheltering and animal control.

The Shelter Manager is responsible for monitoring the shelter's inventory of supplies and equipment. He or she is additionally responsible for monitoring the inventory of drugs and medications used in the shelter. This is especially important in shelters where drugs used for euthanasia and chemical captures are present.

No one wants to walk into a shelter that is dirty and smells. It is also unhealthy for animals to be in poor conditions. It is therefore essential that the Shelter Manager make sure the facility is kept clean and sanitized. This includes the public areas as well as the kennels. While the Shelter Manager will assign these tasks to staff members, he or she must make sure that these things are taken care of consistently.

The Shelter Manager is also responsible for the maintenance and care of the shelter. Depending on the specific job, this may include the actual shelter facility, the building, and/or the outer areas. The individual may assign various employees to care for the facility or retain outside contractors to handle these tasks.

A major part of the job of the Shelter Manager is developing programs to assist in the adoption of animals. He or she may also develop special events to help boost the adoptions of shelter animals. These might include events on shelter premises or off-site. The Shelter Manager generally works with other staff members, developing and implementing these programs. He or she may also develop programs to help the public learn about responsible pet ownership and the humane treatment of animals.

The Shelter Manager frequently deals with the public. He or she is expected to take care of any complaints people have regarding the shelter, its employees, or policies quickly and effectively. The Shelter Manager is also expected to either personally handle or oversee the shelter's public relations campaign. This may include public relations and advertising efforts directed toward the public as well as efforts that target shelter members and donors.

The Shelter Manager will often speak at events, do media interviews, and send out membership materials, among other things, in order to give the shelter publicity, increase membership, and spread the word.

Shelters, like many other not-for-profit groups, depend on the help of volunteers. The Shelter Manager is responsible for coordinating the efforts of all volunteers. In some cases, an assistant manager or director of volunteers will handle this task.

The Shelter Manager is ultimately responsible for everything that happens in the shelter. A good manager can make the difference between a successful shelter with a great reputation and a high adoption rate for healthy pets and a shelter where no one feels comfortable adopting a pet.

It should be noted that some shelters, called "no-kill" shelters, never kill a healthy animal. Others routinely use euthanasia when animals have been in the shelter "too long." These policies may be set by any number of people, including a board of directors, depending on the situation and facility. The Shelter Manager must be comfortable with the shelter policies in order to be able to follow them.

Salaries

Earnings for Shelter Manager can vary greatly. There are some Shelter Managers who earn approximately $24,000 annually and others who earn $47,000 or more. Factors affecting earnings include the experience, education, and responsibilities of the individual as well as the size, budget, and geographic location of the specific shelter.

Employment Prospects

Employment prospects for Shelter Managers are fair. Individuals may work in a variety of settings, including private or public animal shelters, refuges, rescues, and sanctuaries. Employment opportunities will be greatest in areas hosting a large number of animal shelters, societies for the prevention of cruelty to animals, humane societies, and similar organizations. These are generally located throughout the United States.

Advancement Prospects

Advancement prospects for Shelter Managers are fair. Some individuals find similar work in larger shelters with bigger budgets. This generally results in increased earnings and responsibilities. Others may secure positions as shelter directors.

Education and Training

Most animal shelters require or prefer their applicants have a minimum of a four-year college degree. There may, however, be smaller shelters that accept an applicant with an associate's degree or even a high school diploma coupled with experience.

Courses, seminars, and workshops in fund-raising, grant-writing, public relations, business, management, presentation skills, and administration will be useful in honing skills and making new contacts.

Experience, Skills, and Personality Traits

While experience requirements vary from job to job, as a rule individuals must have some sort of supervisory experience. This is often obtained in various positions in animal shelters, refuges, animal hospitals, or veterinary offices.

Individuals should enjoy being around animals and be committed to their welfare. They also need to be compassionate, patient, kindhearted people. A working knowledge of breeds is also vital.

Keen business acumen is necessary, as are management skills. Time-management skills are additionally needed, as is the ability to multitask effectively. Individuals should have an understanding of grant-writing and fund-raising. Successful Shelter Managers are creative, personable people with excellent verbal and written communication skills.

Special Requirements

In some situations Shelter Managers may be required to be certified or licensed as a veterinary technician. Depending on the state, individuals may also be required to be licensed by the state.

Unions and Associations

Shelter Managers may be members of a variety of local, regional, and national animal advocacy organizations and associations dedicated to the humane treatment of animals. These include the Humane Society of the United States, the American Humane Association, and the American Society for the Prevention of Cruelty to Animals (ASPCA), among others. Individuals may also be members of the Society of Animal Welfare Administrators and the National Animal Control Association.

Tips for Entry

1. Get experience working with animals by volunteering at a local shelter, humane society, Society for the Prevention of Cruelty to Animals (SPCA), or other organizations. Then, when an opening exists, you will already have your foot in the door.
2. Send your résumé and a short cover letter to shelters, humane societies, and SPCAs to see if they have openings. Remember to ask that your résumé be kept on file if there are no current openings.
3. Check out openings online. Start with some of the more traditional job sites such as Monster.com. Expand your search from there.
4. Openings are often advertised in the classifieds section of newspapers. Look under headings such as "Animal Shelter Manager," "Animal Shelter," "Animal Shelter Director," "Humane Society," "ASPCA," or "Animal Jobs."
5. Openings may be listed on the Web sites of specific shelters, humane societies, and SPCAs.
6. Network as much as you can in the industry. Go to conferences, conventions, and educational seminars and workshops to meet industry insiders.
7. An internship with a shelter or an animal advocacy organization will also be useful for both the experience and the opportunity to make contacts.

ANIMAL SHELTER CLERK

CAREER PROFILE

Duties: Greet shelter visitors; complete paperwork; answer the phones; maintain files; enter data; show pets to potential adoptive families; handle animal intake; process stray and abandoned animals

Alternate Title(s): Receptionist

Salary Range: $7.25 to $8.00+ per hour

Employment Prospects: Good

Advancement Prospects: Fair

Best Geographical Locations for Position: Positions located throughout the United States

Prerequisites:

Education or Training—Minimum of high school diploma or equivalent; on-the-job training; see text

Experience and Qualifications—Entry level

Special Skills and Personality Traits—Computer skills; typing skills; animal-care skills; ability to follow directions; strong stomach; compassion; communication skills; time-management skills; organizational skills; office skills

CAREER LADDER

Animal Shelter Clerk in Larger Shelter; Animal Attendant; Veterinary Technician

↑

Animal Shelter Clerk

↑

Volunteer or Entry Level

Position Description

Animal shelters, the Society for the Prevention of Cruelty to Animals (SPCA), humane societies, and other organizations house, shelter, and care for unwanted pets, strays, and abandoned and abused animals. These animals may be brought in by former owners, animal control officers, or kindhearted people who see an abandoned puppy or kitten on the side of the road and want to make sure it is cared for.

Within the shelter there are various people who care for the animals. There may be shelter managers, assistant managers, veterinarians, veterinary technicians and technologists, adoption counselors, humane educators, investigators, animal attendants, and Animal Shelter Clerks.

Clerks working in animal shelters perform many of the same tasks and routine duties that clerks or receptionists perform in other offices. The Animal Shelter Clerk is often the first person an individual sees when he or she walks in the door of the shelter. The Animal Shelter Clerk is expected to greet each visitor in a pleasant and welcoming manner.

The individual generally asks visitors the purpose of their visit. For example, are they looking for a new pet? Do they want to turn in an animal? Are they interested in volunteering? Do they want to make a donation? Once the Animal Shelter Clerk ascertains the purpose of the visit, he or she will be able to direct them to the appropriate party.

Animal Shelter Clerks may direct visitors to the kennels where dogs and puppies are kept or the area where kittens are kept. In some cases, Animal Shelter Clerks may accompany visitors into the kennel area.

Animal Shelter Clerks are often involved in the intake process. When someone is relinquishing ownership of an animal, the Animal Shelter Clerk may take the animal from the owner. As part of this process, he or she may then take a report of any information the person has regarding the animal being turned in. Animal Shelter Clerks additionally may handle the processing of stray and abandoned animals that are brought into the shelter.

In some cases people who have lost a dog or cat may call the shelter in hopes of finding their lost pet. The Animal Shelter Clerk, responsible for answering the phone, may receive these calls and reunite the pet and owner.

Animal shelters have a lot of paperwork. Animal Shelter Clerks are expected to maintain files, records, and statistics regarding the shelter's animal population as well as intake and adoption. They must also keep records on any euthanasia performed on animals at the shelter. Animal Shelter Clerks additionally maintain records on animals that have been spayed and neutered. If accidents or other incidents occur within the shelter, the Animal Shelter Clerk is expected to log them and make sure incident reports are filled in and filed with the appropriate people. Animal Shelter Clerks may input information into computers using various software programs.

Animal Shelter Clerks are responsible for making copies, printing out information, and filing. They may complete records and forms, logs of drugs that have been dispensed, and daily activity sheets.

Animal Shelter Clerks are expected to answer the phones and direct calls to the appropriate people within the shelter. They screen incoming calls and often take messages. Depending on the specific shelter, Animal Shelter Clerks may be responsible for taking payment for the pet adoption fees and issuing payment receipts.

In some shelters, Animal Shelter Clerks are responsible for taking digital pictures of animals that are ready for adoption and posting them to the shelter Web site. Clerks may also take animals out of the cages or pens to walk and socialize them.

Salaries
Animal Shelter Clerks are generally paid an hourly wage. This can range from approximately $7.25 to $8.00 an hour or more. Factors affecting earnings include the experience, training, and responsibilities of the individual. Other factors affecting earnings include the size and budget of the specific shelter as well as the geographic location.

Employment Prospects
Employment prospects for Animal Shelter Clerks are good. Employment opportunities may exist throughout the United States. Full-time and part-time opportunities may be available.

Advancement Prospects
Advancement prospects for Animal Shelter Clerks are fair. Some individuals find similar work in larger shelters with bigger budgets. This generally results in increased earnings. With increased experience, education, and training, others may go on to become veterinary assistants, technicians, or technologists.

Education and Training
Most employers prefer their full-time employees to have a minimum of a high school diploma or its equiva-

lent. Individuals generally receive on-the-job training. In some situations, employers will hire individuals who are still in high school for a part-time job.

Experience, Skills, and Personality Traits
While experience requirements vary from job to job, this is considered an entry-level position. Individuals should enjoy being around animals and be committed to their welfare. They also need to be compassionate, patient, kindhearted people.

Animal Shelter Clerks need basic office skills. The ability to type accurately, file, and answer phones in a pleasant manner is vital. Computer skills are mandatory, and a working knowledge of various software programs such as the Microsoft Office applications is helpful. The ability to follow instructions is essential. Time-management skills are also needed.

Unions and Associations
Animal Shelter Clerks may be members of a variety of local, regional, and national animal advocacy organizations and associations dedicated to the humane treatment of animals. These may include the Humane Society of the United States, the American Humane Association, and the American Society for the Prevention of Cruelty to Animals (ASPCA), among others.

Tips for Entry
1. Get experience by volunteering at a local shelter, humane society, or SPCA. Then, when an opening pops up, you will already have your foot in the door.
2. Send your résumé and a short cover letter to shelters, humane societies, and SPCAs to see if they have openings. Remember to ask that your résumé be kept on file if there are no current openings.
3. Check out openings online. Start with some of the more traditional job sites such as Monster.com. Expand your search from there.
4. Openings may also be located on the Web sites of animal shelters, SPCAs, humane societies, and other organizations.
5. Openings are often advertised in the classifieds section of newspapers. Look under headings such as "Clerk–Animal Shelter," "Animal Shelter," "Humane Society," "ASPCA," or "Animal Jobs."

ANIMAL ATTENDANT

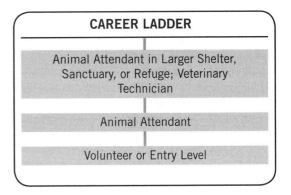

Position Description

Animal shelters, the Society for the Prevention of Cruelty to Animals (SPCA), humane societies, and similar organizations are full of unwanted pets, strays, and abandoned and abused animals. They may be brought in by former owners, animal control officers, or kindhearted people who see an abandoned animal on the side of the road and want to make sure it is cared for.

Within shelters there are several people who care for the animals. There are shelter managers, assistant managers, veterinarians, veterinary technicians and technologists, clerks, adoption counselors, humane educators, investigators, and Animal Attendants, among others.

Animal Attendants are the primary caregivers for animals in a shelter. They provide the bulk of the physical and emotional care of the animals at the shelter.

Animals such as dogs and cats are generally kept in cages, pens, or other types of enclosures. Animal Attendants are responsible for cleaning the animals' cages, pens, and other housing enclosures at the shelter.

Individuals, for example, will remove soiled bedding and feces from the cages. They may also hose out animal pens, making sure all animal waste is cleaned out. Animal Attendants are expected to wash and sanitize the cages and put clean bedding in if necessary. They are also expected to clean up any accidents animals may have when they are out of their cage or pen.

Animal Attendants working at shelters have close contact with the animals. They are often the ones who physically take the animals into the shelter after people turn them in or leave them at the door.

Once animals are brought into the shelter, Animal Attendants are expected to clean the animals. People are more apt to adopt animals that look clean and happy. If necessary, Animal Attendants may bathe and groom animals, brushing out matted fur and taking out any burs. They may also clip the animal's nails or do other simple grooming procedures. Animal Attendants are expected to check animals for fleas, ticks, and other pests. If they see evidence of pests, they may bathe the animals in flea baths or apply flea powder.

The Animal Attendant is expected to keep an eye out for any problems or health concerns with the animals. While observing the animals, he or she may notice unusual behavior. Perhaps a dog is exhibiting aggressive behavior or a puppy is barking insistently. Perhaps a kitten is acting lethargic. Maybe there is blood in a cage. The attendant must be alert to each animal's behavior. If the Animal Attendant sees any problems, he or she must report it to his or her supervisor so it can be attended to.

Animal Attendants working at shelters are responsible for feeding and giving water to animals according to the daily schedule. They may prepare the food, measuring out the correct amounts, and place the food dishes in cages or the animal's pen. Individuals are also responsible for checking that each animal has clean water throughout the day.

Most shelters have a veterinarian visit on a regular basis to assure the animals are healthy and to attend to any problems. Animal Attendants may work alongside the vets when they are at the shelter, assisting with any treatments. They may also be responsible for administering medications or any other treatments that have been prescribed by the veterinarian.

Animal Attendants are responsible for taking the animals out of their cages to show to people who are interested in adopting potential pets. They may hold the animals themselves or put the animal on leashes so people can get to know them. Animal Attendants may walk through the shelter with people, telling them about the various animals that are there. If the animals have accidents while out of their cage or pen, Animal Attendants are responsible for cleaning them up.

Animal Attendants are also responsible for taking animals out of their cages regularly to exercise them, take them for walks, or to help socialize them.

Salaries

Animal Attendants working in shelters are generally paid an hourly wage. This can range from approximately $7.25 to $8.50 an hour or more. Factors affecting earnings include the experience, training, and responsibilities of the individual. Other factors affecting earnings include the size and budget of the specific shelter, as well as the geographic location.

Employment Prospects

Employment prospects are good for Animal Attendants who want to work in shelters.

Employment opportunities may exist throughout the country in areas hosting animal shelters, SPCAs, and humane societies.

Advancement Prospects

Advancement prospects for Animal Attendants working in shelters are fair. Some individuals find similar work in larger shelters with bigger budgets. Others may go on to become veterinary assistants, technicians, or technologists. This generally results in increased earnings and responsibilities.

Education and Training

Most employers prefer their full-time employees to have a minimum of a high school diploma or its equivalent. Individuals generally receive on-the-job training. In some situations, employers will hire individuals who are still in high school for a part-time job.

Experience, Skills, and Personality Traits

While experience requirements vary from job to job, as a rule, this is generally an entry-level position. Individuals should enjoy being around animals and be committed to the welfare of animals. They also need to be compassionate, patient, and kindhearted.

The ability to follow instructions is essential. A strong stomach is needed in order to perform certain tasks and duties. Time-management skills are also needed.

Unions and Associations

Animal Attendants working at shelters may be members of a variety of local, regional, and national animal advocacy organizations and associations dedicated to the humane treatment of animals. These may the Humane Society of the United States, the American Humane Association, and the American Society for the Prevention of Cruelty to Animals (ASPCA), among others.

Tips for Entry

1. Get experience working with animals by volunteering at a local shelter, humane society, or SPCA. Then, when an opening pops up, you will already have your foot in the door.
2. Send your résumé and a short cover letter to shelters, humane societies, and SPCAs to see if they have openings. Remember to ask that your résumé be kept on file if there are no current openings.
3. Check out openings online. Start with some of the more traditional job sites such as Monster.com. Expand your search from there.
4. Openings are often advertised in the classifieds section of newspapers. Look under heading classifications such as "Animal Attendant," "Animal Shelter," "Humane Society," "ASPCA," or "Animal Jobs."

HUMANE EDUCATOR

CAREER PROFILE

Duties: Provide humane education on behalf of shelter; teach kindness and compassion toward animals; teach responsible animal care; develop and present programs and activities regarding animal issues and advocacy to schools and organizations; visit schools; prepare humane education materials; assist with outreach programs; give shelter tours

Alternate Title(s): Educator; Humane Teacher

Salary Range: $22,000 to $35,000+

Employment Prospects: Poor

Advancement Prospects: Fair

Best Geographical Locations for Position: Positions located throughout the United States

Prerequisites:

Education or Training—Educational requirements vary; see text

Experience and Qualifications—Experience working in outreach, education, public relations, public speaking, fund-raising, and/or administration

Special Skills and Personality Traits—Excellent verbal and written communication skills; creativity; persuasiveness; public-speaking skills; good judgment; common sense

Special Requirements—Voluntary certification available; certain positions may require teaching certificate

CAREER LADDER

Humane Educator for Larger, More Prestigious Animal Shelter or Animal Advocacy Organization; Director of Humane Education or Director of Education and Outreach for Animal Shelter

Humane Educator

Teacher; Intern; Volunteer

Position Description

Humane Educators working at animal shelters have a very important job. Individuals in this position are responsible for educating the public about the humane treatment of animals. Within the scope of the job, the individual may have varied responsibilities.

One of the responsibilities of Humane Educators working in animal shelters may be to speak to new and prospective adoptive families about animal welfare and choosing the correct pet. They may instruct individuals on the proper and acceptable ways to treat dogs and cats or other animals they are planning to adopt.

Humane Educators often arrange tours of the shelter for community groups, students, teachers, and other individuals. During these tours, the Humane Educator will show the various areas of the facility and explain the services offered by the shelter. Individuals may chaperone groups of children when they are touring the shelter.

Humane Educators working in shelters frequently develop programs for special events and classroom presentations. They may, for example, bring pets to schools or special events. When doing this, the Humane Educator will choose animals from the shelter that he or she knows will get along well with people.

The Humane Educator is responsible for developing and preparing educational materials designed to promote humane attitudes toward animals and the proper treatment of pets. These materials may be used by schools or the general public as components of outreach programs.

Humane Educators working at shelters may work with others at the shelter in developing newsletters, flyers, and other educational materials geared toward the humane treatment of pets and other animals. They may assist in mailings and distribution of these materials.

Humane Educators are expected to represent the shelter at special events. They may prepare presentations for special informational events or scheduled classes. These might touch on various subject areas, including pet safety, responsible pet ownership, and choosing the correct pet.

The duties of Humane Educators may vary depending on the specific shelter for which they work. In larger shelters, their duties will generally be more specific, focusing on going out into the public and speaking about humane issues. In smaller shelters, individuals may be responsible for the entire education and outreach program. It should be noted that every shelter does not have a Humane Educator on staff. In these cases, the responsibilities of the Humane Educator will fall onto other shelter employees, such as the shelter manager.

Humane Educators working in shelters teach and promote humane attitudes toward animals. They develop, coordinate, and present programs regarding animal issues and the concerns of the specific organization to local schools, youth groups, civic groups, colleges, conferences and other organizations. Since children in various grades have different comprehension levels, when preparing presentations, individuals are expected to develop programs suitable for the appropriate audience. In many cases, Humane Educators working with shelters discuss careers working with animals.

Humane Educators working in shelters help educate people to help prevent animal abuse, cruelty, and neglect. To accomplish this, the Humane Educator is responsible for researching pertinent topics for programs, presentations, and activities that help further the specific organization's mission.

Individuals may seek out additional opportunities to reach the public. They may, for example, attend community events and fairs to educate the public about the shelter and its mission and goals.

The Humane Educator may also appear on television and the radio to discuss various topics on behalf of the shelter. The educator may write columns for newspapers, magazines, or Web sites in order to help educate the public on relevant issues.

Salaries

Depending on a number of factors, earnings for Humane Educators working in animal shelters can range from approximately $22,000 to $35,000 or more. These factors include the size, structure, budget, and geographic location of the specific shelter. Other factors affecting earnings include the responsibilities, professional reputation, and experience of the individual.

Employment Prospects

Employment prospects for individuals aspiring to become Humane Educators in shelter situations are poor. While most shelters have someone who handles the responsibilities of a Humane Educator, not every shelter employs a full-time professional dedicated to educating the public on the humane treatment of animals.

With that being said, those seeking positions in this field may find a variety of part-time opportunities.

Advancement Prospects

Advancement prospects for Humane Educators, once they get their foot in the door, are fair. Individuals may climb the career ladder in a number of ways depending on their career aspirations. Many individuals find similar positions in larger, higher-budget shelters. Others find similar positions in other animal advocacy organizations. There are some Humane Educators who climb the career ladder by becoming either the director of education and outreach of an animal advocacy organization or even a shelter manager or director.

Education and Training

While there may be small shelters that accept an applicant with an associate's degree, or even a high school diploma coupled with experience, almost every shelter prefers their Humane Educator to have a minimum of a four-year degree.

A four-year college degree is also helpful in career advancement. Good choices for majors include education, communications, business administration, journalism, public relations, animal sciences, or a related area.

Courses, seminars, and workshops in education, training, public speaking, grant-writing, public relations, business, management, and presentation skills will be useful in honing abilities and making new contacts.

Experience, Skills, and Personality Traits

Experience requirements depend to a great extent on the size, structure, and reputation of the specific animal shelter. Individuals seeking positions in larger shelters generally will need to have more experience than their counterparts working at smaller shelters. In some situations, Humane Educators gain experience speaking on behalf of animal advocacy organizations or animal shelters on a volunteer basis.

Some Humane Educators have a background in education. Others have experience working with other animal advocacy organizations in various capacities or in public relations, journalism, fund-raising, grant-writing, and nonprofit organizations. What they all generally have in common is a passion for animal welfare.

Humane Educators must be creative, articulate, confident, and enthusiastic individuals with excellent verbal communication skills. The ability to discuss issues persuasively is essential. Public speaking skills are crucial as Humane Educators often speak in front of groups of people. The ability to relate to children is also necessary.

People skills and motivational skills are important. Humane Educators should be competent in media relations, as there will be times when they will be speaking to the media regarding organization issues.

Special Requirements

A voluntary certification is available from the Humane Society Youth. This organization is an affiliate of the Humane Society of the United States (HSUS). The certification provides a professional development program for individuals committed to humane education. Courses are offered online. Those completing the program and passing an exam will earn the designation Certified Humane Education Specialist.

Unions and Associations

Humane Educators employed by animal shelters may belong to a number of organizations that help them make contacts and get professional support. These include the Association of Professional Humane Educators and the Institute for Humane Education. Individuals might also join the American Society for the Prevention of Cruelty to Animals, the American Humane Association, and the HSUS.

Tips for Entry

1. Become an active member of an animal shelter in your area. Ask to help in the education and outreach department.
2. Volunteer at an animal shelter. It will give you shelter experience and help you make important contacts.
3. Look for internships in animal shelters, refuges, rescues, or animal advocacy organizations. Talk to directors of education and outreach at these organizations and other Humane Educators about your career goals.
4. Look for job openings in the classifieds sections of newspapers. Headings for such jobs might include "Humane Educator," "Humane Education," "Education and Outreach," "Outreach and Education," and "Animal Shelter." Jobs may also be advertised under the names of specific animal shelters.
5. Openings may be listed on the Web sites of specific animal shelters, so explore these.

PET ADOPTION COUNSELOR

Duties: Greet shelter visitors; explain adoption policies; handle adoption paperwork; interview potential adoptive families; review applications

Alternate Title(s): Adoption Coordinator; Adoption Counselor; Shelter Adoption Clerk

Salary Range: $8.50 to $15.00+ per hour

Employment Prospects: Fair

Advancement Prospects: Fair

Best Geographical Locations for Position: Positions located throughout the United States

Prerequisites:

Education or Training—High school diploma or equivalent; on-the-job training; see text

Experience and Qualifications—Experience working in animal shelters

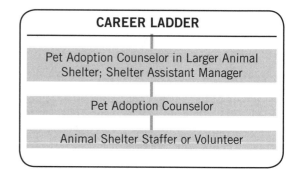

Special Skills and Personality Traits—Animal-care skills; people skills; compassion; communication skills; time-management skills; organizational skills

---

Position Description

Often when people want to add pets to their family, they buy them at pet stores or from breeders. Others may decide that they want to save the life of an animal or may want to give an animal another chance at a good life; these people choose adoption. Animal shelters, the Society for the Prevention of Cruelty to Animals (SPCA), humane societies, and animal rescues are full of unwanted pets, strays, and abandoned and abused animals. They may be brought in by former owners, animal control officers, or kindhearted people who see an abandoned animal on the side of the road and want to make sure it is cared for.

One of the goals of animal shelters, SPCAs, humane societies, and rescues is finding ways to adopt out the animals in their care to families who will love and care for them. Every family is not right for every pet. Conversely, every pet might not be right for every family. Pet Adoption Counselors are the individuals who assist people in finding just the right pet for them. They are also the people who find just the right family for each pet. Within the scope of their job, they have varied responsibilities.

The objective for most Pet Adoption Counselors is to place animals in the shelter in a safe, secure, lifelong home. When doing this, individuals are expected to make potential owners aware of the responsibility they have toward the animal when they adopt.

In order to be effective, the adoption counselor learns as much as possible about animals that come into the shelter. If a pet owner relinquishes a pet, this may be easier. The owner will know the animal's medical history, what immunizations have been administered, and any illnesses he or she has had. The owner may also be able to discuss the animal's temperament, personality, and things such as whether it gets along well with children or other animals.

In some cases, animal control officers or other individuals bring animals to the shelter. In these cases, the adoption counselor may observe the animal him- or herself and talk to shelter personnel to learn as much as possible about the animal's temperament and health.

Pet Adoption Counselors often greet visitors when they come into the shelter. They may speak to people informally about the types of pets they are looking for as well as what animals are available in the shelter. Often, during this process, the counselor may think about a potential match and bring a person or family over to a specific animal to see if there is any interest.

Pet Adoption Counselors at animal shelters are expected to interview prospective people who are interested in adopting animals. It is essential that they explain to each individual the commitment involved in adopting an animal.

Pet Adoption Counselors may inquire about type of home a potential adoptive family or individual has to assure that it is appropriate for specific pets. A small apartment, for example, may not be the optimum home for a large dog. Counselors may also discuss the living situation of the adoptive family. Are there small children? Other pets? Will the pet be alone for long periods of time? Is someone home during the day? These are all questions that need to be answered.

The Pet Adoption Counselor is responsible for explaining the shelter's adoption policies to adoptive families. The counselor may work with the shelter manager in developing these policies, or may develop the policies him- or herself. Depending on the specific situation, the Pet Adoption Counselor may also be responsible for developing questionnaires, forms, and contracts for the shelter to use in regard to adoptions.

Once people have chosen a pet for adoption, the Pet Adoption Counselor is responsible for advising them about the animal's history, if available. He or she may also discuss the feeding and care of the pet. In order to control the pet population, in many shelters one of the rules regarding adoption includes the promise that owners of adopted animals spay or neuter their new pet if the procedure has not already been performed. The Pet Adoption Counselor is expected to explain the services or programs the shelter has in regard to spaying and neutering. Many shelters spay and neuter all animals before adopting them out.

The Pet Adoption Counselor is expected to handle all adoption paperwork. He or she may review applications and check people's references. The adoption counselor generally has the authority to approve or reject an application.

In shelters that charge an adoption fee, the Pet Adoption Counselor may be responsible for obtaining the fees and giving the new owners receipts. In some shelters other staff members are responsible for this task.

Other responsibilities of the adoption counselor working at shelters may include creating a database of names of individuals who are interested in adopting certain breeds of pets. When a specific breed of animal comes into the shelter, the Pet Adoption Counselor then has a reference list to help place the animal. Adoption counselors may also contact specific breed rescue organizations in an attempt to find the perfect home for specific breeds of animals in the shelter.

Salaries

Pet Adoption Counselors working in shelters are generally paid an hourly wage. This can range from approximately $8.50 to $15.00 per hour or more. Factors affecting earnings include the experience, training, and responsibilities of the individual. Other factors affecting earnings include the size and budget of the specific shelter as well as the geographic location.

Employment Prospects

Employment prospects for Pet Adoption Counselors working in animal shelters are fair. Employment opportunities may exist throughout the country in areas hosting animal shelters, SPCAs, and humane societies. It must be noted that while every shelter has someone who performs the duties of the Pet Adoption Counselor, not every shelter has a Pet Adoption Counselor. As a result, individuals may need to relocate for jobs.

Advancement Prospects

Advancement prospects for Pet Adoption Counselors working in shelters are fair. Some individuals find similar work in larger shelters with bigger budgets. Others may go on to become the assistant shelter manager or even the shelter manager. These career advancements generally result in increased earnings and responsibilities.

Education and Training

Most employers prefer their full-time employees to have a minimum of a high school diploma or its equivalent. Individuals generally receive on-the-job training. Those interested in going on to become shelter managers may find that a college degree or extensive experience will help in promotion.

Experience, Skills, and Personality Traits

While experience requirements vary from job to job, most shelters prefer someone who has some sort of experience working in animal shelters. Individuals in this type of job should enjoy being around animals as well as people. They should be compassionate, kindhearted people who are committed to the welfare of animals in the shelter's care.

Time-management skills are necessary, as are organizational skills. The ability to multitask effectively is essential.

Unions and Associations

Pet Adoption Counselors working at shelters may be members of a variety of local, regional, and national animal advocacy organizations and associations dedicated to the humane treatment of animals. These include the Humane Society of the United States, the American Humane Association, and the American Society for the Prevention of Cruelty to Animals (ASPCA), among others.

Tips for Entry

1. Get experience working in shelters by volunteering at a local shelter, humane society, SPCA, or similar organization. Then, when an opening exists, you will already have your foot in the door.

2. Send your résumé and a short cover letter to shelters, humane societies, and SPCAs to see if they have openings. Remember to ask that your résumé be kept on file if there are no current openings.

3. Check out openings online. Start with some of the more traditional job sites such as Monster.com. Expand your search from there.

4. Openings are often advertised in the classifieds section of newspapers. Look under headings such as "Pet Adoption Counselor," "Animal Adoption Counselor," "Animal Shelter," "Humane Society," "ASPCA," or "Animal Jobs."

5. Openings may also be located on the Web sites of specific animal shelters, humane societies, SPCAs, and related organizations, so monitor these for postings.

ANIMAL CRUELTY INVESTIGATOR

Duties: Investigate animal abuse and cruelty; aid animals in distress; feed starving animals; remove animals from inhumane conditions; interview witnesses to abuse; report violators to police

Alternate Title(s): Investigator; Animal Treatment Investigator; Animal Cruelty Officer

Salary Range: $24,000 to $47,000+

Employment Prospects: Fair

Advancement Prospects: Fair

Best Geographical Locations for Position: Positions located throughout the United States

Prerequisites:

Education or Training—Educational requirements vary; college background or degree generally required or preferred; see text

Experience and Qualifications—Experience working in animal control helpful; see text

Special Skills and Personality Traits—Compassion; animal-care skills; strong stomach; people skills; communication skills

Special Requirements—Driver's license; gun permit or license may be required; state licensing may be required; see text

Position Description

While most people are kind and compassionate to animals, there are some people who are not. Although animals do not have the same rights as people, there are a number of laws on the books to help protect them. These laws are useless unless someone notifies a shelter, refuge, sanctuary, or even the police about animals who are in trouble.

When a call is made, or a suspected incident of abuse or neglect is reported, Animal Cruelty Investigators often step in. Animal Cruelty Investigators check into the allegation of cruelty, abuse, or neglect. Once notified of a problem, they are expected to physically go to see the animal. Their job is similar to that of child protective services workers who protect the rights of children.

Animal Cruelty Investigators have a number of responsibilities. They investigate animal abuse and cruelty, aid animals in distress, remove animals from inhumane conditions, and report violators to police.

As part of the job, Animal Cruelty Investigators must interview those who witnessed the abuse to determine the status of the problem. Individuals may begin by trying to speak to the animal's owner. Sometimes the owner will willingly speak to the investigator. Often he or she will not.

If the investigator is successful in speaking to the owners, he or she will notify them that there has been a complaint made and ask to see the animal. The investigator will often speak to others in the vicinity. Have neighbors witnessed abuse? Have neighbors seen the animal outside with no food or shelter for extended periods of time? Has anyone witnessed someone hitting or abusing the animal? There are a lot of questions to ask.

Investigators are responsible for inspecting the home that animals stay in to determine that an animal is safe. During this process they also must ascertain that the home and setting in which the animal lives is in compliance with the humane laws on the books in that particular geographic area.

Sometimes the investigator must look for the animal. The pet owner, for example, may tell the investigator that the pet ran away or the animal is not his or hers. If the animal is not in the owner's home or yard, the investigator may look around the neighborhood for the animal until it is located.

If an animal is being abused or neglected, the investigator will inform the owner (or abuser) of the laws that are being violated and report the matter to the police for action. The investigator is also responsible for removing the animal from an unsafe or abusive situation. If animals are not being fed, the investigator will feed them, give them water, and then take them to the shelter. Individuals drive vehicles equipped with cages to transport animals. The shelter will then have them checked out by a veterinarian and care for them pending further investigation. If animals have been beaten or otherwise abused, the investigator will make them as comfortable as possible and bring them to either the shelter or a veterinarian to be examined and treated. After treatment, the animal will stay at the shelter until further investigation is completed.

In the case of a trapped animal, investigators will locate the animal, free it, and try to find its owner. If the owner cannot be found, the investigator will take the animal back to the shelter for medical care and feeding.

Pet owners are not always responsible for the abuse. In some cases, a neighbor, passerby, or family member might hurt an animal. The investigator is responsible for getting to the bottom of the situation and making sure the animals involved are safe.

Animal Cruelty Investigators work to protect all animals. Some are domesticated. Others are not. They may deal with situations such as cockfights or pit bull fights or animal sacrifices performed by cults. The investigator may need to involve the local police department in some of these situations.

There is a fair amount of paperwork that goes with this job. Animal Cruelty Investigators are expected to write reports regarding each case of animal abuse and neglect. They additionally must write reports of findings and resolutions. In some cases, investigators will take photographs of abused or neglected animals as well as their living conditions. These photos may be used in legal cases in which people are prosecuted for animal abuse or neglect.

It should be noted that there are two areas of specialty for Animal Cruelty Investigators. One is general investigation and the other is arrest. Those who work in the arrest area generally work with the local police department or municipality and often must carry guns.

Animal Cruelty Investigators may see horribly abused or neglected animals on a daily basis. Unfortunately, because of the nature of the job, they cannot save all of them. However, knowing that they are the ones who can step in and make a difference to at least some of the animals can be a very rewarding experience.

Salaries

Earnings for Animal Cruelty Investigators vary dramatically. There are some individuals who earn approximately $24,000 and others who earn $47,000 or more annually. Factors affecting earnings include the experience, education, training, and responsibilities of the individual. Other factors affecting earnings include the size and budget of the specific shelter, municipality, or community as well as geographic location. Investigators who are part of the local police department or work with municipalities generally earn more than those who work for shelters.

Employment Prospects

Employment prospects for Animal Cruelty Investigators are fair but getting better each year. Employment opportunities may exist throughout the country in areas hosting animal shelters, a Society for the Prevention of Cruelty to Animals (SPCAs), humane societies, and similar organizations.

As noted previously, there are two areas of specialty for Animal Cruelty Investigators: general investigation and arrest. Those working in general investigation often work for shelters, humane societies, and SPCAs. Those who work in the arrest area generally work with municipalities or the local police department.

Full- and part-time jobs are available.

Advancement Prospects

Advancement prospects for Animal Cruelty Investigators are fair. Some individuals find similar work in larger shelters with bigger budgets. This generally results in increased earnings. With increased experience, education, and/or training, others may go on to become director of animal treatment investigations. After obtaining experience, individuals who are working for a municipality or the police department may move up the ranks. This generally results in increased responsibilities and earnings.

Education and Training

Educational requirement vary from job to job and state to state. While a college background or degree may not be required for every job, it is almost always preferred. Courses in psychology, sociology, and criminal justice will be helpful. There are some colleges throughout the country that offer courses on animal cruelty investigation.

Many humane societies, SPCAs, and shelters offer courses and programs in animal treatment investigation and animal cruelty investigation. In some jobs with local police departments, individuals may be required to enroll in and graduate from the police academy.

Experience, Skills, and Personality Traits

Experience requirements vary from job to job. Experience handling and caring for animals will be helpful. Experience in law enforcement and investigation will also be useful.

To be successful in this area, individuals need to be compassionate and kindhearted with a love for animals and a commitment to their welfare. The ability to make difficult decisions is vital. Investigators may need to take an abused animal from its owner or recommend euthanasia for a severely abused animal near death. People skills are needed. Investigators must often deal with defensive pet owners and other difficult people. The ability to mediate is helpful.

Animal Cruelty Investigators should have calm, even temperaments. Communication skills are essential.

Special Requirements

Some states may require Animal Cruelty Investigators to hold special licenses or credentials. In positions that require individuals to carry a gun, a permit or license will be required. These are more common in positions with law enforcement agencies.

As Animal Cruelty Investigators are required to drive, a license and a clean driving record are necessary.

Unions and Associations

Animal Cruelty Investigators working at shelters may be members of a variety of local, regional, and national animal advocacy organizations and associations dedicated to the humane treatment of animals. These include the Humane Society of the United States, the American Humane Association, and the American Society for the Prevention of Cruelty to Animals (ASPCA), among others.

Tips for Entry

1. Check with your local police department to see if they have an animal cruelty investigation unit.
2. Some police departments offer volunteer opportunities in their animal cruelty investigation unit. Call or write to inquire about these types of programs.
3. Get experience by volunteering at a local shelter, humane society, or SPCA. Ask about the opportunity to volunteer in the animal cruelty investigation area.
4. Send your résumé and a short cover letter to shelters, humane societies, and SPCAs to see if they have openings. Remember to ask that your résumé be kept on file if there are no current openings.
5. Check out openings online. Start with some of the more traditional job sites such as Monster.com. Expand your search from there.
6. Openings may also be located on the Web sites of animal shelters, SPCAs, and humane societies, so check them frequently.
7. Openings are often advertised in the classifieds section of newspapers. Look under heading such as "Animal Treatment Investigator," "Animal Cruelty Officer," "Animal Shelter," "Humane Society," "ASPCA," or "Animal Jobs."

SHELTER VETERINARY TECHNICIAN

Duties: Assist veterinarians in caring for animals at animal shelters, sanctuaries, or refuges; collect specimens; assist in surgery; monitor animals after surgery; change dressings; draw blood; perform medical and laboratory tests

Alternate Title(s): Animal Health Technician; Technician

Salary Range: $8.50 to $20.00+ per hour

Employment Prospects: Good

Advancement Prospects: Fair

Best Geographical Locations for Position: Positions located throughout the United States in areas hosting animal shelters, sanctuaries, and refuges

Prerequisites:

    Education or Training—Minimum of two-year associate's degree from program accredited by American Veterinary Medical Association.

    Experience and Qualifications—Experience requirements vary; see text

CAREER LADDER

Veterinary Technician in Larger or Bigger-Budget Shelter, Sanctuary, Refuge, or Veterinary Office, Clinic, Animal Hospital, etc.; Veterinary Technologist

Veterinary Technician at Animal Shelter, Sanctuary, or Refuge

Veterinary Assistant; Volunteer; Intern

Special Skills and Personality Traits—Animal-care skills; good judgment; ability to follow directions; strong stomach; compassion; communication skills

Special Requirements—State licensing, registration, or credentialing required; see text

Position Description

Shelter Veterinary Technicians working in animal shelters, sanctuaries, or refuges work closely with animals. These individuals assist veterinarians in much the same way that nurses help physicians. Duties and responsibilities of Shelter Veterinary Technicians vary with each individual job.

It should be noted that while the job titles Shelter Veterinary Technician and veterinary technologist are often used interchangeably, there is a difference. Although a great many of the duties are the same, veterinary technologists are required to have more education than Shelter Veterinary Technicians.

Shelter Veterinary Technicians working in animal shelters, refuges, or animal sanctuaries work under the supervision of veterinarians. Individuals may perform many of the functions of veterinarians with the exception of diagnosing medical problems, performing surgery, and prescribing medication. It should be noted that every shelter, refuge, and animal sanctuary does not have a veterinarian on staff at all times. In these situations, vets often rely heavily on Shelter Veterinary Technicians to keep them abreast of the status of animals under their care.

Shelter Veterinary Technicians are responsible for assisting in the treatment of animals. Shelter Veterinary Technicians are expected to clean animals, change their dressings, and hold and comfort them while the veterinarian performs procedures. They may perform various medical and laboratory tests, draw blood, and collect specimens to check for diseases and parasites as well as prepare tissue samples.

In many situations, animals turned in to shelters have not had optimal care. They may have fleas or ticks and may not be up to date on their immunizations. Individuals are responsible for checking for fleas and ticks on each animal when they come into the shelter and then taking the appropriate action to make the animals as healthy as possible. If this is not done, animals throughout the entire shelter can become infested with fleas or ticks.

In shelters that perform surgical procedures, Shelter Veterinary Technicians are expected to help prepare animals for surgery. They may, for example, calm an animal, lift him or her up on the examination table, and assist in the anesthesia process. The technician often assists the veterinarian during surgeries by handing him or her instruments. A lot of the responsibilities will depend, of course, on exactly what services the shelter, refuge, or sanctuary provides and what services they outsource.

Depending on the specific shelter and its policies, Shelter Veterinary Technicians may deal with individuals turning in unwanted animals to the shelter. In some cases, these animals may have been badly neglected or abused by their owners. It is essential that the Shelter Veterinary Technician have the ability to remain calm when dealing with pet owners.

Shelter Veterinarian Technicians are responsible for monitoring animals under their care. They are expected to check on animals coming out of anesthesia and be sure that the animal is recovering according to the prescribed schedule. They may also administer medications under the direction of the veterinarian.

Animals cannot communicate verbally to tell anyone what is wrong. Shelter Veterinary Technicians are expected to watch animals, reporting any suspected problems to veterinarians. They must keep tabs not only on an animal's physical symptoms and well-being, but on its psychological attitude as well. This is especially important when dealing with animals in shelters that need to be assessed for adoption.

Shelter Veterinary Technicians are responsible for keeping any instruments the veterinarian uses clean and sterile. They are expected to keep inventory of instruments, medications, and other supplies and either order required supplies or inform the veterinarian or shelter manager of what is needed.

Shelter Veterinary Technicians working in shelters, refuges, and sanctuaries often witness abused, injured, neglected, and unwanted animals. This may be very difficult to see, but it is part of the job. Individuals who work in some shelters may also be expected to assist when animals must be euthanized. This too may be very difficult and emotionally draining.

Despite the drawbacks, for individuals who have a true love for animals, this type of position can be very fulfilling and rewarding. Shelter Veterinary Technicians have a lot of interaction with animals, whether in shelters, refuges, or sanctuaries. They may play with them, give them special attention, or comfort them when they are in physical or emotional pain. This one-on-one ability to make a difference in animals' lives is the reason many love their job.

Salaries

Shelter Veterinary Technicians working in animal shelters, sanctuaries, or refuges are generally paid an hourly wage. This can range from approximately $8.50 to $20.00 per hour or more. Factors affecting earnings include the experience, education, and

responsibilities of the individual. Other factors affecting earnings include the type and size of the specific employer as well as the specific geographic location of the facility.

Employment Prospects

Employment prospects for Shelter Veterinary Technicians seeking employment in animal shelters, refuges, and sanctuaries are good. Individuals may find employment throughout the United States.

Advancement Prospects

Advancement prospects for Shelter Veterinary Technicians working in animal shelters, refuges, or sanctuaries are fair. Individuals may climb the career ladder in a number of ways depending on their career aspirations. Some find similar positions in larger facilities or facilities with bigger budgets, generally resulting in increased responsibilities and earnings. Others go back to school and obtain a four-year degree in veterinary technology and become veterinary technologists.

Education and Training

Regardless of the employment setting, Shelter Veterinary Technicians need a minimum of a two-year associate's degree from a program accredited by the American Veterinary Medical Association (AVMA). These programs are generally offered in community colleges and encompass both clinical and laboratory settings. There are also four-year programs for individuals who want to earn a bachelor's degree.

Experience, Skills, and Personality Traits

Experience requirements for Shelter Veterinary Technicians working in animal shelters, refuges, and sanctuaries vary from job to job. Some positions may be entry-level. Others may require or prefer experience.

Shelter Veterinary Technicians need to be compassionate, patient, kind individuals with a true love for animals. Many animals in shelters, refuges, and sanctuaries have been abused, neglected, or abandoned and need extra care.

The ability to follow instructions is essential. Verbal communication skills are necessary as well. A strong stomach is needed in order to perform certain tasks and duties. The ability to deal with stressful situations is vital.

Special Requirements

While each state regulates Shelter Veterinary Technicians in a different manner, all states require them to pass a credentialing examination. This exam includes oral, written, and practical sections and is regulated by either the specific state's board of veterinary examiners or another state agency. Depending on the specific state, Shelter Veterinary Technicians may become registered, licensed, or certified upon passing the test.

Most states use the National Veterinary Technician exam. As a result, individuals who want to have their scores transferred from one state to another can, as long as both states use the exam.

Unions and Associations

Shelter Veterinary Technicians can obtain additional career information by contacting the AVMA. Individuals may also be members of the National Association of Veterinary Technicians in America. This organization offers its members professional support and educational opportunities.

Tips for Entry

1. Get experience by volunteering at a shelter, sanctuary, or refuge. This will help you make sure this is the line of work you want to go into as well as a chance to gain valuable experience and make important contacts.

2. Send your résumé and a short cover letter to animal shelters, sanctuaries, and refuges. Remember to ask that your résumé be kept on file if there are no current openings.

3. Check out openings online. Start with some of the more traditional job sites such as Monster. com. Expand your search from there.

4. Openings are often advertised in the classifieds section of newspapers. Look under headings such as "Animal Shelter," "Animal Refuges," "Refuges," "Animal Sanctuaries," and "Veterinary Technician."

SHELTER VETERINARY TECHNOLOGIST

Duties: Care for animals in shelter; supervise technicians; assist shelter veterinarians; assist in surgery; monitor animals after surgery; change dressings; perform medical and laboratory tests; draw blood and collect specimens; train new staff; look for signs of abuse or neglect in animals; assess animal's temperament

Alternate Title(s): Animal Health Technologist; Technologist; Vet Technologist

Salary Range: $9.50 to $25.00+ per hour

Employment Prospects: Good

Advancement Prospects: Good

Best Geographical Locations for Position: Positions located throughout the United States

Prerequisites:

Education or Training—Bachelor's degree in veterinary technology

Experience and Qualifications—Experience requirements vary; see text

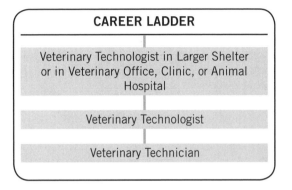

CAREER LADDER

Veterinary Technologist in Larger Shelter or in Veterinary Office, Clinic, or Animal Hospital

Veterinary Technologist

Veterinary Technician

Special Skills and Personality Traits—Animal-care skills; good judgment; supervisory skills; ability to follow directions; strong stomach; compassion; communication skills; ability to deal with stress

Special Requirements—State licensing, registration, or credentialing required; see text

Position Description

Shelter Veterinary Technologists work closely with the animals in their care. Duties and responsibilities vary with each job. While the job titles Shelter Veterinary Technologist and shelter veterinary technician are often used interchangeably and a great many of the duties are the same, Shelter Veterinary Technologists are required to have more education. This prepares them for supervisory and management duties, responsibilities, and positions.

Shelter Veterinary Technologists work under the supervision of the shelter manager and veterinarians. They may perform many of the functions of veterinarians with the exception of diagnosing medical problems, performing surgery, and prescribing medication. They do, however, work next to the veterinarian in these situations, assisting in these functions. As every shelter does not have a veterinarian on duty at all times, this is an important position.

Shelter Veterinary Technologists often witness abused, injured, neglected, and unwanted animals. While this can be very difficult, it is unfortunately part of the job. Individuals who work in some shelters also may

assist when animals must be euthanized. This too may be very difficult and emotionally draining.

Technologists are responsible for assisting in the treatment of animals. This may include cleaning them, changing dressings, or holding them while the veterinarian performs procedures. The technologist may also perform various medical and laboratory tests, draw blood, prepare tissue samples, and collect specimens to check for diseases and parasites.

Depending on the specific shelter and its policies, Shelter Veterinary Technologists may deal with individuals turning in unwanted animals to the shelter. In some cases, these animals may have been badly neglected or abused by their owners. It is essential that the Shelter Veterinary Technologist have the ability to remain calm when dealing with owners of pets who have not cared for them properly.

Depending on the situation, Shelter Veterinary Technologists may be responsible for supervising veterinary technicians and veterinary assistants in the shelter. They may also be expected to train these individuals in performing procedures.

In many shelters, animals are taken to a veterinary office or clinic when surgery is required. There are, however, some larger shelters that have the facilities to perform surgery. In these cases, Shelter Veterinary Technologists may help prepare animals for surgery. Individuals may, for example, help calm an animal, get him or her up on the examination table, and assist in the administration of anesthesia. Technologists may prepare the operating room for surgery and often assist the veterinarian during surgeries by handing him or her instruments.

Shelters are full of animals. Shelter Veterinary Technologists are expected to monitor the health of each of the animals under their care. If an animal has had surgery, the technologist must be sure it is recovering according to schedule. The technologist may also administer medications under the direction of the veterinarian.

While monitoring animals in their care, Shelter Veterinary Technologists are expected to report any problems or issues to the veterinarian. This might includes an animal's physical symptoms and well-being as well as its psychological attitude. This is essential when assessing the temperament of animals for adoption.

Technologists may be responsible for taking inventory of instruments, medications, and other supplies. They may also be expected to order and store needed equipment and supplies on behalf of the shelter.

Shelter Veterinary Technologists have a lot of interaction with animals. They may play with them, give them special attention, or comfort them when they are in physical or emotional pain.

Animals that are in shelters often are under a great deal of stress and may be frightened. They may have been abused, neglected, or abandoned. They may be there because their owner didn't want them. Or they may simply be there because they are strays.

Although all Shelter Veterinary Technologists have the opportunity to provide care to animals, individuals working in shelters often provide the only loving touch or snuggle an animal has experienced in a long while. Making that kind of difference to an animal is the reason many love their job. For individuals who have a true love for animals, yet aren't prepared to commit to veterinary school, this type of position can be very fulfilling and rewarding.

Salaries

Shelter Veterinary Technologists are generally paid an hourly wage. This can range from approximately $9.50 to $25.00 an hour or more. Factors affecting earnings include the experience, education, and responsibili-

ties of the individual. Other factors affecting earnings include the size and budget of the specific shelter as well as its geographic location.

Employment Prospects

Employment prospects for Shelter Veterinary Technologists are good. Individuals may find employment throughout the United States in large or small shelters, humane societies, and sanctuaries. Full- and part-time employment may be available.

Advancement Prospects

Advancement prospects for Shelter Veterinary Technologists are good. Individuals may climb the career ladder in a number of ways, depending on their career aspirations. Those working in shelters may find similar positions in larger shelters with bigger budgets, resulting in increased responsibilities and earnings. Some individuals also find similar positions in larger animal hospitals and clinics or other larger facilities. This, too, generally results in increased earnings and responsibilities.

Some decide that they want more and go back to school to become veterinarians.

Education and Training

Shelter Veterinary Technologists must complete a four-year program accredited by the American Veterinary Medical Association (AVMA). Approximately 16 colleges offer veterinary technology programs that culminate in a four-year degree.

A period of clinical experience in a veterinary practice is required for all students in an AVMA-accredited veterinary technology program. This hands-on training is called a preceptorship, practicum, or externship.

Experience, Skills, and Personality Traits

As noted previously, no matter where Shelter Veterinary Technologists want to work, they must complete hands-on training with a veterinarian before they graduate. Experience requirements for Shelter Veterinary Technologists vary from job to job. Some positions may be entry level. Other employers may require or prefer experience in other shelters, veterinary offices, clinics, or animal hospitals.

In order to be successful in this line of work, individuals must have a true love for animals. Shelter Veterinary Technologists need to be compassionate, patient, and kindhearted.

The ability to follow instructions is essential. Supervisory and management skills are needed as well. Verbal communications skills are a must. A strong stomach is needed in order to perform certain tasks and duties, as is the ability to effectively cope with stressful situations.

Special Requirements

While each state regulates Shelter Veterinary Technologists in a different manner, all states require them to pass a credentialing examination. This exam includes oral, written, and practical components and is regulated by either the specific state's board of veterinary examiners or another state agency. Depending on the specific state, Shelter Veterinary Technologists become registered, licensed, or certified upon passing the exam.

Most states use the National Veterinary Technician exam. As a result, individuals who want to have their scores transferred from one state to another can, as long as both states use the exam.

Unions and Associations

Shelter Veterinary Technologists can obtain career information by contacting the AVMA. Individuals may also be members of the National Association of Veterinary Technicians in America. This organization offers professional support and educational opportunities to members.

Tips for Entry

1. Get experience by volunteering at a shelter, veterinary office, humane society, or sanctuary before you enter school.
2. Send your résumé and a short cover letter to shelters to see if they have openings. Remember to ask that your résumé be kept on file if there are no current openings.
3. Check out openings online. Start with some of the more traditional job sites such as Monster. com. Expand your search from there.
4. Openings are often advertised in the classifieds section of newspapers. Look under headings such as "Veterinary Technologists," "Veterinary Technicians," and "Shelters," among others.
5. Don't forget to ask your veterinarian (if you have a pet) for advice. He or she might become a mentor, or if you have graduated from school, an employer.
6. Check out the Web sites of shelters and similar organizations. Many list job openings.

WILDLIFE REHABILITATOR

Duties: Rescue injured animals; treat injured or ill animals; care for injured, ill, or abandoned wildlife; prepare wildlife to go back to its natural habitat; capture and transport injured animals; assist with administering therapies

Alternate Title(s): Rehabilitator; Wildlife Rehabber

Salary Range: $19,000 to $35,000+

Employment Prospects: Fair

Advancement Prospects: Fair

Best Geographical Locations for Position: Positions may be located throughout the country

Prerequisites:

Education or Training—Educational requirements vary; see text

Experience and Qualifications—Experience working with wildlife

CAREER LADDER

Lead Wildlife Rehabilitator; Assistant Rehabilitator Manager

Wildlife Rehabilitator

Intern; Wildlife Rehabilitator Technician

Special Skills and Personality Traits—Affection for animals; communication skills; observation skills; physical fitness; interest in conservation; people skills; ability to be a team player; ability to work alone

Position Description

When domesticated animals are injured or become ill, their owners or Good Samaritans generally seek medical attention to help nurse them back to health. They may be given medication for illness or disease. They may have bones set or have surgery to correct a problem.

Animals and birds living in the wild, like domestic animals, may also be injured or become ill. Like all other animals, they may be prone to disease. They may also be abandoned by their parents or orphaned before they are ready to care for themselves. Sometimes these animals are left to fend for themselves. Sometimes individuals known as Wildlife Rehabilitators come to their rescue.

Wildlife Rehabilitators are individuals who help injured, ill, or abandoned wildlife. Some equate their job to that of emergency medical technicians who treat people.

While over the years there always were those who helped injured or abandoned wildlife as a hobby, today wildlife rehabilitation has evolved into a career.

Wildlife Rehabilitators rescue animals in need. They then treat and care for them. The ultimate goal of Wildlife Rehabilitators is to rehabilitate animals so that they can be returned to their natural habitat to live independently. Within the scope of their job, individuals may

have a variety of responsibilities. Specific duties will depend, of course, on exactly where the Wildlife Rehabilitator works.

Wildlife Rehabilitators are responsible for capturing animals that are hurt, ill, or orphaned and transporting them to a location where they can be cared for. This is not an easy job. Wild animals instinctively are frightened of humans and may try to escape or defend themselves in some way.

Wildlife Rehabilitators locate animals in need in a number of ways. Sometimes an animal in need is found by another individual and reported to either a Wildlife Rehabilitator or an agency. Sometimes animals are seized from poachers. People who may have tried to turn them into pets bring other animals in.

Some animals are turned over to Wildlife Rehabilitators when an automobile has struck them. Other animals may be turned over to Wildlife Rehabilitators when someone finds them stuck in inhumane traps. Someone may also see a hurt bird, or birds that have fallen out of their nests, and call an agency to see who might be able to help.

When Wildlife Rehabilitators are called in, one of the first things they need to do is to assess the situation. They may examine animals to determine the type and extent of injuries or illnesses. While doing this, individuals must determine the likelihood that each animal can be successfully rehabilitated.

If, in the opinion of the rehabilitator, the animal can be rehabilitated and returned to its environment, the individual will do everything in his or her power to help it. This might include bringing it to a rehabilitation center for treatment. He or she will establish a course of treatment that may include making sure the animal gets a proper diet, medications, surgery, and/or treatments for wounds, among other things. Sometimes the animal just needs to be fed and cared for in a safe environment while it recovers from injuries. Other times animals may need to be taught survival or foraging techniques.

One of the more difficult parts of the job for Wildlife Rehabilitators is when they determine that an animal cannot be rehabilitated or will not be able to be returned to the wild. In these cases, depending on the circumstances, the individual may humanely euthanize the animal, bring it to a wildlife rescue center to live, or on occasion, keep the animal as its foster parent. This may happen, for example, if an animal is orphaned and would not be able to live on its own.

Wildlife Rehabilitators have many functions. In addition to capturing and transporting animals, they may act as animal caretakers, animal behaviorists, nutritionists, emergency medical technicians, and educators, among other things. Wildlife Rehabilitators are in the unique position of not only helping animals in a hands-on manner, but making a difference in their life as well.

Wildlife Rehabilitators are expected to treat any illnesses, injuries, or wounds animals have. They often work with veterinarians who provide specialized medical care to animals in need. A veterinarian may, for example, perform surgery on an animal. The rehabilitator is then responsible for caring for the animal while it recovers. This is usually done at a wildlife or rehabilitation center or rescue or animal hospital. In certain cases, however, the Wildlife Rehabilitator may take animals home to give them around-the-clock care. This may be necessary for a number of reasons. Sometimes, for example, animals or birds need to be monitored 24 hours a day. In other situations, animals may need to be fed every hour or so.

After surgery, Wildlife Rehabilitators are expected to provide aftercare to animals. This may include providing nursing care, physical therapy, and preparing animals to go back to the wild. Wildlife Rehabilitators must often teach young animals how to hunt for prey. Seeing animals killing others for food can be difficult for some rehabilitators, but it is necessary for survival in the wild.

Wildlife Rehabilitators sometimes must replicate the natural environment of animals under their care. Trained rehabilitators know that every animal has specialized housing needs. Some birds, for example, may need special perches. Other animals may need other types of housing. In the wild, appropriate housing helps keep animals safe from predators. During rehabilitation, proper housing is equally important.

Wildlife Rehabilitators must have a broad knowledge of the species with which they work as well as their habitats. They must also know what various animals need to survive. It is essential that individuals be realistic in rehabilitating animals. They need to accept the fact that not every animal can be saved.

Wildlife Rehabilitators are responsible for not only feeding the animals under their care, but also making sure they get enough to eat and drink. This may be difficult when animals are wounded or injured. The task may be made even more difficult when rehabilitators are trying to train animals to find their own food, as they would when they are in the wild.

Wildlife Rehabilitators are responsible for preparing animals to be released back into the wild. They must work to assure that animals can defend themselves, find food, and exist without the help of man. In order to do that, individuals must teach animals needed skills.

Wildlife Rehabilitators determine when animals can be returned to their own environment. For many rehabilitators, seeing animals going "home" and knowing that they are prepared to survive is the ultimate reward.

Wildlife Rehabilitators provide education regarding wild animals, rehabilitation, conservation, and other topics. They may be expected to prepare programs for community groups, schools, or the general public.

Salaries

Earnings for Wildlife Rehabilitators can vary greatly depending on the specific employment situation. Individuals can earn between $19,000 and $35,000 or more. Factors affecting earnings include the specific employment environment as well as the size, location, and type of facility for which the individual works. Other variables affecting salary include the individual's education, experience, and responsibilities. Those taking part in internships will generally earn a small weekly stipend.

Employment Prospects

While the Bureau of Labor Statistics projects slower than average growth for Wildlife Rehabilitators through

2016, employment prospects are still fair for individuals seeking positions in this field. As the field of wildlife rehabilitation grows, there will be more and more opportunities.

Individuals may find jobs throughout the country in federal or state conservation departments, county or city environmental departments, and public or private rehabilitation centers, rescues, nature centers, or hospitals for animal wildlife. Jobs may also be located within nonprofit foundations.

It should be noted that all privately run rehabilitation centers must operate on a not-for-profit status. The reason for this is that according to law, Wildlife Rehabilitators in the United States are not permitted to charge for treating wild animals.

Advancement Prospects

Advancement prospects for Wildlife Rehabilitators are fair. Individuals may climb the career ladder by being promoted to supervisory positions such as a lead wildlife rehabilitator or an assistant rehabilitator manager. Some Wildlife Rehabilitators find similar positions in larger facilities. This often results in increased responsibilities and earnings.

Education and Training

Educational requirements for Wildlife Rehabilitators can vary from job to job. While a college degree may not be required to become a Wildlife Rehabilitator, it does give individuals necessary knowledge for their career and an edge over other applicants who may not hold a degree.

For many positions, employers prefer or require a minimum of a bachelor's degree in biology, ecology, animal sciences, wildlife management, or a related field. Courses in animal behavior, ecology, mammalogy, ornithology, and related wildlife areas are helpful.

There are a number of schools that offer biology and animal ecology degrees that specialize in wildlife, wildlife care, and pre-veterinary medicine. Some offer classes in wildlife rehabilitation, including wildlife management, behavior, field techniques, ecology, animal restraint, raptor physiology, and related areas. Other programs may offer veterinary technology or animal health technology programs.

Many veterinary schools also offer courses in wildlife medicine as well as their own wildlife rehabilitation centers. These are helpful because they provide the opportunity for individuals to get hands-on training in diagnosing and treating ill or injured wildlife.

As Wildlife Rehabilitators often come from diverse backgrounds, there may be individuals who hold degrees in veterinary medicine or veterinary science. Most Wildlife Rehabilitators continue with their education and training in this field by attending additional seminars, conferences, and workshops.

Experience, Skills, and Personality Traits

Wildlife Rehabilitators need practical experience working with animals. Many individuals accomplish this by volunteering at wildlife preserves or zoos. Others get practical experience through internships or by working as veterinary assistants. Some work in shelters, veterinary offices, or on farms.

Wildlife Rehabilitators should be compassionate individuals with a respect for wildlife. They should like animals and enjoy working with them. They should also be interested in research, conservation, the environment, and helping animals.

Wildlife Rehabilitators must know and be able to perform wildlife first aid. Communication skills, both written and verbal, are needed, as are listening skills. Keen observation skills are critical.

Individuals should be energetic and physically fit. A strong stomach is necessary in performing some procedures and handling stressful or traumatic situations. The ability to handle a crisis is mandatory. Creativity and resourcefulness are helpful in solving difficult problems. Successful Wildlife Rehabilitators should enjoy learning new things and be able to work as part of a team while still having the ability to work alone.

Special Requirements

Regulations for becoming Wildlife Rehabilitators vary from state to state. Individuals may be required to hold a variety of permits or licenses. Depending on the situation, these may be issued from state and/or federal agencies. Individuals who work with a licensed rehabilitator or in a facility that is licensed may or may not be required to hold their own licenses or permits.

Requirements for licenses and permits vary from state to state as well. Special permits may be needed for certain tasks such as transporting wild animals or taking orphaned wildlife home for an evening or a weekend. Agencies such as the U.S. Fish and Wildlife Service, the Migratory Bird Program, the Natural Resources Conservation Service, and state fish and game departments can provide information about necessary permits.

Generally, Wildlife Rehabilitators in the United States are licensed in the state in which they work. They are normally only licensed to care for animals native to that state.

Voluntary certification is available for Wildlife Rehabilitators from the International Wildlife Rehabilitation

Council (IWRC). In order to obtain the Certified Wildlife Rehabilitator (CWR) designation, individuals must pass an exam administered by the IWRC. Continued education is required in order to renew certification.

Unions and Associations

Wildlife Rehabilitators may be members of a number of organizations that bring together individuals interested in wildlife rehabilitation as well as provide professional support and educational opportunities. These include the National Wildlife Rehabilitators Association (NWRA) and the IWRC. Other helpful organizations include the U.S. Fish and Wildlife Service, the Wildlife Management Institute, and the Wildlife Society. There are also many state associations and councils dedicated to wildlife rehabilitation.

Tips for Entry

1. When looking for a school, try to find one associated with a wildlife rehabilitation facility.
2. Get hands-on experience by contacting wildlife rehabilitation facilities to learn about volunteer opportunities.
3. Find a Wildlife Rehabilitator and ask if you can shadow him or her and volunteer. It is a great way to get good hands-on experience and make sure this is the career path you want to follow.
4. Look for job openings in the classified section of the newspaper under headings such as "Wildlife Rehabilitator," "Wildlife," "Rehabilitator," and "Wildlife Rehabilitation Facility." Positions may also be listed under the name of specific wildlife rehabilitation facilities or parks.
5. Send your résumé with a short cover letter to wildlife rehabilitation facilities, parks, and zoos. Remember to ask that your résumé be kept on file if there are no current openings.
6. Don't forget to check traditional job sites such as Monster.com.
7. Join the NWRA. In addition to providing professional support and educational opportunities, it posts job openings on its Web site.
8. Contact state and federal wildlife agencies. Most post job openings.

ANIMAL ADVOCACY ORGANIZATIONS

EXECUTIVE DIRECTOR

Duties: Oversee operations of organization; manage business affairs of organization; implement programs; develop budgets; promote organization

Alternate Title(s): Association Executive; Association Director; Organization Director; Chief Executive Officer (CEO)

Salary Range: $24,000 to $150,000+

Employment Prospects: Fair

Advancement Prospects: Fair

Best Geographical Locations for Position: Positions located throughout the United States

Prerequisites:

Education or Training—Bachelor's degree required or preferred by most organizations; see text

Experience and Qualifications—Experience working in public relations, grant-writing, fund-raising, and/or administration

Special Skills and Personality Traits—Management skills; grant-writing skills; fund-raising skills; creativity; personableness; verbal and written communication skills; understanding of and passion for animal advocacy

CAREER LADDER

Executive Director of Larger, More Prestigious Animal Advocacy Organization; Executive Director of Advocacy Organization or Trade Association in Other Industry

↑

Executive Director of Animal Advocacy Organization

↑

Assistant Director of Animal Advocacy Organization; Public Relations Director; Grant Writer; Administrator; Journalist

Position Description

Animal advocacy organizations improve the lives of animals. There are many animal advocacy organizations throughout the United States. Each has its own issues of interest, philosophies, and concerns.

One of the best-known animal advocacy organizations is People for the Ethical Treatment of Animals (PETA). Other well-known organizations include the National Wildlife Federation, Save the Dolphins, the Humane Farming Association, and the National Anti-Vivisection Society, among others. There are hundreds more. Each is dedicated to its own set of causes.

As a rule, animal advocacy organizations are classified as not-for-profit groups. This means that they are not publicly owned. Monies earned by the organizations are generally put back into the organization to pay for services, buy equipment, further the cause of the organization, and so on.

Not-for-profit organizations do not have owners. Instead, they are headed by a board of directors and run by an Executive Director. This individual, who may also be referred to as the CEO, holds a very important position in the animal advocacy organization.

In this position, the individual is in charge of overseeing the operation of the animal advocacy organization. The Executive Director of an animal advocacy organization generally works under the direction of board of directors. Together they establish the direction that the organization will go as well as the organization's policies.

The Executive Director is expected to make sure that the organization runs efficiently and smoothly. He or she does this by overseeing the group's business on a day-to-day basis. The individual works with the various departments to develop methods for the organization to work toward meeting its goals.

Executive Directors of animal advocacy organizations can have a variety of responsibilities depending on a number of factors. These factors include the specific organization and its mission, size, structure, prestige, and budget. In smaller organizations, the Executive Director may handle everything him- or herself, or perhaps with the help of committees of volunteers and interns. In these situations, he or she may, for example, act not only as the Executive Director, but also as the public relations director, copywriter, fund-raiser, education, business manager, lobbyist, and human resources director. In larger organizations, the Executive Director generally has a large staff and assistants who help handle the various duties.

The Executive Director is responsible for supervising all assistants and other administrators within the organization. He or she is ultimately responsible for approving publications, campaigns, special event ideas, and budgets. The director is often also responsible for the final approval on the hiring of staff.

The Executive Director of an animal advocacy organization is heavily involved in the budget and finances of the association. Usually, one of the major responsibilities of the individual is the preparation of the annual budget. Depending on the size and structure of the organization, this may be difficult because many of these organizations work with limited financial resources.

In order to help increase the funds of the organization, the Executive Director is often responsible for fund-raising. The individual may develop, implement, and execute a number of special events during the year to raise needed money. These events may include dinners, membership drives, auctions, galas, golf tournaments, and more. If the association is large, there may a fund-raising director who handles this function.

Grants are another source of funds that animal advocacy organizations depend on to sustain themselves. The Executive Director is responsible for locating grants from federal, state, or local agencies as well as from private foundations and industry. He or she must then write and prepare the grant application. In some situations, the Executive Director of the organization oversees either a staff grant writer or a consultant who is expected to find and apply for these grants. If successful in securing a grant, the Executive Director is responsible for assuring that all rules and regulations of the grant are followed. A grant administrator may be assigned this task as well.

The Executive Director is often expected to solicit donations from the corporate world and private donors. In order to be effective at this task, the individual needs to be comfortable asking for money. Some people are very good at this. Others find it difficult or uncomfortable. Gaining a comfort level in this type of task helps ensure the success of the organization's director and the organization itself.

The Executive Director is expected to either personally handle or oversee the association's public relations and advertising. This may include communications and advertising efforts directed toward the public as well as internally, within the organization's member-ship. As part of this responsibility, press releases, calendar schedules, and newsletters must be developed and prepared. In addition, brochures, leaflets, and booklets must be developed and designed to promote the organization. In smaller organizations, the Executive Director may handle these personally. In larger organizations, the Executive Director is responsible for overseeing the public relations and publications departments and staffers.

The Executive Director is also responsible for finding ways to increase the organization's membership. Depending on the size and structure of the organization, the individual may work with a membership director or handle the task personally. The director will often speak at events, do media interviews, and send out memberships materials, among other things, in order to make the organization better known, spread the word about its cause and mission, and increase membership.

Animal advocacy organizations, like many other not-for-profit groups, depend on the help of volunteers. The Executive Director is responsible for coordinating the efforts of all volunteer groups and committees within the organization's membership.

The Executive Director of an animal advocacy organization must be the champion of that organization. He or she will often attend meetings and events and handle media appearances on behalf of the group to help further its mission.

Salaries

Earnings for Executive Directors of animal advocacy organizations can range tremendously depending on a number of factors. These include the size, structure, budget, and geographic location of the specific organization as well as its specific cause. Other factors affecting earnings include the responsibilities, professional reputation, and experience of the individual. There are some directors who earn approximately $24,000 and others who earn $150,000 or more.

Employment Prospects

Employment prospects for individuals seeking positions as Executive Directors of animal advocacy organizations are fair. Individuals may find employment with organizations focusing on a wide assortment of animal advocacy issues. Some are large and well known. Others are smaller and not as well known, but have important missions just the same.

Opportunities may be found throughout the country. It should be noted that individuals might need to relocate for positions.

Advancement Prospects

Advancement prospects for Executive Directors of animal advocacy organizations are fair. Individuals may climb the career ladder in a number of ways. Many Executive Directors advance their careers by successfully building their organization into a larger, better-known entity. This generally results in increased responsibilities and earnings. Others climb the career ladder by finding similar positions with larger, better-known, or more prestigious organizations, including those not related to animal advocacy.

Education and Training

Most animal advocacy organizations require or prefer that their applicants have a minimum of a four-year college degree. There may, however, be smaller organizations that may accept an applicant with an associate's degree or even a high school diploma coupled with experience, especially if the applicant has a passion for the cause.

Courses, seminars, and workshops in fund-raising, grant-writing, public relations, business, management, presentation skills, and administration will be useful in honing skills and making new contacts.

Experience, Skills, and Personality Traits

Experience requirements depend to a great extent on the size, structure, and prestige of the specific animal advocacy organization. Individuals seeking positions with large, well-known organizations are generally required to have a minimum of three years of experience working with animal advocacy organizations, trade associations, or another not-for-profit group. Experience in public relations, journalism, fund-raising, grant-writing, and working with not-for-profit organizations will also be helpful.

Executive Directors of animal advocacy organizations need to have a passion for the cause. They should be creative visionaries with the ability to think creatively. Individuals must be well-spoken with excellent verbal and communication skills. An understanding of grant-writing is usually necessary as is the ability to develop and adhere to budgets. People skills are essential. Management and supervisory skills are also crucial. The ability to speak in front of groups of people comfortably is necessary.

Unions and Associations

Individuals interested in careers as Executive Directors of animal advocacy organizations may want to become members of various organizations to make contacts. These organizations include the Public Relations Society of America, the Association of Fundraising Professionals, and associations specific to various areas of animal advocacy.

Tips for Entry

1. Get experience working with not-for-profit organizations by volunteering with a local civic or community organization. If you can find an animal advocacy group, great. If not, any experience will be helpful.
2. An internship with an animal advocacy organization will be useful for both the experience and the opportunity to make contacts.
3. Look for job openings in the classifieds sections of newspapers. Headings might include key words such as "Executive Director," "Animal Advocacy Organization," or "Animal Rights Organization." Jobs may also be advertised under the names of specific organizations.
4. Openings may be listed on the Web sites of specific animal advocacy organizations.
5. Network as much as you can in the industry. Go to conferences, conventions, and educational seminars and workshops to meet industry insiders.
6. Offer to do the publicity or fund-raising for a local not-for-profit organization. It doesn't matter if the organization is related to animal advocacy or not. If you can do publicity or fund-raising for one organization, you can do it for any type of group.
7. Become a member of one or more animal rights organizations, humane societies, animal shelter, or rescues.
8. When considering organizations with which to work, it is important to choose one with causes and issues in which you strongly believe.

DIRECTOR OF PUBLIC RELATIONS

CAREER PROFILE

Duties: Handle public relations for organization; develop public relations campaigns; develop internal and external communications; promote positive image of organization; keep organization in the public eye; organize media events; represent organization to reporters and media; handle media inquiries

Alternate Title(s): Public Relations Director; PR Director; Director of PR

Salary Range: $24,000 to $75,000+

Employment Prospects: Fair

Advancement Prospects: Fair

Best Geographical Locations for Position: Positions located throughout the United States in areas hosting animal advocacy organizations

Prerequisites:

Education or Training—Bachelor's degree in public relations, communications, journalism, or related field required or preferred by most organizations; see text

Experience and Qualifications—Experience working in public relations, journalism, or related field

CAREER LADDER

Director of Public Relations of Larger, More Prestigious Animal Advocacy Organization; Executive Director of Animal Advocacy Organization

↑

Director of Public Relations for Animal Advocacy Organization

↑

Assistant Director of Public Relations for Animal Advocacy Organization or Other Industry; Grant Writer or Administrator; Journalist

Special Skills and Personality Traits—Creativity; personableness; verbal and written communication skills; understanding of and passion for animal advocacy; ability to multitask

Position Description

The public relations department of an animal advocacy organization is very important. Its efforts help to influence public opinion about the organization and its goals, issues, and projects.

Animal advocacy organizations improve the lives of animals. There are many animal advocacy organizations throughout the United States. Each has its own issues, philosophies, concerns, and mission.

Generally, animal advocacy organizations are formed when a number of people believe that one or more of the rights of animals are being exploited. The group gets together to find ways to stop the exploitation. Its members work to make others aware of the problems in the belief that the more people know, the more likely it is that they will take action.

Without the help of public relations efforts, many of the goals of animal advocacy organizations might never be known outside of their memberships.

The Director of Public Relations of an animal advocacy organization thus holds a very important position. He or she is ultimately responsible for developing the overall public relations campaign for the organization.

Within the scope of the job, the individual may have varied responsibilities depending on the specific organization and its mission, size, structure, and budget.

In larger organizations, the individual may have more specific duties. In smaller organizations, the Director of Public Relations may personally handle everything within the department or perhaps with the help of committees of volunteers and interns. In larger organizations, the individual may have more specific duties and a staff and assistants who help handle the various duties. Regardless of the organization's size, however, the director is responsible for promoting the organization's image.

Done correctly, public relations can help people form opinions and make them change existing ones. It can make people feel good about certain situations and want to change unpleasant ones. This is especially significant to the Director of Public Relations of an animal advocacy organization when he or she is trying to enlighten the public about an animal advocacy issue.

Additionally, as animal advocacy organizations are generally not-for-profit organizations, they usually depend heavily on donations from the public. As public relations can help determine where people donate their money, campaigns that the Director of Public Relations develops can seriously affect the financial health of the organization.

The Director of Public Relations is responsible for developing methods to publicize and promote the organization as well as formulating campaigns. He or she is expected to develop and prepare internal and external communications and publications. These may include staff and member newspapers and newsletters, programs and promotional materials, letters, and internal memos. The individual may also develop feature stories and draft press releases and special-request articles for the press and other media. In larger organizations, the director may oversee a staff that handles these functions.

It is essential that the individual understands the organization's policies, issues, causes, and mission and has the ability to speak passionately about them in an informed manner. The director is expected to represent the organization to reporters and other media. He or she may handle inquires from the media either in writing or verbally, or may assign this task to a subordinate.

In order to obtain publicity and secure favorable coverage in newspapers, magazines, and on television and radio, the Director of Public Relations must maintain a professional and honest relationship with the media. This can mean the difference between getting a story in the paper or on the air and getting no exposure at all.

It is important to realize that just because the Director or Public Relations or one of his or her staffers issues a press release, the media will not necessarily use it. Those who are successful in this position must know how to develop a good "hook" or angle to draw attention to their particular press release among the dozens of others that are generated every day. This is also necessary when pitching stories to the media about the organization's issues or special events.

The Director of Public Relations may be called on to write or deliver speeches to other groups about the organization and its causes and issues. In many cases, the individual will also be expected to attend meetings or conferences on behalf of the organization.

The Director of Public Relations is expected to either develop or supervise the development of press kits and other materials for the media and the general public. These kits may consist of press releases, information about the organization, photographs, reprints or reviews of articles, fact sheets, and more. They are given or sent to editors, TV and radio producers, and talent coordinators. The Director of Public Relations or his staff must know how to get through to these people in order to get their spokesperson on television or radio or to have feature articles developed and written.

Individuals who hold this position in well-known animal advocacy organizations often have an easier time getting media exposure than their counterparts in lesser-known organizations. In cases where an organization is not very well known, the individual must have the ability to come up with unique ideas and angles to gain the attention of the media. These may include a wide assortment of special events.

In some organizations, the Director of Public Relations may be expected to handle media relations, community relations, and public affairs. In other organizations, other departments or directors may handle these responsibilities.

The Director of Public Relations in an animal advocacy organization is responsible for supervising all assistants and other administrators within the department. He or she is ultimately responsible for approving publications, campaigns, special event ideas, and budgets. The individual is often also responsible for the final approval on the hiring of staff within the department. He or she works closely with the executive director and other department heads, finding ways to further the organization's mission and promote its causes and issues.

Salaries

Earnings for Directors of Public Relations of animal advocacy organizations can range tremendously depending on a number of factors. These include the size, structure, budget, and geographic location of the specific organization as well as its specific mission. Other factors affecting earnings include the responsibilities, professional reputation, and experience of the individual. There are some individuals who earn $24,000 annually, while others earn $75,000 or more. Those at the top of the pay scale generally work for very large, high-budget organizations.

Employment Prospects

Employment prospects for individuals seeking positions as Directors of Public Relations for animal advocacy organizations are fair. Individuals may find employment with organizations dedicated a wide assortment of animal advocacy issues. Some are large and well known. Others are smaller and not as well known, but with important causes just the same.

Opportunities are located throughout the United States. It should be noted that individuals might need to relocate for positions.

While every organization needs someone to handle public relations, every organization does not employ a Director of Public Relations. In smaller organizations, the executive director may handle the responsibilities of the Director of Public Relations along with his or her other duties.

Advancement Prospects

Advancement prospects are fair for Directors of Public Relations of animal advocacy organizations. Individuals may climb the career ladder in a number of ways, depending on their career aspirations. Some advance their career by finding similar positions at larger animal advocacy organizations with bigger budgets, resulting in increased responsibilities and earnings. Some may find similar positions in other industries. Individuals who are passionate about animal advocacy and want to stay in the field may also advance by being promoted to other administrative positions, such as the assistant director or executive director of an animal advocacy organization.

Education and Training

Most animal advocacy organizations require or prefer that their applicants have a minimum of a four-year college degree. There may, however, be smaller organizations that accept applicants with an associate's degree or even a high school diploma coupled with experience, especially those with a passion for the cause.

Good choices for majors include public relations, communications, journalism, marketing, or related areas. Courses, seminars, and workshops in public relations, publicity, promotion, writing, marketing, fund-raising, development, and presentation skills will be useful.

Experience, Skills, and Personality Traits

Experience requirements depend to a great extent on the size, structure, and prestige of the specific animal advocacy organization. Experience in public relations, journalism, and working with not-for-profit organizations will be helpful.

It is essential that the candidate have a total understanding of the issues, causes, and mission of the animal advocacy organization. A belief in the causes of the group is also helpful.

The Director of Public Relations of an animal advocacy organization should have the ability to define problems logically, clearly, and concisely as well as to analyze them from a variety of points of view. Creativity is essential. It is necessary to develop and implement public relations campaigns, generate effective press releases, and create special events.

The Director of Public Relations needs to have excellent verbal and written communication skills. A good writing style is helpful. The ability to communicate on the telephone in a polite, friendly, and effective manner is necessary. A proficiency in public speaking is also needed. Individuals must be comfortable dealing with the media and answering questions.

Interpersonal skills are essential. Management and supervisory skills are also crucial. Successful Directors of Public Relations are enthusiastic people who have the ability to effectively multitask without getting flustered.

Unions and Associations

Individuals interested in careers as Directors of Public Relations for animal advocacy organizations should become members of various organizations to make contacts. These organizations include the Public Relations Society of America and associations focused on various areas of animal advocacy.

Tips for Entry

1. Get experience doing public relations with not-for-profit organizations by volunteering with a local civic or community organization. If you can find an animal advocacy group, great. If not, any experience will be helpful.
2. An internship with an animal advocacy organization in the public relations department will be useful for both the experience and the opportunity to make contacts.
3. Look for job openings in the classifieds sections of newspapers. Headings might include key words such as "Director of Public Relations," "Public Relations Director," "Animal Advocacy Organization," or "Animal Rights Organization." Jobs may also be advertised under the names of specific organizations.
4. Don't forget to look online for job opportunities. Start with some of the general career sites such as Monster.com. Then search out sites specific to working with animals.
5. Openings may be listed on the Web sites of specific animal advocacy organizations, so check these frequently.
6. Network as much as you can in the industry. Go to conferences, conventions, and educational seminars and workshops to meet industry insiders.
7. Become a member of one or more animal advocacy organizations, humane societies, animal shelters, or rescues. Membership will help you make contacts and get you involved in the animal advocacy world.
8. When considering organizations with which to work, it is important to choose one with causes and issues that you believe in.

PUBLICIST

Duties: Develop and write press releases; promote positive image of organization; keep organization in public eye; handle media inquiries; assist in creating media events; be the public face of the organization with reporters and media

Alternate Title(s): Press Representative

Salary Range: $21,000 to 44,000+

Employment Prospects: Fair

Advancement Prospects: Fair

Best Geographical Locations for Position: Positions located throughout the United States

Prerequisites:

Education or Training—Bachelor's degree in public relations, communications, journalism, or related field required or preferred by most organizations; see text

Experience and Qualifications—Experience working in public relations, journalism, or related field

Special Skills and Personality Traits—Creativity; written and verbal communication skills; good judg-

---

CAREER LADDER

Publicist for Larger, More Prestigious Animal Advocacy Organization; Assistant Director or Director of Public Relations for Animal Advocacy Organization

↑

Publicist for Animal Advocacy Organization

↑

Publicist in Different Industry; Journalist; Intern

---

ment; knowledge of graphic arts; good telephone style; persuasiveness; understanding of and passion for appropriate area of animal advocacy

Position Description

Virtually every organization, both for-profit and non-profit, needs and uses public relations in one form or another. Animal advocacy organizations are no different. The public relations department of an animal advocacy organization is responsible for helping to spread the word about its issues, goals, and projects.

Public relations campaigns help people form opinions and change existing ones. They can also make people feel good about certain situations and want to change unpleasant ones. This is especially important in animal advocacy organizations.

Animal advocacy organizations improve the lives of animals. There are many animal advocacy organizations throughout the United States and around the world. Each has its own issues, philosophies, and concerns. The public relations department is responsible for bringing those issues and concerns to the attention of the public. Without the help of public relations, many of the goals and concerns of animal advocacy organizations might never be known outside of their membership. The hope is that when people become aware of a problem, they will help change the situation.

Some animal advocacy organizations have large public relations departments, complete with a director, assistants, writers, graphic artists, photographers, and Publicists. Smaller organizations might have either a director of public relations or an executive director and one or more Publicists.

The Publicist works under the direction of the director of the department or the executive director of the organization and is responsible for carrying out the various public relations campaigns of the organization. He or she also assists in promoting the organization's image as well as helping with the day-to-day public relations duties. Within the scope of the job, the individual may have varied responsibilities.

One of the functions of the Publicist is to develop methods to publicize and promote the organization. He or she may brainstorm with the director of the department or the executive director of the organization when formulating these campaigns.

The Publicist working in an animal advocacy organization generally does a great deal of writing. For example, he or she is generally is responsible for developing and drafting press releases on a variety of subjects. These might include press releases on the organization, special events, issues, concerns, and so on.

It is important to realize that just because a Publicist writes a press release and gives it to members of the media, the media will not necessarily use it. Publicists must know how to develop a good "hook" or angle to draw attention to their particular press release, because there are dozens of others generated every day.

Depending on the specific situation, Publicists working for animal advocacy organizations may be responsible for the preparation of internal and external communications and publications. These may include staff and member newspapers and newsletters, programs and promotional materials, letters, and internal memos.

Publicists working for animal advocacy organizations are often given writing assignments geared toward the Internet. Individuals may, for example, develop the content for the organization's Web site. Others may be assigned to write blogs focused on the organization and its issues.

In order to generate interest in the organization and promote its causes, many Publicists try to develop feature stories and special-request articles for the press and other media. In order to be successful in this task, as with press releases, individuals must have the ability to develop a good angle or "hook" to grab the attention of editors and assignment editors.

It is essential that the individual fully understand the organization's policies, issues, and causes and have the ability to speak passionately about them in an informed manner. At times, the director of the department might ask the Publicist to speak to reporters and other media. The Publicist is also expected to handle inquiries from the media both in writing or verbally.

Publicists are often asked to give speeches to other groups about the organization, its causes, and issues. They may also be responsible for attending meetings or conferences on behalf of the organization.

Publicists assist in the development of press kits and other materials generated for the media and the general public. These kits may consist of press releases, information about the organization, photographs, reprints or reviews of articles, fact sheets, and more. These are distributed to editors, TV and radio producers, and talent coordinators so that the media understand what the organization is all about.

The Publicist working at an animal advocacy organization is expected to manage day-to-day press relations with both traditional and nontraditional media. He or she is responsible for building and maintaining lists of media contacts. It is essential to the success of the Publicist to develop relationships with key editors, reporters, and other journalists. As part of the job, the Publicist must not only pitch stories to these individuals, but successfully place them as well.

Many animal advocacy organizations hold special events to bring attention to their cause, increase membership, or raise needed funds. Depending on the specific situation, the Publicist may be expected to develop events, execute them, and bring them to fruition as well as publicize them.

Other duties of the Publicist may include scheduling and running press conferences, handling community relations and public affairs for the organization, and doing everything possible to find ways to foster the organization's public image.

Salaries

Earnings for Publicists working for animal advocacy organizations can range greatly depending on a number of factors. These include the size, structure, budget, membership, and geographic location of the specific organization as well as its cause. Other factors affecting earnings include the responsibilities, professional reputation, and experience of the individual. There are some individuals who earn $21,000 annually; others earn $44,000 or more. Those at the higher end of the pay scale generally have a great deal of experience and are working for large, well-known animal advocacy organizations.

Employment Prospects

Employment prospects for individuals seeking positions as Publicists for animal advocacy organizations are fair. Individuals may find employment with organizations dedicated to a wide assortment of animal advocacy issues. Some are large and well known. Others are smaller and not as well known, but pursue important goals just the same.

Opportunities are located throughout the United States. It should be noted that individuals might need to relocate for positions.

Advancement Prospects

Advancement prospects for Publicists working for animal advocacy organizations are fair. Individuals may climb the career ladder in a number of ways. Some advance their career by finding similar positions at larger animal advocacy organizations with higher budgets, resulting in increased responsibilities and earnings. Others find positions as the assistant director of public relations or director of public relations for either the organization for which they work or another animal advocacy organization. Individuals who are passionate about animal advocacy and want to stay in the field may also climb the career ladder by being promoted to other administrative positions, such as assistant director or executive director of an animal advocacy organization. Some individuals may find similar positions in other industries.

Education and Training

Most animal advocacy organizations require or prefer a minimum of a four-year college degree. There may, however, be smaller organizations that accept an otherwise qualified applicant with an associate's degree or even a high school diploma coupled with experience, especially if the individual has a passion for the cause.

Good choices for majors include public relations, communications, journalism, marketing, or related areas. Courses, seminars, and workshops in public relations, publicity, promotion, writing, marketing, fundraising, development, and presentation skills will be useful.

Experience, Skills, and Personality Traits

Experience requirements depend to a great extent on the size, structure, and prestige of the specific animal advocacy organization. Experience in public relations, journalism, and working with not-for-profit organizations will be helpful.

It is essential that the individual have a total understanding of the mission of the animal advocacy organization. A belief in the cause is helpful.

Publicists working with animal advocacy organizations should be creative, with the ability to define problems logically, clearly, and concisely. Individuals need to be articulate and have excellent communication skills, both verbal and written. The ability to multitask effectively is critical.

As Publicists spend a great deal of time on the phone pitching stories and speaking to the media, the ability to communicate on the telephone in a polite, friendly, and effective manner is necessary. A proficiency in public speaking is also needed. Individuals must be comfortable dealing with the media and answering questions.

Unions and Associations

Individuals interested in careers as Publicists for animal advocacy organizations may want to become members of various organizations for professional support and to help make contacts. These include the Public Relations Society of America as well as various animal advocacy organizations.

Tips for Entry

1. Network as much as you can. Go to conferences, conventions, and educational seminars and workshops to meet industry insiders.
2. Become a member of one or more animal advocacy organizations, humane societies, animal shelter, or rescues. Membership will help you make contacts and get you involved in the animal advocacy world.
3. When considering organizations with which to work, it is important to choose one dedicated to causes and issues you believe in.
4. Get experience handling publicity for not-for-profit organizations by volunteering with a local civic or community organization. If you can find an animal advocacy group to volunteer with, great. If not, any experience will be helpful.
5. An internship with an animal advocacy organization in the public relations department will be useful for both the experience and the opportunity to make contacts.
6. Look for job openings in the classifieds sections of newspapers. Headings might include key words such as "Publicist," "Public Relations," "Public Relations, Animal Advocacy Organization," "Animal Advocacy Organization," or "Animal Rights Organization." Jobs may also be advertised under the names of specific organizations.
7. Don't forget to look online for job opportunities. Start with some of the general sites such as Monster.com. Then find other career sites specific to working with animals.
8. Openings may also be listed on the Web sites of specific animal advocacy organizations.

PUBLICATIONS EDITOR

CAREER PROFILE

Duties: Determine the content of organization's news-letters or magazines; decide what types of articles, columns, photographs, and additional information will be included; assign projects to copywriters, graphic artists, desktop publishers, and other staffers; develop and write articles; review and edit articles; write revisions

Alternate Title: Editor

Salary Range: $22,000 to $48,000+

Employment Prospects: Fair

Advancement Prospects: Fair

Best Geographical Locations for Position: Positions located throughout the United States

Prerequisites:

Education or Training—Four-year college degree preferred or required for most positions; see text

Experience and Qualifications—Experience working in public relations, journalism, or related field helpful

CAREER LADDER

Publications Editor of Larger Animal Advocacy Organization; Publications Manager for Animal Advocacy Organization; Public Relations Director of Animal Advocacy Organization

Publications Editor

Publication Assistant; Journalist; Publicist

Special Skills and Personality Traits—Creativity; verbal and written communications skills; command of the English language

Position Description

Animal advocacy organizations generally produce a broad range of both internal and external publications. These may include newsletters, magazines, brochures, annual reports, legislative alerts and leaflets, manuals, fact sheets, letters, press releases, marketing materials, and more. Publications Editors are in charge of the development of publications needed by the organization. In very large organizations, there may also be publications managers who head the publications department.

Depending on the size and structure of the organization, a Publications Editor may have varied responsibilities. In organizations where there is no publications manager, he or she may be responsible for hiring copywriters, graphic artists, and various members of a desktop publishing staff. The Publications Editor works with various departments in the organization preparing publications.

The Publications Editor is ultimately responsible for setting the direction, concept, and tone for each publication the organization puts out. He or she additionally is responsible for overseeing the execution and production of each publication.

Many animal advocacy organizations publish one or more newsletters or magazines to inform the public and their membership about happenings in the organization as well as to inform people about their cause. A major function of the Publications Editor is determining the content of these newsletters or magazines. He or she must decide what types of articles, columns, photographs, and additional information will be included in each issue.

Staff writers, freelancers, or volunteers write articles, stories, and columns. Photographers, art directors, and graphic designers may also be employed. The Publications Editor is responsible for assigning projects to these individuals. He or she is also responsible for supervising them, ensuring that they turn in assigned work in a timely manner. In smaller animal advocacy organizations, the Publications Editor generally writes most, if not all, of the copy.

Once articles and other copy have been turned in, the Publications Editor is responsible for reviewing and editing them. He or she may need to do rewrites. The Publications Editor will determine where in the publication each article, column, and graphic will best fit.

It is the responsibility of the Publications Editor to ensure that each newsletter or publication is the best it can be in terms of appearance and content. At very large organizations, there may be a staff of copywriters, researchers, graphic designers, and photographers. In smaller organizations, the Publications Editor might be responsible for producing the entire newsletter from the development stage to publication.

In order to get information for articles, the Publications Editor might conduct interviews with various members of the organization, including the executive director, department heads, volunteers, and donors, as well as others who support the organization. Depending on the size and structure of the organization, these tasks may be assigned to copywriters.

The editor is responsible for reviewing and editing articles and other copy as well as managing communications. The Publications Editor works with the publications manager (if there is one), managing relationships with external vendors. In organizations where there is no publications manager, the Publications Editor is expected to handle these responsibilities.

The Publications Editor also must assist in managing budgets as well as ensuring that each publication is released on time. The Publications Editor may work with the publications manager (if there is one), coordinating timetables and production schedules for printers, graphic artists, copywriters, photographers, and others involved in the preparation of the publication. If there is not a publications manager, these tasks are assumed by the Publications Editor.

The Publications Editor might be expected to do research for specific publications or may assign this task to researchers, assistants, or copywriters. Once copy comes in, the editor is responsible for editing it and checking it for accuracy. When working with graphic artists or photographers, the individual will additionally be responsible for explaining exactly what he or she wants artistically and graphically.

The Publications Editor might work with the publications manager preparing publications in-house instead of at commercial printers. This may be accomplished with desktop publishing software. This not only saves money, but it also means that the Publications Editor and/or manager can have more control over the appearance of the publication. With desktop publishing, copy can be typed directly into a computer and then laid out in a graphically pleasing format, complete with photographs, artwork, logos, and graphics. This means that printer-ready mechanicals can be produced in-house and then simply brought or transmitted to a printer for reproduction. They can then be prepared for publication in the form of newsletters, newspapers, and magazines.

Those who have a strong commitment to animal advocacy and who are talented writers and editors often find this job the perfect career match.

Salaries

Earnings for Publications Editors working for animal advocacy organizations can range widely depending on a number of factors. These include the size, structure, budget, membership, and geographic location of the specific organization, as well as its cause. Other factors affecting earnings include the responsibilities, professional reputation, and experience of the individual.

There are some individuals who earn as little as $22,000 annually, while others earn $48,000 or more. Those at the higher end of the pay scale generally have a great deal of experience and are working for well-known animal advocacy organizations with larger memberships and bigger budgets.

Generally, those working at larger, well-known animal advocacy organizations with large memberships and big budgets will earn more than their counterparts at smaller organizations even though they may perform similar tasks.

Employment Prospects

Employment prospects for Publications Editors aspiring to work at animal advocacy organizations are fair. There are many animal advocacy organizations dedicated to a wide range of animal advocacy issues located throughout the United States. Some are large and well known. Others are smaller and not as well known, but working for important causes just the same.

Most employment opportunities exist in larger, high-budget organizations. Individuals may need to relocate for job opportunities.

Advancement Prospects

Advancement prospects for Publications Editors seeking to work for animal advocacy organizations are fair. There are a number of paths for career advancement. Individuals may locate a similar position in a larger, higher budget or better-known animal advocacy organization. This will generally result in increased responsibilities and earnings. Some individuals might become publications managers. Others might be promoted to either the position of assistant director of public relations or public relations director. Advancement possibilities for the individual depend to a large extent on the structure of the organization.

Education and Training

Most larger animal advocacy organizations require or prefer a minimum of a four-year college degree for Publications Editors. There may, however, be smaller organizations that may accept qualified applicants with an associate's degree or even a high school diploma, coupled with experience, especially if he or she has a passion for the cause and a proven ability in this area.

Good choices for majors include public relations, communications, journalism, English, and liberal arts. Seminars and courses related to all phases of writing, desktop publishing, computers, graphics, and layout should prove to be extremely useful to job candidates.

Experience, Skills, and Personality Traits

Experience requirements for Publications Editors depend on the size, structure, and prestige of the specific animal advocacy organization. Many people get experience in this field working with a smaller organization and then locate a better job with a larger one. Others come from a journalism background or have worked as publicists.

It is essential that the individual has a total understanding of the mission of the animal advocacy organization. A passion for the cause is also helpful.

Publications Editors should be creative and have excellent writing skills. They need a working knowledge of language, grammar, and spelling. A good writing style is a must. The ability to research and check facts and figures for accuracy is imperative.

An understanding of graphics, layout, and the printing industry is needed. Verbal communications skills are mandatory, as are supervisory skills. Computer competency is necessary, and a working knowledge of desktop publishing is helpful.

Unions and Associations

Individuals interested in pursuing a career as a Publications Editor for an animal advocacy organization may join a number of organizations that provide professional support as well as the opportunity to make important contacts. These include the Association of Fundraising Professionals, the Council for the Advancement and Support of Education, and the Public Relations Society of America. Publications Editors might also belong to animal advocacy associations and organizations specific to their area or areas of interest.

Tips for Entry

1. Writing experience is essential to this job. If you are still in school, volunteer to work on your school newspaper or yearbook.
2. Put together a portfolio of your best writing samples. Bring it to interviews to illustrate your skills and style.
3. To get editing experience, consider volunteering to edit a newsletter for a not-for-profit or civic organization.
4. Volunteer to write and develop press releases, brochures, and flyers for local humane societies, animal shelters, nonprofit, or civic organizations.
5. Positions may be advertised in the classifieds section of newspapers under the headings "Publications Editor," "Editor," "Publications," or "Animal Advocacy Organization." Positions might also be located under the names of specific animal advocacy organizations.
6. Check out the Web sites of animal advocacy organizations. Many post employment opportunities online.
7. Employment Web sites such as Monster.com may advertise openings, so monitor them often.
8. Network as much as you can in the industry. Go to conferences, conventions, and educational seminars and workshops to meet industry insiders.
9. Become a member or supporter of one or more animal advocacy organizations, humane societies, animal shelters, or rescues. Membership will help you make contacts and get you involved in the animal advocacy world.
10. When considering organizations with which to work, it is important to choose one dedicated to causes and issues in which you believe.

PUBLICATIONS MANAGER

Duties: Oversee the writing and development of all internal and external publications; develop written materials to promote the organization's objectives; develop outlines, proposals, and budget estimates for publications; work with editors, copywriters, assistants, graphic artists, designers, and printers; coordinate timetables and production schedules; perform research; edit copy for accuracy, content, and style

Alternate Title(s): Publications Director; Director of Publications

Salary Range: $24,000 to $60,000+

Employment Prospects: Poor

Advancement Prospects: Fair

Best Geographical Locations for Position: Positions located throughout the United States in areas with animal advocacy organizations

Prerequisites:

Education or Training—Bachelor's degree required or preferred by most organizations; see text

Experience and Qualifications—Experience working in public relations, journalism, and related areas helpful

CAREER LADDER

Publications Manager of Larger, More Prestigious Animal Advocacy Organization; Public Relations Director of Animal Advocacy Organization

Publications Manager

Publications Assistant; Publications Editor; Journalist; Publicist

Special Skills and Personality Traits—Creativity; verbal and written communication skills; attentiveness to details; interpersonal skills; computer competency; ability to multitask; organizational skills; understanding of and passion for animal advocacy; good command of the English language; supervisory skills

Position Description

Depending on the specific animal advocacy organization's size, prestige, and purpose, it may issue a wide range of internal and external publications to help disseminate information about its mission. Animal advocacy organizations offer a variety of career opportunities for individuals who are talented in writing or interested in various aspects of publishing. In some organizations, the public relations, communications, fund-raising, and development or education departments handle writing duties. In other organizations, there is a special publications department. The individual who heads this department is called the Publications Manager or director.

The Publications Manager is responsible for overseeing the writing and development of all internal and external publications put out by the organization. These publications might include newsletters, magazines, brochures, annual reports, legislative alerts, or leaflets. They could also include letters, press releases, and marketing materials designed to achieve the fund-raising,

marketing, and promotional objectives of the animal advocacy organization or to simply increase public awareness of the organization's specific animal advocacy issue. The Publications Manager might also be responsible for preparing written materials for volunteers and members. These might include instructional sheets, fact sheets, volunteer manuals, and newsletters.

The Publications Manager is expected to work closely with the other departments in the organization to assure that each publication is the best it can be. He or she may, for example, work with the directors of the public relations, marketing, fund-raising and development, membership, and volunteer departments as well as the organization's executive director to develop the written materials that will be used to promote the organization's objectives.

The manager's responsibilities range from ancillary functions to full responsibility for the development of publications required by the organization. The Publications Manager may develop outlines, proposals, preliminary sketches, and budget estimates for publications. He or she may work with editors, copywriters, assistants, graphic artists and designers, layout artists, printers, and other outside vendors and freelancers to implement whatever publication decisions are made.

The Publications Manager is expected to coordinate timetables and production schedules for printers, graphic designers, copywriters, and others who are involved in the preparation of each publication. The manager must see to it that projects are completed on time. A late publication may throw off the timing of anything from upcoming promotions, fund-raisers, or news conferences.

In order to be effective, the Publications Manager must know a great deal about the printing industry. He or she will be responsible for choosing the correct paper stock, type styles, and graphic formats for each publication. This is an involved project as there are many different types, weights, and colors of paper available, as well as thousands of different varieties of type to choose from.

The individual must also be aware of the various sizes in which publications can be printed. While paper can be cut into almost any size, certain sizes and shapes will be more economical. For example, a fund-raising letter for potential donors would probably be best if it fit into a standard #10 business envelope. While a square or oversized shape might look more creative, it could pose problems in the mailing process.

In smaller organizations, the Publications Manager may have more general duties. He or she may, for example, be responsible for laying out brochures, newsletters, leaflets, and other materials in a graphically pleasing manner. In larger organizations, the individual might simply be responsible for overseeing the project and giving suggestions to a printer on his or her ideas for layout.

The Publications Manager might be expected to do research for specific publications or might assign this task to an assistant or copywriter. If the individual is working with writers on a project, he or she will be responsible for editing the copy and checking it for accuracy. When working with graphic artists or photographers, the manager will be responsible for explaining exactly what he or she wants artistically and graphically.

Before any publication is printed, the Publications Manager is expected to review it for accuracy, content, and style. He or she will also ask the appropriate department head to review it as well.

Today, with desktop publishing, the Publications Manager may prepare more projects in-house instead of at commercial printers. With desktop publishing, the Publications Manager can have copy typed into a computer and laid out in a graphically pleasing format complete with photographs, artwork, logos, and graphics. This means that the Publications Manager can produce printer-ready mechanicals and then simply bring or send them to a printer for reproduction.

Most Publications Managers find it gratifying to see publications in print that they helped create, knowing that they had a part in spreading the message for their animal advocacy organization.

Salaries

Earnings for Publications Managers working for animal advocacy organizations can range tremendously depending on a number of factors. These include the size, structure, budget, membership, and geographic location of the specific organization as well as its mission. Other factors affecting earnings include the responsibilities, professional reputation, and experience of the individual.

Some individuals earn as little as $24,000 annually, while others earn $60,000 or more. Those at the higher end of the pay scale generally have a great deal of experience and are working for well-known animal advocacy organizations with large memberships and big budgets.

Employment Prospects

There are many animal advocacy organizations encompassing a wide array of animal advocacy issues located throughout the country. Some are large and well known. Others are smaller and not as well known, but support important causes just the same.

Despite the large number of organizations, employment prospects are poor for individuals seeking this type of position. While most animal advocacy organizations have an individual who handles the responsibilities of the Publications Manager, not all organizations employ one. Sometimes, for example, the public relations director or an editor handles the responsibilities.

The greatest number of employment opportunities will exist in larger, high-budget organizations. It should be noted that individuals might need to relocate for specific job opportunities.

Advancement Prospects

Once a Publications Manager finds a job with an animal advocacy organization, advancement prospects are fair. There are a number of options for career advancement. Individuals may locate a similar position in a larger, higher budget or better-known animal advocacy organization. This will generally result in increased responsibilities and earnings. Some individuals may become the director of public relations. Others may even become the executive director of the organization. Advancement possibilities depend to a large extent on the individual's career aspirations as well as the structure of the specific organization.

Education and Training

Most large animal advocacy organizations require or prefer their applicants have a minimum of a four-year college degree. Smaller organizations may accept qualified applicants holding associate's degrees or even high school diplomas coupled with experience, especially if applicants have a passion for the cause and a proven ability in this area.

Good choices for majors include public relations, communications, journalism, English, and liberal arts. Seminars and courses related to all phases of writing, desktop publishing, computers, graphics, and layout should prove to be extremely useful.

Experience, Skills, and Personality Traits

Experience requirements depend to a great extent on the size, structure, and prestige of the specific animal advocacy organization. Many people get experience in this field by working with a smaller organization, and then go on to a better job with a larger one. It is essential to have a total understanding of the issues and causes of the animal advocacy organization. A belief in the organization's mission is helpful as well.

Publications Managers should be creative and have excellent writing skills. They need strong knowledge of language, grammar, and spelling. A good writing style is a must. The ability to research and check facts and figures for accuracy is imperative.

An understanding of graphics, layout, and the printing industry is needed. Verbal communication skills are mandatory, as are supervisory skills. Computer competency and a working knowledge of desktop printing are also necessary. The ability to multitask effectively is vital.

Unions and Associations

Individuals interested in pursuing a career as a Publications Manager for an animal advocacy organization can join a number of organizations that provide professional support as well as the opportunity to make important contacts. These include the Association of Fundraising Professionals, the Council for the Advancement and Support of Education, and the Public Relations Society of America. Individuals may also belong to associations and organizations dedicated to specific areas of animal advocacy.

Tips for Entry

1. Volunteer to write and develop press releases, brochures, and flyers for local humane societies, animal shelters, and nonprofit or civic organizations.
2. Positions may be advertised in the classifieds section of newspapers under the heading "Publications Manager," "Public Relations," "Publications," or "Animal Advocacy Organization." Positions might also be located under the names of specific animal advocacy organizations.
3. Check out the Web sites of animal advocacy organizations. Many post employment opportunities.
4. Career employment Web sites such as Monster. com might advertise relevant openings.
5. Network as much as you can in the industry. Go to conferences, conventions, educational seminars, and workshops to meet industry insiders.
6. Become a member of one or more animal advocacy organizations, humane societies, animal shelters, or rescues. Membership will help you make contacts and get you involved in the animal advocacy world.
7. When considering organizations with which to work, it is important to choose one dedicated to causes and issues in which you believe.

COPYWRITER

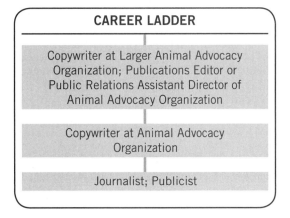

Special Skills and Personality Traits—Creativity; verbal and written communication skills; command of the English language

Position Description

Most animal advocacy organizations produce a broad range of publications. These might include newsletters, magazines, brochures, leaflets, letters, press releases, marketing materials, and more. The individual who writes a great deal of the copy for these publications is called the Copywriter.

Copywriters are important to animal advocacy organizations. The way in which words and ideas are presented can make the difference between a reader committing to the cause and just reading about it. The copy they develop must stimulate the reaction of readers.

Copywriters must have the ability to not only write clearly, concisely, and factually, but powerfully and convincingly as well. The pieces they write must make people aware of and sympathetic to the situations faced by animals and how those situations can be remedied.

Besides writing copy for one or more publications, Copywriters may also craft letters used by the organization for informational purposes, fund-raising appeals, and membership and organization development. They also may write press releases for various departments in the organization.

Copywriters are sometimes expected to develop scripts used in audio and visual projects prepared by the organization. These may include, for example, promotional films, advertisements, and radio copy.

Depending on the specific situation, the Copywriter might work directly with publication assistants or with the director of public relations, marketing, fund-raising, or special events, depending on the particular project.

Before writing articles, stories, or any other copy, the Copywriter is expected to gather facts and verify information. In some organizations, the publication department uses researchers to locate and check required information. Names, numbers, dates, and factual statistical data must be checked and spelling must be verified for accuracy.

At times, the Copywriter working for an animal advocacy organization is expected to cover newsworthy events, special events, meetings, dinners, or promotions in order to obtain information for press releases or articles.

In small animal advocacy organizations, there might just be one Copywriter who is responsible for handling the copywriting needs of the entire organization. In these situations, the Copywriter might also be expected to develop outlines, proposals, or budget estimates for publications. In larger organizations in which there is more than one Copywriter, individuals may have more specialized responsibilities.

Salaries

Earnings for Copywriters working for animal advocacy organizations can range from approximately $21,000 to $40,000 annually, depending on a number of factors. These include the size, structure, budget, membership, and geographic location of the specific organization, as well as its mission. Other factors affecting earnings include the responsibilities, professional reputation, and experience of the individual.

Those at the higher end of the scale generally are working for well-known animal advocacy organizations with large memberships and big budgets.

Employment Prospects

Employment prospects for Copywriters aspiring to work at animal advocacy organizations are fair. There are many animal advocacy organizations focusing on a wide array of animal advocacy issues located throughout the country. Some are large and well known. Others are smaller and not as well known, but support important causes just the same.

As noted, some organizations may employ just one Copywriter, while larger animal advocacy organizations may employee a number of individuals to fill these positions.

Most employment opportunities will exist in larger, high-budget organizations. Individuals might need to relocate for specific job opportunities.

Advancement Prospects

Advancement prospects for Copywriters interested in working for animal advocacy organizations are fair. There are a number of paths for career advancement. Individuals may locate a similar position in a larger or better-known animal advocacy organization with a higher budget. This will generally result in increased responsibilities and earnings. Some individuals become publications editors. Still others are promoted to assistant director of public relations at the organization. Some individuals become Copywriters in other industries.

Education and Training

Most larger animal advocacy organizations require or prefer a minimum of a four-year college degree. However, smaller organizations may accept a qualified applicant with an associate's degree or even a high school diploma coupled with experience, especially if he or she has a passion for the cause and a proven ability in this area.

Good choices for majors include public relations, communications, journalism, English, and liberal arts.

Seminars and courses related to all phases of writing, desktop publishing, computers, graphics, and layout should prove to be extremely useful.

Experience, Skills, and Personality Traits

Experience requirements for Copywriters depend on the size, structure, and prestige of the specific animal advocacy organization. Many people get experience in this field by working with a smaller organization, and then locate a better job with a larger organization. Others come out of a journalism background or have worked as publicists.

It is essential to have a total understanding of the issues and mission of the animal advocacy organization. A belief in the cause is helpful.

The Copywriter should have the ability to write powerful, attention-grabbing copy. He or she should be creative and have excellent writing skills. Strong knowledge of language, grammar, and spelling is essential. A good writing style is a must. The ability to research and check facts and figures for accuracy is imperative.

An understanding of graphics, layout, and the printing industry may be helpful. Individuals should be articulate and have good verbal communication skills. Computer competency and a working knowledge of various software programs are also necessary.

Unions and Associations

Individuals interested in pursuing a career as a Copywriter for an animal advocacy organization might find it useful to join a number of organizations that provide professional support as well as the opportunity to make important contacts. These include the Association of Fundraising Professionals, the Council for the Advancement and Support of Education, and the Public Relations Society of America. They might also join associations and organizations dedicated to specific animal advocacy issues.

Tips for Entry

1. Writing experience is essential to this job. If you are still in school, volunteer to work on your school newspaper or yearbook.
2. Put together a portfolio of your best writing samples. Bring it to interviews to illustrate your skills and style.
3. Volunteer to write and develop press releases, brochures, and flyers for local humane societies, animal shelters, and nonprofit or civic organizations.

4. Positions are sometimes advertised in the classifieds section of newspapers under the headings such as "Copywriter," "Writer," or "Animal Advocacy Organization." Positions might also be located under the names of specific animal advocacy organizations.

5. Check out the Web sites of animal advocacy organizations. Many post employment opportunities.

6. Career employment Web sites such as Monster. com might advertise relevant openings.

7. Network as much as you can in the industry. Go to conferences, conventions, and educational seminars and workshops to meet industry insiders.

8. Become a member of one or more animal advocacy organizations, humane societies, animal shelters, or rescues. Membership will help you make contacts and get you involved in the animal advocacy world.

9. When considering organizations with which to work, it is important to choose one dedicated to causes and issues in which you believe.

DIRECTOR OF FUND-RAISING AND DEVELOPMENT

CAREER PROFILE

Duties: Direct fund-raising efforts; develop strategies for obtaining financial support from individuals and businesses; cultivate corporate sponsorship; write and apply for grants; develop and execute fund-raising events

Alternate Title(s): Director of Development; Fund-raising Director; Director of Philanthropy; Director of Planned Giving

Salary Range: $22,000 to $100,000+

Employment Prospects: Fair

Advancement Prospects: Fair

Best Geographical Locations for Position: Positions located throughout the United States

Prerequisites:

Education or Training—Bachelor's degree required or preferred by most organizations; see text

Experience and Qualifications—Experience working in fund-raising, grant-writing, public relations, journalism, or related field helpful

Special Skills and Personality Traits—Creativity; verbal and written communication skills; attention to detail; interpersonal skills; persuasiveness; computer competency; organizational skills; understanding of and passion for animal advocacy

CAREER LADDER

Director of Fund-raising and Development for Larger, Better-Known Animal Advocacy Organization; Public Relations or Marketing Director of Animal Advocacy Organization; Executive Director of Animal Advocacy Organization; Director of Fund-raising and Development of Not-for-Profit Organization in Other Industry

↑

Director of Fund-raising and Development

↑

Assistant Director of Fund-raising and Development; Assistant Director of Corporate Sponsorship; Fund-raising Coordinator; Corporate Sponsorship Coordinator; Publicist; Special Event Coordinator; Grant Writer

Position Description

Animal advocacy organizations generally are classified as not-for-profit groups. This means that they are not publicly owned or publicly funded. They depend to a great extent on donations and contributions. The department that handles donations, contributions, and fund-raising efforts is called the fund-raising or development department. The individual who oversees this department is called the Director of Fund-raising and Development or the fund-raising director.

The Director of Fund-raising and Development in an animal advocacy organization holds an integral position. He or she is responsible for raising the monies to fund the organization. Within the scope of the job, the individual has varied responsibilities.

The Director of Fund-raising and Development does not always have an easy job. There are a great many nonprofit organizations with varied causes, each vying for funds donated by the public. The director must have the ability to grab the attention of potential donors, interest them in the causes of the organization, and get them to contribute money.

Funds are essential to the success of animal advocacy organizations. It costs a great deal of money to spread the word about the causes of each organization. Monies are needed for overhead, rent, utilities, office equipment, and salaries. Funds are also needed to print brochures, send out mailings, lobby government officials, educate people, and place advertisements.

The Director of Fund-raising and Development must first find ways to educate and inform the public about the concerns of the organization. The more people are aware of the concerns and causes of the organization, the easier it is to solicit donations and the more likely the solicitations will have a financial impact.

The individual works closely with the organization's board of directors and executive director in developing goals and programs. The Director of Fund-raising and Development is expected to develop strategies for obtaining this financial support from private individuals and businesses. He or she might run large capital campaigns as well as smaller sustaining programs. The individual may also be responsible for supervising others in fund-raising efforts to assure a cohesive fund-raising plan.

After determining the best programs and events, the Director of Fund-raising and Development must develop and implement them. Programs might include, for example, membership campaigns, annual giving or sustaining campaigns, and more. They might also include fund-raising dinners, galas, auctions, dances, telethons, entertainment events, bake sales, craft shows, and races or similar events. They might consist of coin tosses in strategic locations with a lot of foot traffic or appeals for money in personal letters or media.

Larger animal advocacy organizations usually employ a Director of Fund-raising and Development as well as an assistant and staff members. Smaller organizations might just have a director who works with a staff of volunteers. The individual is responsible for supervising and training the staff as well as motivating volunteers. In organizations where there is no specific volunteer coordinator, the individual might be responsible for recruiting volunteers as well.

The Director of Fund-raising and Development for an animal advocacy organization must develop and court potential private donors. The individual may attend luncheons, dinners, meetings, and other affairs on behalf of the organization. He or she may often speak to civic groups, businesspeople, and other nonprofit groups regarding the organization, its causes, and the need for fund-raising.

Additionally, the Director of Fund-raising and Development often seeks to cultivate corporate sponsorships. Depending on the specific organization, corporate sponsors might include pet food companies, pet stores, hotel chains, supermarket chains, and pharmaceutical companies, among others. In order to secure corporate sponsorship, the director of fund-raising must first identify potential sponsors. He or she will then give them information regarding the organization and its mission, invite them to the headquarters, give tours, introduce them to board members, and discuss what funds would mean to the cause. Sometimes sponsors want to get on board immediately. In other situations, the director might have

to nurture potential donors for a bit until they are willing to become financially involved in the organization. Within the scope of the job, the director is responsible for seeking both annual gifts from individuals and corporations and obtaining sponsorship for various projects the organization undertakes.

Many nonprofit organizations depend on grants, and animal advocacy organizations are no different. The Director of Fund-raising and Development is expected to seek out grants offered by private foundations as well as the government. He or she may be responsible for identifying these grants or applying for and writing them. Depending on the specific organization, these tasks might be handled by grant writers or other assistants.

The Director of Fund-raising and Development working in an animal advocacy organization generally does a great deal of writing. He or she may write fund-raising letters, invitations, speeches, and brochures. The director might also be responsible for drafting press releases and writing membership letters. Other writing responsibilities include direct mail pieces, brochures, advertising copy, flyer copy, and event invitations. The individual may also be expected to write reports regarding the progress of fund-raising projects for the executive director or to present to the board of directors.

A great deal of the work of the Director of Fund-raising and Development involves the development and execution of special events to raise money for the organization. Depending on the specific organization, these events can be quite simple or very elaborate. The director might be expected to develop the events, execute them, or oversee others in the completion of these tasks.

The individual or his or her staff, for example, might need to find locations for dinner dances or galas, plan menus, price out goods and services, locate individuals and businesses that will donate door prizes, identify and secure guest speakers, and solicit donations. Depending on the organization and the event, these events may occur on an annual or monthly basis. If the organization is larger, there may be a special events coordinator or assistant who does a great deal of the legwork under the direction of the Director of Fund-raising and Development.

An important function of the Director of Fund-raising and Development is keeping accurate records. For example, he or she must keep records of donor management and resource development. He or she is also responsible for making sure that each donation is acknowledged in writing. This task is often assigned to a staff member.

The Director of Fund-raising and Development is responsible for preparing budgets for the department and developing reports tracking the progress and success of various projects. In some organizations, the director is also expected to expand the membership of the organization. In other organizations, a membership director or coordinator handles this task.

Salaries

Earnings for Directors of Fund-raising and Development working for animal advocacy organizations can range tremendously depending on a number of factors. These include the size, structure, budget, membership, and geographic location of the specific organization, as well as its cause. Other factors affecting earnings include the responsibilities, professional reputation, and experience of the individual. Some individuals earn as little as $22,000 annually, while others earn $100,000 or more. Those at the higher end of the scale generally have a great deal of experience and are working for well-known animal advocacy organizations with large memberships and big budgets.

Employment Prospects

Employment prospects for individuals seeking this type of position are fair. However, it must be noted that in some organizations, the responsibilities of the Director of Fund-raising and Development may be coupled with those of the executive director or the public relations director.

There are many animal advocacy organizations located throughout the country. Individuals may find employment with organizations encompassing a wide assortment of animal advocacy issues. Some are large and well known. Others are smaller and not as well known, but have important missions just the same. Smaller organizations will not have big budgets and therefore generally will not pay as well.

It should be noted than individuals may need to relocate for positions.

Advancement Prospects

Advancement prospects for Directors of Fund-raising and Development at animal advocacy organizations are fair. There are a number of paths for career advancement. Some individuals locate a similar position in a larger, higher-budget, or better-known animal advocacy organization. This will generally result in increased responsibilities and earnings. Other individuals become either the director of public relations or marketing of an animal advocacy organization. Still others even become the executive director of the orga-

nization. A great deal of the advancement possibilities for those in this position depend on the structure of the organization. Those who want to stay in the fund-raising and development area may seek a position with a large, high-budget nonprofit organization outside of the animal advocacy industry.

Education and Training

Most larger animal advocacy organizations require or prefer a minimum of a four-year college degree. There may, however, be smaller organizations that accept an otherwise qualified applicant with an associate's degree or even a high school diploma coupled with experience, especially if he or she has a passion for the cause and a proven ability to raise funds.

Good choices for majors include public relations, communications, journalism, marketing, or related areas. Additional courses, seminars, and workshops in fund-raising techniques, development, special events, public relations, publicity, promotion, writing, marketing, dealing with media, and presentation skills will be useful.

Experience, Skills, and Personality Traits

Experience requirements depend to a great extent on the size, structure, and prestige of the specific animal advocacy organization. Many people get experience in this field working with a smaller organization and then locate a better job with a larger organization. It is essential that the individual have a comprehensive understanding of the issues, causes, and mission of the animal advocacy organization. A personal belief in the cause is helpful.

The Director of Fund-raising and Development should be pleasantly assertive, organized, and detail-oriented. Interpersonal skills and the ability to deal with people in a variety of situations are essential. A proficiency in public speaking is also needed. People skills are vital. The ability to multitask effectively is critical.

Creativity is a necessity in this profession. Individuals need excellent communications skills, both verbal and written, so a good command of the English language is vital.

Computer competency is mandatory. The ability to use fund-raising software is a plus. Supervisory skills are also needed.

Unions and Associations

Individuals interested in pursuing a career as a Director of Fund-raising and Development for an animal advocacy organization can join a number of organizations that provide professional support as well as the opportunity to make important contacts. These include the Association of Fundraising Professionals, the Direct Marketing Association, and the Public Relations Society of America. It is also helpful to belong to associations and organizations dedicated to specific areas of animal advocacy.

Tips for Entry

1. Network as much as you can in the industry. Go to conferences, conventions, and educational seminars and workshops to meet industry insiders.
2. Become a member of one or more animal advocacy organizations, humane societies, animal shelters, or rescues. Membership will help you make contacts and get you involved in the animal advocacy world.
3. When considering organizations with which to work, it is important to choose one dedicated to causes and issues you believe in.
4. An internship with an animal advocacy organization in the fund-raising and development department will be useful for both the experience and the opportunity to make contacts.
5. Look in the classifieds section of newspapers under headings such as "Fund-raising," "Public Relations," "Director of Fund-raising," "Fund-raising and Development Director," or "Animal Advocacy." Job openings might also be located under the names of specific animal advocacy organizations.
6. Don't forget to look online for job opportunities. Start with some of the general career sites such as Monster.com. Then search out sites specific to working with animals.
7. Openings are sometimes listed on the Web sites of specific animal advocacy organizations, so check these frequently.

MEMBERSHIP DIRECTOR

CAREER PROFILE

Duties: Build organization membership; find ways to recruit new members; help the organization flourish; run recruitment campaigns; keep membership records; supervise staff

Alternate Title(s): Director of Development; Director of Membership

Salary Range: $23,000 to $60,000+

Employment Prospects: Poor

Advancement Prospects: Fair

Best Geographical Locations for Position: Positions located throughout the United States in areas hosting animal advocacy organizations

Prerequisites:

Education or Training—Bachelor's degree required or preferred by most organizations; see text

Experience and Qualifications—Experience working in membership department of nonprofit organization

CAREER LADDER

Membership Director for Larger, Better-Known Animal Advocacy Organization; Public Relations or Marketing Director; Executive Director

↑

Membership Director

↑

Assistant Membership Director; Membership Department Staffer

Special Skills and Personality Traits—Creativity; verbal and written communication skills; attention to detail; interpersonal skills; persuasiveness; computer competency; organizational skills; understanding of and passion for animal advocacy

Position Description

A large membership is important to animal advocacy organizations for a number of reasons. To begin with, there is strength in numbers. The more interested and dedicated members that a group can generate, the larger and more prestigious the organization will be.

Individuals who believe in the specific mission of the animal advocacy organization are helpful in spreading the word regarding the issues for which the group advocates. Members also help the organization financially by paying dues, making contributions, and supporting fund-raising events.

The individual in charge of developing the membership of an animal advocacy organization is called the Membership Director. He or she has varied responsibilities depending on the specific organization, its size, and its structure.

To build the organization membership, the individual is expected to develop and run a variety of membership drives or campaigns. These might include mass telephone campaigns, direct mail campaigns, and/or e-mail campaigns, among others. He or she must continually find ways to get people interested in the organization and its causes and encourage new members to join.

In order to familiarize people with the mission of the organization and spark their interest, the Membership Director seeks out opportunities to speak before groups of professionals, associations, service and civic groups, school groups, or meetings of those who have expressed interest. Depending on the situation, these might include local, regional, or national groups. The Membership Director is often asked to speak at special events, conferences, fairs, meetings, and conventions.

The Membership Director is sometimes also called upon to be a guest on television, cable, or radio news shows. He or she uses these opportunities to discuss the organization and its causes, goals, and mission. The hope is that after getting the word out about the organization, people listening will be interested enough to become members.

One of the mechanisms Membership Directors utilize to increase membership and spread the word about the organization is placing advertisements in newspapers, magazines, billboards, and on the Internet. Others take out commercials to be aired on television or radio stations.

Membership Directors are expected to develop a variety of membership materials. These include things like fact sheets about the organization, letters inviting people to become members, articles, reprints of news stories, information on the organization's mission, and membership applications. When requests for membership are received, the Membership Director or staff members are responsible for sending out applications and other pertinent information.

The director targets both individual memberships and corporate memberships. In doing so, he or she might develop various levels of membership. These might include, for example, friends, supporters, sustainers, sponsors, and patrons, among others. Each level of membership generally costs a different amount and provides different benefits.

In some situations, the Membership Director seeks out individual or corporate sponsors for the organization as a whole. In other situations, he or she instead seeks out sponsorship for specific programs such as exhibitions, conferences, or projects such as video production or brochures.

The Membership Director is responsible for compiling and updating lists of organization members. The individual or one of his or her staff is also expected to make sure annual renewal materials are sent to members on a timely basis.

It is essential that membership departments keep precise records. In addition to the names of each member, the membership department must be sure to have up-to-date phone numbers, physical addresses, e-mail addresses, and payment and renewal information. Much of this information is maintained in computer databases. In this manner, new members can be easily added and information updated when needed.

The Membership Director often works closely with other departments in the animal advocacy organization. He or she may, for example, work with the public relations department on press releases, the publications department on putting together brochures or letters, the fund-raising department on securing funds, the education department on educating new and existing members about the cause, and the special events department on putting together events for members. The goal is to do everything possible to both cultivate new members and retain those who are already part of the organization.

The Membership Director is expected to oversee the office and any staff members in the department. For individuals in this position, seeing the membership of the organization grow is very gratifying.

Salaries

Salaries for Membership Directors of animal advocacy organizations range from approximately $23,000 to $60,000 or more. Variables affecting earnings include the size and budget of the specific organization as well as the experience and responsibilities of the individual. Those at the higher end of the scale generally have a great deal of experience and are working for well known animal advocacy organizations with big budgets.

Employment Prospects

There are many animal advocacy organizations located throughout the country. Individuals may find employment with a wide variety of organizations encompassing an assortment of animal advocacy issues. Some are large and well known. Others are smaller and not as well known but support important causes just the same.

With that being said, employment prospects are poor for individuals seeking this type of position. While every organization has someone who handles the duties of the Membership Director, every organization does not employ one. In these organizations, the public relations director, the fund-raising director, or the executive director handles the responsibilities of Membership Directors. Occasionally, a volunteer performs this function.

It should be noted that individuals might need to relocate for positions.

Advancement Prospects

Advancement prospects for Membership Directors working for animal advocacy organizations are fair. There are a number of paths for career advancement. Some locate a similar position in a larger, higher budget, or better-known animal advocacy organization. This will generally result in increased responsibilities and earnings. Some individuals become either the director of public relations or marketing of a large animal advocacy organization. Others become the executive director. Advancement possibilities depend to a large extent on the structure of the organization.

Some individuals locate positions in trade associations in or out of the animal advocacy world.

Education and Training

Most larger animal advocacy organizations require or prefer a minimum of a four-year college degree. There are, however, smaller organizations that might accept a qualified applicant with an associate's degree or even a high school diploma coupled with experience.

Good choices for majors include public relations, communications, journalism, marketing, or related areas. Additional courses, seminars, and workshops in fundraising techniques, development, special events, public relations, publicity, promotion, writing, marketing, dealing with media, and presentation skills will be useful.

Experience, Skills, and Personality Traits

Experience requirements depend to a great extent on the size, structure, and prestige of the specific animal advocacy organization. Many people get experience in this field working with a smaller organization and then locate a better job with a larger organization. It is essential to have a comprehensive understanding of the issues and causes of the animal advocacy organization. A belief in the cause is helpful.

Creativity is a necessity in this profession. Individuals need to be articulate and have excellent communication skills, both written and verbal. In order to prepare effective membership materials, a good command of the English language is vital as is a firm grasp of grammar and spelling. The ability to communicate verbally is indispensable when speaking to people on either an individual or group basis.

The Membership Director should be organized and detail-oriented. Interpersonal skills and the ability to deal well with people in a variety of situations are essential. The ability to multitask effectively is critical.

Computer competency is mandatory. Supervisory skills are also needed.

Unions and Associations

Membership Directors working for animal advocacy organizations may join a number of organizations that provide professional support as well as the opportunity to make important contacts. These include the Association of Fundraising Professionals and the Public Relations Society of America. They may also belong to associations and organizations specific to the area of interest in animal advocacy.

Tips for Entry

1. Network as much as you can in the industry. Go to conferences, conventions, and educational seminars and workshops to meet industry insiders.

2. Become a member of one or more animal advocacy organizations, humane societies, animal shelters, or rescues. Membership will help you make contacts and get you involved in the animal advocacy world.

3. When considering organizations with which to work, it is important to choose one dedicated to causes and issues in which you believe.

4. An internship with an animal advocacy organization in the membership department or volunteering in any other department will be useful for both the experience and the opportunity to make contacts.

5. Look in the classifieds section of newspapers under headings such as "Membership Director," "Director of Membership," or "Animal Advocacy," among others. Job openings might also be located under the names of specific animal advocacy organizations.

6. Don't forget to look online for job opportunities. Start with some of the general employment sites such as Monster.com. Then search out sites specific to working with animals.

7. Openings are sometimes listed on the Web sites of specific animal advocacy organizations, so check these often.

DIRECTOR OF
EDUCATION AND OUTREACH

CAREER PROFILE

Duties: Provide humane education on behalf of organization; develop, coordinate, and implement outreach projects and activities to educate the public about the causes and issues of the organization; develop printed materials and other educational resources; visit schools, civic groups, and other organizations

Alternate Title(s): Education and Outreach Director; Outreach Director; Education Director

Salary Range: $23,000 to $50,000+

Employment Prospects: Poor

Advancement Prospects: Fair

Best Geographical Locations for Position: Positions located throughout the United States in areas hosting animal advocacy organizations

Prerequisites:

Education or Training—Bachelor's degree required or preferred by most organizations; see text

Experience and Qualifications—Experience working in outreach, education, public relations, grant-writing, fund-raising, and/or administration

Special Skills and Personality Traits—Verbal and written communication skills; persuasiveness; public speaking skills; good judgment; common sense; supervisory skills; ability to multitask; creativity; grant-writing skills; motivation; understanding of and passion for animal advocacy

Special Requirements—Voluntary certification available; some positions may require teaching certificates; see text

CAREER LADDER

Director of Education and Outreach of Larger, More Prestigious Animal Advocacy Organization; Executive Director

Director of Education and Outreach

Assistant Director of Education and Outreach; Humane Educator

Position Description

Animal advocacy organizations improve the lives of animals. There are many animal advocacy organizations throughout the United States and around the world. Each has its own issues, philosophies, and concerns.

Education of the public is extremely important to every animal advocacy organization. To make people think about taking action, they must be made aware of the treatment of animals. Animal advocacy organizations direct a great deal of their efforts to this type of education. The department within the animal advocacy organization that handles education is called the education and outreach department, the education department, or the department of educational activities.

Most organizations feel that if people know about a problem, they will try to change the situation. The education and outreach department is responsible for making the public aware of not only the problems and issues of concern to the specific organization, but also the possible solutions.

The individual in charge of this department is called the Director of Education and Outreach. He or she may also be called the director of education or the director of educational activities.

In large animal advocacy organizations, there may be a director as well as one or more assistants, humane educators, and even speakers. In smaller organizations the director may work alone. In very small organizations, the executive director or the director of public relations may handle education and outreach.

The Director of Education and Outreach is responsible for developing, coordinating, and implementing a variety of activities designed to help educate the public about the causes and issues of the organization. He or she may, for example, develop printed materials such as brochures, booklets, articles, manuals, and other educational resources.

The Director of Education and Outreach is also expected to develop educational programs and materials for courses, workshops, and other presentations. It is his or her responsibility to research and select topics pertinent to the organization and the needs of the population they hope to reach.

The director must search out opportunities to present educational programs to various groups in an array of different situations. Depending on the specific organization and its mission, these might include presentations to civic groups, school assemblies, college audiences, conferences, and conventions.

The director may form partnerships with schools and colleges to offer classes or workshops in various areas of humane education. He or she may also form partnerships with businesses and corporations that believe in the mission of the organization and want to help educate the public.

As young people are often the key to change, the Director of Education and Outreach may develop special programs to send humane educators and speakers into schools to talk to students about various phases of animal advocacy and animal rights. Depending on the organization and its mission, they may talk about the humane treatment of pets with young children, alternatives to dissection to middle or high school students, and careers working with animals and animal advocacy organizations with college students.

The Director of Education and Outreach must have a thorough understanding of the organization's polices and causes. It is essential that he or she have the ability to speak about them persuasively and passionately. In some situations, the individual may speak and educate people about the group's mission, compassionate treatment of animals, inhumane treatments, exploitation of animals, and what can be done to help. In other situations, the individual might assign this task to humane educators, speakers, or assistants.

The Director of Education and Outreach is often responsible for coordinating outreach actions and campaigns. Depending on the specific organization and its mission, these might include boycotts, protests, letter-writing campaigns, marches, fur burnings, and so on. A possible campaign, for example, could be a nationwide boycott of manufacturers that test products on animals. In some organizations, a special events director or an activist coordinator handles campaigns.

Depending on the specific mission of the advocacy group, there might be grants available from federal, state, and local agencies as well as private industry to help educate the public. In some organizations, the Director of Education and Outreach is responsible

for finding grants as well as preparing and writing the applications. In other organizations, a staff grant writer handles this task.

The Director of Education and Outreach might seek out additional opportunities to reach the public. He or she may, for example, attend community events and fairs, setting up booths to educate the public on the specific issues relevant to the animal advocacy organization.

The Director of Education and Outreach is responsible for providing training and supervision of the employees and volunteers within the education and outreach office. He or she might also be expected to train other staff and volunteers within the organization.

The individual might often appear on television or radio news and talk shows discussing various topics regarding the issues of the specific animal advocacy organization. He or she might also write columns for newspapers or magazines in order to help educate the public on the humane treatment of animals.

Many Directors of Education and Outreach use the Web to help educate the public on humane issues. Some develop online columns. Others have found blogging to be very effective.

The Director of Education and Outreach holds an important position in an animal advocacy organization. He or she not only helps spread the word about the mission and issues of the organization, but helps teach others what they need to do to make things better in the lives of animals. Through the efforts of the education and outreach department, more people learn about the poor treatment of animals. These people can then work toward freeing animals from suffering and/or exploitation.

Salaries

Earnings for the Director of Education and Outreach of an animal advocacy organization can range tremendously depending on a number of factors. These include the size, structure, budget, and geographic location of the specific organization as well as its cause. Other factors affecting earnings include the responsibilities, professional reputation, and experience of the individual. There are some who earn approximately $23,000 and others who earn $50,000 or more.

Employment Prospects

Employment prospects are poor for individuals seeking these types of positions. As noted previously, while most animal advocacy organizations have someone who handles the duties of education and outreach, not every organization hires a Director of Education and

Outreach. In some organizations, the responsibilities of this individual may fall on the director of public relations or the executive director.

Individuals may find employment with organizations dedicated to a wide assortment of animal advocacy issues. Some are large and well known. Others are smaller and not as well known but are concerned with important causes just the same. Opportunities may be located throughout the United States. It should be noted that individuals might need to relocate for positions.

Advancement Prospects

Advancement prospects for the Director of Education and Outreach are fair once he or she gets a foot in the door and finds a job. Individuals may climb the career ladder in a number of ways. Many find similar positions in larger, better-known organizations, resulting in increased responsibilities and earnings. Others climb the career ladder by being promoted to the position of executive director. Some seek similar jobs in other industries.

Education and Training

Most animal advocacy organizations require or prefer a minimum of a four-year college degree for this position. Certain positions require a master's degree. Some also require a teaching certificate.

With that being said, there are also smaller organizations that may accept an applicant with an associate's degree or even a high school diploma coupled with experience, especially if he or she has a passion for the cause.

Good choices for majors include education, communications, business administration, journalism, public relations, or a related area.

Courses, seminars, and workshops in education, training, public speaking, fund-raising, grant-writing, public relations, business, management, presentation skills, and administration will be useful in honing skills and making new contacts.

Experience, Skills, and Personality Traits

Experience requirements depend to a great extent on the size, structure, and prestige of the specific animal advocacy organization. Individuals seeking positions with large, well known organizations generally need to have at least a couple of years of experience working with either animal advocacy organizations, trade associations, or another not-for-profit group.

Some individuals have a background in education. Others have experience working with other animal advocacy organizations in various capacities or in public relations, journalism, fund-raising, grant-writing, or working with not-for-profit organizations.

The Director of Education and Outreach of an animal advocacy organization needs to have a true passion for the cause. He or she must have a full understanding and commitment to the specific animal advocacy group and its specific beliefs. Those successful in this area truly enjoy helping people learn more about the issues of the organization.

Individuals must be well-spoken, with excellent verbal communication skills. The ability to discuss issues persuasively is essential. Public speaking skills are crucial.

People skills are needed, as are supervisory and leadership skills. An understanding of grant-writing is helpful. The ability to work on a number of different projects at the same time without getting flustered is necessary. Motivational skills are the key to success in any outreach campaign.

Special Requirements

A voluntary certification is available from the Humane Society Youth, formerly known as the National Association for Humane and Environmental Education. This organization is an affiliate of the Humane Society of the United States (HSUS).

Certification provides a professional development program for individuals committed to humane education. Courses are given online. Those completing the program and passing an exam will earn the designation Certified Humane Education Specialist.

Some positions may require applicants to hold teaching certificates.

Unions and Associations

Individuals interested in pursuing careers in this area might want to join various organizations to make contacts and get professional support. These include the Association of Professional Humane Educators and Humane Society Youth. Individuals can also join the American Society for the Prevention of Cruelty to Animals, the American Humane Association, and HSUS. They might also belong to the Public Relations Society of America.

Tips for Entry

1. Join one or two animal advocacy organizations that have concerns and issues in which you believe and get involved as an active member. Ask to help in the education and outreach department.
2. When considering organizations with which to work, it is important to choose one dedicated to causes and issues in which you believe. If you are still in school, consider starting a student chapter

of that organization. It will help you make important contacts.

3. Look for internships in animal advocacy organizations, animal shelters, refuges, or rescues. Talk to the Director of Education and Outreach about your career goals and get his or her advice.

4. Get experience working with not-for-profit organizations by volunteering with a local civic or community organization. If you can find an animal advocacy group, great. If not, any experience will be helpful.

5. Look for job openings in the classifieds section of newspapers. Headings might include key words such as "Director of Education and Outreach," "Outreach and Education," "Animal Advocacy Organization," or "Animal Rights Organization." Jobs might also be advertised under the names of specific organizations.

6. Openings are sometimes listed on the Web sites of specific animal advocacy organization, so check these often.

7. Network as much as you can in the industry. Go to conferences, conventions, and educational seminars and workshops to meet industry insiders.

8. Offer to do the publicity or fund-raising for a local not-for-profit organization. It doesn't matter if the organization is related to animal advocacy or not. If you can do publicity or fund-raising for one organization, you can do it for any type of group.

DIRECTOR OF
RESEARCH AND INVESTIGATION

Position Description

Unfortunately, there are many animals that are mistreated, abused, and exploited every day. Sometimes people see the problem. They might, for example, see a dog being beaten. In a pet store, someone might see puppies in small cages with no room to walk and no water.

Sometimes people don't actually see abuse, but they hear of it happening or know of it occurring. For example, individuals may hear about puppy mills where dogs are kept in horrible conditions to breed puppies for pet stores. They may hear that there are organized dogfights or cockfighting rings. And although no one wants to think it is true, there are people who respond to "free to good home" advertisements only to sell the animals to labs for use in testing.

Often the exploitation is not as easily recognized, but that does not mean it is not there. Animals in certain circuses or zoos may not be cared for properly. Owners of horse-drawn carriages might be making the horses work on days when it is just too hot. The list goes on.

There are some who feel that animals should not be experimented on for research for cosmetics or even for medical research. Others may feel that animals on certain farms are not being treated humanely. Some find that certain animals are being killed in an inhumane manner.

Animal advocacy organizations generally have research and investigation offices to look into these and similar situations. The Director of Research and Investigation is the individual in charge of the research and investigation office. Responsibilities can vary depending on the specific type of advocacy organization and its mission.

The Director of Research and Investigation in a shelter, humane society, or Society for the Prevention of Cruelty to Animals (SPCA), for example, generally looks into problems on a local level. The investigations may deal specifically with pets or animal cruelty in general. It might deal with animals that are being tortured or sacrificed by cult members.

The Director of Research and Investigation for specialized organizations might deal with specific types of animal exploitation. PETA (People for the Ethical Treatment of Animals), however, deals with ending the suffering and exploitation of all animals. Their investigations include the treatment of animals on farms, in the wild, in zoos, circuses, rodeos, carnivals, and racetracks, to name a few. Other investigations include the exploitation of animals used for fur, clothing, food, nonfood products, and those used in labs and other research.

Some animal advocacy organizations have more specific commitments. The Humane Farming Association, for example, investigates the improper treatment of farm animals. Save Japan Dolphins works to stop the killing of dolphins in Japan and to stop the capture and live trade of dolphins to zoos and aquariums around the world.

The Director of Research and Investigation for an animal advocacy organization has a lot of responsibility. He or she must direct all investigations of abuse, neglect, and exploitation. Within the scope of the job, the individual performs various duties.

The Director of Research and Investigation must first learn about the problem. All exploitation and abuse to animals is not done in the open. Sometimes a disgruntled employee of a company complains. Sometimes there is an anonymous tip. Other times, people who see nothing wrong with a situation may just talk about something that is occurring. This brings the situation to the attention of the animal advocacy organization.

In very small animal advocacy organizations, the research and investigation department just consists of the director. If the organization is slightly larger, there might be one or two staff members or even volunteers who help with research and investigations. In large organizations, the research and investigation department might include the director, an assistant director, coordinators, investigators, clerks, and numerous other staff members.

Once the animal advocacy organization learns about a potential case of abuse, neglect, or exploitation, the Director of Research and Investigation develops a plan of action. He or she is expected to research the complaint and launch an appropriate investigation.

The type of investigation will be dependent on the specific animal advocacy organization, its mission, and the severity of suspected abuse, neglect, or exploitation. The director may assign one or more staff members to the case to research the complaint thoroughly.

In some cases, the Director of Research and Investigation finds that the complaint warrants an undercover investigation. This often occurs when a company is not open about its treatment of animals or when the director thinks that the abuse, neglect, or exploitation is so severe that it needs more documentation than usual. In these situations, the Director of Research and Investigation may assign undercover investigators to infiltrate a company. Depending on the situation, investigators might get jobs on farms, in research labs, puppy mills, pet stores, slaughterhouses, zoos, racetracks, circuses, and so on.

Undercover investigators witness abuse and exploitation firsthand. As no one knows they are part of an animal advocacy organization, people often speak and act freely around them. The undercover investigators gather information, document what is happening, and take photos and/or videos of the conditions and the violations.

Once this documentation is brought to the Director of Research and Investigation, he or she can get a more realistic picture of what is going on. Depending on the size of the organization, the director of the department may take part in undercover investigations.

The director is responsible for debriefing investigators and then analyzing and collating information. After reviewing the documentation, the director then works with others in the animal advocacy organization to make sure that what is happening is brought to the attention of the membership, the public, the media, and/or law enforcement officials. Without documentation and evidence showing otherwise, a company or individual can easily deny any allegations of wrongdoing. With incriminating documentation, offenders are trapped.

The Director of Research and Investigation frequently works with other departments in the animal advocacy organization to determine what to do with the information they have uncovered. Sometimes, the organization decides to organize a boycott of a company or an industry. In other situations, they may hold demonstrations. Depending on the situation, the Director of Research and Investigation may also contact law enforcement officials or the media, or authorize a seizure of animals. In some cases, the organization is successful in making big changes to the way animals are treated. Unfortunately, this is not always the case.

There is a fair amount of paperwork that goes with this job. The Director of Research and Investigation working at an animal advocacy organization is expected to document each investigation and write reports regarding each case of animal abuse, neglect, and exploitation he or she investigates. The individual also must write reports of findings and resolutions.

The Director of Research and Investigation working with an animal advocacy organization is in a position to make a difference in the lives of animals. By launching investigations that can help all kinds of animals and ultimately show the public what is really happening in a company in relation to its treatment of animals, the Director of Research and Investigation plays a role in helping to change things for the better.

Salaries

Earnings for the Director of Research and Investigation of an animal advocacy organization can vary dramatically. Some individuals earn approximately $24,000, while others earn $48,000 or more annually. Factors affecting earnings include the experience, education, training, and responsibilities of the individual. Other factors affecting earnings include the size and budget of the specific animal advocacy organization. Those with earnings at the higher end of the scale generally work at well known organizations with large budgets.

Employment Prospects

Employment prospects for individuals seeking positions as the Director of Research and Investigation of animal advocacy organizations are poor. While many animal advocacy organizations have someone who handles research and investigations, not every organization has the resources to employ an individual for this position. With that being said, opportunities exist throughout the United States in areas hosting animal advocacy organizations with large budgets.

Advancement Prospects

Advancement prospects for individuals once they have a job as the Director of Research and Investigation of an animal advocacy organization are fair. Some find similar work in larger, better-known animal advocacy organizations with bigger budgets. This generally results in increased earnings and responsibilities. Some go on to become the director of animal treatment investigations for large municipalities. This, too, can result in increased responsibilities and earnings. Some individuals may become the executive director of animal advocacy organizations. As there are no hard-and-fast rules for climbing the career ladder in animal advocacy organizations, advancement opportunities depend to a large extent on an individual's career aspirations and the specific organization.

Education and Training

Educational requirements vary from job to job. While a college background or degree is not required for every job, it is almost always preferred. Courses in psychology, sociology, and criminal justice will be helpful. There are some colleges throughout the country that offer courses on animal cruelty investigation, animal welfare, and the law.

There are Directors of Research and Investigation who have degrees in veterinary medicine, master's degrees in communications, and bachelor's degrees in everything from the sciences to journalism to education. There are others who hold associate's degrees in liberal arts as well as some who are high school graduates with a sincere desire to help animals.

Experience, Skills, and Personality Traits

Experience requirements vary from job to job. Most individuals who hold jobs in this field have experience working in the cruelty or investigation area of animal advocacy organizations, shelters, SPCAs, police departments, or municipalities.

Individuals need a strong stomach for this type of work. Directors of Research and Investigation cannot always take action immediately. As a result, they often see horrible acts of animal cruelty, exploitation, and abuse while performing investigations.

A love of animals and commitment to their welfare is essential. It is also vital that directors have a commitment to the mission of the specific animal advocacy organization. The ability to make difficult decisions is essential.

People skills are needed, as are communication skills. The ability to multitask is also necessary. Supervisory and administrative skills are a must. Research skills are also needed.

The Director of Research and Investigation should have a calm, even temperament. It is often difficult to see animals being abused and exploited. The ability to analyze problems and determine effective plans of action is necessary in planning investigations. In order to maintain the integrity of undercover investigations and keep investigators safe, the ability to keep information confidential is vital.

Special Requirements

Some states require the Director of Research and Investigation to hold a special license or credential. If the individual is required to drive, a driver's license and a clean driving record are necessary.

Unions and Associations

Individuals can become members of local shelters, SPCAs, and animal advocacy organizations.

Tips for Entry

1. Check with your local police department to see if they have an animal cruelty investigation unit and, if it does, offer to volunteer. This will give

you experience working in the investigation area.

2. Contact animal advocacy organizations to inquire about internships in the research and investigation office.

3. Contact shelters, SPCAs, and humane societies to see if they have internship opportunities.

4. Get experience by volunteering at a local shelter, humane society, SPCA, or animal advocacy organization. Ask about the opportunity to volunteer in the animal cruelty investigation area.

5. Send your résumé and a short cover letter to animal advocacy organizations to see if they have openings. Remember to ask that your résumé be kept on file if there are no current openings.

6. Check out openings online. Start with some of the more traditional job sites such as Monster.com. Expand your search from there.

7. Openings are sometimes posted on the Web sites of specific animal advocacy organizations, so look into these.

8. Openings are often advertised in the classifieds section of newspapers. Look under headings such as "Director of Research and Investigation–Animal Advocacy Organization," "Animal Advocacy Organization Jobs," "Animal Advocacy Organization Investigation Director," "Animal-Related Jobs," or "Animal Jobs."

UNDERCOVER INVESTIGATOR

Position Description

There are many acts of animal cruelty, neglect, mistreatment, and exploitation that are not visible to the public. A pet store, for example, might deprive ill animals of health care. Cruelty and abuse might be common on a specific dairy farm; ducks might be force-fed at a duck farm; animals might be tortured at research laboratories; puppy mills sometimes house dogs in inhumane conditions while having litter after litter of puppies; dogs, cocks, or even hogs are sometimes forced into fighting for the sake of entertainment and money; and animals are trapped in an inhumane fashion for fur.

Animal advocacy organizations bring together people who want to assure that animals are treated in a humane manner. There are many different animal advocacy organizations throughout the United States dedicated to improving the lives of animals. Some try to protect the lives of animals in general. Others work with specific types and breeds of animals. Many of these organizations have research and investigation

departments whose focus is looking into complaints or allegations of wrongdoing.

Shelters, humane societies, or societies for the prevention of cruelty to animals (SPCA) generally look into problems on a local level. Their investigations might deal specifically with pets or with cruelty to other types of animals. They may also deal with animals that are being tortured or sacrificed by cult members. They may additionally deal with dog-, cock-, and hog-fighting rings.

One of the largest and best-known animal advocacy organizations is PETA (People for the Ethical Treatment of Animals), which deals with ending the suffering and exploitation of all animals. Their investigations include the treatment of animals on farms, in the wild, and in zoos, circuses, rodeos, carnivals, and racetracks, to name a few. Other investigations involve the exploitation of animals used for fur, clothing, food, nonfood products, and those used in labs and other research. Some animal advocacy organizations have even more specific commitments. The Humane

Farming Association, for example, investigates the improper treatment of farm animals.

Once an animal advocacy organization learns about a potential case of wrongdoing, it takes action. The director of research and investigation develops a plan of action, launching an investigation to gather evidence and document the situation.

The type of investigation launched depends on the specific animal advocacy organization, its mission, and the level of suspected abuse, neglect, or exploitation. In some cases, the organization thinks the problem warrants an undercover investigation. This often occurs when a company is not open about its treatment of animals or when the abuse, neglect, or exploitation is so horrific that it needs more documentation than usual.

In these situations, the research and investigation department may assign Undercover Investigators to infiltrate a company. Undercover Investigators work for animal advocacy organizations in the research and investigation department. As part of their job, they infiltrate companies by getting jobs with the particular company or organization in question.

Depending on the situation, investigators might get jobs on farms, in research labs, puppy mills, zoos, slaughterhouses, racetracks, circuses, etc. Undercover Investigators witness the abuse and exploitation firsthand. As no one knows they are part of an animal advocacy organization, other employees generally speak and act freely around them. By gaining access into the inner circle of a company, Undercover Investigators can gather information, document what is happening, and take photos and/or videos of the conditions, the abuse, neglect, and/or exploitation.

Undercover Investigators have an interesting but difficult job. Once assigned to a case, the Undercover Investigator is expected to go to the company being investigated and get a job. Depending on the specific situation, he or she often takes on a different identity provided by the animal advocacy organization. The investigator might have to travel to a different part of the country depending on where the company being investigated is located. The length of the assignment varies from job to job.

Once hired by the company being investigated, the Undercover Investigator goes about his or her day as a "normal" worker. What no one knows is that he or she is also gathering evidence and documentation regarding the animal abuse, neglect, or cruelty. As part of the job, the investigator is expected to be an employee of the investigated company doing whatever is asked of him or her.

Undercover Investigators working for animal advocacy organizations believe animals should be treated humanely and with respect. Having to be "part of the company" that does not conduct itself in accordance with that belief causes distress for some investigators. Individuals might be asked to do things they are morally or ethically opposed to, but they must do them to protect the integrity of the investigation. The Undercover Investigator is responsible for observing what is happening and documenting it, not trying to change the situation while undercover.

Undercover Investigators use a variety of tools to document evidence, including cameras, video cameras, and voice recorders. Sometimes individuals use hidden cameras that look like shirt buttons or tiny video cameras and recorders in order to get pictures, videos, and sound bites as evidence of animal abuse, cruelty, exploitation, or living conditions. Other times, they may use the camera or video camera in a cell phone to secure evidence.

Undercover Investigators must be very careful not to "break their cover" when gathering evidence. Individuals must try to blend in with the other workers of the company they are infiltrating. They cannot appear to be too curious or show any emotion, even when offensive things are happening right in front of them. With that being said, talented Undercover Investigators know how to engage with other workers and often find ways to get them to discuss details relevant to the investigation.

Undercover Investigators are expected to write regular reports on the status of their investigations. These may be done on a daily basis or a few times a week. Depending on the situation, reports and photos may be mailed, e-mailed, or hand delivered.

For those who love animals, this job can be both difficult and rewarding. While seeing animals being abused, neglected, exploited, or treated in an inhumane fashion without being able to step in and stop it can be heart-wrenching for Undercover Investigators, knowing that they are ultimately working to make a change can be very gratifying.

Depending on the situation, Undercover Investigators can stay on a case for a short time or for months. Once an investigation is completed, individuals must move to another location to perform another investigation.

After the Undercover Investigator secures evidence of wrongdoing, it is brought back to the animal advocacy organization. It can then be used to help bring the situation to the attention of the public, the media, or law enforcement officials.

There is a saying that states that a picture is worth a thousand words. Nothing could be truer in the case of animal cruelty. Bringing documentation such as photographs and videos to the attention of the public can be instrumental in changing the way animals are treated by a company. Showing a video or pictures of a horrific case of animal abuse, cruelty, or exploitation on television, in print media, or online can often be the impetus to making companies change the way they treat animals in their care.

To some, Undercover Investigators are like spies. They are expected to take on a different identity while undercover. As a result, it is difficult to make real friends during that time. During some investigations, especially those involving long-distance travel, the individual can't see his or her real friends or family for logistical reasons or because they might blow his or her cover.

The investigator is expected to gather evidence, take photos, and in essence spy on the people he or she is working with. It is very easy to get paranoid in a situation like this, so he or she must remain calm and collected under pressure.

Successful Undercover Investigators are committed to the cause, know why they are on the job, and are ready to do what they have to do to help change the way companies treat animals.

Salaries

Earnings for Undercover Investigators working with animal advocacy organizations can range from approximately $24,000 to $35,000 or more. Factors affecting earnings include the experience, education, training, and responsibilities of the individual as well as the size and budget of the specific animal advocacy organization.

Those with earnings at the higher end of the scale generally work at well known organizations with larger budgets. It should be noted that some Undercover Investigators work on a contract basis and are therefore paid by the project.

Employment Prspects

Employment prospects for individuals seeking positions as Undercover Investigators for animal advocacy organizations are fair. Opportunities exist throughout the country in areas hosting animal advocacy organizations. PETA (People for the Ethical Treatment of Animals) and other similar organizations often advertise for people to work as Undercover Investigators and infiltrate companies. The greatest number of opportu-

nities will exist in animal advocacy organizations with larger budgets. It is important to note that individuals may need to relocate for positions.

Advancement Prospects

Advancement prospects for Undercover Investigators working in animal advocacy organizations are fair. Once an individual obtains some experience, he or she often lands better assignments or may find similar positions in organizations with larger budgets. Both scenarios generally result in increased responsibilities and earnings. Some Undercover Investigators may go on to become the assistant director of research and investigation of the organization, or perhaps the director of research and investigation.

As there are no hard-and-fast rules for climbing the career ladder in animal advocacy organizations, advancement opportunities depend to a great deal on an individual's career aspirations and the specific organization.

Education and Training

Educational requirement vary from job to job. While a college background or degree may not be required for every job, it is almost always preferred. Courses in psychology, sociology, and criminal justice will be helpful. There are some colleges throughout the country that offer courses on animal cruelty investigation, animal welfare, and the law. There are also some animal advocacy organizations that offer on-the-job training for Undercover Investigators.

Undercover Investigators come from a variety of educational backgrounds. There are some who have degrees in veterinary medicine, master's degrees in communications, or bachelor's degrees in everything from the sciences to journalism to education. There are others who hold associate's degrees in liberal arts as well as some who are high school graduates with a sincere desire to help animals.

Experience, Skills, and Personality Traits

Experience requirements vary from job to job. Undercover Investigators working with animal advocacy organizations often have experience in the cruelty or investigation area of animal advocacy organizations, shelters, SPCAs, police departments, or municipalities.

Individuals need a strong stomach for this type of work. In order to get the proper documentation, Undercover Investigators frequently must witness abuse, neglect, exploitation, and other poor treatment of animals while doing nothing immediately to help them.

A love of animals and commitment to their welfare is essential. It is also vital for the individual to have a commitment to the mission of the specific animal advocacy organization. The ability to make difficult decisions is essential. Attention to detail is mandatory. As noted, Undercover Investigators in essence are leading two lives, so a calm and collected demeanor is necessary.

People skills and communication skills are essential. The ability to multitask is also necessary. In order to maintain the integrity of undercover investigations and keep themselves safe, investigators must have the ability to keep the investigation confidential.

Special Requirements

Some states require investigators to hold a special license or credential. If the individual is required to drive, a driver's license and a clean driving record are necessary.

Unions and Associations

Individuals can become members of local shelters, SPCAs, and animal advocacy organizations whose missions they believe in.

Tips for Entry

1. Check with your local police department to see if it has an animal cruelty investigation unit. If it does, offer to volunteer. This will give you experience working in the investigation area.

2. Contact animal advocacy organizations, shelters, SPCAs, and humane societies to inquire about internships in the research and investigation office.

3. Get experience by volunteering at a local shelter, humane society, SPCA, or animal advocacy organization. Ask about the opportunity to volunteer in the animal cruelty investigation area.

4. Send your résumé and a short cover letter to animal advocacy organizations to see if they have openings. Remember to ask that your résumé be kept on file if there are no current openings.

5. Check out openings online. Start with some of the more traditional job sites such as Monster.com. Expand your search from there.

6. Openings are sometimes posted on the Web sites of specific animal advocacy organizations.

7. Openings are often advertised in the classifieds section of newspapers. Look under headings such as "Investigator," "Research and Investigation," "Animal Advocacy Organization," "Undercover Investigator–Animals," etc.

HUMANE EDUCATOR

Duties: Provide humane education on behalf of organization; teach kindness and compassion toward
animals; teach responsible animal care; develop and
present programs and activities regarding animal
issues and advocacy to schools and organizations;
visit schools; prepare humane education materials;
assist with outreach programs

Alternate Title(s): Educator; Humane Teacher

Salary Range: $22,000 to $45,000+

Employment Prospects: Fair

Advancement Prospects: Fair

Best Geographical Locations for Position: Positions
located throughout the United States in areas hosting animal advocacy organizations

Prerequisites:

    Education or Training—Bachelor's degree required
or preferred by most organizations; see text

    Experience and Qualifications—Experience work-
ing in outreach, education, public relations, public
speaking, grant-writing, fund-raising, and/or administration

    Special Skills and Personality Traits—Excellent
verbal and written communication skills; persua-

Humane Educator for Larger,
More Prestigious Animal Advocacy
Organization; Director of Humane
Education or Director of Education
and Outreach of Animal Advocacy
Organization

Humane Educator

Intern; Volunteer

siveness; public speaking skills; good judgment;
common sense; supervisory skills; ability to multitask; creativity; grant-writing skills; motivation;
understanding of and passion for animal advocacy

Special Requirements—Voluntary certification
available; certain positions may require teaching
certificate

Position Description

To make people think about making a change, they
must be made aware of a problem. Therefore, education
of the public is extremely important to every animal
advocacy organization. Animal advocacy organizations
direct a great deal of their efforts to this type of education.

The department within animal advocacy organizations that handles education is called the education and
outreach department, the education department, or the
department of educational activities.

The education and outreach department is responsible for making the public aware of not only the problems and issues the specific organization targets, but the
possible solutions as well. Depending on the size and
structure of the organization, there may be a director of
education and outreach, assistants, speakers, and one or
more Humane Educators.

The duties of Humane Educators vary depending
on the organization for which they work. In larger

organizations, their duties will generally be specified,
focused on going out into the public and speaking
about humane issues. In smaller organizations, especially those without a director of education and outreach, individuals might be responsible for the entire
education and outreach program for the organization.
Humane Educators working with animal advocacy
organizations teach and promote humane attitudes
toward animals. They develop, coordinate, and present
programs regarding animal issues and the concerns of
the specific organization to local schools, youth groups,
civic groups, and other organizations. Since children
in various grades have different comprehension levels,
when preparing presentations, individuals are expected
to develop audience-appropriate programs.

As young people are often the key to change, animal
advocacy organizations frequently send their Humane
Educators into schools to speak to students about various phases of animal advocacy. Depending on the specific organization and its mission, they might speak,

for example, on the humane treatment of pets, compassionate treatment of animals in general, alternatives to dissection, careers working with animals, animal rights, etc.

The goal of Humane Educators is to educate people to help prevent animal abuse, cruelty, and neglect. To accomplish this, the Humane Educator is responsible for researching pertinent topics for programs, presentations, and activities that help further the specific organization's mission.

The Humane Educator is responsible for developing and preparing humane education materials designed to promote humane attitudes toward animals. Schools or the general public can use these materials to assist with outreach programs.

The Humane Educator might work with schools in developing educational programs and materials for courses, workshops, programs, and other presentations. He or she may work with teachers in setting up a syllabus for an educational learning program.

The Humane Educator often searches out opportunities to present educational programs to various groups in an array of different situations. Depending on the specific organization and its mission, these might include presentations to civic group meetings, school assemblies, clubs on college campuses, conferences, and conventions.

It is essential that the Humane Educator have a thorough understanding of the organization's polices and causes so he or she can speak about them persuasively, passionately, and knowledgeably.

The Humane Educator works with the director of education and outreach to coordinate outreach actions and campaigns. In situations where the organization is planning a boycott, protest, or letter-writing campaign, the Humane Educator is expected to educate people on why the organization is holding these events and how they can help the organization's mission.

The individual may seek additional opportunities to reach the public. He or she may, for example, attend community events and fairs, setting up booths to educate the public on the specific issues of the animal advocacy organization.

The Humane Educator might also appear on television or radio news and talk shows discussing various topics regarding the issues of the specific animal advocacy organization. He or she may write columns for newspapers, magazines, or Web sites in order to help educate the public on the humane treatment of animals.

In organizations without grant writers or a director of education and outreach, the Humane Educator is responsible for searching out, preparing, and writing grant applications to help fund the humane education programs.

Salaries

Earnings for Humane Educators of animal advocacy organizations can range tremendously depending on a number of factors. These include the size, structure, budget, and geographic location of the specific organization as well as its specific mission. Other factors affecting earnings include the responsibilities, professional reputation, and experience of the individual. There are some individuals who earn as little as $22,000, while others earn $45,000 or more.

Employment Prospects

Employment prospects for individuals aspiring to become Humane Educators are fair. While every animal advocacy organization does not have a director of education and outreach, many have one if not more Humane Educators.

Individuals can find employment with organizations dedicated to a wide assortment of animal advocacy issues. Some are large and well known. Others are smaller and not as well known, but support important causes just the same. Opportunities are located throughout the United States. It should be noted that individuals might need to relocate for positions.

Advancement Prospects

Advancement prospects for Humane Educators are fair. Individuals can climb the career ladder in a number of ways, depending on their career aspirations. Many individuals find similar positions in larger, better-known organizations, resulting in increased responsibilities and earnings. Others climb the career ladder by becoming either the director of education and outreach of an animal advocacy organization or director of humane education.

Education and Training

Most animal advocacy organizations require or prefer a minimum of a four-year college degree for this position. Certain positions may require a master's degree as well.

There are smaller organizations that accept applicants with just an associate's degrees or even a high school diploma coupled with experience.

Good choices for majors include education, communications, business administration, journalism, public relations, animal sciences, or a related area.

Courses, seminars, and workshops in education, training, public speaking, grant-writing, public relations, business, management, and presentation skills will be useful for honing skills and making new contacts.

Experience, Skills, and Personality Traits

Experience requirements depend to a great extent on the size, structure, and reputation of the specific animal advocacy organization. Individuals seeking positions with large, well known organizations generally need to have more experience than their counterparts working at smaller animal advocacy groups. In some situations, Humane Educators gain experience speaking on behalf of animal advocacy organizations on a volunteer basis.

Some Humane Educators come from a background in education. Others have experience working with other animal advocacy organizations in various capacities or in public relations, journalism, fund-raising, grant-writing, and working with not-for-profit organizations. What they all have in common is a passion for the cause.

Humane Educators must have a full understanding and commitment to the specific animal advocacy group and its beliefs and issues. Those successful in this area truly enjoy helping people learn more about the issues of the organization.

Humane Educators should be articulate, confident, creative, and enthusiastic individuals with excellent verbal communication skills. The ability to discuss issues persuasively is essential, as are public speaking skills. As Humane Educators often speak in front of groups of people, the ability to be comfortable speaking in front of others is mandatory.

People skills are needed. Motivational skills will be helpful. Humane Educators should be competent in media relations as there will be times that they will speak to the media regarding organization issues. Good judgment and common sense are necessary as well.

Special Requirements

A voluntary certification is available from the Humane Society Youth, (formerly known as the National Association for Humane and Environmental Education.) This organization is an affiliate of the Humane Society of the United States (HSUS).

The certification provides a professional development program for individuals committed to humane education. Courses are offered online. Those who have completed the program and passed an exam earn the designation Certified Humane Education Specialist.

Unions and Associations

Individuals interested in pursuing careers in this area might want to join various organizations to make contacts and get professional support. These include the Association of Professional Humane Educators and Humane Society Youth. Individuals can also join the American Society for the Prevention of Cruelty to Animals (ASPCA), the American Humane Association (AHA), and the Humane Society of the United States (HSUS).

Tips for Entry

1. Join one or two animal advocacy organizations that have concerns and issues in which you believe and get involved as an active member. Ask to help in the education and outreach department.
2. When considering organizations with which to work, it is important to choose one with causes and issues in which you believe strongly. If you are still in school, consider starting a student chapter of that organization. It will help you make important contacts.
3. Look for internships in animal advocacy organizations, shelters, refuges, or rescues. Talk to the director of education and outreach and other Humane Educators about your career goals.
4. Look for job openings in the classifieds section of newspapers. Heading titles might include key words such as "Humane Educator," "Humane Education," "Education and Outreach," "Outreach and Education," "Animal Advocacy Organization," and "Animal Rights Organization." Jobs might also be advertised under the names of specific organizations.
5. Openings are sometimes listed on the Web sites of specific animal advocacy organizations, so check these often.
6. Network as much as you can in the industry. Go to conferences, conventions, and educational seminars and workshops to meet industry insiders.

SPECIAL EVENTS COORDINATOR

Duties: Coordinate special events for animal advocacy organization; develop ideas; plan special events; develop budgets; monitor expenditures; bring ideas to fruition

Alternate Title: Special Events Manager

Salary Range: $21,000 to $45,000+

Employment Prospects: Fair

Advancement Prospects: Fair

Best Geographical Locations for Position: Positions located throughout the United States in areas hosting animal advocacy organizations

Prerequisites:

Education or Training—Bachelor's degree in public relations, communications, journalism, or related field required or preferred by most organizations; see text

Experience and Qualifications—Experience planning and executing special events

Special Skills and Personality Traits—Creativity; ability to multitask; verbal and written communica-

tion skills; attention to detail; good telephone style; ability to multitask; people skills; understanding of and passion for animal advocacy

Position Description

There are many animal advocacy organizations throughout the United States and around the world. Each has its own issues, philosophies, concerns, and missions. Each works in some way to improve the lives of animals.

Nearly all animal advocacy organizations hold special events throughout the year. These events are scheduled for any number of reasons. Some events, for example, are put together to bring in additional funds to the organization. They might be simple, like bake sales, or large, elaborate events such as dinner dances, galas, golf tournaments, and so on.

Fund-raising is not the only reason animal advocacy organizations hold special events. Many groups hold special events to enhance their public image. They also are held to heighten public awareness of the group's key issues and causes. These might include, for example, demonstrations in front of department stores selling fur coats, save-the-whales demonstrations, or even events where groups attempt to liberate animals being used for product testing. Some events are used to bring organization members together.

Others are developed to honor members or others who have made a difference to the organization's causes and mission.

The individual responsible for putting together animal advocacy organization events is called the Special Events Coordinator. In some organizations, the public relations department handles the duties of this position. In others, there is a separate special events department run by a Special Events Coordinator. Depending on the specific organization's size, structure, and mission, the individual in this position might have a variety of duties.

The Special Events Coordinator must set up an annual calendar of events for the organization. This includes smaller events as well as larger ones. The calendar might, for example, contain regularly scheduled events such as organizational meetings. It might also include any fund-raisers or entertainment events the organization may host. These events can consist of bake sales, dinners, dances, galas, golf tournaments, concerts, etc. The annual calendar might additionally include conferences, boycotts, walks, and runs to bring attention to the organization's cause.

Scheduling events is just the beginning. The Special Events Coordinator is also responsible for developing ideas for special events and programs for the animal advocacy organization, planning the events, developing budgets, monitoring expenditures, and bringing ideas and events to fruition.

Some of these events might be planned for the local area. Others may be scheduled to take place in one or more locality. This will, of course, depend on the size and structure of the organization and its mission. Large animal advocacy groups, for example, might plan a nationwide protest at department stores selling fur coats. Smaller organizations, on the other hand, might plan demonstrations at local stores. In some situations, the Special Events Coordinator of one chapter of an organization will work with the Special Events Coordinator of another chapter of the organization in putting together events. This might happen, for example, when a larger demonstration is being scheduled in front of a chain of stores.

Special Events Coordinators are often contacted by the executive director or public relations department of the animal advocacy organization in regard to the need for an event. The individual must get the general information about the program, including the type of event that is needed and its purpose, size, time frame, and proposed budget.

Armed with that information, the Special Events Coordinator is expected to develop an appropriate event. Successful Special Events Coordinators come up with exciting, novel, and workable ideas. While the individual might do this on his or her own, a number of people in the organization usually are called on to brainstorm. After the rough ideas have been developed, the Special Events Coordinator is expected to work out the details and develop the basic plan. Depending on the structure of the organization, he or she might need to get approval before moving forward.

The Special Events Coordinator must develop budgets for each event and make sure to stick to them. He or she is responsible for handling all the logistics of the event. This includes, for example, finding appropriate locations, people, and items needed to make the event successful. Depending on where the event is being held, the individual may need to find caterers, tents, chairs, stages, promotional items, and special food.

A lot of thought needs to be put into every aspect of the event. An animal advocacy group that doesn't believe in killing animals for food, for example, cannot serve meat as a main course. The organization would need to find vegetarian caterers or at least caterers who know how to cook vegetarian food.

Depending on the event, the Special Events Coordinator might need to find entertainment. He or she will often seek out entertainers or celebrities who believe in the cause and mission of the organization. The individual is expected to scout out locations, dates, and times. Every detail of the entire event is the responsibility of the Special Events Coordinator.

Sometimes the pubic relations department of the animal advocacy organization handles the marketing and publicity for events. In other situations, the Special Events Coordinator is responsible for marketing. He or she may be expected to prepare press releases and other publicity for events before they occur as well as post-publicity on portions of the program that have already occurred. The individual might be required to write, design, and/or lay out programs, booklets, flyers, leaflets, or brochures about the program. Writing reports on the status or the result of promotions and events is usually necessary. At times the Special Events Coordinator may function as a public relations person. He or she may call the media and arrange interviews, articles, feature stories, photo opportunities, and broadcasts. The individual may be required to arrange and execute press conferences, cocktail parties, luncheons, and dinners.

The Special Events Coordinator is expected to be present at most if not all events. Many events take place in the evening or on weekends. Individuals usually work on many projects at one time.

The Special Events Coordinator is often judged by his or her last event. The individual can execute 100 successful programs, but if one is deemed a failure, people remember it. This can be stressful. However, for those who want to be part of the animal advocacy world and enjoy fast-paced workdays where no two days are the same, this can be a great career.

Salaries

Earnings for Special Events Coordinators working for animal advocacy organizations can range tremendously depending on a number of factors. These include the size, structure, budget, membership, and geographic location of the specific organization as well as its mission. Other factors affecting earnings include the responsibilities, professional reputation, and experience of the individual. Some earn as little as $21,000 annually, while others earn $45,000 or more. Those at the higher end of the pay scale generally have a great deal of experience and are working for large, well known animal advocacy organizations.

Employment Prospects

Employment prospects for individuals seeking positions as Special Events Coordinators are fair. Individuals can find employment with organizations dedicated to a wide assortment of animal advocacy issues. Some are large and well known. Others are smaller and not as well known, but support important causes just the same.

Opportunities are located throughout the country. It should be noted that individuals might need to relocate for positions.

Advancement Prospects

Advancement prospects for Special Events Coordinators working for animal advocacy organizations are fair. Individuals can climb the career ladder in a number of ways. Some advance their career by finding similar positions at larger animal advocacy organizations with higher budgets, resulting in increased responsibilities and earnings. Others find positions as the director of special events for a large animal advocacy organization or zoo. Some find similar positions outside the animal advocacy area.

Individuals who are passionate about animal advocacy and want to stay in the field can also climb the career ladder by being promoted to other administrative positions such as the director of public relations or the assistant director or executive director of the animal advocacy organization.

Education and Training

Most animal advocacy organizations require or prefer a minimum of a four-year college degree for this position. There are, however, smaller organizations that accept qualified applicants with associate's degrees or even high school diplomas coupled with experience, especially if the applicant has a passion for the cause.

Good choices for majors include public relations, communications, journalism, marketing, or related areas. Courses, seminars, and workshops in special events, public relations, publicity, promotion, writing, marketing, fund-raising, business development, media relations, and presentation skills will be useful.

Experience, Skills, and Personality Traits

Experience requirements depend to a great extent on the size, structure, and prestige of the specific animal advocacy organization. Experience, even on a volunteer basis, running special events and working with not-for-profit organizations will be useful.

Special Events Coordinators need to be creative and have the ability to think "outside of the box." They need to be able to conceptualize an idea and then bring it to fruition. The ability to look at a project and then break it up into logical, clear, concise phases is crucial to the success of a Special Events Coordinator.

Special Events Coordinators should be articulate and have excellent communication skills, both verbal and written. A good command of the English language is essential. People skills are vital.

The ability to communicate on the telephone in a polite, friendly, and effective manner is necessary. A proficiency in public speaking is helpful. Special Events Coordinators should be comfortable dealing with the media and answering their questions. They also need to be energetic, detail-oriented multitaskers.

An understanding of the issues and causes of the animal advocacy organization and a belief in its mission is also helpful.

Unions and Associations

Individuals interested in careers as Special Events Coordinators for animal advocacy organizations should consider becoming members of various organizations for professional support and to help make contacts. These include the Public Relations Society of America and various associations dedicated to assorted areas of animal advocacy.

Tips for Entry

1. Get experience and make valuable contacts by volunteering to put together events for a local animal advocacy organization, zoo, or other not-for-profit group.
2. Network as much as you can in the industry. Go to conferences, conventions, and educational seminars and workshops to meet industry insiders.
3. Become a member of one or more animal advocacy organizations, humane societies, animal shelters, or rescues. Membership will help you make contacts and get you involved in the animal advocacy world.
4. When considering organizations with which to work, it is important to choose one dedicated to causes and issues in which you believe.
5. An internship with an animal advocacy organization in the special events or public relations department will be useful for both the experience and the opportunity to make contacts.
6. Look for job openings in the classifieds section of newspapers. Headings might include key words such as "Special Events," "Special Events Coordina-

tor," "Animal Advocacy Organization," or "Animal Rights Organization." Jobs might also be advertised under the names of specific organizations.

7. Don't forget to look online for job opportunities. Start with some of the general sites such as Monster.com. Then search out sites specific to working with animals.

8. Openings may be listed on the Web sites of specific animal advocacy organizations, so check these regularly.

ATTORNEY

CAREER PROFILE

Duties: Handle legal matters for animal advocacy organization; handle contractual matters; negotiate deals; provide legal advice and counsel; litigate and negotiate on behalf of organization

Alternate Title(s): Lawyer; Animal Welfare Attorney

Salary Range: $45,000 to $125,000+

Employment Prospects: Poor

Advancement Prospects: Fair

Best Geographical Locations for Position: Positions located throughout the United States in areas hosting animal advocacy organizations

Prerequisites:

Education or Training—Law degree

Experience and Qualifications—Experience requirements vary from job to job; see text

Special Skills and Personality Traits—Negotiation skills; knowledge of animal advocacy issues; ability to read and understand contracts; ability to focus; organization skills; verbal and written communication skills; analytical mind; flexibility

Special Requirements—Must pass the bar exam and be licensed in the specific state in which individual works

CAREER LADDER

Attorney at Larger, Better-Known Animal Advocacy Organization; Partner in Law Firm Handling Animal Advocacy Issues; Attorney in Private Practice Handling Large Roster of Clients

Attorney

Law School Student

Position Description

Many animal advocacy organizations rely on outside or part-time counsel or law firms for their legal needs. There are some organizations, however, that have an in-house Attorney or legal department. These are usually the larger, better-known organizations. Depending on the size, budget, and structure of the organization, the legal department might consist of one or more Attorneys, paralegals, legal assistants, and clerical workers.

Attorneys have a number of functions at animal advocacy organizations. One of the most important functions is to advise the organization administration, staff, or board of directors of their legal rights and obligations. They additionally are responsible for counseling the organization on the legal ramifications of their actions so that the members of the organization can make good choices. Often the Attorney will work in conjunction with the organization administration, the board, and even volunteers to help focus the organization on its mission and causes so they do not overstep their legal boundaries in advocating for their goals and mission.

The duties of Attorneys working for animal advocacy organizations depend to a great extent on the organization's issues and goals as well as the tactics used to attain those objectives. There might, for example, be times when the organization decides to hold a march to stop the euthanizing of animals at shelters or a demonstration against a store that sells fur coats. The administration and members need to know the local rules and regulations regarding permits, gatherings, and distribution of material. The Attorney is often called upon to assist in this process.

Many of the responsibilities of Attorneys revolve around contracts. Depending on the specific situation, an Attorney would be responsible for negotiating and preparing contracts and agreements or reviewing those written by others to assure the meaning and intent is clear. The goal is always to make sure that the organization is protected. When working on contracts, the Attorney must always strive to be thorough and clear while acting in the best interest of the organization.

An important function of all Attorneys is conflict resolution, whether by negotiation or litigation. Those working in animal advocacy address such issues as the legal right to demonstrate, animal cruelty, or situations regarding the agency's issues and mission.

Attorneys are required to go to court when an agency's actions are brought into question or when the agency wishes to challenge the actions of an individual or business. They defend the organization if it is sued or start court proceedings when necessary.

These Attorneys may also perform an array of other duties for the organization, including negotiating leases or purchases of facilities or services and setting up business entities such as not-for-profit corporations. It is critical that that the Attorney assures that the organization is in full compliance with federal, state, and local laws and regulations. The Attorney may additionally be responsible for tax or financial advice or guidance.

Attorneys working in animal welfare not only have the opportunity to practice their chosen profession; they are also able to help protect innocent animals in the process.

Salaries

Earnings for Attorneys working for animal advocacy organizations vary dramatically. Salary ranges for these Attorneys will generally be lower than those working in private practice or corporate law.

Salary ranges for Attorneys in smaller organizations start at approximately $40,000 to $45,000. While salaries for Attorneys working for larger organizations may go as high as $125,000 or more, these jobs are few. Many law firms have Attorneys who are assigned to specific organizations or have special training and expertise in representing animal welfare and advocacy organizations. Associates at large firms and Attorneys in private practice have a much higher income potential.

Employment Prospects

Given the current economic climate, employment prospects for high-end employees such as Attorneys in animal advocacy organizations are limited. The greatest number of opportunities will exist with large, nationally known organizations. As noted previously, some positions may be part-time or on a contract basis.

Advancement Prospects

Advancement prospects for Attorneys working in animal advocacy organizations are fair. Advancement prospects will increase as an individual becomes known as an expert or specialist in this area.

Individuals can climb the career ladder in a number of ways. Some find similar positions in larger, better-known animal advocacy organizations. Others climb the career ladder by finding positions with law firms specializing in animal welfare. Still others either open their own practice or become a partner in a law firm specializing in animal welfare or advocacy.

Education and Training

Attorneys must have a four-year college degree and then go through three years of law school. Law schools must be approved by the American Bar Association (ABA). In order to apply to these law schools, applicants must first take the Law School Admission Test, better known as the LSAT. In order to practice, individuals must pass a written bar exam and be admitted into the bar of the particular state in which they wish to practice.

Various law schools offer classes in animal law, animal rights, and animal advocacy. Additionally, schools, bar associations, and national associations often offer continuing legal education, allowing Attorneys to develop specialized skills and expertise.

Experience, Skills, and Personality Traits

Experience requirements for Attorneys working for animal advocacy organizations differ from job to job. Large, well known organizations may want staff Attorneys to have three to five years or more of experience working in animal advocacy, animal welfare law, or a similar area. Smaller organizations may just require a year or so of experience after law school.

All Attorneys, no matter what their specialty, need to have good written and verbal communication skills. The ability to think analytically and objectively is essential, as are research skills.

Individuals need to be responsible, organized, ethical, and professional. Attorneys working with animal advocacy organizations need an understanding of the mission, issues, and concerns of the specific organization.

Attorneys are often privy to sensitive information. The ability to keep this information confidential is essential. The ability to show discretion is critical. The individual must also be extremely trustworthy.

Public speaking skills are necessary when trying a case in front of a judge or jury or addressing groups.

Special Requirements

Attorneys working with animal advocacy organizations, like all other Attorneys, need to pass the bar exam for the state or states in which they will be practicing, and be licensed and/or registered in the state in which they will be practicing.

Unions and Associations

Attorneys working in animal advocacy organizations can join the ABA and specific state bar associations. They might also be members of the Animal Legal Defense Fund, the Young Lawyers Division, and the Animal Protection Committee of the American Bar

Association. Individuals in some areas might also belong to the ABA's or local animal law committees. They may also be members of the American Society for the Prevention of Cruelty to Animals, the American Humane Association, and the Humane Society of the United States.

Tips for Entry

1. Become a member or supporter of animal advocacy organizations, humane societies, animal shelters, and rescues. Volunteer your services in any area needed. These groups help you make important contacts.
2. Try to find an internship in the legal department of an animal advocacy organization or with Attorneys who handle animal welfare law. It will help you obtain important experience.
3. Join trade associations in areas that interest you. These are helpful in building a career and making contacts.
4. Once you have some college under your belt, you might consider an internship or job as a paralegal at a law firm specializing in animal welfare or an animal advocacy organization.
5. Send your résumé with a short cover letter to animal advocacy organizations and law firms specializing in animal welfare. You might get lucky.
6. Positions in this field might be advertised in the newspaper classifieds section in areas hosting animal advocacy groups. Look under headings such as "Animal Welfare Attorney," "Animal Advocacy Attorney," "Animal Advocacy Organization," "Attorney," "Legal Affairs–Animal Advocacy," etc. Positions are also listed under the names of specific animal advocacy organizations.
7. Don't forget to check traditional job sites such as Monster.com.
8. Animal advocacy organizations sometimes list job openings on their Web sites, so check these, too.

PARALEGAL

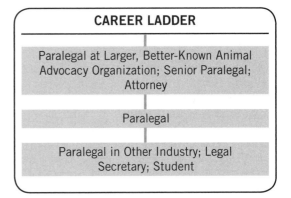

Position Description

Many animal advocacy organizations have legal departments to deal with an assortment of legal needs. Depending on the size, budget, and structure of the specific animal advocacy organization, this department may consist of one or more attorneys, Paralegals, or legal assistants and clerical workers.

Paralegals work under the supervision of attorneys and may perform many of the same tasks. While attorneys assume ultimate responsibility for legal work in the organization, they often delegate many of their tasks to Paralegals. With that said, Paralegals working in an animal advocacy organization, as well as any other situation, are specifically prohibited from carrying out specific tasks that include things such as presenting cases in court, giving legal advice, and setting legal fees.

The duties of Paralegals working in animal advocacy organizations vary from job to job. If the organization, for example, is dealing with any type of litigation, Paralegals might be expected to analyze legal materials. They may additionally be responsible for maintaining reference files for the case. Individuals are often expected to collect and analyze evidence used for agency hearings.

Paralegals are expected to perform research on issues related to specific matters for attorneys. They often are responsible for conducting investigations related to issues the animal advocacy organization may have. For example, the organization may be involved in litigation regarding animal cruelty. The Paralegal might participate in the investigation by interviewing witnesses and others involved in the case.

Many of the duties of Paralegals working in animal advocacy organizations involve writing. Individuals might prepare legal documents such as contracts, leases, or documents related to litigation. They might additionally draft advisory opinion letters, research memos, and other documents. At times, Paralegals also prepare statements regarding the organization's policies and procedures. These are used internally or distributed to the public.

While they cannot practice law, Paralegals working in animal advocacy organizations perform quasi-legal functions. This might be the ideal type of job for those interested in the legal aspect of animal advocacy but not prepared to invest the time or finances necessary to become full-fledged attorneys.

Salaries

Earnings for Paralegals working for animal advocacy organizations vary dramatically. Salary ranges for individuals working in organizations such as this will generally be lower than those working in similar positions in private practice.

Earnings for Paralegals working in smaller organizations start at approximately $27,000 and may go to $40,000 or more. Those working in larger organizations or those with more experience may have earnings of $47,000 or more.

Employment Prospects

Employment prospects for Paralegals are fair. As Paralegals can perform work that is sometimes done by attorneys, but at a lower cost, they are frequently hired to do preliminary work when a lawyer is not on staff. The greatest number of opportunities will exist with large, nationally known animal advocacy organizations.

Advancement Prospects

Advancement prospects for Paralegals working in animal advocacy organizations are fair. Individuals can climb the career ladder in a number of ways, depending on their career aspirations. Some become senior Paralegals in the organization in which they work. Others find similar positions in larger, better-known animal advocacy organizations. Some individuals also find they can advance their career by locating similar positions with law firms specializing in animal welfare. Still others find positions as Paralegals in industries outside of the animal welfare and advocacy industries. There are also many Paralegals who go to law school and become attorneys.

Education and Training

There are a number of different ways to become a Paralegal. Individuals can go through a two-year program at a community college, culminating in an associate's degree. They can also complete a specialized program in which they earn a certificate in paralegal studies. There are also a limited number of colleges offering a bachelor's degree and master's degree in paralegal studies. Some Paralegals are also trained on job.

Certificate programs vary in length and generally provide intensive training. While degrees or certificates are not essential, they enhance an individual's marketability, salary potential, and advancement prospects.

There are approximately 1,000 colleges, universities, law schools, and proprietary schools offering formal paralegal training programs. Two hundred and sixty of those programs are approved by the American Bar Association (ABA). While ABA-approved programs are not required, many employers prefer the training they provide.

Experience, Skills, and Personality Traits

Experience requirements for Paralegals working for animal advocacy organizations differ from job to job. Larger organizations generally prefer that their Paralegals have more experience than smaller organizations might. However, many organizations, no matter the size, will forgo experience requirements if individuals are trained and can demonstrate a true understanding and deep passion for the cause and mission of the organization.

Paralegals working with animal advocacy organizations need an understanding of the mission, issues, and concerns of the specific organization. Communication skills, both written and verbal, are essential. The ability to think analytically is helpful. Research and investigative skills are mandatory for this type of job.

Individuals should have a full understanding of legal terminology as well as the terminology used in animal advocacy and animal welfare. The ability to work effectively under pressure is critical.

Special Requirements

There are a number of voluntary certifications available to Paralegals. The National Federation of Paralegal Associations (NFPA) offers the Registered Paralegal designation to Paralegals who hold a bachelor's degree, have a minimum of two years of experience, and pass an exam. Continuing education is required to maintain the credential.

NALS: The Association for Legal Professionals offers the Professional Paralegal certification to individuals passing a four-part exam. Continuing education is required to maintain the credential.

The American Alliance of Paralegals, Inc. (AAPI) offers certification in the form of the American Alliance Certified Paralegal credential to individuals who have a minimum of five years of paralegal experience and meet certain educational criteria. Individuals must renew their certification every three years and complete 18 hours of continuing education in that time.

Unions and Associations

Paralegals working in animal advocacy organizations can join of a number of organizations that can be helpful for professional support and networking purposes. These include the National Association of Legal Assistants and the AAPI.

Other organizations that may be helpful include the ABA, the NFPA, the Animal Legal Defense Fund, the Young Lawyers Division, and the Animal Protection Committee of the American Bar Association. Individuals can also join the American Society for the Prevention of Cruelty to Animals, the American Humane Association, and the Humane Society of the United States.

Tips for Entry

1. Become a member or supporter of animal advocacy organizations, humane societies, animal shelters, and rescues. Volunteer your services in any area needed. These groups help you make important contacts.
2. Try to find an internship in the legal department of an animal advocacy organization or with attorneys who handle animal welfare law. It will help you obtain important experience.
3. Join trade associations in areas that interest you. These are helpful in building a career and making contacts.
4. Consider an internship in the legal department of an animal advocacy organization or at a law firm specializing in animal welfare or an animal advocacy organization.
5. Send your résumé with a short cover letter to animal advocacy organizations and law firms specializing in animal welfare. You might get lucky.
6. Positions in this field might be advertised in the newspaper classifieds section. Look under headings such as "Animal Welfare Paralegal," "Animal Advocacy Paralegal," "Animal Advocacy Organization," "Paralegal," "Legal Affairs–Animal Advocacy," and "Legal Assistant." Positions might also be listed under the names of specific animal advocacy organizations.
7. Don't forget to check traditional job sites such as Monster.com.
8. Animal advocacy organizations sometimes list job openings on their Web sites, so keep an eye on these.
9. Get the best training you can. It will help your marketability when looking for a job and your earnings once you obtain one.

GRANT WRITER

Position Description

The majority of animal advocacy organizations are classified as nonprofits. In order to remain solvent, these groups need money, which they often seek from donations, contributions, membership fees, and merchandising.

Most animal advocacy organizations also seek out financial assistance in the form of grants. Grants are funds given to support a particular project, organization, or cause. Foundations, corporations, or individuals in the private, public, or governmental sector offer them. Grant Writers are the individuals who actively research, write, and solicit grants.

Some animal advocacy organizations have an entire department dedicated to dealing with grants. Others may just have one or two Grant Writers. There are also some organizations that may depend on individuals in the public relations or fund-raising departments or even the executive director to write grants. Still others outsource grant-writing responsibilities.

Grant Writers have a number of responsibilities. To begin with, they are expected to find applicable grants for the animal advocacy organization. Grants may be located in a number of ways. Some are advertised or listed in corporate publications. Others are located in newspapers or periodicals or through press releases. Still others are found in publications dealing specifically with grants. Some Grant Writers also send letters of inquiry directly to foundations, corporations, or individuals in hopes of piquing their interest to provide grant money.

There is a wide array of grants available to animal advocacy organizations. Each has its own set of requirements that must be met in order to qualify. As there is often more than one organization vying for the same grant money, it is necessary for the Grant Writer to do everything possible to ensure that grant applications are answered clearly, completely, and in an attention-grabbing and persuasive manner.

Some grant applications are straightforward, simply asking applicants to fill in forms identifying the organization, funds needed, and the proposed use of funds. Others can be very complicated, often requiring the Grant Writer to do extensive research, development, and preparation.

In larger organizations, the Grant Writer might work with a researcher or an assistant in the preparation of the grant. In smaller organizations, he or she may be expected to do the work independently.

Grant Writers must be sure each grant proposal is prepared in accordance with the instructions. While instructions differ from proposal to proposal, most ask the applicant to identify the organization and its qualifications and credibility. For example, the Grant Writer might discuss a bit about the animal advocacy organization and explain what its mission is, who it helps, and what are some of its projects. Somewhere in this information, he or she must be sure to note that the animal advocacy group is a nonprofit, 501(c)(3) organization.

The Grant Writer will describe the request for the grant, the amount of monies needed, and why the funds are needed or what they will be used for. In many cases, he or she is expected to detail the budget for the project for which the grant is being requested. Depending on the project, the individual might need to do quite a bit of research in order to provide this information.

Some grants are very generic. Grant Writers in these cases may simply need to explain a bit about the organization, why funds are needed, and how funds could further the causes of the animal advocacy organization or a particular project.

Some of the grants that Grant Writers apply for, on the other hand, are very specific in nature. For example, the Grant Writer might apply for a grant that specifically funds a research project, educational outreach, or even the salary of an individual. A grant might offer funds to an animal advocacy organization that helps with the adoption of older dogs and cats or may offer funds to an organization that works in an area of animal rights.

Whatever the grant, the Grant Writer must be sure to adequately describe each project, explaining in a persuasive manner why funds are needed and how the funds can help. He or she must be sure that each grant applied for is applicable to the organization's goals and objections.

An effective Grant Writer can win funding for an animal advocacy organization that it might not ordinarily get. The individual is expected to prepare each proposal to fit the requirements of the grantor. While doing this, the writer gives information on the organization, including its goals, objectives, and mission. The individual may explain the manner in which the organization hopes to achieve those goals and objectives and further its mission. Grant Writers often work on more than one grant at a time.

It is essential that the individual understand the organization's policies, issues, and causes and have the ability to passionately convey them, both in writing and verbally.

Depending on the specific organization and its size and structure, the Grant Writer might also be the grant administrator. In this capacity, he or she will additionally be responsible for evaluating the grant application, administering the grant, dispersing grant funds, and overseeing their use. In other organizations, a special grant administrator handles these duties.

Salaries

Earnings for Grant Writers working for animal advocacy organizations range from approximately $24,000 to $65,000 or more. Factors affecting earnings include the size, structure, budget, and geographic location of the specific organization as well as its cause and mission. Other factors affecting earnings include the responsibilities, professional reputation, and experience of the individual.

Employment Prospects

Employment prospects for individuals seeking positions as Grant Writers for animal advocacy organizations are fair. Individuals can find employment with organizations dedicated to a wide assortment of animal advocacy issues. Some are large and well known. Others are smaller and not as well known, but have important missions just the same.

Opportunities are located throughout the country. It should be noted that individuals might need to relocate for positions.

Some organizations hire more than one Grant Writer. However, while most organizations need someone to write grants, not every organization employs Grant Writers. As noted earlier, in some organizations, a staffer from the public relations or fund-raising department, or even the executive director, handles grant-writing.

Advancement Prospects

Advancement prospects for Grant Writers employed by animal advocacy organizations are fair. Individuals can climb the career ladder in a number of ways, depending on their career aspirations. Some advance their career by finding similar positions at larger, higher-budget animal advocacy organizations, resulting in increased responsibilities and earnings. Others find similar positions in other industries. Individuals who are passionate about animal advocacy and want to stay in the field can also climb the career ladder by being promoted to other administrative positions, such as the director of grants, director of public relations, director of fund-raising and development, or even executive director. Some individuals become grant-writing consultants.

Education and Training

Most animal advocacy organizations require or prefer a minimum of a four-year college degree for this position. There are, however, smaller organization that may accept an applicant with an associate's degree or even a high school diploma coupled with experience, especially if the applicant has a passion for the cause and a demonstrated ability to write successful grants.

Good choices for majors include public relations, communications, journalism, marketing, liberal arts, or related areas. Courses, seminars, and workshops in grant-writing, writing, marketing, fund-raising, and development will be useful.

Grant-writing courses are located throughout the United States in a variety of settings. They are often offered at community colleges and through governmental programs.

Experience, Skills, and Personality Traits

Prior experience writing grants, whether on a voluntary or paid basis, is generally necessary. Experience working with nonprofit organizations and animal advocacy organizations will always be helpful as well. This experience is often obtained through volunteer opportunities and internships.

Grant Writers must have excellent writing skills. A working knowledge of grammar, spelling, and language is essential. Research skills are also vital. Creativity is a must. Grant Writers must have the ability to follow instructions, as grants must be prepared in the manner required by the funding organization.

It is essential that Grant Writers have a total understanding of the causes and mission of the animal advocacy organization. A belief in the cause is helpful as well.

Grant Writers should be well spoken. The ability to communicate on the telephone in a polite, friendly, and effective manner is necessary.

Special Requirements

Voluntary certification for Grant Writers is available through the American Grant Writers Association (AGWA). The AGWA offers the Certified Grant Writer credential to individuals who pass a proficiency exam in grant researching and writing. While most employers do not require this certification, it may provide an edge over another applicant with similar qualifications who does not hold certification.

Unions and Associations

Grant Writers for animal advocacy organizations belong to a number of organizations that provide professional support, educational opportunities, and networking possibilities. These include the AGWA, the Association of Fundraising Professionals, and the Public Relations Society of America. Individuals can also join organizations and associations specific to various animal advocacy issues.

Tips for Entry

1. Get experience by volunteering or interning in the grant department of a nonprofit organization. While an animal advocacy organization would be ideal, getting experience with any type of organization is well worth it.
2. Be on the lookout for new grant-writing classes. If you can pick up even one new idea or tip, it will be worth the time.
3. If you can't find a job as a Grant Writer, consider getting involved in grant writing for animal advocacy organizations on a consulting basis.
4. Send your résumé and a short cover letter to animal advocacy organizations. Ask that your résumé be kept on file if there are no current openings.
5. Check out openings online. Start with some of the more popular job sites such as Monster.com. Then look for job Web sites specific to animal advocacy organizations and other nonprofits.
6. Don't forget to check out the Web sites of animal advocacy groups. Many list their openings online.
7. When considering organizations with which to work, it is important to choose one dedicated to causes and issues in which you believe.

LOBBYIST

CAREER PROFILE

Duties: Draft bills for legislators; work to have bills passed or defeated; influence legislators to pass legislation; meet with legislators; study proposed legislation

Alternate Title(s): Government Affairs Representative; Legislative Assistant; Legislative Associate

Salary Range: $26,000 to $125,000+

Employment Prospects: Fair

Advancement Prospects: Fair

Best Geographical Locations for Position: Positions located throughout United States in areas hosting animal advocacy organizations; large concentration of lobbying firms in Washington, D.C.

Prerequisites:

Education or Training—Educational requirements vary; minimum of bachelor's degree required or preferred

Experience and Qualifications—Experience requirements vary from job to job; see text

Special Skills and Personality Traits—Written and verbal communication skills; persuasiveness; negotiation skills; knowledge of animal advocacy issues; understanding of political process; people skills; time-management skills; ability to multitask effectively

CAREER LADDER

Lobbyist for Larger, Better-Known Animal Advocacy Organization; Lobbyist for Larger Nonprofit Organization Outside of Animal Advocacy Organization; Partner in Lobbying Firm; Independent Lobbyist; Executive Director of Large Animal Advocacy Organization

↑

Lobbyist

↑

Congressional Aide; Legislative Aide; Attorney; Public Relations Staffer; Policy Assistant; Animal Advocacy Activist

Position Description

Many methods and tactics are used by animal advocacy organizations to further their goals and accomplish their mission. They might, for example, try to educate the public about situations regarding the way animals are treated through writing, speaking, and advertising. They might hold protests, boycott certain products, and mount letter-writing campaigns in an effort to bring about change. Many animal advocacy organizations also have found that lobbying is a very effective way of influencing legislators and society as a whole.

Lobbying is a process by which one or more people try to persuade legislators to vote a certain way on a given piece of legislation. Lobbyists attempt to sway lawmakers to their way of thinking. Legislation might include a variety of bills, rules, or regulations.

An effective Lobbyist can mean the difference between success and failure in getting a piece of legislation passed or defeated. For example, a Lobbyist for an animal advocacy group might lobby for a bill that prohibits transporting animals going to slaughter in an inhumane manner. If legislation is passed, using that method of transportation will be illegal.

Lobbyists working for animal advocacy organizations attempt to change or push through legislation that directly affects the lives of animals. As part of the job, the Lobbyist must determine what legislation the animal advocacy group wants passed or defeated. Once that is done, the Lobbyist drafts a bill and takes it to a legislator.

In some cases, the Lobbyist finds that a bill related to the animal advocacy organization is already before the legislature. Depending on the specific legislation, the Lobbyist will either work to have the bill passed or defeated.

Lobbyists meet with legislators to discuss the reason why the animal advocacy group wants a proposed bill passed or defeated. Depending on the level of the government the Lobbyist is dealing with, he or she may arrange meetings with local, state, or federal officials. In some instances, the Lobbyist works with a local legislator and asks him or her to put pressure on a state or federal legislator in order to get legislation passed.

When meeting with legislators, Lobbyists are expected to point out the strengths and weaknesses of a specific bill. This is done to try to sway the legislator's opinion regarding the passage of the bill. In some cases, while the Lobbyist cannot totally change the legislator's mind, the Lobbyist can at least get that bill amended so that it is more acceptable to the animal advocacy organization.

Lobbyists must do a great deal of preliminary preparation work and research before meeting with legislators. They must study the proposed legislation to determine its potential effects on the animal advocacy organization and animals in general.

Depending on the size and structure of the specific animal advocacy organization, Lobbyists might be responsible for developing and writing letters, press releases, and other communications to publicize proposed legislation that the animal advocacy group supports or opposes. Individuals might also schedule and hold press conferences, appear on radio and television talk and news shows, and provide written information to the media. In other organizations, some or all of these tasks may be done by an assistant or staff member or may be assigned to the public relations or publications department.

Lobbyists often collect signatures on petitions urging passage of specific bills. These petitions are taken to legislators when discussing the bill. Lobbyists also frequently must speak to groups, testify at hearings, and seek support for the animal advocacy organization's mission.

Salaries

Earnings for Lobbyists working for animal advocacy organizations vary dramatically. There are some Lobbyists working with animal advocacy organizations who earn $26,000 and others who may earn $70,000 or more. Factors affecting earnings include the specific animal advocacy organization and its size and budget. Other variables include the experience, responsibilities, and professional reputation of the individual.

In some cases, the Lobbyist of an animal advocacy organization is also its attorney. These individuals can have a higher earning potential, with some earning $125,000 or more annually. Jobs at this pay, however, are rare.

Employment Prospects

Employment prospects are fair for individuals seeking positions as Lobbyists for animal advocacy organizations. Positions are located throughout the country in areas hosting animal advocacy organizations. The greatest opportunities exist with large, nationally known animal advocacy groups.

Animal advocacy groups recruit some Lobbyists from lobbying consulting firms or as independent Lobbyist consultants. There is a large concentration of lobbying firms located in Washington, D.C., because of the proximity to federal legislators.

Advancement Prospects

Advancement prospects for Lobbyists working with animal advocacy organizations are fair. Lobbyists who are able to develop a network of contacts and are successful in getting bills passed can climb the career ladder by locating similar positions with better-known, better-funded organizations. This results in increased responsibilities and earnings. Some individuals become independent Lobbyists. Others become partners in lobbying firms. Still others who have a very deep passion for a specific animal advocacy organization may become the organization's executive director. There are also some Lobbyists who find similar positions outside the animal advocacy field.

Education and Training

Educational requirements for Lobbyists vary from job to job. The minimum requirement for most positions is a bachelor's degree. Good majors include political science, communications, liberal arts, journalism, public affairs, public relations, conservation, environmental studies, law, or a related field. Some positions require or prefer a graduate degree.

There are some animal advocacy organizations that require or prefer their Lobbyists to be attorneys. In order to become a lawyer, individuals are required to have a four-year college degree and then complete three years of law school. Law schools must be approved by the American Bar Association (ABA). In order to apply for these law schools, applicants must first take the Law School Admission Test, better known as the LSAT. In order to practice, individuals must pass a written bar exam and be admitted into the bar of the particular state in which they wish to practice.

Various law schools offer classes in animal law, animal rights, and animal advocacy. Additionally, schools, bar associations, and national associations may offer continuing legal education, allowing attorneys to develop specialized skills and expertise.

Experience, Skills, and Personality Traits

Experience requirements for Lobbyists working for animal advocacy organizations differ from job to job. Large, well known organizations generally require their

Lobbyists to have a great deal more experience than smaller ones do. Experience in lobbying as well as animal advocacy, animal welfare law, or a similar area is generally needed.

One of the most important traits of a Lobbyist working with animal advocacy organization is a passion for the cause. Individuals must strongly believe in the cause and the issues of the group in order to lobby effectively. A broad knowledge of the legislative process is essential. Research skills are vital.

Strong interpersonal skills are necessary in this position. Individuals must have the ability to make contacts and keep them. Lobbyists must be persuasive in a non-threatening manner. They must be well groomed and have a good public presence. Public speaking skills are helpful.

Individuals need to be articulate, with excellent written and verbal communication skills. The ability to think analytically and objectively is essential. Negotiation skills are helpful. Time-management skills and the ability to multitask effectively will also be useful to the success of Lobbyists.

Unions and Associations

Lobbyists can join a variety of organizations that provide professional support, the opportunity to make contacts, and educational resources. These include the American League of Lobbyists, the American Association of Political Consultants, and the American Society of Association Executives. Lobbyists might also join Women in Government Relations.

If Lobbyists are attorneys, they can be members of the ABA as well as specific state bar associations. They might also be members of the Animal Legal Defense Fund, the Young Lawyers Division, and the Animal Protection Committee of the American Bar Association. Individuals in some areas also belong to Animal Law Committees. Many Lobbyists are also members of the American Society for the Prevention of Cruelty to Animals, the American Humane Association, and the Humane Society of the United States.

Tips for Entry

1. Become a member or supporter of animal advocacy organizations, humane societies, animal shelters, and rescues. Volunteer your services in any area needed. These groups help you make important contacts.

2. Try to find an internship with a Lobbyist of an animal advocacy organization, an independent Lobbyist, or a lobbying firm. It will help you obtain important experience.

3. Consider an internship with a governmental agency on either the state or federal level. The contacts you make will be invaluable.

4. Look for job openings in the classifieds section of newspapers in areas hosting animal advocacy organizations under headings such as "Lobbyist," "Animal Advocacy Organization," "Animal Rights Organizations," "Animal Welfare Attorney," "Animal Advocacy Attorney," "Attorney," "Legal Affairs–Animal Advocacy," etc. Positions might also be listed under the names of specific animal advocacy organizations.

5. Send your résumé with a short cover letter to animal advocacy organizations asking about openings. Remember to ask that your résumé be kept on file if there are no current openings.

6. Don't forget to check traditional job sites such as Monster.com.

7. Animal advocacy organizations may also list job openings on their Web sites, so check these too.

WEB SITE CONTENT PRODUCER

Duties: Create, write, and maintain content for organization's Web site; develop content to attract and retain members and other Web site visitors; oversee the implementation of Web content; edit Web site content

Alternate Title(s): Web Site Content Manager; Web Site Content Editor

Salary Range: $25,000 to $60,000+

Employment Prospects: Fair

Advancement Prospects: Fair

Best Geographical Locations for Position: Positions located throughout United States in areas hosting animal advocacy organizations

Prerequisites:

Education or Training—Educational requirements vary; see text

Experience and Qualifications—Writing and editing experience necessary

CAREER LADDER

```
Executive Web Site Content Producer;
Web Site Content Producer for
More Prestigious Animal Advocacy
Organization; Web Site Content Producer
in Other Industry
```

```
Web Site Content Producer
```

```
Journalist; Writer; Publicist; Webmaster
```

Special Skills and Personality Traits—Creativity; command of the English language; writing skills; passion; Internet savvy; organization; innovation; understanding and passion for the causes and mission of the specific animal advocacy organization

Position Description

Animal advocacy organizations, like other organizations, use the Internet as a marketing tool. Depending on the specific organization, its mission, and its popularity, a Web site can potentially get thousands of hits a day.

In order to spread the word about the missions and causes of animal advocacy organizations, many groups now utilize the services of Web Site Content Producers. These individuals are responsible for creating and maintaining the content of the organization's Web site.

In this position, individuals are expected to develop and execute a strategic online content plan. In order to be successful, Web Site Content Producers must constantly come up with fresh, innovative content that makes people want to keep coming back to the site.

Web sites give animal advocacy organizations a necessary presence on the Web. This presence makes it easy for members to obtain general information on the organization as well as to stay informed about news and events. Web sites also give organizations a simple way to promote the group and their cause. With every hit, the organization gets a chance to bring in much-needed funds, add new members, and educate the public about

the specific causes and missions of the group. Web sites also help animal advocacy groups build communities. These communities can dramatically help the organization raise awareness of the mission, become better known, and raise funds.

One of the best things about a Web site is that if the media or anyone else needs information, it is available with a click of the mouse. In a world where people want information *now,* this can be priceless.

Web Site Content Producers are responsible for the content of every aspect of the Web site. It is essential that the Web sites are full of great information, user friendly, and make people want to keep coming back. Individuals in this position are responsible for researching and writing engaging stories and articles in a variety of areas and categories. Their role is like a combination of a print journalist and editor.

Web Site Content Producers are expected to develop a variety of stories for the Web site that are of interest to both current and potential members of the organization. These articles might be about the organization itself, notable members, or animal advocacy issues in general, among other topics.

Sometimes these articles are short blurbs. Other times, they might be longer and more in-depth. The Web Site Content Producer must be sure each article will both catch the eye of those visiting the site and keep visitors' attention.

The home page is the location where most people start at a Web site and it must entice visitors to keep exploring the site. The Web Site Content Producer must be sure the home page stays fresh and is constantly updated. No one wants to go to an organization's Web site to see what is happening and find that the news on the page is six months old.

The home page might include breaking news about the organization, announcements regarding events, photos, and links to other information.

Other pages on the site might include information on the organization itself, profiles of board members, feature stories, reprints of interviews, forums, photos, and videos. The Web Site Content Producer must be sure all copy is interesting and easy to read.

In an effort to increase interest in the organization as well as give people a reason to visit the site, Web Site Content Producers might develop blogs, webcasts, chats, and podcasts. These techniques help get people involved and attract media attention.

Web Site Content Producers often find ways to develop mailing lists of people who visit the site. They accomplish this using a variety of methods, including developing "contact us" forms, surveys, or even sweepstakes. These mailing lists can be extremely valuable to an animal advocacy organization. They can be used to get news out as well as to let members know about events or campaigns such as boycotts, marches, or other events.

Some Web Site Content Producers develop e-mail blasts that they send out to members. These may be used to spread news quickly as well as to ask large groups of members to call radio stations, television stations, news media, or corporations when they want an issue addressed. If the organization has developed a large enough e-mail list, these e-mail blasts can often draw a great deal of attention to an issue in a short amount of time.

Depending on the size and structure of the animal advocacy organization Web site, there may be more than one content producer. One might be a senior or executive Web Site Content Producer who oversees the entire site. Another might develop and monitor blogs. Still another might develop podcasts. Some may be responsible just for researching and writing feature stories about the organization, while others are expected to do interviews. Everything really depends on the size of the site and how comprehensive the organization wants it to be.

Web Site Content Producers are often responsible for overseeing staff copywriters, photographers, and graphic artists. Some content producers are also responsible for finding and retaining freelancers to write articles on specific subjects or in specific areas.

The content producer is responsible for getting all stories, editing them when necessary, and giving them to the webmaster to put online. As a picture is often worth a thousand words, the Web Site Content Producer is often responsible for finding pictures, animations, videos, and other graphics to make the content more appealing and interesting. He or she may utilize the services of graphic artists, photographers, or others to accomplish this task.

The Web Site Content Producer might, for example, put a video on a page dedicated one of the organization's large demonstrations. In the same vein, he or she might put a link to a television news story showing how a puppy mill was closed down and hundreds of dogs were saved. The Web Site Content Producer might also utilize videos of individuals in the organization being interviewed or compelling videos illustrating why animals need to be treated better. It is essential in this process that the individual works with the webmaster to find images that are appropriate and appealing but do not affect the ease of opening the site.

One of the exciting things about the Internet for animal advocacy organizations is that it can be interactive. The Web Site Content Producer can develop surveys, questionnaires, or other interactive content to involve those visiting the site. In some instances, the interactive part of the site is related to promotions, events, campaigns, or other happenings.

In order to keep people returning to the site, it is vital that the Web Site Content Producer keeps the site fresh. This is often done with daily updates. These might include information on television or radio interviews or stories regarding the organization, dates of events, and other interesting or current information regarding the group and its causes.

Salaries

Web Site Content Producers who work for animal advocacy organizations earn between $25,000 and $60,000 or more annually. Factors affecting earnings include the experience, responsibilities, and professional reputation of the individual as well as the size, budget, and popularity of the specific animal advocacy organization. Other variables include the size of the Web site as well as the importance the organization places on its online presence.

Individuals who work on a consulting basis are paid a monthly fee ranging from $2,000 to $5,000 or more. Some are also compensated on a per-project basis.

Employment Prospects

Employment prospects for Web Site Content Producers for animal advocacy organizations are fair. Individuals can work for large, well known, established animal advocacy organizations or smaller groups or even organizations that are just starting up.

Depending on the situation, individuals might be employed directly by the animal advocacy organization or work on a consulting or freelance basis.

Advancement Prospects

Advancement prospects for Web Site Content Producers working for animal advocacy organizations are fair. To a great extent, advancement prospects depend on how established the individual is in his or her career.

Web Site Content Producers handling Web sites for lesser-known organizations, for example, can climb the career ladder by finding similar positions with larger, better-known organizations. This generally results in increased responsibilities and earnings. Those at the top of their game find similar positions with even larger organizations. Some move into similar positions in areas and industries other than animal advocacy.

Education and Training

While there might be exceptions, most positions require or prefer individuals to hold a minimum of a four-year college degree. Good choices for majors include journalism, communications, English, public relations, marketing, animal sciences, or liberal arts.

Courses, workshops, and seminars in public relations, writing, promotion, journalism, animal advocacy issues, and Web journalism will be helpful in honing skills and making new contacts.

Experience, Skills, and Personality Traits

Experience requirements depend to a great extent on the specific animal advocacy organization and the emphasis it places on its online presence. Organizations that are just starting up might only require an individual to be able to demonstrate competency in this area. Well known, large-budget organizations that place a great deal of importance on their Web site generally

prefer that individuals have a proven track record and a minimum of two or three years of experience developing, creating, editing, and managing Web and interactive content.

Writing and editing experience will be useful whether it is Web-related or not. Web Site Content Producers need to be innovative, creative, and organized. A command of the English language is necessary, as are excellent communication skills, both written and verbal.

Web Site Content Producers need the ability to multitask effectively. A full understanding and working knowledge of the area in which the specific animal advocacy organization is involved is essential. Individuals must also be Internet savvy, with an understanding of Web analytic and search engine optimization. While it may not be required, individuals who know HTML (a programming language) will have a leg up on other candidates.

Unions and Associations

Web Site Content Producers can join a number of animal advocacy organizations, such as the American Society for the Prevention of Cruelty to Animals, the American Humane Association, and the Humane Society of the United States. Individuals can also join the Internet Professionals Association.

Tips for Entry

1. Positions are sometimes advertised in the classifieds section of newspapers in areas where there are larger numbers of animal advocacy organizations. Look under headings such as "Web Site Content Producer," "Web site Content Manager," "Animal Advocacy Organization–Web site," "Web sites," and "Web Careers."
2. This is the perfect type of job to look for online. Start with some of the more popular job sites such as Monster.com and expand your search from there.
3. Jobs openings can also be located on career sites specific to animal advocacy organizations.
4. Get as much writing experience as you can. If you are still in school, get involved in your school newspaper and/or Web site.
5. Offer to put together a Web site for your local shelter or humane society. It will give you good experience and a line to add to your résumé.
6. Consider a part-time job for a local newspaper to get some writing experience and to build up your contacts.

7. Look for internships at animal advocacy organizations, shelters, humane societies, etc. These will give you on-the-job training, experience, and the opportunity to make important contacts. Contact the human resource department to see what is available.

8. Send your résumé and a short cover letter to animal advocacy organizations. You can never tell when an opportunity exists.

9. Many advocacy organizations advertise openings on their Web sites. Look for the section of the site that lists job opportunities.

ZOOS AND AQUARIUMS

ZOO VETERINARIAN

Position Description

Zoo Veterinarians are responsible for the medical care of animals in zoos. They are expected to care for sick animals and handle the preventive care of healthy ones.

Zoological medicine integrates ecology, conservation, and veterinary medicine. It then applies these principles to wild animals living within both natural and artificial environments such as zoos.

Veterinarians working in zoos work with a variety of wild animals in captivity, including lions, tigers, bears, foxes, moose, elephants, elk, giraffe, antelopes, birds, various primates, and more. Responsibilities of Zoo Veterinarians vary depending on the specific situation in which they are working. Instead of practicing in an office environment, Zoo Veterinarians visit animals in their cages or enclosures at the zoo.

Just as doctors give checkups to people, Zoo Veterinarians give checkups to animals. They check the animal's heart, lungs, skin, and coat. They also check the animal's eyes, ears, and teeth. Of course, this is not as easy as working with people or pets. The specialized training Zoo Veterinarians receive helps them accomplish these tasks. In many cases, however, animals will need to be anesthetized when they receive certain types of checkups.

When performing checkups, vets often discuss the animal's health with its zookeepers. They discuss any issues the animals have, health concerns, and behavior problems. The vet prescribes a nutritionally sound diet or makes changes in the foods the animal has been eating. In some cases, the vet needs to deal with allergies in certain zoo animals.

Zoo Veterinarians vaccinate animals to protect them from disease. If they are sick, vets prescribe and administer medications. They set broken bones when animals are injured.

Zoo Veterinarians are expected to provide preventive, proactive animal care to animals in the zoo, such as testing for disease or parasites. They are responsible for diagnosing health problems of animals in their care. Once the problem is diagnosed, the vet is responsible for developing a course of treatment. He or she will also follow up after the treatment to be sure it has been effective.

At times, Zoo Veterinarians need to quarantine animals. This often occurs when new animals come to the zoo or are being disbursed to other zoos.

Zoo Veterinarians often perform surgery. They may anesthetize animals, insert IVs, and provide postoperative care. Individuals are frequently assisted by veterinary technicians and technologists in these tasks.

Other responsibilities of Zoo Veterinarians include performing postmortems or necropsies on animals that have died at the zoo. This might be necessary for a number of reasons, including to make sure that the animal did not harbor any virus or parasite that could be contagious to other animals at the zoo. Necropsies are also conducted for research reasons.

Some zoos have a variety of consulting veterinarians who come to the zoo to treat specialized illnesses or problems. Specialties include, for example, ophthalmology, dentistry, specialized surgery and so on. Other consulting vets who have specialized training in the care of certain breeds of animals might also come into the zoo. The Zoo Veterinarian is expected to coordinate the visits of these veterinarians.

Zoo Veterinarians are responsible for purchasing supplies, equipment, and medications needed to care for animals at the zoo. They also must prepare reports and records. Individuals are responsible for the maintenance of health records for all animals in the zoo. This is necessary to ensure compliance with all regulatory agencies.

As animals are frequently bred in captivity, in many zoos, the veterinarian is responsible for overseeing, planning, and running the facility's reproductive program.

Zoo Veterinarians are just one part of the medical team that cares for animals in zoos. The vet often meets with zookeepers, veterinary technicians, and interns to discuss any issues regarding the animals.

Salaries

Earnings for Zoo Veterinarians vary greatly. There are some Zoo Veterinarians who have earnings starting at approximately $45,000, while others have earnings of $120,000 or more. Factors affecting earnings includes the specific zoo and its size, popularity, and geographic location. Other variables affecting earnings include the responsibilities, experience, education, and professional reputation of the individual.

Employment Prospects

While employment prospects for veterinarians in general are good, they are only fair for individuals seeking positions as Zoo Veterinarians. There are more people who want to work in this area than there are jobs. That is not to say that it is impossible to find a job, only that it is competitive.

Many large cities as well as some smaller metropolitan areas throughout the United States host zoos. Larger zoos often have more than one veterinarian. Some Zoo Veterinarians do research. Others work on a relief basis.

Advancement Prospects

Advancement prospects for Zoo Veterinarians are good. Individuals can climb the career ladder in a number of ways, depending on their career aspirations and their current career status. Some find similar positions in larger zoos. Some advance their career by teaching. Others climb the career ladder by being promoted to supervisory positions. Some individuals end up teaching part of the time, and still others strike out on their own, taking consulting projects of interest to them.

Education and Training

In order to become any type of veterinarian, an individual must graduate with a doctor of veterinary medicine degree from an accredited college of veterinary medicine. There are 28 colleges in 26 states that are accredited by the Council on Education of the American Veterinary Medical Association (AVMA) offering this four-year program. Once an individual has graduated, he or she receives either the designation D.V.M. or V.M.D.

While prerequisites for admission to this program vary by school, each requires at least 45 to 90 semester hours of undergraduate work. With that being said, most individuals entering these programs hold a bachelor's degree. Because there are only 28 programs, competition for admission is fierce.

Those interested in pursuing a career in this field should take classes in the sciences such as organic and inorganic chemistry, physics, biochemistry, biology, animal biology, animal nutrition, and zoology.

In order to be accepted into one of these programs, individuals must also take a number of exams, such as the Graduate Record Examination, the Veterinary College Admission Test, or the Medical College Admission Test, depending on the specific school.

While those who graduate with a doctor of veterinary medicine can practice once they become licensed, those who want to become Zoo Veterinarians must acquire additional education. Some complete a one-year internship. Others go through a three- to four-year residency program in a specialty such as zoological medicine. Those who want to be board certified in a specific area such as zoological medicine must complete an internship and residency in zoological medicine. They then must take and pass an examination given by the American College of Zoological Medicine (ACZM).

Individuals are expected to take continuing education classes in order to maintain their license.

Experience, Skills, and Personality Traits

The American Association of Zoo Veterinarians (AAZV) offers a number of opportunities to individuals interested in becoming Zoo Veterinarians while they are still going through training to become vets as well as after they have completed their training. These include a variety of internships, externships, preceptorships, fellowships, and residencies. Those who complete internships or residencies get experience working in zoos.

Others may get experience by working in veterinary offices, clinics, or shelters before graduating from veterinary programs. Some get experience working or volunteering in wildlife rehabilitation clinics, captive wildlife facilities, and zoos.

Zoo Veterinarians should be compassionate, kindhearted individuals. An inquisitive mind and scientific aptitude are requirements. A strong love for wildlife is necessary, and an interest in conservation is also helpful. Excellent judgment is mandatory, as vets must think quickly and make effective decisions. Verbal communication skills are essential. Physical strength and stamina are also helpful.

Special Requirements

Veterinarians in every state are required to be licensed before they can practice. Licensing is governed by each state. Therefore, requirements for licensure are not federally standardized. Generally, in order to become licensed, individuals must have graduated from an accredited veterinary program with a D.V.M. and have passed a national board examination called the North American Veterinary Licensing Exam. This test is an eight-hour exam composed of 360 multiple-choice questions that cover veterinary medicine in addition to a section covering diagnostic skills.

As mentioned previously, there are continuing education requirements for licensed veterinarians that are necessary to demonstrate the individual's knowledge of medical and veterinary advancements.

Certification is available from the American College of Zoological medicine (ACZM) for veterinarians with expertise in zoological medicine such as Zoo Veterinarians or wildlife veterinarians. The ACZM is an international specialty organization recognized by the AVMA. In order to become certified, individuals must complete an approved training program and then pass an examination.

Unions and Associations

Zoo Veterinarians can belong to a number of organizations that provide professional support and educational opportunities. These include the AAZV, the AVMA, and the American Association of Wildlife Veterinarians. Individuals might also contact the Association of American Veterinary Medical Colleges and the ACZM to obtain information on education.

Tips for Entry

1. If you are still in school and considering becoming a Zoo Veterinarian, make sure you take classes in the sciences.
2. Get experience by volunteering at a zoo, wildlife rehabilitation clinic or center, or a captive wildlife facility.
3. Send your résumé and a short cover letter to zoos and captive wildlife facilities. Remember to ask that your résumé be kept on file if there are no current openings.
4. Check out openings online. Start with some of the more traditional job sites such as Monster. com. Then check out career Web sites specific to zoos and the veterinary field. (Be sure to look in the appendix for some ideas.)
5. Join the AAZV. This organization provides educational opportunities and professional support.

ZOO VETERINARY TECHNICIAN

Duties: Assist veterinarians in caring for zoo animals; collect specimens; assist in surgery; monitor animals after surgery; change dressings; perform medical and laboratory tests; draw blood; assist in design of treatment plan

Alternate Title(s): Animal Health Technician; Technician

Salary Range: $9.00 to $22.00+ per hour

Employment Prospects: Good

Advancement Prospects: Fair

Best Geographical Locations for Position: Positions located throughout the United States in areas hosting zoos

Prerequisites:

Education or Training—Minimum of associate's degree from program accredited by American Veterinary Medical Association

Experience and Qualifications—Experience requirements vary; see text

CAREER LADDER

Veterinary Technician in Larger Zoo; Veterinary Technician Supervisor; Veterinary Technician Researcher Supervisor; Veterinary Technologist

Veterinary Technician

Veterinary Assistant; Intern; Volunteer

Special Skills and Personality Traits—Animal-care skills; good judgment; ability to follow directions; strong stomach; compassion; communication skills

Special Requirements—State licensing, registration, or credentialing required; see text

Position Description

Zoos are filled with animals of a variety of sizes and breeds. It is the responsibility of the zoo to keep all animals in the facility as healthy as possible. Veterinarians are ultimately responsible for the health of zoo animals. Zoo Veterinary Technicians work closely with veterinarians, assisting them in much the same way that nurses help physicians. Duties and responsibilities of Zoo Veterinary Technicians vary with each individual job. Zoo Veterinary Technicians are vital to the zoo's health-care team.

It should be noted that while the job titles Zoo Veterinary Technician and veterinary technologist are often used interchangeably, there is a difference. Although a great many of the duties are the same, veterinary technologists are required to have more education than Zoo Veterinary Technicians.

Zoo Veterinary Technicians work in a number of different areas. Some work in clinical care. Others may choose to focus on research. These individuals are often called veterinary technician researchers. Some individuals work in both areas; it all depends on career aspirations and the size and structure of the specific zoo.

Zoo Veterinary Technicians working in the clinical care area work under the supervision of zoo veterinarians. Individuals perform many of the functions of veterinarians with the exception of diagnosing medical problems, performing surgery, and prescribing medication.

They change dressings and hold and comfort animals while the veterinarian performs procedures. They perform various medical and laboratory tests, prepare tissue samples, draw blood, and collect specimens to check for diseases and parasites.

Animals, like people, become sick or have accidents. Zoo Veterinary Technicians frequently assist with these situations. They give animals needed vaccinations or bandage wounds.

Zoo Veterinary Technicians assist vets with neonatal care as well as hand-raising animals when necessary. They also prepare animals that are being shipped to other facilities as well as animals that have arrived from other locations.

As zoo animals aren't in their natural habitat, veterinarians and Zoo Veterinary Technicians must often check for any signs of stress or illness. If something is found, a plan of care must be developed and implemented.

Zoo Veterinary Technicians are expected to help prepare animals for surgery. They might, for example, calm an animal, lift him or her up onto the examination table or the space where the operation will take place, and assist in the anesthesia process. As many zoo animals are large, this process is often difficult. The technician often assists the veterinarian during surgeries by handing him or her instruments.

Zoo Veterinary Technicians are responsible for monitoring animals under their care. They are expected to check on animals coming out of anesthesia and be sure that they recovering according to the prescribed schedule. They might also administer medications under the direction of the veterinarian.

Animals cannot communicate verbally to tell anyone what is wrong. Zoo Veterinary Technicians are expected to watch animals, reporting any suspected problems to veterinarians. They must not only keep tabs on an animal's physical symptoms and well-being, but also on its psychological state.

Zoo Veterinary Technicians are responsible for keeping any instruments the veterinarian uses clean and sterile. They are expected to keep inventory of instruments, medications, and other supplies and either order required supplies or inform the veterinarian or supervisor of what is needed.

Zoo Veterinary Technicians who work in research are expected to set up and carry out various experiments in the lab. This type of job is generally done in zoos that have research facilities and large labs. Other responsibilities of Zoo Veterinary Technicians include drawing blood and other samples from animals and gathering data.

Salaries

Zoo Veterinary Technicians are generally paid an hourly wage. This can range from approximately $9.00 to $22.00 an hour or more. Factors affecting earnings include the experience, education, and responsibilities of the individual. Other factors affecting earnings include the geographic location, size, budget, and prestige of the specific zoo. Individuals with more experience and education working in zoos with larger budgets will generally earn more than their counterparts in smaller facilities.

Employment Prospects

Employment prospects for Zoo Veterinary Technicians are good. Employment can be located throughout the country in areas hosting zoos. It should be noted that individuals might need to relocate for positions.

As noted previously, Zoo Veterinary Technicians working may work in either the clinical care area or research.

Advancement Prospects

Advancement prospects for Zoo Veterinary Technicians are fair. Individuals can climb the career ladder in a number of ways, depending on career aspirations. Some find similar positions in larger zoos with bigger budgets, generally resulting in increased responsibilities and earnings. Others are promoted to supervisory positions. Still others go back to school and obtain a four-year degree in veterinary technology and become veterinary technologists.

Zoo Veterinary Technicians who are working in the clinical-care area may move to the research area and find positions in larger zoos that have research facilities.

Education and Training

Zoo Veterinary Technicians must have a minimum of an associate's degree from a program accredited by the American Veterinary Medical Association (AVMA). These programs are generally offered in community colleges and provide preparation for both clinical and laboratory roles. There are also four-year programs for individuals who want to earn bachelor's degree.

Experience, Skills, and Personality Traits

Experience requirements for Zoo Veterinary Technicians vary from job to job. Some positions are entry level. Others require or prefer experience working with animals in some manner.

Zoo Veterinary Technicians must be physically fit and have a great deal of endurance. Unlike veterinary technicians who work in traditional veterinary offices, individuals working in zoos must often move around the zoo from exhibit to exhibit to care for various species. They also need the strength and the ability to lift heavy animals.

Zoo Veterinary Technicians need to be compassionate, kind individuals with a true love for animals. They should be patient and have the ability to follow instructions. Verbal communication skills are necessary as well. A strong stomach is needed in order to perform certain tasks and duties. The ability to deal with stressful situations is vital.

Special Requirements

While each state regulates Zoo Veterinary Technicians in a different manner, all states require them to pass a credentialing examination. This exam includes oral, written, and practical components and is regulated by either the specific state's board of veterinary examiners or another state agency. Depending on the specific state, after passing the exam, Zoo Veterinary Technicians become registered, licensed, or certified. They can, for example, become registered veterinary technicians, licensed veterinary technicians, or certified veterinary technicians.

Most states use the National Veterinary Technician exam. As a result, individuals who want to have their passing scores transferred from one state to another can as long as both states use the same exam.

Unions and Associations

Zoo Veterinary Technicians can obtain additional career information by contacting the AVMA. Individuals can also join the National Association of Veterinary Technicians in America. This organization provides professional support and educational opportunities for its members. Individuals and the zoos they work with can be members of the Associations of Zoos and Aquariums.

Tips for Entry

1. Get experience by volunteering at a zoo, shelter, sanctuary, or refuge. This will help you make sure this is the right line of work for you and give you valuable experience and the ability to make important contacts.
2. Send your résumé and a short cover letter to zoos in which you are interested in working. Remember to ask that your résumé be kept on file if there are no current openings.
3. Check out openings online. Start with some of the more traditional job sites such as Monster. com. Expand your search from there.
4. Many zoos post job openings on their Web sites, so check these regularly.
5. Openings are often advertised in the classifieds section of newspapers. Look under heading such as "Zoos," "Zoo Jobs," "Work with Animals," "Veterinarian Technician," or "Zoo Veterinary Technician."
6. The career placement office at your school might be able to help you locate job openings.

ZOO MEMBERSHIP DIRECTOR

CAREER PROFILE

Duties: Build zoo membership; find ways to recruit new private and corporate members; help the zoo flourish; develop membership benefit programs; run recruitment campaigns; maintain membership records; supervise staff; design special events for members

Alternate Title(s): Director of Membership; Membership Service Director; Membership Manager

Salary Range: $23,000 to $65,000+

Employment Prospects: Poor

Advancement Prospects: Fair

Best Geographical Locations for Position: Positions located throughout the United States in areas hosting zoos

Prerequisites:

Education or Training—Bachelor's degree required or preferred by most zoos; see text

Experience and Qualifications—Experience working in membership department of zoo, animal advocacy organization, or other nonprofit group

CAREER LADDER

Membership Director for Larger, Better-Known Zoo; Director of Development

Membership Director

Membership Manager; Assistant Membership Director; Membership Staffer

Special Skills and Personality Traits—Creativity; excellent verbal and written communication skills; attention to detail; interpersonal skills; persuasiveness; computer competency; organizational skills; understanding of nonprofit membership processes; analytical skills; customer service skills

Position Description

Zoos offer membership programs to individuals and businesses that want to support the facility. Funds generated from these memberships help support the zoo and its exhibits and programs. Membership funds also help care for the animals as well as make it possible to bring in new exhibits.

The individual responsible for developing the membership is called the Zoo Membership Director. He or she has varied responsibilities, depending on the specific zoo and its size and structure. For individuals in this position, seeing the zoo membership grow can be very gratifying.

To build the zoo membership, the director is expected to develop and run a variety of membership drives or campaigns. These might include mass telephone campaigns, direct mail campaigns, and/or e-mail campaigns, among others. He or she must continually find ways to get people interested in the zoo and encourage new members to join.

In order to familiarize people with the zoo and pique their interest, the Zoo Membership Director might seek out opportunities to speak before groups of professionals, associations, service and civic groups, and school

groups. The Zoo Membership Director might also be asked to speak at special events, conferences, fairs, meetings, and conventions.

The Zoo Membership Director may also be called upon to be a guest on television or radio news and interview shows. He or she uses these opportunities to discuss the zoo, its exhibits, and the facility's goals and mission. After getting the word out, people who hear the show often are interested enough to become members.

One of the methods Zoo Membership Directors use to increase membership and spread the word about the zoo is placing advertisements in newspapers, magazines, and on the Internet. He or she might also develop commercials to be aired on television and radio stations. These ads tout the benefits of zoo membership. The Zoo Membership Director might also work in conjunction with the zoo's marketing director in assuring that every advertisement, commercial, and marketing piece includes a line about membership.

Zoo Membership Directors are expected to develop a variety of written membership materials. These might include fact sheets about the zoo, fact sheets listing membership benefits, letters inviting people or businesses to become members, reprints of news and feature stories, information on the zoo's missions and goals, and membership applications.

The Zoo Membership Director directs his or her staff to send out pertinent information and membership applications when appropriate. The office is also responsible for processing applications and payments.

The individual might target both individual memberships and corporate memberships. In doing so, he or she might develop various levels and types of memberships. These might include, for example, friends, supporters, sustaining memberships, sponsors, and so on. Each level of membership generally costs a different amount and provides different benefits. Other membership options might include, for example, single memberships, family memberships, corporate memberships, and patron memberships.

It is the responsibility of the Zoo Membership Director to develop various membership programs and then come up with ways to market them effectively. Creative Zoo Membership Directors find effective ways to market these membership benefits. These benefits may include, among others, free admission to the member zoo, free admission to other zoos in reciprocal programs, discounts at zoo gift shops, discounts at zoo eateries, free zoo parking, discounts on educational programs, and so on.

Zoo Membership Directors also are expected to develop special events exclusively for members and bring them to fruition. These might include things like parties, picnics, gala dinners, educational events, and presentations. Other events may include nighttime tours of exhibits, Thanksgiving at the zoo, Halloween at the zoo, and more.

Many Zoo Membership Directors create special programs so people can help support the zoo. Exciting programs for many supporters include adopt-an-animal, adopt-a-species, or adopt-an-exhibit. In these programs, members have an opportunity to support the care of an animal, species, or exhibit by making a financial donation earmarked for the specific cause. Depending on the specific zoo, Zoo Membership Directors might provide adoption certificates, signs on cages, pictures of the "adoptee," etc.

The Zoo Membership Director is responsible for compiling and updating lists of zoo members. The individual or a member of his or her staff is also expected to make sure annual renewal materials are sent to members on a timely basis.

It is essential that the membership department keep precise records. In addition to names of each member, member level, and payment information, the membership department must be sure to have up-to-date phone numbers, physical addresses, e-mail addresses, payment information, and renewal information. Much of this is maintained in computer databases for easy access and management.

The Zoo Membership Director is expected to oversee the office and any staff members in the department. Depending on the specific zoo, there may be an assistant membership director, an events coordinator, and one or more membership staff members. Many zoos also have membership kiosks in one or more areas of the zoo.

The Zoo Membership Director often works closely with other zoo departments. He or she might, for example, work with the public relations department on press releases, the publications department on putting together brochures or letters, the fund-raising and development department on securing monies and grants, the education department to educate new and existing members about the zoo's exhibits and programs, and the special events department putting together members-only events. The goal is to do everything possible to both cultivate new members and retain current members.

Salaries

Salaries for Zoo Membership Directors can range from approximately $23,000 to $65,000 or more. Variables affecting earnings include the size and budget of the zoo as well as the experience and responsibilities of the individual. Those at the higher end of the scale generally have a great deal of experience and are working for well known zoos with bigger budgets.

Employment Prospects

As of this writing, there are 224 zoos and aquariums accredited by the Association of Zoos and Aquariums (AZA). Additionally, there are hundreds of other facilities that are not accredited by the AZA.

Despite the large number of zoos, employment prospects are poor for individuals seeking this type of position. While every zoo has someone who handles the duties of the Zoo Membership Director, every zoo does not employ one. Instead, a membership manager or staffer or the fund-raising and development department might handle the responsibilities of this individual.

This does not mean that it is impossible to get a job in this area; it just means it might be more difficult. It should be noted that individuals might have to relocate for openings.

Advancement Prospects

Advancement prospects for Zoo Membership Directors are fair. There are a number of paths for career advancement. Some locate a similar position in a larger, higher-budget zoo, resulting in increased responsibilities and earnings. Some individuals climb the career ladder by becoming the director of development. Still others may become the zoo's marketing director. Advancement prospects for individuals in this position depend to a great extent on the size and structure of the zoo as well as the individual's career aspirations.

Education and Training

Most larger zoos require or prefer that their applicants have a minimum of a four-year college degree. There are, however, be smaller zoos that might accept a qualified applicant with an associate's degree or even a high school diploma coupled with relevant experience.

Good choices for majors include public relations, communications, journalism, marketing, business, or related areas. Additional courses, seminars, and workshops in fund-raising techniques, development, special events, public relations, publicity, promotion, writing, marketing, media relations, and presentation skills will be useful.

Experience, Skills, and Personality Traits

Experience requirements depend to a great extent on the size, structure, and prestige of the specific zoo. Most zoos prefer that their Zoo Membership Directors have some sort of experience in the membership department of either zoos or another nonprofit agency.

Creativity is a necessity for Zoo Membership Directors, as they must come up with innovative methods to attract new members. Individuals should be articulate, with excellent communication skills, both written and verbal. In order to prepare effective membership materials, a good command of the English language is vital, as is a working knowledge of grammar and spelling. A proficiency in public speaking is helpful as well.

Successful Zoo Membership Directors are organized and detail-oriented. Interpersonal skills and the ability to deal well with people in a variety of settings are also essential. Customer service skills are also essential. The ability to multitask effectively is critical. Supervisory skills are also needed.

Computer competency is mandatory. Knowledge of membership database software is a plus.

Unions and Associations

Zoo Membership Directors can join a number of organizations that provide professional support as well as the opportunity to make important contacts. These include the Association of Fundraising Professionals and the Public Relations Society of America. Individuals can also become members of the AZA. This organization provides helpful professional guidance and support to members.

Tips for Entry

1. Network as much as you can in the industry. Go to conferences, conventions, and educational seminars and workshops to meet industry insiders.
2. Join the AZA and take part in its programs.
3. You might also want to become a member of one or more animal advocacy organizations, humane societies, animal shelters, or rescues. Membership will help you make contacts.
4. If you are still in school, look for an internship with a zoo in the membership or develop department. It is another great way to get experience and make helpful contacts.
5. Look in the classifieds section of newspapers under headings such as "Membership Director," "Director of Membership," and "Zoos," among others. Job openings might also be located under the names of specific zoos.
6. Don't forget to look online for job opportunities. Start with some of the general sites such as Monster.com. Then search out sites specific to working with animals.
7. Openings might be listed on zoo Web sites, so check these regularly.

GIFT SHOP MANAGER

CAREER PROFILE

Duties: Provide day-to-day management of zoo gift shop; supervise and train sales associates; create employee schedules; provide accounting of sales; assist customers; oversee loss prevention; display merchandise in store

Alternate Title: Retail Supervisor

Salary Range: $22,000 to $35,000+

Employment Prospects: Fair

Advancement Prospects: Fair

Best Geographical Locations for Position: Positions located throughout the United States in areas hosting zoos

Prerequisites:

Education or Training—Educational requirements vary from job to job; minimum of high school diploma or equivalent; some jobs require or prefer college background; on-the-job training; see text

CAREER LADDER

Gift Shop Manager in Larger Zoo; Store Manager in Other Industry

Gift Shop Manager

Assistant Gift Shop Manager

Experience and Qualifications—Experience working in retail management

Special Skills and Personality Traits—Customer service skills; personableness; excellent verbal and written communication skills; people skills; sales skills

Position Description

In addition to exhibits showcasing animals, most zoos host on-site amenities designed to make a guest's visit to the zoo a complete experience. These might include restaurants, food stands, and picnic areas. Most zoos also host one or more gift shops and/or kiosks where visitors can purchase souvenirs or gifts.

Zoo gift shops carry a wide array of merchandise. Some may be branded, such as T-shirts and other clothing, mugs, key chains, and other "must have" items with the zoo name and logo prominently displayed. Others items might be zoo-oriented, such as stuffed animals, posters, books, and other toys. There might be postcards, cameras, film, CDs, DVDs and more. The gift shop might also be stocked with candy, soda, and other snack items. Some zoo gift shops carry jewelry and other eye-catching items.

The individual in charge of the day-to-day management of the zoo gift shop is the Gift Shop Manager. Responsibilities vary depending on the size and structure of the specific gift shop and zoo.

No matter what the size of the zoo gift shop, the zoo Gift Shop Manager holds the bottom-line responsibility for the achievement of sales plans and profit margins. He or she is expected to establish and imple-

ment policies, goals, objectives, and procedures for the store. This might be done in conjunction with zoo administrators.

The zoo Gift Shop Manager is responsible for supervising the sales associates working in the shop. As part of this function, the manager is expected to train associates in all necessary functions. These might include, for example, writing sales slips, using the cash register, processing credit cards, and approving checks. The Gift Shop Manager should be a leader. He or she is expected to motivate the staff of the shop to exceed the expectations of customers.

The Gift Shop Manager is responsible for scheduling employees. As part of this task, he or she must take into account the days and hours the store is expected to be busiest and to make sure enough employees are on hand to adequately service customers. It is the responsibility of the Gift Shop Manager to assign duties to sales associates as well as oversee their activities. Duties include, among other things, pricing and ticketing merchandise, placing merchandise on display, and cleaning and organizing shelves, displays, and inventory in the stockroom.

In order to maximize sales, the Gift Shop Manager is expected to make sure merchandise is prominently displayed in an attractive manner in the store, making it easy for customers to find what they are looking for and helping to entice spur-of-the-moment purchases. Gift Shop Managers might handle this duty on their own or assign the task to other gift shop staffers. The Gift Shop Manager is additionally responsible for making sure the sales associates know where merchandise is located.

One of the essential job functions of the Gift Shop Manager at a zoo is to identify new ways to generate sales. In order to do this, the individual is responsible for developing and coordinating sales promotions. He or she may put items on sale or create special sales in conjunction with zoo events. Some Gift Shop Managers have promotions, for example, where individuals receive a free gift on their birthday. Others create senior citizen discounts or other promotions.

In order to maximize sales, successful Gift Shop Managers know that they need to have the right products in the store. By listening to customer feedback, individuals can often get an idea of what people want. Are customers asking for T-shirts in 3-X large? Are customers looking more zoo-branded baby items? Having the right merchandise can translate into increased sales.

Some Gift Shop Managers have found a way to make the gift shop a destination. Through effective merchandising, people think of the shop as a venue to buy unique birthday presents, Christmas and holiday gifts, or just gifts in general.

In some situations, the Gift Shop Manager may act as the merchandise buyer for the store. In others, this responsibility is handled by a buyer or buying service. If the Gift Shop Manager is dealing with a buyer, he or she must be sure to communicate the merchandise that is selling, merchandise that is not selling, and things for which people have asked.

The Gift Shop Manager is ultimately responsible for everything that happens in the shop. He or she is expected to maintain customer satisfaction, often working on the sales floor, greeting and assisting customers with purchases. If a customer has a problem related to the shop, the Gift Shop Manager is responsible for finding a way to make it right.

Customer service is very important in all areas of retail, and zoo gift shops are no exception. The Gift Shop Manager must work with employees in following the zoo's customer service programs. The successful Gift Shop Manager at a zoo knows that customers come first. A bad experience in the gift shop may not only affect the shop; the customer's memories of the day at the zoo itself might be tainted. With that in mind, the Gift Shop Manager is expected to do everything possible to be sure that the store exceeds patrons' expectations and that their total visit to the zoo was a good experience.

The Gift Shop Manager must train his or her staff to assure that customer service issues are dealt with appropriately. The individual must be sure that his or her staff always makes customers feel that their needs come first. In the event that there is a problem or issue, the manager is expected to be on hand to deal with it personally.

The zoo Gift Shop Manager is expected to review sales records and account for sales. He or she might handle this task alone or with the help of one or more assistant managers or other staff members.

A major responsibility of the zoo Gift Shop Manager is overseeing loss prevention in the store. He or she must train employees to look for signs of shoplifting and report it as directed. The manager must also do everything possible to assure that shoplifting and theft, both internal and external, are as limited as possible.

Salaries

Earnings for zoo Gift Shop Managers range from approximately $22,000 to $35,000 or more per year. Factors affecting earnings include the size, structure, budget, and geographic location of the specific zoo. Other factors affecting earnings include the responsibilities, professional reputation, and experience of the individual.

Employment Prospects

Employment prospects for individuals seeking positions as zoo Gift Shop Managers are fair. Opportunities can be located throughout the United States in areas hosting zoos. Some zoos have more than one gift shop. Some gift shops also have more than one manager. It should be noted that individuals might need to relocate for positions.

Advancement Prospects

With experience and training, advancement prospects for zoo Gift Shop Managers are fair. Individuals climb the career ladder in a number of ways. Some advance their career by finding similar positions in larger gift shops in larger, better-known zoos. This results in increased responsibilities and earnings.

Some zoo Gift Shop Managers also find similar positions in larger gift shops outside of zoos. This, too, will result in increased responsibilities and earnings.

Education and Training

Educational requirements vary from job to job. All positions generally require individuals to have a minimum of a high school diploma or the equivalent. Some positions require or prefer a college education. Others accept experience in lieu of education.

Any training in retail, store management, or buying will be useful. Most zoo Gift Shop Managers have moved up the career ladder by starting as sales associates and learning on the job. Some individuals go through management training programs.

Experience, Skills, and Personality Traits

The job of a zoo Gift Shop Manager is not an entry-level position. Experience in retail sales and management is usually necessary. Individuals should have supervisory and management skills.

Zoo Gift Shop Managers should be personable, customer service–oriented individuals. Sales and merchandising skills are necessary. Problem-solving skills are mandatory. Creativity is a plus in creating customer-oriented sales promotions.

Gift Shop Managers working in zoos need to be well-spoken, articulate individuals. People skills are essential. The ability to effectively multitask without getting frazzled is vital.

Unions and Associations

Gift Shop Managers working in zoos can learn more about careers in retail by contacting the National Retail Federation.

Tips for Entry

1. Send a short cover letter with your résumé to zoos. Remember to ask that your résumé be kept on file if there are no current openings.

2. Get experience by working as a sales associate at a zoo gift shop. When a key holder (or management) position opens up, you'll know about it first.

3. Look for job openings in the classifieds section of newspapers. Headings might include key words such as "Zoo Gift Shop Manager," "Gift Shop Manager," "Retail Jobs," or "Zoo Jobs." Jobs might also be advertised under the names of specific zoos.

4. Don't forget to look online for job opportunities. Start with some of the better-known general career sites such as Monster.com. Then search out sites specific to working in zoos.

5. Openings may be listed on zoo Web sites, so keep an eye on these.

DEVELOPMENT DIRECTOR

Duties: Coordinate annual giving activities, capital campaigns, and deferred giving opportunities for donors and potential donors to zoo; direct fund-raising efforts; develop strategies for obtaining financial support from individuals and businesses; cultivate corporate sponsorship

Alternate Title(s): Director of Development; Fund-Raising Director; Director of Philanthropy; Director of Planned Giving; Fund-Raising and Development Director

Salary Range: $30,000 to $125,000+

Employment Prospects: Fair

Advancement Prospects: Fair

Best Geographical Locations for Position: Positions located throughout the United States in areas hosting zoos

Prerequisites:

Education or Training—Minimum of bachelor's degree required or preferred

Experience and Qualifications—Experience working with nonprofit organizations in fund-raising,

CAREER LADDER

```
┌─────────────────────────────────────────┐
│  Development Director for Larger, Better-  │
│      Known Zoo; Zoo Director               │
└─────────────────────────────────────────┘
                    ▲
┌─────────────────────────────────────────┐
│       Development Director, Zoo            │
└─────────────────────────────────────────┘
                    ▲
┌─────────────────────────────────────────┐
│  Assistant Director of Fund-raising and   │
│   Development; Assistant Director of       │
│   Corporate Sponsorship; Fund-raising      │
│  Coordinator; Assistant Public Relations   │
│              Director                       │
└─────────────────────────────────────────┘
```

development, grant-writing, public relations, journalism, etc.

Special Skills and Personality Traits—Creativity; excellent verbal and written communication skills; attention to detail; interpersonal skills; persuasiveness; computer competency; organizational skills; enthusiasm; people skills

Position Description

While there are exceptions, most zoos are classified as nonprofit entities. This means that they are not publicly owned or publicly funded. They depend to a great extent on donations and contributions to sustain themselves.

Getting people to donate money is never easy, particularly when there are so many organizations and causes vying for funds. The department that handles donations, contributions, and fund-raising efforts at a zoo is called the development department. The individual who oversees this department is called the Development Director.

The Development Director holds an integral position in the zoo. He or she is responsible for raising the monies to fund the zoo, its exhibits, and its programs. The Development Director works with the zoo director and/or the managing director, planning and implementing strategies for fund-raising and development. Within the scope of the job, the individual is expected to develop a variety of cultivation and solicitation strategies aimed at both the general public and corporate business.

The Development Director does not always have an easy job. As noted, there are a great many nonprofit organizations with varied causes, each trying to get funds donated by the public. The director must have the ability to grab the attention of potential donors, to interest them in the zoo and its mission and programs, and to get them to contribute money.

He or she does this in a number of ways. The Development Director is expected to plan, organize, coordinate, direct, and execute the annual fund-raising and giving activities, capital campaigns, and deferred giving opportunities for donors and potential donors.

In implementing a strategic annual giving plan for the zoo, the Development Director comes up with a number of different projects. These might include, for example, the development of direct mail campaigns that help build the zoo's membership. The director might also develop special events at the zoo and programs such as telephone and telethon fund-raisers, as well as balls, dinners, and cocktail parties designed to support the zoo financially. These programs might increase membership or even generate direct financial support to the zoo.

The Development Director must find ways to reach individuals who will potentially become members or donors or the zoo. He or she must often do research to find these people. This research might include a variety of surveys and questionnaires. It might also include talking to public and various community contacts to learn about the needs of the community in relation to the zoo. Are more educational programs needed? Do people in the community want to know more about the conservation of animals? Can the zoo be used for community or private events in off-hours? What kinds of programs and events can the zoo have that will develop the zoo as a whole? Finding the answers to these types of questions is often helpful to the Development Director in seeking donors. The Development Director acts as a liaison between donors, potential donors, and the zoo management and board of directors. He or she informs the zoo management and the board of any occurrences affecting donors.

The Development Director is expected to create fund-raising and development literature and audiovisual materials such as brochures, booklets, pamphlet, programs, volunteer training, films, slide shows, and DVDs.

The Development Director works closely with the zoo's director in developing goals and programs. The Development Director is expected to develop strategies for obtaining financial support from private individuals and businesses. He or she might run large capital campaigns as well as smaller sustaining programs. The individual might also be responsible for supervising others in fund-raising efforts to assure a cohesive fund-raising plan.

The zoo Development Director must constantly work to develop potential private donors. The individual attends luncheons, dinners, meetings, and other affairs on behalf of the zoo. He or she may often speak to civic groups, businesspeople, and other nonprofit groups regarding the zoo, its mission, and the need for fund-raising.

The Development Director is expected to cultivate corporate sponsorships. Corporate sponsors might include local, regional, and national businesses and companies. In order to secure corporate sponsorship, the Development Director must first identify potential sponsors. He or she will then give them information regarding the organization and its mission, invite them to the zoo, give tours, introduce them to key members of the zoo staff and board, and discuss what funds would mean to the zoo. Sometimes sponsors want to get on board immediately. In other situations, the director might have to nurture them for a bit until they are willing to become financially involved in the zoo.

As part of the job, the Development Director is responsible for seeking both annual gifts from individuals and corporations and obtaining sponsorship for various projects and programs the zoo undertakes. The Development Director is responsible for developing strategies for individual major donor cultivation and solicitation. He or she often works with the zoo director in developing plans for the solicitation of planned gifts. The zoo, for example, may need money for a new primate exhibit or a new education center. Once the determination is made of what is needed, it is often easier to find the funds.

Many nonprofit organizations depend on grants, and zoos are no exception. The Development Director is expected to seek out grants offered by private foundations as well as by the government. He or she may be responsible for identifying these grants or may be responsible for applying for and writing them. Depending on the zoo and its structure, these tasks may be handled by grant writers or other assistants.

The Development Director of the zoo is expected to do a great deal of writing. He or she may write fund-raising letters, invitations, speeches, and brochures. In addition to writing grant applications, he or she may also be responsible for drafting press releases and writing membership letters. Other writing responsibilities include direct mail pieces, brochures, advertising copy, flyer copy, and invitations. The director might also be expected to write reports regarding the status of development or fund-raising projects for the zoo director or the board of directors.

A great deal of the work of the Development Director often involves the development and execution of special events to raise money for the organization. Depending on the specific organization, these events can be quite simple or very elaborate. The director may be expected not only to develop the events, but to execute them and bring them to fruition or to oversee others performing these functions.

The individual or his or her staff, for example, may need to find locations for dinner dances or galas, plan menus, price out goods and services, locate individuals and businesses that will donate door prizes, identify and secure guest speakers, solicit donations, etc. Depending on the event, these events may be annual or monthly. In some zoos, there is a special events coordinator or assistant who does a great deal of the legwork under the direction of the Development Director.

Programs might include, for example, membership campaigns, annual giving or sustaining campaigns, and more. They might also encompass fund-raising dinners, galas, auctions, dances, telethons, entertainment events, bake sales, craft shows, and races or similar events. They might consist of appeals for money in personal letters or via the media.

It is essential that the Development Director keep accurate records. He or she (or staff members) must keep records of donor management and resource development. The director is also responsible for making sure that each donation is acknowledged in writing. This task is often assigned to a staff member.

The Development Director is responsible for preparing budgets for the department and developing reports tracking the progress and success of various development and fund-raising projects.

The Development Director is expected to oversee the development office as well as supervise the staff. Depending on the specific zoo and its structure, the individual may also be responsible for supervising the special events department.

Zoos often employ volunteers in various areas of fund-raising and development. The Development Director is sometimes responsible for overseeing these volunteers. In many cases, the individual will serve as a staff adviser to the volunteer committees who work on various fund-raising and development projects. He or she might also coordinate one or more committees that work directly with the zoo board, helping to develop strategies to meet fund-raising and development goals.

The Development Director is expected to serve as a spokesperson for any of the zoo's fund-raising and development activities. He or she is also responsible for keeping the zoo's board of directors abreast of all fund-raising and development goals, programs, and activities. The Development Director must monitor fund-raising results in all areas, including those from individuals, corporations, and foundations, and then report the results to the zoo director and the board of directors.

Salaries

Earnings for Development Directors working at zoos range tremendously depending on a number of factors. These include the size, structure, budget, membership, and geographic location of the specific zoo. Other factors affecting earnings include the responsibilities, professional reputation, and experience of the individual. Some earn as little as $30,000 annually, while others may earn $125,000 or more. Those at the higher end of the scale generally have a great deal of experience and are working for large, well known zoos in metropolitan areas.

Employment Prospects

Employment prospects for talented individuals seeking positions as zoo Development Directors are fair. Those who have a proven record of results are always in demand. Individuals might find employment in large, midsize, and smaller zoos throughout the United States. It should be noted that relocation might be necessary for some positions.

Advancement Prospects

Advancement prospects for Development Directors working at zoos are fair. There are a number of paths for advancement. Some individuals locate a similar position in a larger, better-known zoo, resulting in increased responsibilities and earnings. Others become the zoo's managing or executive director. Those who want to stay in the development area might seek a position with a large, high-budget nonprofit organization in a different industry.

Education and Training

Generally, most employers require or prefer a minimum of a four-year college degree for this position. Good choices for majors include business, public relations, communications, journalism, marketing, or related areas. Additional courses, seminars, and workshops in fund-raising techniques, development, special events, public relations, publicity, promotion, writing, marketing, dealing with media, and presentation skills will be useful.

Experience, Skills, and Personality Traits

Experience requirements depend to a great extent on the specific zoo. Normally, the bigger the zoo, the more experience is needed. Many people get experience in this field through internships or volunteering at a zoo or other nonprofit organization in the development or fund-raising office. Others work with a smaller animal advocacy organization or similar group.

Development Directors should be pleasantly assertive, with good interpersonal skills and the ability to deal well with people in a variety of areas. As a rule, Development Directors are persuasive but not off-putting. They know how to bring in potential donations; they also know how to get others to volunteer to help. Individuals should be organized and detail-oriented. The ability to multitask effectively is essential. A proficiency in public speaking is also needed.

Creativity is a necessity for Development Directors. Individuals need to be articulate with excellent communication skills, both verbal and written. A good command of the English language is vital.

Computer competency is mandatory. The ability to use fund-raising and development software is a plus. Supervisory skills are also needed. An understanding and belief in the mission of the zoo is essential.

Unions and Associations

Individuals interested in pursuing a career as a Development Director for a zoo can join a number of organizations that provide professional support as well as the opportunity to make important contacts. These include the Association of Fundraising Professionals, the Direct Marketing Association, and the Public Relations Society of America. Individuals can also join the Association of Zoos and Aquariums.

Tips for Entry

1. Contact zoos to check the availability of internships in the development office. These are valuable for the experience as well as for making contacts.

2. While an internship in a zoo would be optimal, an internship in the development office of any nonprofit organization will prove useful.

3. Go to conferences, conventions, and educational seminars and workshops to meet industry insiders.

4. Become a member of a zoo and go to its events. It is a great way to network and meet people.

5. There are many seminars offered in both the development and fund-raising field, so look into these.

6. Look in the classifieds section of newspapers under job headings such as "Development Director," "Fund-Raising and Development," "Director of Development," "Fund-Raising," and "Zoo Jobs." Job openings can also be located under the names of specific zoos.

7. Don't forget to look online for job opportunities. Start with some of the general career sites such as Monster.com. Then search out sites specific to zoos and fund-raising and development jobs.

8. Openings are sometimes listed on zoo Web sites, so monitor these.

9. Send your résumé and a short cover letter to zoos in which you are interested in working.

MARKETING DIRECTOR

Position Description

In all towns and cities, there are usually many options for people to choose from to spend their time. Even in smaller areas where there might not be a lot to do, people can choose to just stay home and watch television.

People have a lot of options in how they spend their free time and money. Some go shopping. Some go to concerts. Others go to movies. Some choose to spend their day at a museum. Still others go to a zoo.

People visit zoos for a variety of reasons. Some view a visit to the zoo as an educational event; others just go for a fun day. Some like to see animals up close. Others simply find a visit to the zoo a great family activity.

The challenge for a zoo is finding ways to market its facility to entice people to come spend their time and money. The individual in charge of this task at a zoo is called the Marketing Director.

The Marketing Director is expected to develop and implement concepts and campaigns necessary to successfully market the zoo, its exhibits, and events. Within the scope of the job, the individual has varied duties, depending on the size and structure of the facility.

The Marketing Director is expected to determine the most effective techniques and programs for promoting the zoo. As part of the job, he or she is responsible for planning and coordinating the facility's marketing goals and objectives. If the zoo is large, the Marketing Director oversees a staff of people including those in the public relations, publicity, and advertising departments. If the zoo is smaller, the individual might handle many of the tasks of those departments personally.

The Marketing Director creates a variety of programs designed to draw positive attention to the zoo. This attention can result in zoo memberships, admissions, and media exposure.

A great deal of the marketing strategy the individual develops will be tailored to the demographics of the people the zoo is attempting to attract. Are they trying to attract children? Seniors? Families? Singles? Is the zoo attracting local people or are people coming to visit the zoo from out of town? What types of exhibits does the zoo have? What type of events is it planning or can be planned? Determining the answers to these questions can help the Marketing Director choose just the right marketing strategies and campaigns to put in place. The individual must do a great deal of research to determine the demographics of the people who attend the zoo on a one-time basis as well as those who are members.

He or she must also do research on other zoos, museums, and entertainment options in the area. This type of research might be accomplished by utilizing surveys, questionnaires, focus groups, and so on. Information might be obtained in person at the zoo. In some cases this information can also be obtained through direct mail. Other times it might be accomplished via the Internet.

The individual might come up with simple, traditional marketing ideas such as "two for one" promotions where people can buy two tickets to the zoo for the price of one or where there are discounts for seniors, children, or families. The Marketing Director might also work with other tourist attractions in the area and the local chamber of commerce in putting together promotions for out-of-town visitors.

Some zoo Marketing Directors plan special events at the zoo such as Halloween parties, nighttime at the zoo, sleepovers at the zoo, Thanksgiving dinner at the zoo, concerts, and more. Others work with local radio stations, television stations, or newspapers, putting together promotions, contests, and sweepstakes and giving away zoo tickets or memberships.

Very successful zoo Marketing Directors come up with innovative and creative ideas to attract people and get them to buy tickets and zoo memberships. These ideas might cover a wide array of promotions and special events.

Once ideas are developed, the Marketing Director might work with the public relations director and the advertising director and their staff to publicize and advertise the promotions. In smaller zoos, the Marketing Director is often responsible for handling the public relations and advertising functions.

The Marketing Director is responsible for overseeing all of the advertising for the zoo. As noted previously, an advertising staff or the Marketing Director handles this task. In some cases, the Marketing Director will also work with an advertising agency.

The Marketing Director must determine the most effective places to advertise the zoo and its new exhibits and events. In order to do this, he or she might meet with representatives from various newspapers, periodicals, television and radio stations, and Web sites. Once the director decides where to advertise, he or she must decide how much advertising to do. This is often done in conjunction with the advertising director.

The Marketing Director is expected to design and develop marketing materials for the zoo. These might include brochures, posters, pamphlets, newsletters, etc. The individual might do this him- or herself, or assign the tasks to a staff member or an outside vendor.

The zoo Marketing Director is expected to develop annual budgets detailing projected spending for the implementation of marketing campaigns, advertising, promotion, publicity, staffing, etc. It is the responsibility of the individual to stay within the budget.

The zoo Marketing Director is responsible for searching out corporate partners for unique alliances. He or she might seek out new sponsorship opportunities for exhibits or programs or even capital projects. As part of the job, the individual will work with the membership department in promoting and securing new corporate memberships.

The Marketing Director works closely with the public relations and special events departments in securing publicity for the zoo and its events. Once again, depending on the size and structure of the zoo, the Marketing Director might handle this task personally or oversee the public relations department or a publicist. The individual might do interviews on the radio, on television, or in the newspaper to keep the zoo in the public eye. The director might also arrange for interviews or feature stories on the zoo and its exhibits and events.

The Internet has changed the way everyone does business, and zoos are no exception. People often look online to check out upcoming events, new exhibits, information on memberships, ticket prices, etc. Marketing the site is essential. In some cases, the Marketing Director handles the marketing of the site; in others, the director oversees a Web site marketing manager.

As part of the job, the Marketing Director must plan and coordinate the site's marketing goals and objectives. How will people know about the Web site? How will they know the Web address? Who is the site being marketed to? What will bring them there? The Marketing Director must answer these questions and find ways to bring people to the site.

No matter who is in charge of the zoo's Web site, the Marketing Director must always be sure that the zoo's Web address is displayed in as many places as possible. This includes all advertising, brochures, newsletters, and so on. If the Marketing Director makes the Web address known, people will be able to access information on the zoo in an easy and efficient manner.

The Marketing Director works to develop e-mail blasts and other forms of e-mail marketing. Utilizing e-mail and the Internet means that with the click of a mouse, the zoo Marketing Director can let people know about breaking news relevant to the zoo.

The zoo Marketing Director must continually monitor the effectiveness of marketing campaigns. If a campaign is working, it will continue. If not, the director must revamp the program.

For individuals who want a career in marketing and love zoos and animals, this might be the perfect career choice.

Salaries

Earnings for Marketing Directors at zoos can range from approximately $25,000 to $73,000 or more. Variables affecting earnings include the size, budget, location, and prestige of the specific zoo as well as the experience, qualifications, professional reputation, and responsibilities of the individual.

Employment Prospects

Employment prospects for individuals seeking positions as Marketing Directors at zoos are fair. Opportunities are located throughout the United States in areas hosting zoos. It should be noted that individuals might need to relocate for positions.

Advancement Prospects

Advancement prospects for Marketing Directors working at zoos are fair. Individuals may climb the career ladder in a number of ways. Some advance their career by finding similar positions at larger, better-known zoos, resulting in increased responsibilities and earnings. Some climb the career ladder by becoming the vice president of marketing at a large zoo. Still others become Marketing Directors in other industries.

Education and Training

Most zoos require or prefer a minimum of a bachelor's degree for this position. Good choices for majors include marketing, public relations, advertising, business, communications, or a related field.

Courses, seminars, or workshops in publicity, marketing, advertising, public relations, promotion, etc. will be helpful for educational purposes and for the opportunity to make contacts.

Experience, Skills, and Personality Traits

Experience requirements for zoo Marketing Directors vary depending on the specific zoo and its prestige, size, and location. Generally, the larger or more well known the zoo, the more experience the individual needs.

Zoo Marketing Directors need to be extremely creative individuals. The ability to develop and conceptualize unique ideas is essential. Individuals must be highly articulate in this type of job. Excellent verbal and written communication skills are critical. Zoo Marketing Directors should be outstanding public speakers with good business presentation skills.

A working knowledge of publicity, promotion, public relations, advertising, and research techniques is necessary, as is a full understanding of the inside workings of zoos. Individuals must be extremely organized and have the ability to multitask effectively. Supervisory skills and people skills are also a must.

Unions and Associations

Zoo Marketing Directors can join a number of trade associations that provide professional support and guidance. These include the American Marketing Association, the Marketing Research Association, and the Public Relations Society of America. Individuals and the zoos they work for can also join the Association of Zoos and Aquariums (AZA).

Tips for Entry

1. Send your résumé and a short cover letter to zoos. Request that your résumé be kept on file if there are no current openings. Just because you don't see a job advertised doesn't mean one doesn't exist. The "hidden job market" is your opportunity to let people know you are available.
2. Openings may be advertised in the classifieds section of newspapers. Look under headings such as "Zoos," "Marketing Director," "Director of Marketing," "Marketing Manager," "Marketing," etc.
3. Look for openings online. Check out some of the more traditional job sites such as Monster.com. Then surf the Internet for other options. Use key words such as "Zoo Marketing Director" and "Zoo Jobs."
4. Don't forget to check individual zoo Web sites for openings. Many zoos post their openings online.
5. The AZA posts openings on its site, so keep an eye on that.
6. If you are still in school, consider finding an internship in the marketing department of a zoo. Contact zoos or aquariums in your area to check into the possibilities.
7. Look for seminars, workshops, and courses on all aspects of marketing, publicity, public relations, and promotion. In addition to the education they provide, these courses help you hone your skills and give you the opportunity to make valuable contacts.

WEB SITE MARKETING DIRECTOR

CAREER PROFILE

Duties: Develop and implement marketing plans and campaigns for zoo's Web site; handle day-to-day Web site marketing functions; plan and implement special Web site promotions; oversee Web site advertising and public relations programs

Alternate Title(s): Marketing Director; Online Marketing Director; Online Director of Marketing

Salary Range: $24,000 to $55,000+

Employment Prospects: Fair

Advancement Prospects: Fair

Best Geographical Locations for Position: Positions located throughout the United States

Prerequisites:

Education or Training—Bachelor's degree usually required or preferred

Experience and Qualifications—Marketing experience; experience handling Web site marketing

Special Skills and Personality Traits—Creativity; good verbal and written communication skills;

CAREER LADDER

Web Site Marketing Director for Better-Known or More Prestigious Zoo; Web Site Marketing Director in Other Industry; Marketing Director for Zoo

↑

Zoo Web Site Marketing Manager

↑

Assistant Zoo Web Site Marketing Director; Marketing Director in Other Industry

promotion skills; marketing skills; Internet savvy; understanding of specific zoo Web site targets

Position Description

We go online when we are looking for information and when we want to conduct research. Information that once might have taken days to locate can now be found almost instantaneously online. It is not surprising, then, that most zoos have Web sites.

With a click of the mouse, people can easily find information on zoo happenings, special events, exhibits, hours, and more. They can find out about memberships, entrance fees, and on-site restaurants. People can buy tickets in advance, shop for merchandise, and even join online communities of individuals interested in animals and the zoo. Zoos need a Web presence to market their facility effectively. Individuals responsible for handling the marketing of zoo Web sites are called Web Site Marketing Directors.

Responsibilities of individuals in this position vary depending on the specific zoo as well as the importance it places on its Web site. The zoo Web Site Marketing Director is expected to develop the concepts and campaigns that determine how the site will be marketed and how people will be attracted to it. He or she is responsible for determining the most effective tech-

niques and programs to market the site and its content, and then find ways to implement them.

As part of the job, the zoo Web Site Marketing Director plans and coordinates the site's marketing goals and objectives. How will people know about the Web site? How will they know the Web address? How will they find it? What is the site's target audience? What will bring them there?

Zoo Web Site Marketing Directors use traditional marketing techniques or come up with innovative methods to promote and market the zoo's Web site. For a very creative Web Site Marketing Director, the sky is the limit on marketing activities.

Zoo Web Site Marketing Directors must constantly find innovative ways to get the Web address known so that when people think of the specific zoo, they can easily find it on the Web. This might be done through promotions, advertising, and/or public relations. The Web Site Marketing Director is expected to be sure that the zoo's Web address, or URL, is added to all television commercials, print advertisements, brochures, billboards, stationery, products, and branded merchandise.

The zoo Web Site Marketing Director will often use various forms of e-mail marketing and e-mail blasts to get people to visit the site. The individual must find ways to track visitors to the site so he or she knows what areas of the site people are visiting, how long they are staying, and what brought them there.

People might just visit the site for a couple of minutes to get some information on zoo hours or membership, or they may visit the site for a half an hour or more to watch a live streaming webcam of one of the zoo exhibits. Once the Web Site Marketing Director determines what is bringing people to the site, he or she can often find new ways to market the site, and the zoo.

The zoo Web Site Marketing Director frequently works with the zoo's public relations department, sending out press releases to develop ways to attract media attention that will help garner the attention of the general public. The more places the public sees the Web address, the more likely they are to remember it and visit it.

The zoo Web Site Marketing Director also works with the zoo's general marketing director to coordinate marketing efforts. These might include advertisements, promotions, and publicity efforts.

The zoo Web Site Marketing Director might decide it is advantageous to advertise the zoo's Web site on other Web sites. This is often done with banner ads. When an individual clicks on one of these banner ads, he or she is taken to the site of the advertiser. The individual, may, for example, advertise the zoo's site on a local newspaper, television, or radio Web site. He or she may advertise on other entertainment or animal-related sites as well.

Zoo Web Site Marketing Directors might be expected to perform research in order to obtain information about visitors to the site. They can do this by preparing questionnaires or surveys placed strategically on the site. In order to entice people to answer questionnaires as well as to attract new visitors to the site, the Web Site Marketing Director might offer gifts, discounted tickets to the zoo, memberships, or entries into sweepstakes.

Zoo Web Site Marketing Directors often work with external promotion companies developing these contests, sweepstakes, and other online promotions. These promotions give people an extra incentive to go to the zoo's Web site. The more people who visit the Web site, the more hits the site gets. This is important not only because it publicizes the zoo, but also because many zoos charge other companies to put their online advertisements on their site. The more traffic a site gets, the more expensive it is to advertise on it.

Additionally, Web Site Marketing Directors have found that sweepstakes or contests are an excellent way to build mailing lists. When people enter sweepstakes, they generally are asked to provide their name, address, phone number, age, and e-mail address. In many cases, with the enticement of possibly winning a prize, people are also enticed to give additional information they might not normally give out.

This information is useful to the zoo Web Site Marketing Director as well as to the general marketing director for a variety of reasons. It can help target what potential visitors to the site and to the zoo want. It can also help build information for e-mail lists that in turn can be used for informing people about site changes, zoo promotions, specials on tickets and memberships, zoo news, and more.

Zoo Web Site Marketing Directors and zoo marketing directors who come up with innovative and creative ideas often get the attention of media members who are preparing articles or television or radio pieces. A zoo Web site might, for example, have a contest to name a baby panda or simply a sweepstakes where someone can win a lifetime membership to the zoo. Media pieces about these events generate positive media exposure and can also generate thousands of Web site hits. These hits may then turn into zoo visitors, memberships, and sales of zoo-branded merchandise.

One of the newer functions of zoo Web Site Marketing Directors is creating online communities. These include forums, blogs, chats, and more. These online communities help the zoo attract new visitors and friends. The trickle-down effect can mean thousands of dollars in memberships, ticket sales, merchandise sales, media exposure, donations, and more. The zoo Web Site Marketing Director might work on creating online communities with a Web Site Content Producer or an individual who is specifically responsible for handling the online communities. Individuals might also market the site via other social networking sites such as Facebook and Twitter.

Salaries

Earnings of zoo Web Site Marketing Directors range from approximately $24,000 to $55,000 or more annually. Factors affecting earnings include the specific zoo's budget, size, and popularity. Other factors include the emphasis that the zoo puts on its Web site as well as the experience, reputation, and responsibilities of the individual.

Employment Prospects

Employment prospects for zoo Web Site Marketing Directors are fair. Individuals can find employment with larger, better-known zoos as well as smaller zoos throughout the United States.

It should be noted that the duties of the Web Site Marketing Director are sometimes handled by the general zoo marketing director or outsourced. Some zoos allow the Web Site Marketing Directors to telecommute all or part of the time.

Advancement Prospects

Advancement prospects for zoo Web Site Marketing Directors are fair. Individuals climb the career ladder in a number of ways, depending on their career aspirations. Some find similar positions with larger or more prestigious zoos. Others are promoted to the position of general marketing director.

Individuals can also climb the career ladder by finding similar positions in other industries. Some individuals start their own marketing firms.

Education and Training

Most zoos prefer or require a minimum of a four-year college degree for this position. Good choices for majors include marketing, public relations, advertising, journalism, liberal arts, English, communications, business administration, or a related field. Classes, seminars, and workshops in general marketing, promotion, Web marketing, publicity, and public relations will be helpful in honing skills and making important contacts.

Experience, Skills, and Personality Traits

Experience requirements for zoo Web Site Marketing Directors vary depending on the specific position. Large, well known zoos generally require their Web Site Marketing Directors to have more experience than do smaller facilities.

Zoo Web Site Marketing Directors need to have the same skills as traditional marketing directors as well as having an understanding of Web marketing. In order to be successful, they need to be creative, innovative, ambitious, articulate, and highly motivated. Excellent written and verbal communication skills are also essential. Knowledge of publicity, promotion, public relations, advertising, and research techniques is necessary. The ability to multitask, handling many details at one time without getting flustered, is needed.

Unions and Associations

Zoo Web Site Marketing Directors can join a number of trade associations, including the Web Marketing Association, the American Marketing Association, the Marketing Research Association, and the Public Relations Society of America. These organizations provide professional support to members and often offer networking opportunities. Individuals and their zoos can also be members of the Association of Zoos and Aquariums.

Tips for Entry

1. Positions are often advertised in the classifieds section of newspapers in areas hosting zoos. Look under headings such as "Marketing," "Marketing Director," "Marketing Manager," "Web site Marketing," "Web Site Marketing Director," "Zoos," and "Zoo Web Site Marketing Director."

2. Positions can also be located online. Start off by checking out some of the more popular career sites such as Monster.com.

3. Don't forget to check out specific zoo Web sites for job openings.

4. Look for seminars, workshops, and courses in marketing, promotion, public relations, publicity, Web marketing, etc. These are good opportunities to hone skills and make valuable contacts.

DIRECTOR OF EVENTS

Position Description

While the main attractions at zoos are always the animals, most zoos also hold a variety of special events throughout the year. These include events that generate income for the zoo, guest and programming events, and donor cultivation events, among others.

The individual responsible for directing all aspects of these events at the zoo is called the Director of Events. Within the scope of the job, the individual has a great deal of responsibility. He or she is expected to oversee the strategy and planning of all events, from inception to completion. This includes scheduling events, developing ideas, planning the details, developing budgets, and monitoring expenditures to bring ideas and events to fruition.

The Director of Events works in conjunction with other departments at the zoo, coordinating their event-related efforts. These may include the development department, education department, guest relations, government affairs, public affairs, public relations, marketing, and zoo exhibits, among others.

The Director of Events is generally contacted when one of the departments at the zoo wants to hold some sort of special event. The individual must get the general information about the program, including the type of event that is needed and its purpose, size, time frame, and proposed budget.

He or she frequently gets ideas from other parties regarding the event. Is it going to be used to cultivate new donors? Will it be used to attract people to the zoo? Is the event going to be used to bring in new membership? How big an event will it be? When is the best time to hold it?

The Director of Events is expected to develop and implement unique strategies for events. The individual might be asked to develop one or more events to increase attendance at the zoo. He or she might be asked to develop events that connect the local business community or community groups to the zoo. The membership department might want an event to bring members together. The development department might need some sort of fund-raising event. The marketing department might need a unique event to market the zoo more effectively. The zoo director might want to showcase a new exhibit.

Coming up with interesting and unique ideas is not always easy. In order to be successful in this line of work, the individual must be creative and generate exciting, novel, and workable ideas. While the Director of Events might do this alone, in most cases, a number of people at the zoo will brainstorm. After rough ideas have been developed, the Director of Events is expected to work out the details on paper, developing the basic plan. Depending on the specific situation, he or she might need to get approval before moving forward.

The Director of Events must develop a budget for each event and make sure it is adhered to. The director works with his or her staff in executing the logistics of every aspect of the event. Specific tasks might include, for example, designing invitations, getting them printed and mailed, tracking RSVPs, and finding appropriate people and items needed to make the event successful. Depending on the event, the director might need to locate caterers, musical talent, tents, chairs, stages, promotional items, photographers, etc.

The Director of Events is responsible for negotiating for all services. He or she might ask for price quotes from a number of different vendors in order to get the best prices. The individual is also responsible for signing contracts for goods, services, and vendors for each special event.

The Director of Events might work with the public relations and marketing departments when marketing and publicizing events. In some cases, he or she may be personally responsible for this task. Press releases and other publicity items need to be prepared for events before they occur; in addition post-publicity materials must be prepared for events that have already occurred. The Director of Events or a staff member might contact the media and arrange interviews, articles, feature stories, photo opportunities, and broadcasts on the event. He or she is additionally responsible for making sure information on special events is given to the zoo Web content producer so that accurate information is available online in a timely manner.

In some cases, the individual is expected to arrange and execute press conferences, cocktail parties, luncheons, and dinners. The Director of Events might be required to write, design, and/or lay out programs, booklets, flyers, leaflets, and brochures about the program. Whether any of these tasks are outsourced or handled by other departments, the Director of Events is still responsible for overseeing the work.

The Director of Events is generally expected to be present at most if not all events to handle last-minute glitches and be a representative of the zoo. Depending on the calendar of events, the individual might handle more than one project at a time.

The Director of Events is expected to oversee all time lines for events, assuring that deadlines are met and the project is on budget. He or she will continually evaluate every event to see if it has met its purpose, stayed on budget, met its financial goals, and marketed the zoo effectively.

Salaries

Earnings for Directors of Events working in zoos range from approximately $25,000 to $65,000 or more, depending on a number of factors. These factors include the size and budget of the zoo as well as the experience and responsibilities of the individual. Those at the higher end of the pay scale generally have a great deal of experience and are working for well known zoos with bigger budgets.

Employment Prospects

Employment prospects for individuals seeking positions as the Director of Events of zoos are fair. Although there are only 224 zoos and aquariums accredited by the Association of Zoos and Aquariums (AZA) as of this writing, there are hundreds of other facilities not accredited by the AZA that might be potential employers for individuals seeking jobs like this.

It should be noted that individuals might have to relocate for openings.

Advancement Prospects

Advancement prospects for Directors of Events at zoos are fair. Individuals can climb the career ladder in a number of ways. Some advance their career by finding similar positions at larger, better-known zoos, resulting in increased responsibilities and earnings. Others are promoted to other administrative positions such as director of marketing. Some find similar positions outside of the nonprofit area, opting to work in the corporate world.

Education and Training

Most zoos require or prefer their applicants to have a four-year college degree for this position. Good choices for majors include public relations, communications, journalism, marketing, or related areas. Courses, seminars, and workshops in special events, public relations, publicity, promotion, writing, marketing, fund-raising, development, dealing with the media, and presentation skills will be useful.

Experience, Skills, and Personality Traits

Experience requirements depend to a great extent on the specific zoo and its size and structure. Larger, better-known zoos often require three to five years of experience handling large-scale events. Smaller zoos sometimes accept experience in running special events for nonprofit organizations on a volunteer basis.

The Director of Events at a zoo should be creative and have the ability to think outside of the box. The director needs to be able to conceptualize an idea and then bring it to fruition. The ability to look at a project and then break it up into logical, clear, concise components is crucial to success.

The Director of Events needs to be a strategic decision maker who is detail-oriented and organized. The individual also needs to be articulate and have excellent communication skills, both verbal and written. A good command of the English language is essential. People skills are vital.

The ability to communicate on the telephone in a polite, friendly, and effective manner is necessary. A proficiency in public speaking is helpful. The Director of Events should be comfortable dealing with the media and answering their questions.

Unions and Associations

Individuals interested in becoming the Director of Events for zoos often belong to a number of organizations for professional support and networking purposes. These include the Public Relations Society of America and the AZA.

Tips for Entry

1. Get experience and make valuable contacts by volunteering to put together events for a local zoo, animal advocacy organization, or other nonprofit group.

2. Network as much as you can in the industry. Go to conferences, conventions, and educational seminars and workshops to meet industry insiders.

3. An internship with a zoo in the special events, marketing, or public relations department will be useful for both the experience and the opportunity to make contacts.

4. Look for job openings in the classifieds section of newspapers. Headings might include key words such as "Special Events," "Director of Events," "Special Events Director," or "Zoos." Jobs may also be advertised under the names of specific zoos.

5. Don't forget to look online for job opportunities. Start with some of the general careers sites such as Monster.com. Then search out sites specific to working with animals.

6. Openings are sometimes listed on the Web sites of specific zoos.

ZOOKEEPER

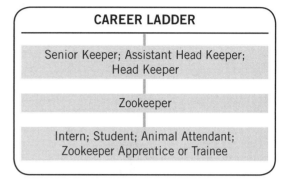

Position Description

Zookeepers are the individuals directly responsible for the care of animals at zoos. They are responsible for keeping animals safe, healthy, and happy. Individuals monitor them, feed them, and clean their living spaces. Within the scope of their job, Zookeepers have a great deal of responsibility.

Animals, unlike people, can't tell the individuals caring for them when they are not feeling well or hurt. Zookeepers must therefore constantly observe animals under their care to see if there are any symptoms of illness or injury. In order to do this, Zookeepers watch and listen to the animals to see if there are any changes in their behavior, mood, or preferences. Even a small change could indicate that there is a problem.

While monitoring animals under their care, Zookeepers are expected to write detailed notes and reports. If they think there is a problem or an animal is sick or injured, Zookeepers are responsible for telling the veterinarian so the animal can be attended to immediately.

While there are exceptions, Zookeepers generally care for wild and exotic animals. Zookeepers spend a great deal of time with the animals they care for. They get to know their habits, likes, and dislikes. The animals, in turn, start recognizing their keepers. After a while, they even begin to depend on them.

Zookeepers work with a broad range of animals, including mammals, birds, and reptiles, or they may be assigned to work with limited collections such as primates, large cats, or elephants, among others. Some Zookeepers work exclusively on special projects such as research or breeding in captivity. Duties and assignments depend on the specific zoo and its structure.

Zookeepers try to keep animals comfortable and active while enriching their lives. They provide animals with objects such as logs, branches, shells, balls, or even sandboxes to make sure they aren't bored. Zookeepers, for example, frequently hide food for the animals to find so that the animals can forage much as they do in the wild.

Zookeepers often train animals to do certain things. While some of these things may appear to be for the entertainment of zoo visitors, most of them make caring for the animals easier. For example, Zookeepers teach primates to open their mouths wide so that veterinarians can look in their mouth. They train elephants to lift their feet so that veterinarians can examine them. They also train animals to stand still for medical procedures such as inoculations. Training animals is not easy, but it is possible. Most keepers use a mixture of food and praise to train animals.

Zookeepers prepare the food that the animals eat. Depending on the specific animal and its prescribed diet, individuals chop fruits and vegetables and weigh meat, feed, hay, etc. They put the food in bowls in the animals' enclosures or feed them through chutes, depending on the animal.

Zookeepers are responsible for maintaining the exhibit areas and/or enclosures in which the animals live. This includes cleaning up urine, manure, dung, and other droppings. They may use shovels, sprays, or hoses to clean the areas. Keepers must then make sure the enclosures are disinfected. Individuals are also expected to put out fresh straw or similar materials that the animals use to sleep or live.

Keepers are sometimes responsible for the actual cleaning of certain animals as well. While they probably wouldn't give a lion a bath, it is not uncommon for keepers to hose down an elephant or brush its skin.

One of the more interesting responsibilities of keepers is teaching people about the animals for which they are caring. Zookeepers provide a great deal of education to the public not only about the specific animals they care for, but the conservation and biology of animals as well. They give formal or informal presentations and answer visitors' questions. Sometimes the Zookeeper showcases certain animals that are trained and can be taken out of their enclosures so that people can see them up close. Zookeepers also develop special programs for school groups.

Zookeepers sometimes contribute to research done on animals in their care. Depending on the specific assignment, individuals might be responsible for assisting in the repopulation of animals on the brink of extinction.

While Zookeepers often form a close bond with animals they are caring for, it can never really be like the bond people develop with their pets. It is important to remember that most animals in the zoo are wild animals and that the work can be dangerous. Animals may kick, bite, scratch, or trample the Zookeeper instinctively.

Depending on the specific exhibit, Zookeepers might work outside in inclement weather, including rain and extreme heat. Individuals might also have to work weekends and holidays.

Salaries

Earnings for Zookeepers range from approximately $22,000 to $48,000 or more annually. Factors affecting earnings include the size, location, budget, and prestige of the specific zoo. Other factors include the specific area within the zoo in which the individual works and his or her education, experience, and responsibilities.

Employment Prospects

While competition is keen for jobs in this field, employment prospects are fair for individuals seeking positions as Zookeepers. Every zoo employs Zookeepers to care for its animals. The number of keepers is dependent on the size, structure, and budget of the zoo. Jobs are located throughout the United States (or the world, for that matter) in areas that host zoos and zoological parks. It should be noted that individuals might need to relocate for job openings.

As noted previously, Zookeepers work in various areas of the zoo. They may be technical specialists, senior keepers, assistant head keepers, or head keepers. It should be noted that the higher the level of job, the fewer openings there are for positions.

Advancement Prospects

Advancement prospects for Zookeepers are good. Some individuals find similar positions in larger, better-known zoos. This often results in increased responsibilities and earnings. Some are promoted to other assignments working with animals in which they have a special interest or on projects such as captive breeding programs.

Others obtain experience and are promoted to positions such as senior keeper, assistant head keeper, head keeper, or assistant curator.

Education and Training

Educational requirements for Zookeepers vary from job to job. While some zoos will accept applicants with a high school diploma or the equivalent, most zoos require or prefer a bachelor's degree. Good majors include biology, animal science, zoology, animal husbandry, conservation, or a related field.

There are also a small number of certificate and associate's degree programs in zoo keeping and exotic animal training. Zookeepers receive on-the-job training.

Experience, Skills, and Personality Traits

Zookeepers need practical experience working with animals. Many individuals acquire this experience by volunteering at zoos in areas where they have contact with animals. Others get practical experience working as veterinary assistants. Some work in shelters, veterinary offices, or on farms.

Zookeepers need to both like animals and enjoy working with them. They need to be interested in research, conservation, and helping endangered animals.

Zookeepers must be good at math so they can properly measure out food for animals. Communication skills, both written and verbal, are needed. Public speaking skills are vital, since Zookeepers give presentations to groups of people. Keen observation skills are critical.

Whether caring for elephants, tigers, lions, apes, or any other animal at the zoo, the job of a keeper is physically demanding. Physical fitness is a necessity. A strong stomach is also necessary. The ability to handle a crisis is mandatory.

Unions and Associations

Zookeepers can join the American Association of Zookeepers (AAZ). This organization provides professional support and educational opportunities.

Tips for Entry

1. Volunteer at a zoo. This will give you hands-on experience, which is invaluable in this career.
2. If you can't find volunteer opportunities at a zoo, try shelters, humane societies, or veterinary offices.
3. An internship at a zoo will also be invaluable. If you can secure one working with keepers, that is great. If not, any department will be useful.
4. Look for job openings in the classifieds section of newspapers in areas hosting zoos and zoological parks. Look under headings such as "Zookeeper," "Keeper," "Zoo Jobs," etc. Positions might also be listed under the names of specific zoos and zoological parks.
5. Send your résumé with a short cover letter to zoos and zoological parks asking about openings. Remember to ask that your résumé be kept on file if there are no current openings.
6. Don't forget to check traditional job sites such as Monster.com. Zoos might also list job openings on their Web sites.
7. Join the AAZ. In addition to providing professional support and educational opportunities, job openings are posted on its Web site.

AQUARIST

CAREER PROFILE

Duties: Care for and maintain exhibits and tanks at aquariums, zoos, and other institutions; care for fish, marine mammals, and other aquatic animals; feed fish and other animals; keep records of the feeding and condition of fish and other animals; monitor water in tanks; clean tanks; repair tanks and exhibits; design exhibits; train dolphins, sea otters, seals, etc.

Alternate Title(s): Keeper; Mammal Trainer; Diving Aquarist; Gallery Aquarist; Trained Aquarist; Senior Aquarist

Salary Range: $25,000 to $135,000+

Employment Prospects: Fair

Advancement Prospects: Fair

Best Geographical Locations for Position: Positions located throughout the United States in areas hosting zoos, aquariums, and similar facilities

Prerequisites:

Education or Training—Educational requirements vary; bachelor's degree in biological sciences, physiology, or animal behavior required or preferred

CAREER LADDER

Aquarist Supervisor

Aquarist

Aquarist-in-Training

Experience and Qualifications—Experience requirements vary; see text

Special Skills and Personality Traits—Comfort in water environment; strong swimming ability; written and verbal communication skills; quick reflexes; creativity; patience; scientific aptitude; mechanical ability

Special Requirements—Certified scuba diver

Position Description

When visiting aquariums and zoos, most people don't think about how the exhibits are designed and maintained and how the fish and animals are cared for. There are a lot of people who work toward making sure aquariums and zoos are interesting to view and that animals are cared for in the best manner possible. Aquarists are part of this team.

Aquarists work in aquariums caring for fish and other underwater creatures. Their job is much like that of a keeper in a zoo. Duties of individuals vary depending on the specific job and the type of fish or marine animals for which they are caring.

Aquarists are responsible for feeding and monitoring the fish and animals in their care. They also must maintain the exhibits. There are some Aquarists who also are responsible for training animals such as dolphins, seals, and other marine animals.

Fish and other marine animals are very sensitive to temperature variations. As part of the job, Aquarists must check the temperature and condition of the tanks at the aquarium. They also are responsible for looking for any possible medical problems or changes in the conditions of the animals.

Aquarists are responsible for feeding the fish, seals, dolphins, and other marine animals in their care. In order to do this, Aquarists first need to determine the dietary needs of each specimen and then prepare the food. This often entails thawing frozen fish and chopping fish, shrimp, and plants and mixing in any necessary supplements. Individuals feeding fish in small tanks only need to sprinkle the food into the tanks. Aquarists who feed larger fish or fish in larger tanks, however, often need to actually dive into the tanks and feed the fish by hand. Individuals who do this wear gloves, wet suits, and scuba gear.

Aquarists must keep records of what each fish was fed. This is essential, as many fish are predators. If predators do not eat, they will attack other fish of different species in the tank. Aquarists are expected to dive into the tank a number of times a day to feed fish. While feeding the fish, Aquarists are responsible for checking the condition of the fish in the tank. Individuals check for injuries, unusual behavior, changes in appearance, and so on.

Another important task of Aquarists is assuring that the water in each tank is clean. In doing this, individuals must check that the filtration systems are working properly. Aquarists will frequently take water samples and analyze them to be sure everything is as it should be. If there is a problem, individuals must take steps to make sure the problem with the water is rectified quickly. Aquarists might, for example, unclog equipment or change the filter in the tank. They are also responsible for repairing problems with the tank or exhibit. They clean the tanks, too, in a number of ways. Aquarists often dive into the tanks with brushes to scrub the walls and vacuum away debris.

Individuals often help design and build the exhibits so they are exciting to both visitors and the fish and animals themselves. When doing so, they incorporate specific themes to tie exhibits together. Aquarists frequently strive to make the environments in which the fish live more interesting. Fish, like many other living things, flourish in more interesting environments. Aquarists might, for example, build tunnels or place objects in tanks. They might hide food so fish can hunt for it using their innate foraging skills.

Aquarists are expected to collect creatures and plants. They do this in freshwater or salt water. Other Aquarists are expected to repopulate the aquarium through breeding.

The most exciting part of the job for some Aquarists is training marine animals such as seals, sea otters, and dolphins to respond to commands. While these commands also make it easier to care for animals in the aquarium setting, the training of these mammals is used mainly to entertain and educate the public.

As noted, Aquarists often are expected to dive into tanks to feed fish, check the condition of fish and exhibits, and repair exhibits, among other things. When diving into exhibits, individuals generally wear wet suits and other protective gear. Some Aquarists are responsible for one large exhibit, while others are in charge of a number of smaller exhibits.

Salaries

Earnings for Aquarists working in aquariums or similar settings range from approximately $25,000 to $135,000 or more, depending on a number of factors. These include the specific employment situation as well as the experience, education, and responsibilities of the individual. Other factors affecting earnings include the specialization of the individual and the budget of the institution. By and large, individuals earning the highest salaries are those with the most education and experience and those in supervisory positions.

Employment Prospects

Employment prospects are fair for Aquarists. Individuals may work in a number of situations, including public, private, and governmental facilities such as zoos, aquariums, and marine parks. These facilities are located throughout the country. Individuals may need to relocate for positions.

Advancement Prospects

Advancement prospects for Aquarists are fair and based to a great extent on both experience and career aspirations. Aquarists-in-training advance to become full-fledged Aquarists.

Some Aquarists climb the career ladder by finding similar positions in larger, more prestigious facilities. Others are given more prestigious assignments. Some individuals become senior Aquarists or supervisors.

Education and Training

Educational requirements for Aquarists vary from job to job. Most employers require or prefer a minimum of a bachelor's degree in one of the biological sciences such as biology or marine science.

With that said, there are some Aquarists, especially those who train mammals, who hold bachelor's degrees instead in psychology or animal behavior. There are also some Aquarists who hold associate's degrees in animal-related fields or have had extensive experience working with animals. It should be noted that there is often a correlation between education level and earnings.

Experience, Skills, and Personality Traits

Aquarists must be comfortable in the water. Good communication skills, both written and verbal, are necessary. Individuals must have excellent observation skills. Part of their job is watching to see if there are changes in the fish or other marine life.

Whether designing exhibits or simply finding new places to hide food so fish can forage, creativity is a plus in this line of work. A mechanical ability is useful for Aquarists when repairing exhibits.

Aquarists who train animals must have a great deal of patience. Strong swimming skills are also necessary.

Special Requirements

Aquarists must be certified scuba divers. This certification can be obtained through a number of organizations throughout the country such as the YMCA, dive clubs, and colleges and universities.

Unions and Associations

Individuals interested in working as Aquarists can seek additional information from a number of organizations, including the American Association of Zoological Parks and Aquariums, the International Aquarium Society, the National Aquarium Society, the Consortium for Oceanographic Research and Education, the Association of Zoos and Aquariums, and the National Association of Marine Laboratories.

Tips for Entry

1. Make sure you get certified as a scuba diver before you look for a job.
2. If you are interested in a career as an Aquarist, go to a local aquarium or zoo and speak to one of the Aquarist supervisors. Tell him or her of your career aspirations and ask for suggestions for getting ready for your career.
3. See if you can find an internship with a zoo or aquarium. The experience as well as the opportunity to make contacts will be helpful in starting your career.
4. Send your résumé and a short cover letter to zoos, aquariums, marine parks, etc. Ask that your résumé be kept on file if there are no current openings.
5. Openings may be located in the classifieds section of newspapers. Look under headings such as "Aquarium," "Zoo", "Aquarist," "Trainer," and the specific names of aquariums, zoos, and marine parks.
6. Don't forget to search out job possibilities online. Start with some of the more popular job search sites such as Monster.com. Then go to more specific job sites.

PUBLIC RELATIONS MANAGER

CAREER PROFILE

Duties: Handle public relations for zoo; develop public relations campaigns; develop internal and external communications; promote positive image of zoo; represent zoo at media events; handle media inquiries; keep zoo in public eye; organize media events

Alternate Title(s): PR Manager; Manager of Public Relations; Communications Manager

Salary Range: $24,000 to $65,000+

Employment Prospects: Fair

Advancement Prospects: Fair

Best Geographical Locations for Position: Positions located throughout the United States in areas hosting zoos

Prerequisites:

Education or Training—Bachelor's degree in public relations, communications, journalism, or related field required or preferred by most employers; see text

Experience and Qualifications—Experience working in public relations, journalism, etc.

CAREER LADDER

Public Relations Manager at Larger Zoo; Assistant Director of Public Relations at Larger Zoo; Director of Public Relations at Zoo; Zoo Director of Marketing

↑

Public Relations Manager

↑

Public Relations Staffer; Public Relations Coordinator; Public Relations Position in other Nonprofit Organization

Special Skills and Personality Traits—Creativity; personableness; excellent verbal and written communication skills; presentation skills; people skills; persuasiveness; ability to multitask

Position Description

The Public Relations Manager of a zoo holds an important position with a big influence on the success of the facility. He or she is responsible for helping to increase the visibility of the zoo and positioning it as a venue people want to visit and support.

The Public Relations Manager is expected to develop and execute effective public relations, promotion, and communications campaigns for the zoo. The individual assists the zoo marketing director in the development and execution of comprehensive marketing and communications campaigns on both a short- and long-range basis. Together, they must find ways to market the zoo to increase membership, attendance, and visibility.

In larger zoos, the Public Relations Manager might work within a department of assistants, publicists, writers, etc. In smaller zoos, the Public Relations Manager might be expected to handle everything within the department personally or perhaps with the help of one or two assistants, volunteers, and/or interns.

As the Public Relations Manager of the zoo, the individual is the principal representative to the media, press, and public. He or she is expected to be the key spokesperson for the zoo. As part of the job, the individual is responsible for responding to inquiries from the media.

The zoo Public Relations Manager is responsible for researching, developing, and writing copy for zoo promotional materials. These might include, for example, brochures, pamphlets, and member newsletters. They might also include e-mail newsletters, e-mail blasts, zoo blogs, and information for the zoo's Web site.

The Public Relations Manager develops and prepares internal and external communications and publications. These may include staff and member newspapers and newsletters, programs and promotional materials, letters, and internal memos. The individual may also develop feature stories, draft press releases, and write special-request articles for the press and other media.

The Public Relations Manager is responsible for promoting the zoo's image in the best possible light. He or she is expected to develop methods to publicize and promote the zoo and formulate campaigns designed to increase attendance and membership.

In order to obtain publicity and get positive stories in newspapers, magazines, and on television and radio, the Public Relations Manager must maintain a professional and honest relationship with the media. This can mean the difference between getting a story in the paper or on the air and getting no exposure at all.

It is important to realize that just because the Public Relations Manager issues a press release does not mean that the media will use it. Those who are successful in this position know how to develop a good "hook" or angle to draw attention to their particular press release among the dozens of others issued every day. This is also necessary when pitching stories to the media about the zoo, exhibits, or special events.

The Public Relations Manager may be called on to write or deliver speeches to other groups about the zoo. In many cases, the individual will also be expected to attend meetings or conferences on behalf of the zoo.

The Public Relations Manager is expected to represent the zoo at media events. He or she handles inquiries from the media either verbally or in writing. He or she is responsible for either developing or supervising the development of press kits and other materials for the media and the general public. These kits consist of press releases, information about the zoo, photographs, reprints or reviews of articles, fact sheets, and more. They are given or sent to editors, TV and radio producers, and talent coordinators. The Public Relations Manager or his or her staff must know how to get through to these people in order to secure television or radio appearances or to have feature articles developed and written.

The Public Relations Manager must generate media exposure whenever possible. He or she must constantly search out media opportunities. The Public Relations Manager is responsible for developing feature story concepts and then finding ways to get the media interested. Depending on the specific zoo, the individual will seek local media exposure and/or national media exposure.

The Public Relations Manager is responsible for helping reporters and other journalists, photographers, and television and radio crews when they are doing stories or interviews. He or she might provide background information, press kits, photos, tours, and special access to the zoo.

Another responsibility of the Public Relations Manager of a zoo is arranging for publicity photos to be taken. Depending on the zoo, the manager will personally take publicity photos or arrange for a photographer to do so. The individual, may, for example, coordinate a publicity photo shoot of a new zoo exhibit or the introduction of a new baby elephant. Once photos are taken, the Public Relations Manager is expected to select the best ones to use.

A major responsibility of the Public Relations Manager at a zoo is the coordination and execution of media events and press conferences to publicize and promote zoo exhibits, attractions, special programs, educational events, public events, and projects. The individual is expected to handle these events from inception through fruition.

In some zoos, the Public Relations Manager may be expected to handle media relations, community relations, and public affairs. In others, different departments or directors may handle these responsibilities.

Salaries

Earnings for Public Relations Managers working at zoos range from approximately $24,000 to $65,000 or more. Factors affecting earnings include the size, structure, budget, and geographic location of the specific zoo. Other factors affecting earnings include the responsibilities, professional reputation, and experience of the individual.

Employment Prospects

Employment prospects for individuals seeking positions as Public Relations Managers in zoos are fair. Opportunities are located throughout the United States in areas hosting zoos. It should be noted that individuals might need to relocate for positions.

Advancement Prospects

Advancement prospects for Public Relations Managers working in zoos are fair. Individuals climb the career ladder in a number of ways, depending on their career aspirations. Some advance their career by finding similar positions at larger, better-known zoos, resulting in increased responsibilities and earnings. Public Relations Managers working in zoos can be promoted to positions such as the director of communications or marketing director. Some individuals find similar positions in other industries.

Education and Training

Most zoos require or prefer a minimum of a four-year college degree for this position. Some positions may even require a master's degree. On occasion, there are smaller zoos that accept an applicant with an associate's degree or even a high school diploma coupled with experience.

Good choices for majors include public relations, communications, journalism, marketing, or related areas. Courses, seminars, and workshops in public relations, publicity, promotion, writing, marketing, fund-raising, development, dealing with media, and presentation skills will be useful.

Experience, Skills, and Personality Traits

Experience requirements depend to a great extent on the size, structure, and prestige of the specific zoo. Experience in public relations, journalism, and working with nonprofit organizations is helpful.

Public Relations Managers working in zoos need to be well-spoken, articulate individuals with polished communication skills. A proficiency in public speaking is also necessary. Individuals must be comfortable dealing with media inquiries. The ability to think quickly is essential. Excellent writing skills are vital.

Public Relations Managers working in zoos need the ability to define problems logically, clearly, and concisely as well as to analyze them from a variety of points of view. Creativity is essential to developing and growing public relations campaigns, coming up with effective press releases, and creating special events.

The ability to communicate on the telephone in a polite, friendly, and effective manner is necessary. People skills are essential. The ability to multitask without getting flustered is crucial. Successful individuals have the ability to work independently and as part of a team.

Unions and Associations

Individuals interested working as Public Relations Managers for zoos might want to become members of various organizations for professional support and to make contacts. These include the Public Relations Society of America, the premier association for public relations professionals.

Tips for Entry

1. Get experience doing public relations with nonprofit organizations by volunteering with a local civic or community organization. If you can find a zoo or animal advocacy group, great. If not, any experience will be helpful.

2. An internship with a zoo in the public relations department will be useful for both the experience and the opportunity to make contacts.

3. Look for job openings in the classifieds section of newspapers. Heading titles might include key words such as "Public Relations Manager," "Public Relations," and "Zoo Jobs." Jobs may also be advertised under the names of specific zoos.

4. Don't forget to look online for job opportunities. Start with some of the general career sites such as Monster.com. Then search out sites specific to working with animals.

5. Openings may be listed on the Web sites of specific zoos, so check these often.

COMMUNITY RELATIONS DIRECTOR

CAREER PROFILE

Duties: Plan, develop, and execute programs to help local community while enhancing the image of the zoo; coordinate and foster relationship between zoo and local civic and community groups

Alternate Title(s): Community Affairs Director; Public Affairs Director

Salary Range: $24,000 to $60,000+

Employment Prospects: Fair

Advancement Prospects: Fair

Best Geographical Locations for Position Opportunities located throughout the United States in areas hosting zoos

Prerequisites:

Education or Training—Bachelor's degree

Experience and Qualifications—Experience requirements vary; see text

Special Skills and Personality Traits—People skills; verbal and written communication skills; attention to detail; public speaking skills; articulateness; creativity; organization skills; time-management skills; high energy

CAREER LADDER

Community Relations Director for Larger, More Prestigious Zoo; Public Relations Director; Director of Marketing

Community Relations Director

Community Relations Coordinator; Community Relations or Public Relations Staffer

Position Description

The Community Relations Director of a zoo coordinates the relationship between the zoo and local agencies, civic groups, schools, community groups, political entities, and governmental agencies. The Community Relations Director must also find ways to foster the growth of relationships with these groups.

The Community Relations Director has a number of responsibilities. He or she is expected to plan, develop, and execute programs that help the local community while enhancing the image of the zoo. While performing these functions, the Community Relations Director needs to be sensitive to the local community and its needs and values.

The Community Relations Director is responsible for representing the zoo at various events at the zoo and off premises. In many cases, he or she will also act as the zoo's representative on other nonprofit organization boards and committees. As the zoo's Community Relations Director, the individual is additionally expected to be an active member of local civic and community groups.

The zoo Community Relations Director is expected to develop innovative community relations programs in which the zoo can take a leadership role. These might include, for example, fairs, concerts, and lecture series.

Other community projects might include the adoption of zoo animals by local groups such as the Girl Scouts, Boy Scouts, a local elementary school, or a professional group.

The director might bring various members of the zoo's staff into schools so that young people can learn about animals and careers in zoos. The individual might also work with the director of educational activities to bring educational programs pertaining to animal conservation to schools.

The zoo Community Relations Director is frequently asked to give speeches or presentations on behalf of the zoo to local community groups, civic groups, schools, and businesses. These presentations help enhance the image of the zoo and bring it to the attention of potential donors, volunteers, and visitors.

While working on community programs, Community Relations Directors might also work with businesses and corporations that sponsor these programs. Projects and programs like these give the zoo positive publicity.

The zoo Community Relations Director may be asked to appear for television or radio interviews or on news shows to promote the zoo's community projects. These appearances spotlight the zoo's commitment to the community.

The director of community relations at a zoo might work with governmental agencies on a variety of projects and programs. These programs may, for example, be geared toward education, the conservation of animals and wildlife, and related topics.

Community groups frequently call upon the Community Relations Director when they have an idea or a request regarding the zoo. They may simply want to hold a meeting at the zoo or to work on some sort of program or project. It is up to the director of community relations to respond in a timely manner and find ways to honor requests, if possible.

Depending on the size and structure of the specific zoo and the community relations department, the Community Relations Director might be responsible for supervising a staff. He or she might additionally be responsible for developing budgets. Other responsibilities of the individual include writing press releases, developing promotional and marketing material, and writing grants.

The Community Relations Director works with the public relations and marketing departments to assure that the zoo maintains a good public image. He or she also works to assure that the needs of the community are met.

Salaries

Earnings for directors of community relations at zoos range widely depending on a number of factors. These include the size, structure, budget, and geographic location of the specific zoo. Other factors affecting earnings include the responsibilities, professional reputation, and experience of the individual. There are some who earn as little as $24,000 annually, while others earn $60,000 or more. Those at the top of the pay scale generally work for large, high-budget zoos.

Employment Prospects

Employment prospects for individuals seeking positions as Community Relations Directors for zoos are fair. Individuals may find employment with larger, well known zoos as well as smaller facilities. While opportunities are located throughout the United States in areas hosting zoos, it should be noted that individuals might need to relocate for positions.

Advancement Prospects

Advancement prospects for zoo Community Relations Directors are fair. Individuals can climb the career ladder in a number of ways, depending on their career aspirations. Some advance their career by finding similar positions at larger, higher-budget zoos, resulting in increased responsibilities and earnings. Some find similar positions handling community relations and public affairs in other industries. Still others climb the career ladder by being promoted to zoo public relations director or marketing director.

Education and Training

Most zoos require or prefer a minimum of a four-year college degree for this position. There may, however, be smaller zoos that accept an applicant with an associate's degree or even a high school diploma coupled with experience.

Good choices for majors include public relations, communications, journalism, marketing, or related areas. Courses, seminars, and workshops in public relations, publicity, promotion, writing, marketing, fund-raising, development, dealing with media, and presentation skills will be useful. Seminars in grant-writing and working with nonprofit groups will also be helpful.

Experience, Skills, and Personality Traits

Experience requirements vary from job to job. Larger, better-known zoos generally require more experience than smaller zoos. Experience is often obtained by working in the community affairs or public relations department of a zoo as either a coordinator or staffer. Others gain experience working as journalists or in community relations in other industries.

Successful Community Relations Directors are articulate, outgoing, energetic, personable people. They are creative, with a mix of public relations, marketing, and promotional skills. Excellent verbal and written communication skills are necessary. A good command of grammar and the English language is helpful. Public speaking skills are also needed because Community Relations Directors often must give presentations or speak at meetings.

It is essential in this type of position to enjoy working with people. Individuals should be community-minded and have an understanding of nonprofit, civic, and community groups.

Community Relations Directors working in zoos must also be detail-oriented and have good organization and time-management skills. The ability to multitask effectively will be of great use.

Unions and Associations

Zoo Community Relations Directors can join a number of associations and organizations that provide professional support, education, and networking opportunities. These include the Public Relations Society of America and the Association of Fundraising Professionals.

Individuals may also be members of local community and civic groups. In addition, Community Relations Directors and/or their zoo may also be members of the Association of Zoos and Aquariums (AZA).

Tips for Entry

1. If you are still in school, look for an internship with a zoo in the community relations or public relations department. It is a great way to obtain experience, hone skills, and make helpful contacts.

2. Join the AZA and take part in its programs. This is a great way to meet people, network, and find out about job openings.

3. Network as much as you can in the industry. Go to conferences, conventions, and educational seminars and workshops.

4. You might want to become a member of one or more local nonprofit organizations, animal advocacy organizations, humane societies, animal shelters, or rescues. Get involved in their projects so others can start to know who you are. It's great experience, and if someone hears about a job opportunity, he or she might just recommend you.

5. Look in the classifieds section of newspapers in areas hosting zoos. Look under headings including "Community Relations Director," "Director of Community Relations," "Public Affairs Director," "Director of Public Affairs," and "Zoos," among others. Job openings may also be located in advertisements under the names of specific zoos.

6. Don't forget to look online for job opportunities. Start with some of the general job sites such as Monster.com. Then search out sites specific to working in zoos.

7. Openings may be listed on zoo Web sites, so monitor these.

VOLUNTEER COORDINATOR

Duties: Recruit volunteers and docents; schedule volunteers and tour docents; train volunteers and docents; coordinate volunteers; evaluate volunteers

Alternate Title: Coordinator of Volunteers

Salary Range: $25,000 to $51,000+

Employment Prospects: Fair

Advancement Prospects: Fair

Best Geographical Locations for Position: Positions located throughout the United States in areas hosting zoos

Prerequisites:

Education or Training—Bachelor's degree in public relations, communications, journalism, or related field required or preferred; see text

Experience and Qualifications—Experience working with volunteers; experience working in nonprofit organizations

CAREER LADDER

Director of Volunteers; Volunteer Coordinator at Larger, Better-Known Zoo

Volunteer Coordinator

Volunteer Department Staffer; Intern

Special Skills and Personality Traits—People skills; drive; personableness and persuasiveness; resourcefulness; ability to multitask; excellent verbal and written communication skills; attention to detail

Position Description

Many nonprofit organizations use volunteers to supplement staff. Zoos are no exception. Volunteers play a vital role in zoos on a number of levels. Not only do they augment staff in certain areas, but in many instances they provide visitors to the zoo with a unique and personal experience.

While volunteers don't usually go into the lion's den or any other dangerous situation that requires highly trained individuals, they do get an insider's view of the zoo. Volunteers serve as ambassadors of the zoo, enhancing the experience of visitors. Some volunteers assist zoo staff members in caring for animals. Others help with special events, outreach, and the daily operations of the zoo. Still other volunteers assist with the education of zoo visitors. These volunteers are called docents and often give guided tours of the zoo as well as live animal presentations. Docents share their knowledge of animals with zoo visitors.

The individual responsible for overseeing volunteers at a zoo is called the Volunteer Coordinator. Within the scope of the job, this individual has a multitude of responsibilities.

To begin, the Volunteer Coordinator at the zoo is responsible for recruiting volunteers. He or she may use a number of methods to do this. The individual may, for example, speak to community and civic groups about volunteering at the zoo. He or she might also send out press releases to the local media outlets asking for volunteers. The Volunteer Coordinator may appear as a guest on local radio and television shows discussing volunteering at the zoo. Generally, there is a link for volunteer opportunities on zoos' Web sites. There is usually also literature regarding volunteer opportunities placed strategically throughout zoos.

The Volunteer Coordinator must interview and screen volunteers to make sure they are a good fit for the zoo. When doing this, the coordinator talks to potential volunteers to see where their talents might best be utilized and what they are interested in doing. For example, people who like to teach and answer questions might be great docents. Some people might want to help with special events. Some may be interested in preparing food for the animals. Others want to help with administrative duties, be main-gate ambassadors, answer visitors' questions, direct people to various exhibits, or assist keepers with various duties. Successful Volunteer Coordinators help individuals find their niche at the zoo so they are doing something they enjoy.

The Volunteer Coordinator is responsible for making sure all volunteers complete applications and paperwork. The individual must be sure references are checked and, depending on the specific zoo and area where the individual is volunteering, conduct background checks.

Volunteer Coordinators are expected to develop and hold orientation and training sessions for volunteers. These sessions are normally held throughout the year as new volunteers are recruited. While volunteers need only go to an orientation session once, they may go through a number of training sessions. Depending on the area where individuals want to volunteer, training sessions are led by the Volunteer Coordinator or other members of the zoo staff.

The Volunteer Coordinator is responsible for scheduling volunteers. This is often not an easy task as the coordinator is working around the needs of the zoo and the schedules of volunteers.

The coordinator must make sure that all volunteers and docents have everything they need to meet their goals. This included skills, guidance, information, and tools. The individual will have periodic meetings with volunteers to evaluate their performance and make sure that their needs are being met.

Just because volunteers are not paid does not mean they should not be recognized. In addition to saying "thank you," the Volunteer Coordinator must come up with unique ways to show appreciation to volunteers. He or she might, for example, work with the event director to develop a recognition luncheon, dinner, or other special event. He or she might also create awards, pins, or certificates noting how many hours of service volunteers have given. The individual might even recognize a different volunteer every month and write a corresponding story for the zoo's Web site or newsletter.

Every now and then, there will be issues among volunteers or between volunteers and staff members. The Volunteer Coordinator is responsible for mediating these issues and handling any conflicts in a timely manner.

As zoo exhibits frequently change, it is essential that volunteers and docents have the most current information. The Volunteer Coordinator is expected to disseminate new information on current exhibits and the zoo in general. He or she will additionally be the liaison between the various zoo departments and the volunteers and docents.

The Volunteer Coordinator is expected to develop an annual operating budget for the department. As part of the job, he or she also must recommend the most effective ways to use available financial resources. Are more training materials needed? What about training sessions? In order to retain volunteers, do more events need to be planned? These are all questions that need to be answered before developing the budget.

The Volunteer Coordinator might also provide administrative support to volunteers and docents and develop mailing lists, files, and correspondence.

Salaries

Earnings for Volunteer Coordinators working in zoos range from approximately $25,000 to $51,000 or more, depending on a number of factors. These include the size and budget of the zoo as well as the experience, job responsibilities, and professional reputation of the individual. Those at the higher end of the scale generally have a great deal of experience and are working for well known zoos with bigger budgets.

Employment Prospects

Employment prospects for Volunteer Coordinators are fair. While as of this writing there are only 224 zoos and aquariums accredited by the Association of Zoos and Aquariums (AZA), there are hundreds of other facilities that are not accredited by the AZA that employ Volunteer Coordinators.

It should be noted that individuals might have to relocate for openings.

Advancement Prospects

Advancement prospects for zoo Volunteer Coordinators are fair. Individuals climb the career ladder in a number of ways. Some advance by finding similar positions at larger, better-known zoos, resulting in increased responsibilities and earnings. Others are promoted to the position of director of volunteers. Some find similar positions outside of zoos in institutions such as hospitals or libraries.

Education and Training

Most zoos require or prefer a minimum of a four-year college degree for this position. Good choices for majors include education, the biological sciences, public relations, communications, journalism, marketing, or related areas. Courses, seminars, and workshops in public relations, writing, dealing with volunteers, and about the nonprofit sector will be useful.

Experience, Skills, and Personality Traits

Experience dealing with volunteers and docents is generally necessary, as is experience in the nonprofit sector. Experience in zoo education may be preferred.

Experience requirements depend to a great extent on the specific zoo and its size and structure. Larger, better-known zoos often require more experience than their smaller counterparts.

Volunteer Coordinators must enjoy working with people and have great management skills. They should be articulate individuals with excellent communication skills, both verbal and written. A good command of the English language is essential. Proficiency in public speaking is vital.

Volunteer Coordinators need to be detail-oriented and organized. The ability to multitask effectively is necessary. Time-management skills are mandatory. Good judgment and problem-solving skills are required. The ability to use tact and diplomacy are critical. A basic knowledge of animals and conservation is helpful.

Unions and Associations

The Volunteer Coordinator working in a zoo can join a number of organizations that provide educational opportunities and professional support. These include the Association for Volunteer Administration, the American Society of Association Executives, the Society for Nonprofit Organizations, and the AZA.

Tips for Entry

1. Get experience working with volunteers by volunteering with a nonprofit organization and chairing committees. Volunteering in a zoo, shelter, or animal advocacy organization would be great, but any nonprofit organization would provide good experience.

2. If you are in still in college, try to find an internship at your local zoo in the volunteer department.

3. Openings may be advertised in the classifieds section of newspapers. Look under headings such as "Zoo Volunteer Coordinator," "Volunteer Coordinator," "Coordinator of Volunteer Services," "Volunteer Services," and "Zoo Jobs."

4. Send your résumé and a short cover letter to the personnel directors of zoos in which you are interested in working. Remember to ask that your résumé be kept on file if there are no current openings.

5. Don't forget to look online for job opportunities. Start with some of the popular general sites such as Monster.com. Then search out sites specific to working in animal-related fields.

6. Openings may be listed on the Web sites of specific zoos, so check these often.

PET FOOD, PET SUPPLY, AND PET MERCHANDISE STORES

STORE MANAGER

CAREER PROFILE

Duties: Manage store; oversee operations of store; supervise employees; handle customer problems and inquiries; train and develop sales staff; work to achieve store's sales goals

Alternate Title(s): Manager; General Manager

Salary Range: $28,000 to $65,000+

Employment Prospects: Good

Advancement Prospects: Good

Best Geographical Locations for Position: Positions located throughout the United States

Prerequisites:

Education or Training—Educational requirements vary; see text

Experience and Qualifications—Retail management experience

Special Skills and Personality Traits—Supervisory skills; problem-solving skills; negotiation

CAREER LADDER

Store Manager for Larger or More Prestigious Pet Food and Supply Store; Regional Manager; Store Manager for Store in Other Industry

↑

Store Manager

↑

Assistant Store Manager

skills; communication skills; ability to deal well with people; management skills; understanding of retail industry; understanding of pet industry

Position Description

More than ever before, people consider their pets to be part of their family. Pet supplies, accessories, and food have grown into a multibillion-dollar industry. While some of these products are sold in pet departments of big box or department stores, there are many stores that specialize specifically in pet food and merchandise. The individual in charge of overseeing the operations of one of these stores is called the Store Manager.

A good Store Manager is critical to the success of a retail pet food or pet supply store. Stores that have managers who are knowledgeable about their store inventory, pet merchandise, and pets in general as well as those who share that knowledge with their staff generally end up having better sales. Additionally, those who are passionate about the job generally motivate and inspire their employees, also resulting in higher store sales.

Store Managers have an array of duties. An important responsibility is handling personnel matters. The Store Manager is responsible for hiring staff and for the overall management of the store staff.

The manager may find employees in a number of ways. The individual might place advertisements in the newspaper and online. He or she might also notify employment agencies regarding openings or even put

up signs in the store window. In some cases, potential employees just walk into the store and ask to fill in applications. In other situations, prospective employees apply online.

The Store Manager is expected to review employee applications and interview potential employees. He or she must be sure that the staff that is hired is competent, trustworthy, dependable, and dedicated to customer service.

The manager is expected to train employees in various facets of the store operations. This might include everything from running a cash register and deciding on store appearance to providing customer service and setting store policy, and everything in between. Depending on the structure of the specific store, it might also entail training employees in how to help customers choose the right pet food, pet toys, and even how to choose the correct pet. In certain stores, the manager trains employees on how to answer pet-related questions or train pets. In some situations, the Store Manager will run formal training programs for employees. In others, he or she will either train new employees personally as they are hired or assign another staff member to handle training.

The Store Manager is expected to supervise store employees. Depending on the size and structure of the store, staff might include assistant managers, key holders (workers who open and close the store, among other duties), floor supervisors, sales associates, clerks, cashiers, stock people, maintenance people, bookkeepers, animal attendants, pet groomers, and animal trainers. At times, the assistant manager or floor supervisors perform supervisory functions.

The Store Manager, often in cooperation with the assistant store manager, creates schedules for the store staff. This is often a difficult job because the store must always be fully staffed. Having a handle on when the store does the most business is helpful in creating schedules. Generally, stores are busiest on weekends, when people can get out to shop. However, stores may be busy at other times as well, such as after the traditional workday ends or during a lunch hour, so the manager must account for this. Additionally, the manager must always make contingency plans in case any of the scheduled staff calls in sick or has an emergency. In smaller stores, where there are fewer employees, the manager may also be required to fill in when an employee doesn't show up for work.

Store Managers working in pet food and pet supply stores must be knowledgeable about all of the store's stock. They must become an expert on everything in the store. If the store sells pet food, the manager must know the difference between each type of food as well as the benefits of each. If the store is selling dog beds, birdcages, pet toys, or training supplies, the manager must know as much as possible about each item. With so many choices, people are often confused about purchases and want information. Stores that have managers and staff who are knowledgeable attract more customers, resulting in higher sales.

The Store Manager oversees everything and everyone in the store. At times, he or she assumes the duties of a salesperson, clerk, or cashier. During a particularly busy period, for example, the Store Manager might be responsible for approving checks and making sure large bills are not counterfeit.

One of the important roles of the Store Manager is handling customer service problems. When a customer has a problem or issue with the store or its merchandise, policies, or employees, the Store Manager is expected to find an effective solution. Good customer service is essential to the success of all retail outlets, and pet food and supply stores are no exception.

A customer, for example, might return opened merchandise, products without receipts, or pet food their pet didn't like. In order to keep goodwill between customers and the store, the manager might authorize an exchange or refund even if the return does not fall within the requirements in the store policy. He or she might also authorize the acceptance of expired coupons, match prices or competitors, or perform similar activities to keep customers happy and create goodwill.

The Store Manager is expected to handle any problems that may arise between employees and customers. Whether an employee is rude or nasty to a customer or a customer just feels he or she was treated shabbily, the manager must find a way to make the customer feel his or her complaint has been taken seriously and has been addressed. The successful Store Manager's motto must be, "The customer is always right."

In some stores, the Store Manager acts as the buyer for the store. This generally occurs in smaller, privately owned stores. The individual in this situation is responsible for speaking with various representatives of pet food or pet merchandise companies. The manager gets price quotes and then places orders based on inventory in the store and the needs of customers who have come into the store and asked for things.

In larger pet food and pet supply stores, or chain stores, where the Store Manager does not do the purchasing, the individual will instead be responsible for checking inventory and assuring that the main office or warehouse sends needed merchandise. The manager must check inventory regularly to know what items are low in stock or have sold out completely. In some cases, the manager assigns this duty to an assistant or a sales associate.

The Store Manager is also responsible for making sure that when stock arrives, each piece is accounted for. He or she might count and sort merchandise and verify the receipt of items on invoices personally or assign this duty to an assistant or salesperson. Once this is done, the manager will assign someone to make sure all items are priced for sale. The manager must also be sure all merchandise is arranged attractively, shelves and racks are stocked, and merchandise is easy for customers to find.

Depending on the specific situation, the Store Manager might be responsible for advertising store specials. He or she might be expected to work with local newspapers and radio and television stations to create advertisements and place ads and commercials.

Some pet food and pet supply Store Managers receive advertising circulars from their main office. This generally happens when individuals are managing large chain pet food and pet supply stores. In these circumstances, the manager is expected to make sure all items advertised in the circular are available in the store, sale priced, and easy to find. He or she will generally advise all store employees where sale items can be located so items can be found quickly when customers ask for them.

The manager is often expected to obtain time sheets and work hours of employees for payroll purposes. He or she may then be responsible for drawing up payroll checks or giving the information to a payroll service, the store owner, or the main office.

A major responsibility of Store Managers in pet food and supply stores is handling loss prevention. This may include both internal and external theft of store merchandise and money. The manager is expected to ensure that employee training as well as merchandising techniques are utilized to minimize loss due to theft.

Depending on the specific store and its structure, Store Managers may work various hours and shifts. If an employee doesn't show up for a shift and there is no coverage, the manager may be expected to fill in. He or she is also expected to be available in case of emergency.

Store Managers working in pet merchandise and supply stores report to either the owner, if the store is privately owned, or the regional or area manager, if the store is part of a chain.

Salaries

Earnings for Store Managers of pet food and pet supply stores range between $28,000 and $65,000 or more annually. Factors affecting earnings include the specific store and its size and geographic location as well as the experience and responsibilities of the individual.

In addition to salaries, many Store Managers receive bonuses for meeting or exceeding sales quotas.

Employment Prospects

Employment prospects for Store Managers for pet food and supply stores are good. Stores can sell an array of pet food, supplies, and merchandise. Individuals can find employment at one of the well known pet supercenter chains or smaller local or regional stores or boutiques. Jobs are located throughout the United States.

Advancement Prospects

Advancement prospects for Store Managers working in pet food and supply stores are good. The most common way individuals climb the career ladder is by locating similar positions at larger or more prestigious stores. This generally results in increased responsibilities and earnings.

Those working in chains can advance their careers by moving to larger stores within the chain. Some climb the career ladder by becoming regional or area managers or moving into other areas of corporate management.

Education and Training

Educational requirements for pet store managers vary depending on the job. Virtually every position requires a minimum of a high school diploma or its equivalent. Many positions require or prefer a college background or degree.

Good majors include retailing, merchandising, business management, marketing, communications, advertising, liberal arts, or a related field.

Pet superstores and other chain pet stores often have their own formal executive training programs that management recruits complete. These programs train managers in an array of areas, including store policies, management techniques, sales, merchandising, marketing, promotion, human resources, and public and community relations. These programs also familiarize managers with specific store products and merchandise. Completing these programs helps the manager run the store smoothly and profitably.

Experience, Skills, and Personality Traits

Previous retail management experience is almost always required for Store Managers working in pet food and pet supply stores. Experience is generally obtained as individuals work their way up from sales positions to key holders to department managers to assistant managers.

Communication skills, both verbal and written, are essential. Strong organizational skills are critical, as is the ability to deal with details. The ability to solve problems and make quick decisions is vital.

Store Managers are responsible for the organization, administration, and running of the store. They should have supervisory, management, and administrative skills. They should always present a professional appearance and demeanor.

Honesty and dependability are vital traits for individuals in this type of position. Store Managers should like working with people. An understanding of the retail industry and the pet industry is imperative.

Unions and Associations

Store Managers in pet or pet supply stores may belong to a number of professional trade associations, including the American Collegiate Retailing Association, the National Retail Federation, and the Retail Merchants Association. They may also be members of the World Pet Association and the American Pet Products Association.

Tips for Entry

1. Experience in retail sales is vital. Look for a job in a pet or pet supply store as a sales associate. Once you have some experience, you're on your way.

2. Positions are often advertised in the classifieds section of newspapers. Look under headings such as "Store Manager," "Management Positions," "Store Management," "Management Opportunities," "Retail Opportunities," "Pet Food Store," "Pet Supply Store," or under specific store names.

3. Stores may also advertise openings on their Web sites, so check these.

4. Don't be afraid to simply walk into a pet store and inquire about openings. You might get lucky.

5. Many chain pet stores offer management-training programs. Contact the headquarters of these stores to find out about requirements.

6. Jobs may also be located on the Internet. Begin your search on some of the more popular job search sites such as Monster.com.

7. Contact recruiters and executive search firms specializing in management positions in retail.

ASSISTANT MANAGER

CAREER PROFILE

Duties: Oversee store operations; supervise employees; handle customer problems and inquiries; assist in the training and development of sales staff; work to achieve sales goals

Alternate Title(s): Assistant

Salary Range: $24,000 to $48,000+

Employment Prospects: Good

Advancement Prospects: Good

Best Geographical Locations for Position: Positions located throughout the United States

Prerequisites:

Education or Training—Educational requirements vary; see text

Experience and Qualifications—Retail sales and management experience

Special Skills and Personality Traits—Supervisory skills; problem-solving skills; negotiation

CAREER LADDER

Assistant Manager for Larger or More Prestigious Pet Food and Pet Supply Store; Store Manager for Pet Food and Pet Supply Store

↑

Assistant Manager

↑

Third Key

skills; communication skills; ability to deal well with people; management skills; understanding of retail industry; understanding of pet industry

Position Description

Pet supplies, accessories, and food have grown into a multibillion-dollar industry. While some of these products are sold in pet departments of big box or department stores, there are many stores that specialize in pet merchandise and pet food. Some are well known pet supercenter chains, while others are smaller local or regional stores. Still others are privately owned shops or niche pet boutiques. Most stores have managers. Many also have Assistant Managers.

The Assistant Manager is second-in-command. He or she is expected to help the store manager with the day-to-day store operations. When the store manager is off duty or otherwise unavailable, the Assistant Manager is responsible for stepping in and assuming his or her duties.

Assistant Managers work under the direction of the store manager. Specific duties vary depending on the situation. Individuals working in pet superstores may have more specialized duties than those working in smaller stores. Assistant Managers working in smaller stores typically have more general duties.

The Assistant Manager works with the store manager in supervising store employees. Depending on the size and structure of the store, staff might include

key holders (workers who open and close the store, among other duties), floor supervisors, sales associates, clerks, cashiers, stock people, maintenance people, bookkeepers, animal attendants, pet groomers, and animal trainers.

The Assistant Manager is expected to help give the store a pleasant atmosphere. This is important both to keep employees happy and to make the store more comfortable for customers.

In order to meet the store's sales and profit goals, Assistant Managers working in pet food and pet merchandise or supply stores are responsible for helping to motivate the sales staff. There are a lot of choices for people purchasing their pet supplies. Successful Assistant Managers know how to motivate employees to do their job well and to provide excellent customer service.

The Assistant Manager works with the manager in training employees in various phases of store operation. This might include everything from running cash registers and merchandising to store appearance and customer service, store policy, and everything in between. Depending on the structure of the specific store, duties might also include training employees to help customers choose the right pet food, pet toys, and even how to choose the correct pet. The Assistant Manager may additionally train employees on how to answer pet-related questions. These training sessions for employees may be formal or informal.

The Assistant Manager, along with the manager and key holder, often take turns opening the store. Before the gates or doors to the store are even opened to the public, the Assistant Manager works with other employees to make sure the store is ready for customers. This might include performing tasks such as checking to see if shelves, displays, and racks are neat and fully stocked; the floor is clean; and the registers have change.

Some stores just have one Assistant Manager. Others, such as pet merchandise supercenters, have a number of Assistant Managers. Depending on the size and structure of the particular store, the Assistant Manager may oversee department managers and merchandise managers, offering suggestions regarding how to improve their departments and productivity.

Assistant Managers working in pet stores or pet merchandise stores are jacks-of-all-trades. They are expected to check to see if more cashiers are needed, if customers need help, or if problems need to be solved.

The Assistant Manager works with the store manager to make sure all health, legal, and safety rules and regulations are followed. This is especially important in stores selling pets. The individual must also regularly check to see if aisles or entrances are blocked, spills need to be cleaned, and fire exists are obstructed. The Assistant Manager works with the manager to be sure that the store and parking area are as safe as possible. If there are any incidents such as accidents, slips, falls, etc., the manager or Assistant Manager is expected to complete written reports.

The Assistant Manager works with the manager in planning and preparing work schedules and assigning store staff to specific duties. If the Assistant Manager sees something that needs to be done, he or she may reassign an employee to do it.

Customer service is the key to success in any retail store, and pet stores and pet supply stores are no exception. The Assistant Manager works with the manager and other employees to assure good customer service. When a customer isn't happy for some reason, the Assistant Manager is often called upon to help resolve the problem. As the individual has greater authority than sales staff, he or she can resolve more customer complaints.

Depending on the specific store and its structure, the Assistant Manager may work with the manager in developing and implementing advertising campaigns, writing copy, designing ads, and placing them. The Assistant Manager often also helps the store manager develop promotions and special events designed to attract customers.

The Assistant Manager will take turns with the manager and key holder closing the store after business hours. At closing time, the individual will be responsible for going over the day's receipts, reconciling cash with sales receipts, and accompanying another employee when depositing the day's receipts in the bank.

The Assistant Manager may be required to fill in personally when other employees call in sick and replacement staff can't be located. The Assistant Manager is also expected to be available to handle store emergencies.

Salaries

Earnings for Assistant Managers of pet food, supply, and merchandise stores can range between $24,000 and $48,000 or more annually. Factors affecting earnings include the specific store and its size and geographic location as well as the experience and responsibilities of the individual.

In addition to salaries, many Assistant Managers receive bonuses for meeting or exceeding sales quotas.

Employment Prospects

Employment prospects for Assistant Managers of pet food and pet supply stores are good. Stores may sell pets, supplies, food, merchandise, or a combination. Individuals may find employment at one of the well known pet supercenter chains or smaller local or regional stores or boutiques. Jobs may be located throughout the United States.

Advancement Prospects

Advancement prospects for Assistant Managers working in pet food and pet supply stores are good. The most common way individuals climb the career ladder is by being promoted to store manager. Others locate similar positions at larger pet food and pet supply stores. This generally results in increased responsibilities and earnings.

Those working in chain stores may advance their careers by being promoted to work in larger stores within the chain.

Education and Training

Educational requirements for Assistant Managers of pet food and pet supply stores vary depending on the job. Virtually every position requires a minimum of a high school diploma or its equivalent. Many positions require or prefer a college background or degree. Good majors include retailing, merchandising, business management, marketing, communications, advertising, liberal arts, or a related field.

Pet superstores and other chain pet supply stores often have their own formal executive training programs that management recruits complete. These programs train Assistant Managers in an array of areas, including store policies, management techniques, sales, merchandising, marketing, promotion, human resources, and public and community relations. Programs also familiarize recruits with specific store products and merchandise. These programs help Assistant Managers learn how to run a store more effectively and profitably.

Experience, Skills, and Personality Traits

Previous retail management experience is almost always required for Assistant Managers working in pet food and pet supply stores. This is generally obtained as individuals work their way up from sales positions to key holders to department managers.

Communication skills, both verbal and written, are essential. Strong organizational skills are critical, as is the ability to deal with details. The ability to solve problems and make quick decisions is vital.

Assistant Managers need supervisory, management, and administrative skills. They should have a professional appearance and demeanor. Honesty and dependability are vital traits for individuals in this type of position. Successful Assistant Managers are also detail-oriented and highly motivated individuals.

Assistant Managers should like working with people. An understanding of the retail industry and pet industry is imperative.

Unions and Associations

Assistant Managers of pet food and pet supply stores can join a number of professional trade associations, including the American Collegiate Retailing Association, the National Retail Federation, and the National Retail Merchants Association.

Tips for Entry

1. Get experience in retail sales. Look for a job in a pet supply store as a sales associate.
2. Positions are often advertised in the classifieds section of newspapers. Look under heading classifications such as "Assistant Manager," "Management Positions," "Store Management," "Management Opportunities," "Retail Opportunities," "Pet Store," "Pet Superstore," and under specific store names.
3. Stores may advertise openings on their Web sites, so check these often.
4. Don't be afraid to walk into a pet store and inquire about openings. You might get lucky.
5. Many chain pet stores offer management-training programs. Contact the headquarters of these stores to find out about requirements.
6. Job openings may be located on the Internet. Begin your search on some of the more popular job sites such as Monster.com.
7. Contact recruiters and executive search firms specializing in retail management positions.

SALES ASSOCIATE

CAREER PROFILE

Duties: Sell merchandise; conduct transactions; take inventory; arrange merchandise; assist customers

Alternate Title(s): Clerk; Salesperson

Salary Range: $7.25 to $10.00+ per hour

Employment Prospects: Excellent

Advancement Prospects: Good

Best Geographical Locations for Position: Positions located throughout the United States

Prerequisites:

Education or Training—Educational requirements vary; see text

Experience and Qualifications—Sales experience helpful, but not always necessary

Special Skills and Personality Traits—Sales skills; dependability; personableness; articulateness; good communication skills; ability to deal well with people; high energy

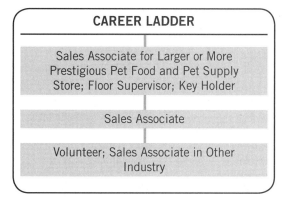

CAREER LADDER

Sales Associate for Larger or More Prestigious Pet Food and Pet Supply Store; Floor Supervisor; Key Holder

Sales Associate

Volunteer; Sales Associate in Other Industry

Position Description

The pet food and pet supply business has turned into multibillion-dollar industry. While there are pet departments at big box and department stores, there are also many stores that specialize in pet food, pet merchandise, and even pets themselves. Some are well known pet supercenter chains. Others are smaller local or regional stores. Still others are privately owned shops or niche pet boutiques.

Each of these stores need informed, knowledgeable Sales Associates. These individuals are responsible for selling food, pet-related merchandise, and supplies. In some cases, the Sales Associate will even be responsible for assisting customers in purchasing pets. Specific responsibilities of Sales Associates vary depending on the store and its management structure. Individuals working in large pet supercenters may have more specialized duties than those working in smaller, privately owned stores. Depending on the specific store, Sales Associates may work on the sales floor, at the cash register, in the stock room, directly with pets, or in a combination of these settings.

Sales Associates are expected to assist customers when they come into the store. It is essential that sales staff know as much about the merchandise in the store as possible. When customers come in, knowledgeable Sales Associates can answer questions regarding the merchandise or make suggestions regarding purchase possibilities.

There are a lot of choices for consumers in pet stores today. Whether the decision is about a pet, a pet toy, pet food, or any other pet supply, it is sometimes difficult for customers to know what the best choice is. A customer, for example, might want to know what type of dog food to buy. He or she might want to know the difference between dog food for senior pets and dog food for puppies or the differences between brands. The customer might not know how much to feed his or her new dog. Well-informed Sales Associates are an asset to the store as they can answer any questions customers might have.

Individuals must also know where merchandise is located within the store. When customers come in asking for a specific product, the Sales Associate must be able to direct them to the merchandise. He or she may also bring the customer to the merchandise and ask if the individual needs any other help.

Sales Associates are often responsible for ringing up purchases and running the cash register. While most registers today are automated, individuals still must be able to make the correct change. Sales Associates must also know how to process credit card transactions in stores where credit card services are not automated. They additionally must know the proper procedures for accepting checks as payment.

Some Sales Associates are responsible for stocking shelves and displaying merchandise. When store circulars come out or a store puts items on sale, Sales Associates may be responsible for moving sales merchandise to where it is sure to be visible. They may also be expected to handle the pricing and ticketing of merchandise.

Individuals may be expected to clean and organize shelves and keep the store neat and orderly. They may sweep the floor or clean shelves when things such as cat litter and dog food spill when bags are ripped or broken. In pet-friendly stores or in stores where pets are being sold, the Sales Associate may additionally be expected to clean up after the animals when there are accidents.

Customer service is very important in all facets of the retail industry, and pet food and supply stores are no exception. There are many retail outlets for consumers to choose from. Successful stores make every customer feel important. Sales Associates are responsible for making sure every person who comes into the store feels comfortable and valued, even if the customer is only browsing.

Sales Associates in some stores are expected to handle merchandise returns. In other stores, managers or the customer service department handles this task. Sales Associates work part time or full time. They may be scheduled to work days, nights, and/or weekends.

Salaries

Sales Associates working in pet food and pet supply stores are generally paid an hourly wage. This can range from minimum wage ($7.25) to approximately $10.00 or more per hour.

Factors affecting earnings include the geographic location and size of the specific store. Other variables include the experience and responsibilities of the individual. Some Sales Associates may be paid a commission on sales in addition to their hourly rate. Depending on the store, some individuals might also receive fringe benefits.

Employment Prospects

Employment prospects are excellent for individuals interested in becoming Sales Associates for pet food and pet supply stores. Stores may sell food, supplies, merchandise, pets, or a combination of these. Individuals may find employment at one of the well known pet supercenter chains or smaller local or regional stores or boutiques. Jobs can be found throughout the United States.

As noted previously, individuals may work part time or full time. One of the great things about this job is that individuals can often use it as a part-time job while they are still in school.

Advancement Prospects

Advancement prospects for Sales Associates working in pet food and pet supply stores are good. There are a number of methods of advancement. After obtaining some experience, individuals can find a similar position in a larger store, resulting in increased responsibilities and earnings. Sales Associates can also climb the career ladder by being promoted to floor manager, department manager, or key holder.

Education and Training

Educational requirements for Sales Associates working in pet food and pet supply stores vary depending on the specific job. Employers generally prefer someone with a minimum of a high school diploma or its equivalent. However, as noted previously, many employers also will hire individuals who are still in school. Once on the job, Sales Associates generally receive on-the-job training.

Experience, Skills, and Personality Traits

Experience requirements for individuals interested in working in a pet food or pet supply store vary. While some positions require or prefer some type of retail sales experience, there are many entry-level positions in this field.

Individuals should be customer service–oriented and like working with people. Excellent customer service skills are mandatory to success in this field. Strong communication skills are necessary as well.

Individuals should be courteous, pleasant, and upbeat. Sales ability and money-handling skills are essential. Honesty and dependability are also vital for this type of position. Any experience in the pet industry will be a plus.

Unions and Associations

Individuals working as Sales Associates in pet food and pet supply stores can get career information from a number of professional trade associations, including the American Collegiate Retailing Association, the National Retail Federation, and the Retail Merchants Association.

Tips for Entry

1. While retail experience is not always needed, it may be preferred. Include any prior retail experi-

ence on your application or résumé, even if it is not related to the pet industry.

2. Positions are often advertised in the classifieds section of newspapers. Look under headings such as "Sales Associate," "Sales Clerk," "Sales," "Retail Opportunities," "Pet Store," "Pet Superstore," or under specific store names.

3. Stores also advertise openings on their Web sites, so check these often.

4. Don't be afraid to simply walk into a pet store and inquire about openings. You might get lucky.

5. Search for jobs online. Begin your search on some of the more popular job sites such as Monster.com. Expand your search from there.

ANIMAL ATTENDANT

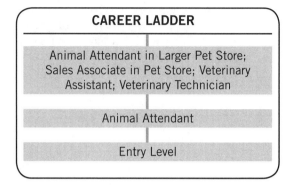

Position Description

When many people want a pet, they go to a local humane society or animal shelter and adopt one. Others buy pets from breeders. Still others go to pet stores. Pet stores sell a variety of animals, including dogs, cats, rabbits, hamsters, gerbils, reptiles, and more. Some sell fish and turtles. Some stores are well known pet supercenter chains. Others are smaller local or regional stores. Still others are privately owned shops or niche pet boutiques.

Animals in pet stores are generally kept in cages at all times. They eat, sleep, and live in their cage. Animal Attendants are responsible for cleaning the animals' cages. They must, for example, remove soiled bedding and any feces in the cages. They will also remove leftover food. Animal Attendants are expected to wash and sanitize the cages and put clean bedding in if necessary.

In stores that sell fish and amphibians, the Animal Attendant is expected to clean the aquariums. He or she must do this in a manner in which the fish are not disturbed. After removing debris, the individual might add new gravel or plants, depending on the situation.

Whether cleaning cages or aquariums, the Animal Attendant is expected to keep an eye out for any problems or health concerns with the animals. While observing the animals, he or she might also notice unusual behavior. Perhaps two puppies in the same cage are fighting. Maybe a dog is exhibiting aggressive behavior.

Does a dog look lethargic? Are there a large number of dead fish in the tanks? Is there blood in a cage? If the Animal Attendant sees any problems, he or she must report it to his or her supervisor or the store manager.

A major function of Animal Attendants at pet stores is feeding and watering the animals in the store according to the daily schedule. They prepare the food, measuring out the correct amounts, and place the food dishes in cages. Individuals are also responsible for checking that each animal has clean water throughout the day.

No one wants to buy a puppy or kitten that looks dirty and scruffy. In many stores, the Animal Attendant is responsible for grooming the animals to ensure that they look their best. They may bathe animals and brush them so they look and smell nice. They may also clip the animals' nails or do other simple grooming procedures.

Animal Attendants working in pet stores are expected to check animals for fleas, ticks, and other pests. If they see evidence of any pests, they bathe the animals in flea baths, apply flea powder, or administer medicine.

Most pet stores have a veterinarian visit on a regular basis to assure the animals are healthy and attend to any problems. The Animal Attendant might work alongside the vet at the store, assisting with any treatments. The attendant may also be responsible for administering medications or any other prescribed treatments.

Animal Attendants are responsible for taking the animals out of their cages to show to customers who are looking for potential pets. They may hold the animals themselves or may help customers hold them. If the animals have accidents, Animal Attendants are responsible for cleaning them up.

Depending on the employment situation, veterinarian assistants might be responsible for assisting in the grooming and cleaning of animals under their care. They may help wash, deflea, and comb or brush them.

Animal Attendants are sometimes responsible for taking animals out of their cages to exercise them or take them for regular walks. Individuals working in some stores may have additional duties. Depending on the specific store and its structure, Animal Attendants may also work on the sales floor, at the cash register, and in the stock room.

Salaries

Animal Attendants working in pet stores are generally paid an hourly wage. This can range from approximately $7.25 (minimum wage) to $9.50 an hour, possibly more. Factors affecting earnings include the experience, training, and responsibilities of the individual. Other factors affecting earnings include the type and size of the specific employer as well as the geographic location, size, and prestige of the store.

Employment Prospects

Employment prospects for Animal Attendants who want to work in pet stores are good. Employment opportunities exist throughout the United States in stores that just sell pets and those that also sell pet food, merchandise, and supplies.

Individuals can find employment at one of the well known pet supercenter chains or smaller local or regional stores or boutiques. Individuals may work full or part time. One of the great things about this job is that individuals can often work part time while they are still in school.

Advancement Prospects

Advancement prospects for Animal Attendants working in pet stores are fair. Some individuals find similar

work in larger stores. Others go on to become veterinary assistants, technicians, or technologists. This generally results in increased earnings and responsibilities.

Education and Training

Most employers prefer their full-time employees to have a minimum of a high school diploma or its equivalent. Individuals generally receive on-the-job training. As noted previously, however, in some situations, employers will hire individuals who are still in high school for a part-time job.

Experience, Skills, and Personality Traits

While experience requirements vary from job to job, this is generally an entry-level position. Individuals should enjoy being around animals. Attendants should be compassionate, patient, and kindhearted.

The ability to follow instructions is essential. A strong stomach is needed in order to perform certain tasks and duties. Time-management skills are also needed.

Unions and Associations

Individuals interested in a career working in pet stores can get career information by contacting the American Pet Products Association or the Pet Care Services Association.

Tips for Entry

1. Get experience working with animals by volunteering at a veterinary office, shelter, humane society, or similar institution.
2. Send your résumé and a short cover letter to pet stores to see if they have openings. Remember to ask that your résumé be kept on file if there are no current openings.
3. Check out openings online. Start with some of the more traditional job sites such as Monster. com. Expand your search from there.
4. Openings are often advertised in the classifieds section of newspapers. Look under heading such as "Animal Attendant" and "Pet Store Jobs."
5. Stores often post openings in their windows, so be on the lookout.
6. Don't be afraid to stop into a store and ask to speak to a manager about possible openings. Remember to bring your résumé and dress appropriately when you stop by.

PETS

PET SITTER

Duties: Care for people's pets when their owners aren't home; feed pets; exercise pets; interact and play with pets

Alternate Title(s): Dog Sitter; Cat Sitter

Salary Range: $20 to $100+ per day

Employment Prospects: Good

Advancement Prospects: Fair

Best Geographical Locations for Position: Positions located throughout United States

Prerequisites:

Education or Training—No formal educational requirements

Experience and Qualifications—Experience caring for dogs, cats, and other pets

Special Skills and Personality Traits—Enjoyment of being with animals; dependability; personable-

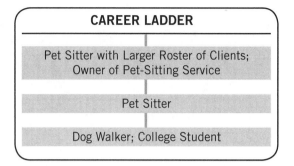

CAREER LADDER

Pet Sitter with Larger Roster of Clients; Owner of Pet-Sitting Service

Pet Sitter

Dog Walker; College Student

ness; articulateness; good communication skills; ability to deal well with people; high energy; time-management skills

Special Requirements—Voluntary certification available; business license may be needed; bonding; liability insurance; see text

Position Description

More than ever before, people consider their pets to be part of the family. Pet supplies, accessories, and food have grown into a multibillion-dollar industry. In a study conducted by the American Pet Products Association in 2009, the organization found that more than three-quarters of the people who owned dogs, cats, birds, or other small animals felt their animals were like a family member and treated them as such. As a matter of fact, those who owned dogs and cats often considered the animals to be like their children. The survey furthermore showed the importance that pets play in people's lives.

With this in mind, it is not a surprise that people are willing to pay others to care for their pets. Today's busy lifestyle means people may want to go on vacations or may need to go on business trips, yet they don't want to leave their pet without the proper care. While some people kennel their animals and others leave their pets in the care of friends or family, many require other arrangements. These people often hire Pet Sitters.

Pet Sitters care for people's animals when they are on vacation, away for business, or need to be away from home for any other reason. Pet Sitters care for pets in people's homes, or they may care for pets in their own home. This is generally up to the pet owner.

Some owners prefer that Pet Sitters care for their pets in the animal's own home. In this manner, the animal is in its own environment. It can roam around the house, receiving personal attention and interaction.

Pet Sitters who care for pets in their own home may have a special area in which the pets stay or the pet may have the run of the house. Sometimes the Pet Sitter has his or her own pet that interacts with the pet being watched. Whatever the environment, Pet Sitters are expected to care for people's pets, keeping them as happy as possible while their owner is gone.

Pet Sitters can care for any type of animal. While the most common are dogs and cats, individuals also care for ferrets, guinea pigs, rabbits, fish, or even horses.

A Pet Sitter is much like a baby-sitter who cares for children. The individual is responsible for feeding the animal, making sure it has water, and taking it outside, if necessary. A significant part of the job is interacting with the pet so that it is not lonely.

A Pet Sitter plays with pets, takes them for walks, exercises them, and on occasion lets them sleep in the bed with him or her (if that is what the owner does). If the pet is taking medication, the Pet Sitter is expected to give the animal its medication as well.

A big responsibility of Pet Sitters is handling any emergencies that may arise when the owner is away.

If the pet is injured or becomes ill, the Pet Sitter is expected to bring the animal to the vet.

Prior to taking a pet-sitting assignment, the Pet Sitter must meet with the owner and the pet. It is essential that the individual is comfortable with the pet and vice versa. The Pet Sitter must get to know the pet's routines and its likes and dislikes.

As mentioned above, the Pet Sitter must know what medications (if any) the animal is taking and when to administer them. He or she should also know the veterinarian's name, address, and phone number in case of an emergency. Many Pet Sitters obtain letters from the pet owner explaining what medical procedures can be performed on the animal in case of emergency when the owner is gone.

Depending on the situation, Pet Sitters may work full time or part time.

Salaries

Pet Sitters are compensated in a number of different ways. Some are paid by the job. Others are paid by the day (or night) they are sitting for the pet.

Daily fees range from $20 to $100 or more. Weekly fees range from $100 to $750 or more. There are a number of factors that can affect earnings for Pet Sitters. One is how the individual is being compensated. Individuals, may, for example be paid by the day (or night), by the week, or by the project. Other factors include the experience and responsibilities of the Pet Sitter. Is he or she staying in the pet owner's home with the pet? Is the Pet Sitter bringing the pet into his or her home? Sometimes, for example, Pet Sitters may go into people's homes, feed and water the pets, play with them, take them outside for a while, and then leave. In other situations, the Pet Sitter visits the home a few times during the day to care for the pet and then sleeps in the owner's home. It all depends on what the pet owner wants.

Another factor affecting earnings is the type and number of pets being cared for. Pet Sitters may charge more for caring for two large dogs than they do for a cat, for example.

Other factors affecting earnings include the number of pets the Pet Sitter cares for in a year and the geographic location of the sitter. The most successful Pet Sitters have multiple clients.

Employment Prospects

With more and more people owning pets and treating them like family, employment prospects are good for individuals interested in becoming Pet Sitters. When people today take vacations or need to travel for work, many look for alternatives to kenneling their pets.

Whether Pet Sitters stay in clients' homes to care for their pet or care for them in their own home, pet sitting is becoming more and more popular as a viable career option. Individuals may pet sit on a full-time or part-time basis. Some people also pet sit in addition to another job.

Advancement Prospects

Advancement prospects for Pet Sitters are fair. As Pet Sitters gain a reputation for being dependable, they will generally obtain a larger roster of clients. This results in increased earnings.

There are also some Pet Sitters who want to build their business by forming partnerships or hiring others to work for them. This also generally results in increased earnings.

Education and Training

There are no formal educational requirements for Pet Sitters. Classes, seminars, and workshops in pet training, animal behavior, and animal first aid will be useful. Individuals may also want to take classes in business management such as accounting, bookkeeping, and marketing.

Experience, Skills, and Personality Traits

Pet Sitters should enjoy being around animals and be comfortable with them. A general knowledge of animals as well as pet first aid is necessary.

Successful Pet Sitters are physically fit and able to handle the demands of various sizes and breeds of pets. Time-management and organization skills are essential.

Individuals should have the ability to accommodate the special and sometimes unusual needs and demands of pets and their owners. People skills are mandatory. The ability to make decisions quickly and effectively in the absence of pet owners is critical, especially in emergency situations.

Honesty and dependability are also vital for this type of position. Any experience with pets will be a plus.

Special Requirements

Pet Sitters can obtain voluntary certification from the National Association of Professional Pet Sitters (NAPPS). In order to obtain this certification, individuals must go through a course of study in pet care, nutrition, and behavior, among other subjects. Individuals must also complete courses in pet first aid.

As Pet Sitters often go into people's homes, it may be helpful for individuals to be bonded. While this is not always required, it may provide an edge over the competition. Individuals may also consider getting liability insurance.

Unions and Associations

Pet Sitters can join the NAPPS. This organization offers members professional support, educational and networking opportunities, and voluntary certification.

Tips for Entry

1. Volunteer at animal shelters. This will give you experience dealing with different types of pets with different personalities. It is also useful in making contacts.

2. Make business cards. Give them out to everyone you know. Even if the people you give cards to don't have pets, they probably have friends or colleagues who do.

3. Put up flyers and signs advertising your services on the bulletin boards of grocery stores, pet stores, and vet offices.

4. Visit veterinary offices and speak to the veterinarian and the receptionist about your services.

5. Get references from satisfied clients. People are very particular about who cares for their pet. A good set of references is essential.

6. Job opportunities can be located in the classifieds section of newspapers. Look under headings such as "Pet Sitter Wanted" or "Care for My Pets."

PET GROOMER

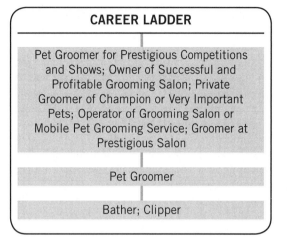

Position Description

Anyone who has ever had a haircut, a massage, a shave, a pedicure, or other similar service knows the pleasure of being pampered. It may be surprising to some that pets are often pampered in much the same way as people. Pet Groomers are the individuals who are responsible for the neat trim on the family pet, as well as the fully manicured, perfect flowing coat on the "best in show" champion. The position involves attention to the appearance of pets, as well as their hygiene. As a result of their hands-on attention to their clients' pets, the Pet Groomer is often the first to notice conditions that need further attention from veterinarians. While Pet Groomers used to be known as dog groomers, groomers now attend to cats and other small animals in addition to dogs.

The everyday responsibilities of a groomer can vary greatly, depending on the type of facility in which the individual performs his or her job. All groomers need to be skilled in handling animals comfortably and safely. At minimum, they are responsible for bathing and shampooing animals, trimming their nails, cleaning their ears, and cutting their hair, which includes styling and blow-drying.

Groomers use various tools, including trimmers, clippers, driers, and products designed to enhance the health and appearance of animals. It is common for a groomer to examine animals, both physically and visually, and to supplement the basic grooming with massage and parasite treatment, as well as special skin and fur treatments.

Groomers develop basic grooming skills while caring for their own pets or observing or working with other groomers in an employment or apprentice situation. These grooming skills are important to individuals who wish to work in pet stores, kennels, or as assistant or junior groomers in salons, where the clientele consists mostly of family pet owners. However, as Pet Groomers develop their skills and expand their clientele, they need to become more familiar with all breeds, including specialty breeds. They also must be familiar with the requirements of kennel clubs and dog shows.

While the grooming of family pets focuses on assuring the pet is clean, neat, and easy to care for, grooming for professional expos, exhibits, or competitions, or for special pets such as those that appear on television or in movies, requires a higher level of skill and knowledge. In these situations, each breed has a standard for the manner of trimming, and specific requirements such as length, style, and appearance of hair or fur.

The groomer may have additional duties when dealing with celebrity or show animals, as these animals may be in the public eye and therefore subject to stressful situations. While some individuals choose to work in kennels, pet stores, veterinary clinics, or pet salons, some individuals aspire to develop a grooming business. These individuals need to have the skills of an exceptional Pet Groomer coupled with the business skills necessary to be a successful entrepreneur.

A recent trend in grooming services are mobile pet grooming services, in which the Pet Groomer travels and performs services, either in the client's home or in a mobile unit such as a van or modified recreational vehicle equipped with necessary tools and equipment.

In addition to grooming skills, a Pet Groomer who maintains a grooming business, salon, or mobile grooming unit may be responsible for training and managing staff. The owner of a grooming business may also schedule appointments, address owner concerns and pet problems, and assure a safe, inviting, healthy, and clean environment for clients and their pets. The owner of a grooming business or an independent Pet Groomer may additionally be required to select appropriate equipment and tools, market products and services, and most important, develop a loyal clientele.

While grooming is a career, some individuals choose to also participate in grooming competitions; these groomers have the opportunity to showcase their skills and expertise while gaining professional recognition. Often there are cash prizes as well. For those who want to work in a hands-on situation caring for animals but don't want to work in a medical or health-care field, this could be a rewarding career option.

Salaries

Earnings for Pet Groomers vary greatly depending on the specific employment situation. Those who work in a pet superstore or salon earn between $10 and $20 or more per hour.

Some also earn commissions on services. Self-employed groomers or those who own a grooming business can earn from $16,000 to $80,000 or more annually, or $20 to $100 or more per service.

Employment Prospects

Employment opportunities for Pet Groomers are excellent due to the growing pet population in the United States, along with the willingness of pet owners and handlers to pay for and invest in the comfort and beauty of their pets. Job openings and business opportunities for Pet Groomers will have extensive growth over the next several years. The U.S. Bureau of Labor Statistics predicts employment in this field to grow, noting that growth and employment prospects will be best in a strong economy due to greater disposable income of pet owners.

Advancement Prospects

Advancement prospects are good for talented Pet Groomers. The potential for advancement as a groomer is directly related to increased skills. Groomers most often begin their careers as trainees or apprentices, performing limited functions such as bathing and clipping; those with more knowledge of pet health and breed standards, and a greater ability to handle animals and enhance their health and appearance, will have the opportunity to establish their own clientele or their own business, salon, or mobile grooming service. Those individuals who excel in grooming, and who choose to develop expertise in specific or rare breeds, may have the opportunity to work with champions, "best in show" animals, or celebrity animals—the most prestigious and lucrative of all grooming jobs.

Education and Training

There are no formal educational or training requirements necessary to become a Pet Groomer. Many groomers have a natural ability and acquire experience by working on their own pets. Pet stores, particularly the national pet chains and superstores, offer on-the-job training. Internships and formal and informal apprenticeships are offered by salons, independent groomers, kennels, and veterinary facilities. Additionally, there are approximately 50 state-licensed grooming schools throughout the country. National grooming associations, as well as state and local associations, offer continuing education programs, seminars, and conferences throughout the year at various locations. Skills may also be sharpened by participation in competitions and expos.

Experience, Skills, and Personality Traits

Above all, Pet Groomers must love pets. Grooming is also, however, a physically demanding (and sometimes dirty) job, and individuals choosing grooming as a career must be hardworking, careful, and patient, both with clients and their pets. Creativity, precision, a sense of style, and knowledge of specific breeds will distinguish the expert groomer from the novice. If a groomer chooses to be self-employed or open a salon, the individual needs to have business, marketing, and financial knowledge.

Special Requirements

Although there are no national certification or licensing requirements in the United States, certification as a Pet Groomer may be obtained by application and testing through many of the national grooming associations. However, it is common for pet grooming facilities and businesses to require operating licenses, which are ordinarily governed by local laws or ordinances, which must be reviewed prior to setting up any salon or shop.

Unions and Associations

Pet Groomers can join a number of professional associations, including the National Dog Groomer Association of America, the National Association of Professional Creative Groomers, International Professional Groomers, the Professional Cat Groomers Association of America, the International Society of Canine Cosmetologists, and various state and local associations.

The national organizations provide opportunities for certification, and all of the associations offer opportunities for education and training, professional support, and networking.

Tips for Entry

1. Job opportunities may be advertised in the classifieds section of newspapers. Look under headings such as "Groomer," "Pet Groomer," "Dog Groomer," etc.
2. Don't forget to look online for job opportunities. Start with some of the more popular career sites such as Monster.com. Expand your search from there.
3. Gain experience and skills by offering to apprentice or intern at local veterinary facilities, kennels, or salons.
4. Acquire clients by offering a free trial service to friends, or donate a grooming session to a local charity to get your name out into the community.
5. Design business cards and flyers or brochures featuring photos of one or more pets that you groomed. Distribute them at dog shows and competitions, pet stores (if permitted), veterinary offices, grocery stores, and coffee shops.

DOG TRAINER

Duties: Train dogs to eliminate problematic behavior; teach dogs to obey commands; help housebreak dogs; train dogs for agility; train dogs for hunting; train therapy dogs for therapy

Alternate Title(s): Trainer; Obedience Instructor; Dog Handler

Salary Range: $12,000 to $150,000+

Employment Prospects: Good

Advancement Prospects: Good

Best Geographical Locations for Position: Positions located throughout the United States; highest concentration in densely populated and affluent areas

Prerequisites:

    Education or Training—No formal education required; apprenticeships, workshops, seminars, etc. helpful; see text

    Experience and Qualifications—Experience handling and training dogs

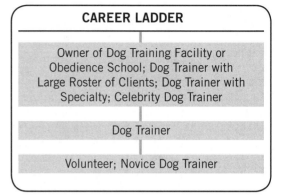

CAREER LADDER

Owner of Dog Training Facility or Obedience School; Dog Trainer with Large Roster of Clients; Dog Trainer with Specialty; Celebrity Dog Trainer

Dog Trainer

Volunteer; Novice Dog Trainer

Special Skills and Personality Traits—Enjoyment of dogs; teaching skills; communication skills; physical ability to handle dogs of all sizes and temperaments; leadership; patience; creativity

Special Requirements—Licensing or certification may be required; see text

Position Description

Dog Trainers are for dogs like schoolteachers are for children. They shape dogs' lives. Some Dog Trainers train dogs starting from puppyhood, including housebreaking and basic skills. Others train older dogs to learn a variety of skills and behaviors.

A Dog Trainer's work with puppies introduces them to appropriate behavior, standard commands such as come, sit, down, and stay, and simple tricks such as fetch and paw waving. As the dog becomes older and can learn new skills and tricks, there is no limit to training possibilities. By teaching simple skills such as retrieving a ball or stick, or more complicated ones such as catching a Frisbee, drinking water from a faucet, or opening a refrigerator, the Dog Trainer assists both the dog and the owner in accomplishing new feats. The Dog Trainer's ability to teach a command, and the dog's ability to learn, keep a family dog safe and happy. For example, a stern "down" command can stop a dog in its tracks, keeping it from running into the street and into harm's way.

Dog Trainers use a plethora of training methods. There are Dog Trainers who still rely on negative reinforcement methods, including choke collars or prong collars. More and more, however, these methods are frowned upon, particularly in the training of family pets, due to the possibility that the dog will become aggressive or unhappy. Currently, the most popular and possibly the most effective methods focus on positive training of both the dog and the owner or handler. This is because only with the cooperation and reinforcement of both the dog and the owner/handler will skills be learned for the lifetime of the animal.

According to some trainers, dogs care most about two things: praise and food. These are the most common means Dog Trainers use to reinforce positive behavior. Some trainers also used clicker training as a positive reinforcement training method. Clicker training is a method of conditioning that uses a clicker that makes an immediate clicking sound when squeezed. The clicker is associated with a positive behavior by the dog, and followed with a treat.

Dog Trainers who work with individuals and their companion pets often work independently and are self-employed, providing private individual sessions, or holding classes for a large group of dogs and their owners. Additionally, there are opportunities to work in shelters, with veterinarians, or in community-based programs, where well-behaved dogs add to the safety and well-being of the community as a whole.

While a majority of Dog Trainers work with family pets, there are many more opportunities and challenges for individuals who want to choose a career in training. Specific breeds, such as hounds, spaniels, pointers, and retrievers, for example, are suited for training as hunting or bird dogs. This special training done by Dog Trainers introduces dogs to water, birds, deer, the sound of gunshots, and the concept of retrieving, all while focusing on the bond between owner and dog. While it is well known that only certain dogs make good hunting dogs, only great training makes great hunting dogs. Likewise, sheepdogs, shepherds, cattle dogs, and collies, which are instinctively suited for herding, may be trained by Dog Trainers to work on farms and ranches across the country.

Dog Trainers may also train dogs to participate in agility competitions. Agility training involves specific obedience commands and focuses on training a dog to navigate various courses and equipment, using skills such as jumping, zigzagging, and about-face turns. The challenges of agility training often require the Dog Trainer to go far beyond basic commands, although the trainer uses the same techniques. Agility training can be rewarding because trainers often see their work pay off not only in happier, more energetic dogs, but also in awards, ribbons, and cash prizes from local and national agility competitions.

The job of a Dog Trainer is not always glamorous. Dogs come with all different personalities, and an individual must be willing to work with difficult (and sometimes dangerous) dogs as well as the timid, docile, or easy to train. In addition to obedience training, Dog Trainers are often called upon to try to modify a dog's aggressive or destructive behavior or bad habits, or to assist in helping the dog get used to a new baby or a new situation. Sometimes the Dog Trainer must train the dogs, but sometimes it is more necessary to change the dog's surroundings or train the dog's owner.

There is also an opportunity to work as a Dog Trainer for dogs with star quality. Dogs (and other animals) have always been regulars in commercials, television shows, and movies. The dogs you recall as household names, such as Lassie, Eddie from *Frasier,* Hooch in *Turner and Hooch,* and Toto from the *Wizard of Oz,* all had Dog Trainers. This career path may be best for an individual who can commit to just a few clients, as each canine client may require a substantial amount of ongoing and on-the-job training. While employment as a Dog Trainer for dog actors or celebrities may not come along every day, when an individual can obtain such a job, he or she will be paid well.

Despite public opinion that Dog Trainers' primary job is to teach dogs new tricks, the job of a Dog Trainer is not all fun and games. Many Dog Trainers perform very serious and important work for the well-being of society. While most people think of dogs as companions and family pets, there are many working dogs that have careers of their own. Dog Trainers are responsible for the rigorous protocols required of police dogs, search and rescue dogs, cadaver dogs, drug detection dogs, and bomb-sniffing dogs. An individual who performs this type of training may be responsible not only for the training of the dogs, but also for selecting those few dogs that may succeed and excel in this type of work. The trainer is also responsible for follow-up training to keep the skills of the dogs, and their handlers, as sharp as possible.

One of the most rewarding jobs, and perhaps one of the most important functions that a Dog Trainer may undertake, may well be his or her part in bringing a dog to an individual who needs assistance. The training of therapy dogs, guide dogs for the blind, and service dogs for the disabled is complicated and possibly the most time-consuming of all training. Such training requires far more than just obedience work. As with other working dogs, the Dog Trainer may be responsible for evaluating and selecting appropriate animals to participate as assistance dogs, choosing only those animals that are highly intelligent and willing to work. In training guide dogs for the blind and service dogs for the disabled, the Dog Trainer must be willing to work even more closely with both the dog and the person in need. After all, the dog is only one half of the team necessary for successful training.

As evidenced by the numerous different paths that an individual may choose, a career as a Dog Trainer can be interesting, exciting, rewarding, and lucrative.

Salaries

Salaries for Dog Trainers vary greatly depending on their specific employment situation. An individual providing private sessions or classes, or running a dog obedience school, can earn between $12,000 and $65,000 or more annually, depending upon the number of dogs trained and clients served.

Hourly fees for training often depend on the geographical location, skill, and professional reputation of the Dog Trainer as well as the needs of the client. These fees may range from $12.00 to $100.00 or more per hour.

Guide dog training and training for narcotics detection, bomb sniffing, or police dog work is ordinarily salaried, with annual earnings ranging from between $35,000 to $85,000 or more depending upon the specific employer (usually in the public or non-profit sector). Dog Trainers for celebrity and performing dogs have the greatest potential for earnings, with salaries of $150,000 or more.

Employment Prospects

Employment prospects for Dog Trainers are good. Career opportunities for Dog Trainers at dog obedience schools are anticipated to increase as a result of the growing dog population along with the willingness of pet owners and handlers to pay others to train their dogs.

Job openings and business opportunities for Dog Trainers will likewise have extensive growth, with an abundance of employment opportunities over the next several years. The U.S. Bureau of Labor Statistics predicts employment in this field to grow due to greater disposable income of pet owners. Individuals may find employment throughout the country.

Advancement Prospects

Advancement prospects for Dog Trainers are good. Advancement depends to a great extent on the individual's skills and professional reputation. Dog Trainers who wish to advance their careers have the opportunity to increase their client base or open dog obedience facilities. Individuals may also advance their career by choosing to do specialized training, such as the training of service dogs, law enforcement dogs, or celebrity dogs; these trainers usually require further training and experience to establish their expertise.

Education and Training:

There are no formal educational or training requirements to be a general Dog Trainer. Individuals can complete internships and apprenticeships with experienced trainers. They may also attend workshops, seminars, and classes in various areas of training and dog behavior. Guide dog trainers may require specific education and testing to obtain certification or licensing in certain states. While rigorous training requirements must be met in order to train guide dogs and service dogs, this training is ordinarily specific to the organization that provides and trains service dogs. Likewise, Dog Trainers that wish to specialize in training dogs for police or law enforcement work require education and training in law enforcement or criminal justice in addition to general dog training experience.

Experience, Skills, and Personality Traits:

The most important trait for a Dog Trainer is a love for dogs. Dog Trainers need to be patient individuals with a gift for teaching both dogs and their owners.

Dog Trainers must have dog-handling experience, an ability to communicate effectively with both dogs and their owners, and knowledge of specific training methods and techniques. Individuals who wish to train guide dogs, therapy dogs, and other service dogs should have knowledge of and experience with the specific disability or needs of the owner or future owner of the dog being trained. Dog Trainers training dogs for bomb sniffing, detection of drugs or other contraband, or similar functions will benefit from experience in law enforcement.

All Dog Trainers must be physically fit, regardless of their specialty.

Special Requirements

Depending on the specific job, certification or licensure may be required or preferred. Dog Trainer certification is offered by many national organizations, including the Certification Council for Professional Dog Trainers.

Individuals may obtain certification as a Certified Pet Dog Trainer or Certified Professional Dog Trainer through private institutions or the Certification Council for Professional Dog Trainers. Certification for guide dog trainers may require specific education and testing. In certain states, individuals in this line of work may need to be licensed.

Most localities require obedience schools and similar businesses to be licensed.

Unions and Associations

Dog Trainers can join a number of professional associations, including the American Dog Trainers Network, Association of Pet Dog Trainers, National Association of Dog Obedience Instructors, National K-9 Dog Trainers Association, International Positive Dog Training Association, and various state and local associations. The national organizations provide opportunities for certification, and all of the associations offer opportunities for education and training, professional support, and networking.

Tips for Entry

1. Search for job opportunities in the classifieds section of newspapers. Look under headings such as "Dog Trainer" and "Trainer."

2. Get dog-training experience by volunteering to do basic training at shelters in your area. It's a great way to hone skills and make contacts.

3. Contact a local obedience school to find out if there are apprenticeship or intern opportunities.

4. Start developing a clientele by donating a free training session to a local charity event. This will help get your name and service out to the community.

5. Design and print business cards and flyers or brochures. Distribute them to pet stores, grocery stores, and coffee shops.

6. If you are interested in training service dogs, find out about volunteer opportunities at an agency that trains and offers service dogs. This will help you hone skills and make contacts.

DOGGIE DAY CARE WORKER

CAREER PROFILE

Duties: Interact with dogs; play with dogs; exercise dogs; feed and give water to dogs; monitor dogs; clean up after dogs

Alternate Title: Doggie Daycare Attendant

Salary Range: $8.50 to $16.00+ an hour

Employment Prospects: Good

Advancement Prospects: Fair

Best Geographical Locations for Position: Positions located throughout the United States

Prerequisites:

Education or Training—Educational requirements vary; some facilities require or prefer training in animal behavior, canine first aid, and animal CPR; see text

Experience and Qualifications—Experience caring for dogs

Special Skills and Personality Traits—Enjoyment of dogs; dependability; high energy; personableness; communication skills; strong stomach; physical fitness

Special Requirements—Certification in dog CPR

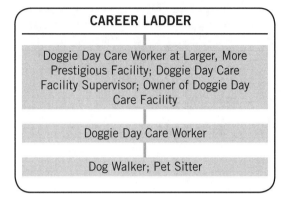

CAREER LADDER

Doggie Day Care Worker at Larger, More Prestigious Facility; Doggie Day Care Facility Supervisor; Owner of Doggie Day Care Facility

Doggie Day Care Worker

Dog Walker; Pet Sitter

Position Description

For many people, pets are part of the family. As a matter of fact, those who own dogs and cats often considered their animals to be like their children. While cats generally care for themselves during the day, dogs often get bored or lonely when left alone. Some have separation anxiety. Others exhibit destructive behavior such as chewing, digging, or barking. Pet owners who work cannot stay home to keep their dogs company.

Many dog owners solve this challenge by bringing their dog to doggie day care. Doggie day care facilities are much like day care facilities for children. Just as the quality of day care for children varies, so does the quality of services and amenities of doggie day care facilities.

Some facilities are simply pet-sitting services that supervise dogs during the day, providing food, water, shelter, and walks. Others may offer a variety of services and activities, such as doggie group play, interactive activities, dog training, socialization with other animals, and dog walking. Some doggie day care facilities also offer spa treatments, boutiques, salons, and veterinary services.

Doggie day care facilities may have separate rooms for playing, exercising, eating, and sleeping. Some are simple, and others are more elaborate with lots of toys, personalized couches for the dogs to stretch out on, and more.

Good doggie day care facilities are dedicated to providing fun-filled days with activities designed to stimulate dogs' minds and exercise their bodies along with time and space for dogs to sleep and rest comfortably. What often sets one facility apart from another, however, are the Doggie Day Care Workers.

These individuals are charged with the responsibility of keeping the dogs in their care happy, safe, and active. While doggie day care facilities may have different structures, Doggie Day Care Workers are generally expected to give personalized attention to each animal. Individuals may be responsible for things such as supervising dog play groups, playing with dogs one-on-one, cleaning up pet messes, feeding dogs meals and snacks, and making sure dogs have clean water. If animals require medication or special food, Doggie Day Care Workers must accommodate them.

Some Doggie Day Care Workers take dogs out for walks. Others exercise dogs by playing with them, throwing balls, or doing other activities. Doggie Day Care Workers in some facilities are responsible for bathing dogs or trimming their nails. Others are responsible for handling customer service in the doggie day care facility.

In doggie day care facilities with no receptionist, Doggie Day Care Workers are expected to greet pet owners and their dogs and bring dogs to a specific play or rest area. Some Doggie Day Care Workers are additionally responsible for taking payment for services or answering phones. Others give tours of the facility and its amenities to prospective clients.

Doggie Day Care Workers are generally responsible for a specific number of dogs at the center. This may range from five to 10 depending on the structure of the specific facility. Doggie Day Care Workers may throw Frisbees or balls and play with dogs. They may also help dogs interact with other dogs.

Doggie Day Care Workers must make sure all dogs are safe. Individuals must monitor dogs and keep an eye out for any situations where animals are playing too roughly with each other. They may need to break up dogfights if necessary. Individuals are expected to find ways to stimulate dogs to keep them occupied, interact with them, and play both one-on-one and in groups.

At times, the Doggie Day Care Worker may bring dogs to comfortable areas where they can nap and have quiet time. When a dog owner comes to pick up his or her pet, the Doggie Day Care Worker is expected to go get the dog and bring it to its owner.

Doggie Day Care Workers are responsible for making sure dogs aren't showing any signs of illness. If they suspect that a dog has a medical problem, they are expected to report it to the supervisor of the facility immediately.

One of the perks of a job in doggie day care is that individuals often get to bring their own dogs to work. For those who enjoy being around dogs, this type of job is an interesting and satisfying alternative to working in an office.

Salaries

Doggie Day Care Workers are generally paid an hourly wage ranging from $8.50 to $16.00 or more. Variables include the size, structure, and prestige of the facility as well as its geographic location. Other factors affecting earnings include the specific training and responsibilities of the individual.

Employment Prospects

Employment prospects for Doggie Day Care Workers are good. Individuals may find both full- and part-time employment in doggie day care facilities throughout the United States. More doggie day care facilities are opening up every day to meet the needs of dog owners who don't want their pets to be home alone all day.

Advancement Prospects

Advancement prospects for Doggie Day Care Workers are fair. Some individuals climb the career ladder by finding similar positions at larger, more prestigious doggie day care facilities. This generally results in increased responsibilities and earnings. Others become facility supervisors. Still others decide to open their own facility.

Education and Training

While there are no formal educational requirements for Doggie Day Care Workers, most employers prefer that their employees have a minimum of a high school diploma or the equivalent. Some also require their workers to be trained in animal behavior, canine first aid, and animal CPR.

Experience, Skills, and Personality Traits

Experience requirements vary from job to job. Most facilities want their Doggie Day Care Workers to have at least some sort of experience working with animals. Working or volunteering in a veterinary office or shelter is a good way to gain experience.

Doggie Day Care Workers should be physically fit and able to handle the demands of various sizes and breeds of dogs. A love of dogs is essential. Knowledge of dog behavior is necessary as well. The ability to be a "pack leader" is vital. The Doggie Day Care Worker might need to deal with stressed or untrained dogs. Individuals must have a strong stomach and not mind cleaning up after dogs.

Individuals should have the ability to accommodate the special and sometimes unusual needs and demands of pets and their owners. People skills are mandatory. Dependability is vital. Individuals who have special skills, such as training or grooming skills, will be especially in demand.

Special Requirements

Doggie Day Care Workers may need to be certified in animal CPR.

Unions and Associations

Doggie Day Care Workers can obtain additional career information by contacting the North American Dog Daycare Association.

Tips for Entry

1. Volunteer at animal shelters. This will give you experience dealing with different types of animals with different personalities.

2. Jobs may be located in the classifieds section of newspapers. Look under heading classifications such as "Doggie Day Care," "Doggie Day Care Worker," and "Pet Jobs."

3. Other job openings may be located online. Start with some of the more common career job sites like Monster.com and Simplyhired.com. Expand your search from there.

4. Doggie day care facilities sometimes advertise openings on their Web sites, so check these often.

5. Visit doggie day care facilities and ask to fill out an employment application.

DOG WALKER

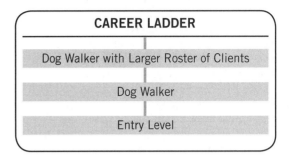

Position Description

There are over 44 million people in the United States who have at least one dog. Some have more than one. Many of these people work long hours. Some also commute a significant distance to work. These people have a difficult time walking their dogs regularly.

Other dog owners are unable to walk their dogs for a variety of reasons. Some are elderly, ill, or incapacitated in some manner. Some dog owners want their pet to get more exercise but don't have enough room in their house or yard.

Dog Walkers help dog owners solve these problems. Dog Walkers go to people's homes, pick up their dogs, and take them for walks. Sometimes the Dog Walker walks a dog once a day. Other times, the Dog Walker may take a dog for a walk twice or more daily. It all depends on the needs of the owner.

Prior to taking a dog walking assignment, the Dog Walker must meet with the owner and the dog. It is essential that the individual is comfortable with the pet and vice versa. The Dog Walker should get to know the pet's routines, personality, and preferences. Does the dog get along with other dogs? Does it go after other dogs or cats? Has the dog been trained to walk on a leash? These are all questions that need to be answered before a Dog Walker accepts a job.

The Dog Walker should also know if the dog has any allergies, what medications (if any) the dog is taking, and if any medications need to be administered. The Dog Walker should know the dog's veterinarian's name, address, and phone number in case of an emergency.

The Dog Walker talks to the dog owner and determines what services he or she is looking for. How long does the owner want the walk to be? How frequently does the owner want the dog to be walked? Are there specific times the owner wants the dog walked? These questions must be answered for the Dog Walker to do the job properly.

The Dog Walker must also establish if the owner wants his or her dog to be walked alone or whether it can be walked with other dogs. It is not an uncommon sight in cities, for example, to see a Dog Walker walking five or more dogs at a time.

In some situations, the Dog Walker will take a dog for a regular walk on a leash and then bring it to a "safe" area where the dog can be let off the leash and run around. This, of course, must be established beforehand with the dog owner.

Most dogs look forward to walks. They need to go out to relieve themselves and get exercise. The human contact and attention also helps make them happier and healthier.

It is essential that the Dog Walker get documentation assuring that the dogs in their care have the proper inoculations. That way, if a dog bites someone, the Dog Walker can give immediate assurance that the dog has been vaccinated. While the dog owner must be notified of such incidents immediately anyway, knowing that the dog has been vaccinated can keep a bad situation from getting worse.

Once the Dog Walker has completed the walk, he or she will return the dog to its home. If the owner is not home, the Dog Walker will make sure the dog has water and perhaps a treat or two before leaving.

Dog Walkers must handle any emergencies that may arise when walking the dog. If the dog bites a person or another dog, the Dog Walker must be sure to get all the pertinent information such as names, addresses, and phone numbers of all parties involved. He or she must also give the name and contact information of the dog's owner as well as the animal's vaccination status.

Dog Walkers may have to deal with dogs that pull, slip their collar, or get loose somehow. A dog may get injured, become sick, or run away. Dealing with emergencies and the unexpected is all part of the job. In order to deal effectively with any problems, the Dog Walker generally gets the owner's contact information and calls him or her immediately if there is an issue. Some Dog Walkers obtain written letters from the dog owner explaining what emergency medical procedures can be performed on the animal in case of emergency when the owner is not available.

Some Dog Walkers specialize in walking large dogs. Others specialize in walking small dogs. Some walk all types of dogs. It all depends on the Dog Walker and what he or she is comfortable with.

Dog Walkers must work in all types of weather conditions. Whether it is hot or cold, sunny or rainy, snowing or icy, dogs still need to be walked. One of the good things about dog walking is that individuals can work as much as they want. Those who want to use dog walking to augment other income can do so. Those who want to expand their dog walking into a bigger business can do that as well. There are Dog Walkers who are students and others who use dog walking as their primary source of income.

Some clients need a Dog Walker only during the week, when they are away from home for extended periods of time. Other clients want their Dog Walker to work on weekends. Successful Dog Walkers are flexible with clients who may have sudden changes in their busy lifestyles. It is vital for Dog Walkers, however, to know what they can physically do and not do so they don't make promises that they can't easily keep.

Dog Walkers generally develop a very good rapport with the dogs they walk. Most are very gratified to see wagging tails when they walk in the door. They feel the unconditional love of dogs in their care and are happy to be paid to do something they enjoy. This is a good job for active people who like to be around dogs and enjoy being outside.

Salaries

Earnings for Dog Walkers vary depending on their location, the way they are compensated, their responsibilities, experience, and professional reputation. Earnings also depend on how many dogs they are walking and how many clients they have.

Dog Walkers may be compensated in a number of different ways. Some are paid an hourly fee. Depending on the geographic area, this may range from approximately $10 to $30 or more per hour. Those walking dogs in larger cities will generally earn more than their counterparts in the suburbs.

Some Dog Walkers are paid daily or by the job. Dog Walkers, may, for example, be paid $200 to $350 or more per week to walk a dog a few times a day.

Many Dog Walkers find it difficult to set fees, worrying that they are either not charging enough or are charging too much. It is essential that individuals know their worth. There is a delicate line between charging enough so an individual is being paid fairly for his or her time and overcharging. When setting fees, the Dog Walker must take a number of factors into account. These include the amount of time he or she will spend walking dogs for a client, the number of dogs a client wants the individual to walk, and any additional duties for which the Dog Walker may be responsible.

Employment Prospects

Employment prospects for Dog Walkers are good. Opportunities exist throughout the United States and can be located in cities, the suburbs, or rural areas. Individuals can work as a Dog Walker on a part-time or full-time basis.

Advancement Prospects

Advancement prospects for Dog Walkers are fair, although advancement prospects depend to a great extent on an individual's career aspirations. Some individuals climb the career ladder in this area by obtaining a larger roster of clients. This will increase the individual's earnings. Others branch out and become pet sitters or start doggie day care businesses. Still others add services such as dog sitting or dog grooming to their repertoire. There are also some Dog Walkers who build their business by forming partnerships or hiring others to work for them.

Some people become Dog Walkers while waiting for other types of job opportunities to materialize or to augment other income.

Education and Training

There are no formal educational requirements for Dog Walkers. Classes, seminars, and workshops in pet training, animal behavior, and animal first aid will be useful.

Experience, Skills, and Personality Traits

Dog Walkers should enjoy being around dogs. Knowledge of animal first aid is necessary in case a dog is injured.

Dog Walkers should be physically fit individuals who enjoy walking. They must be physically able to hold onto strong dogs that may pull when they see other dogs, people, or things that they want to get to. Time-management and organization skills are essential.

Individuals should have the ability to accommodate the special and sometimes unusual needs and demands of pets and their owners. People skills are mandatory.

Honesty and dependability are also vital for this type of position. Any experience with pets is a plus.

Special Requirements

Dog Walkers can obtain voluntary certification from the Professional Dog Walkers Association International (PDWAI). In order to obtain this certification, individuals must complete a course in animal first aid as well as a dog training class taught by a reputable trainer.

As Dog Walkers often go into people's homes to pick up dogs, it may be helpful for individuals to be bonded. While this is not always required, it may give one individual an edge over another. Individuals might also consider getting liability insurance.

Unions and Associations

Dog Walkers can join the National Association of Dog Walkers. This organization brings together small business owners and entrepreneurs who walk dogs, offering professional support, education, and information. Individuals may also be members of the PDWAI. This organization offers a voluntary certification for Dog Walkers.

Tips for Entry

1. Volunteer at animal shelters. This will give you experience dealing with different types of pets with different personalities. It is also useful in making contacts.

2. Get professional-looking business cards made. Give them to everyone you know. Even if the people you give cards to don't have pets, they probably have friends or colleagues who do.

3. Put up flyers and signs on the bulletin boards of groceries, pet stores, and vet offices.

4. Visit veterinary offices and speak to the veterinarian and the receptionist about your services.

5. Get references from satisfied clients. People are very particular about who they allow to care for their pet. A solid set of references is essential.

6. Job opportunities may be located in the classifieds section of newspapers. Look under headings such as "Dog Walker Wanted" or "Pets."

7. Job possibilities might also be located on the Internet. Start with some of the more popular career sites such as Monster.com, Simplyhired.com, and Indeed.com. Expand your search from there.

8. Consider advertising your services in a local newspaper or publication. You might also consider setting up your own Web site. Make sure your URL is simple so your site is easy to find.

HORSES

JOCKEY

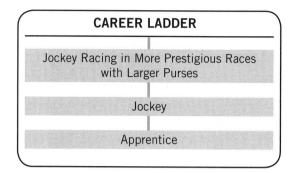

Position Description

Thoroughbreds are a specific breed of horse. In Thoroughbred racing, a Jockey rides the saddled horse. Thoroughbred racing may also be called flat horse racing.

Some of the more popular Thoroughbred races held annually include the Kentucky Derby at Churchill Downs in Lexington, Kentucky, the Belmont Stakes at Belmont Park in Elmont, New York, the Preakness Stakes at Pimlico Race Course in Baltimore, Maryland, and the Travers Stakes at Saratoga Race Course in Saratoga Springs, New York. Some tracks hold racing year-round. Others only have racing dates during specific times of the year.

The main function of Jockeys is to ride horses in competitions at racetracks. These individuals are often crucial to the success of a horse in a race. Jockeys sit on a horse's back when racing. It is therefore imperative for a Jockey to keep his body weight down. Generally, the lighter they are, the better. The average body weight of Jockeys is around 100 pounds. Individuals are usually small in stature.

Most Jockeys begin their careers working in horse stables learning how to care for horses. Individuals must know how to feed them, clean them, and get them ready for exercising. Aspiring Jockeys help trainers exercise and train horses on a daily basis. Once they are 18 years old, they can apply for an apprentice license.

Jockeys prepare their horses for races. They may work with the trainer to try to improve the horse's strengths and alleviate its weaknesses. In some cases, the Jockey is also the trainer.

Jockeys frequently travel in the course of their job. Many tracks are seasonal. Individuals may work at one track for a couple of months and then move on. They may also travel between tracks when a horse is being raced at a number of tracks during a season.

Jockeys must be strong enough to control the horse during a race. They must know how to guide and motivate the horse into a winning position. In order to be successful, the Jockey must know the specific horse well enough to know its strengths, weaknesses, and abilities. By knowing this, he or she can develop a strategy to race the horse effectively. The Jockey must know if the specific horse is a slow starter, quick starter, or quick finisher, among other things. This knowledge and understanding generally comes from the Jockey working with the horse extensively. The individual often helps with the training and general conditioning of the horse.

This job may often be stressful. If the horse does not win, the Jockey is often blamed for the loss. To stay successful in the industry, the Jockey must constantly produce winners.

Jockeys must also always be mindful of potential injuries. Working with animals can be unpredictable. Jockeys are often bitten, kicked, thrown off horses, and trampled. For individuals who love horses and the exciting life of racing, however, none of these drawbacks matter.

Depending on the situation, Jockeys are responsible either to the horse owner or trainer.

Salaries

Earnings can vary tremendously for Jockeys. There are some individuals who earn as little as $23,000 annually; others earn $2,000,000 or more. Factors affecting earnings include the Jockey's experience level and skills as well the number and type of races in which he or she rides. Other factors affecting earnings include the number of winners he or she has. Earnings are also dependent on the type of financial arrangement the Jockey has made with the horse owner or trainer.

Jockeys are paid a small amount for each race. This mount fee is generally somewhere between $25 and $100 or more. Jockeys also earn a percentage of the winning purse. Although percentages vary, an average is usually 10 percent of the purse or prize money if the horse comes in first. Percentages for second, third, fourth, and fifth vary.

For Jockeys riding in races with major purses, such as the Kentucky Derby, earnings can be quite high. Some Jockeys who ride in these types of races earn six-figure incomes. In 2008, Jockey John Velazquez earned over $2.1 million with his share of purses. Most individuals, however, have more modest earnings.

Jockeys may ride for more than one trainer or owner. What this means is that they may sometimes be riding in more than one race during the day at a track, increasing their earnings dramatically.

Employment Prospects

Employment prospects for skilled Jockeys are good. Horse owners usually do the hiring. Jockeys may be under contract with owners or may ride on a freelance basis.

Jockeys who have proven themselves in a number of races will have no problem finding work. Thoroughbred racetracks are located throughout the country. It should be noted, however, that many tracks located in colder climates are seasonal.

Jockeys may work full time or part time depending on the specific situation.

Advancement Prospects

Advancement prospects for Jockeys are fair: They are to a great extent, based on performance. Dedicated individuals who are willing to learn their craft have a good chance of climbing the career ladder.

Jockeys who consistently do well in races advance their career by being sought out to ride either more prestigious horses or in more prestigious races with larger purses. Some Jockeys advance their career by contracting a greater number of horses to ride.

Education and Training

While there are no formal educational requirements for Jockeys, individuals do need to have a complete knowledge of horses and experience working with them. Individuals must be licensed in order to be Jockeys. To obtain a license, Jockeys must first complete an apprenticeship program. Depending on the locations, these programs may be administered by the state or by organizations.

Experience, Skills, and Personality Traits

As noted, Jockeys get experience and training through an apprenticeship. Most Jockeys are small and light. They must know how to ride horses expertly and are skilled in every facet of horsemanship.

Individuals must have a feel for the way horses think, act, and behave. In order to be successful in this job, Jockeys need to love horses. Horses are very sensitive animals and can instinctively tell if a Jockey is comfortable doing his or her job.

Jockeys need to be confident and have quick reflexes. They must be dependable, honest, and trustworthy. Individuals must be able to work under pressure. They must additionally have the ability to accept criticism and advice without taking it personally. In many cases, when a horse does not win, the Jockey must take the blame.

Special Requirements

As noted previously, Jockeys need to be licensed. Licensing may be administered by the state or specific organizations, depending on the state. In order to apply for an apprentice license, individuals need to be at least 18 years old. They may obtain a freelance apprentice certificate or a contract apprentice license. The freelance apprentice certificate means that the individual can ride for any trainer at any stable. A contract apprentice license means that the Jockey can only ride for one specific stable.

While an apprentice, the individual rides in races and gains experience. After winning a number of races, the individual becomes a full-fledged Jockey and receives his or her journeyman's license.

Unions and Associations

Jockeys may belong to the Jockey's Guild and the Jockey's Club as well as a number of other local, state, and national organizations that bring members of this profession together. These groups provide professional support and career guidance to members.

Tips for Entry

1. Get a job working at either a racetrack or a local stable. This will give you hands-on experience and help you make important contacts in the field.

2. Visit the library and get some books on horse racing. The more you know about the industry, the better chance you will have to become successful.

3. Look for one or more trainers or Jockeys to talk to about your career aspirations. They are usually glad to offer advice and help.

4. Go to a racetrack and watch the races. Get a feel for what Jockeys do and how they handle the horses.

HARNESS HORSE RACE DRIVER

CAREER PROFILE

Duties: Race horses in harness races; train horses to race

Alternate Title(s): Driver; Harness Driver; Catch Driver; Harness Race Driver

Salary Range: $23,000 to $1,500,000+

Employment Prospects: Fair

Advancement Prospects: Fair

Best Geographical Locations for Position: Positions located throughout the United States in areas hosting harness racetracks

Prerequisites:

Education or Training—No formal educational requirement; training in working with horses and driving sulky; see text

Experience and Qualifications—Experience as a groom or trainer's assistant

Special Skills and Personality Traits—Knowledge of horse care and training; ability to drive sulkies; love of working with horses; self-confidence; quick reflexes

Special Requirements—State licensing required; additional licenses may be needed; see text

CAREER LADDER

Harness Horse Race Driver in More Prestigious Races with Larger Purses

Harness Horse Race Driver

Harness Horse Race Driver Apprentice; Harness Horse Race Driver/Trainer Apprentice

Position Description

In harness racing, instead of riding the horse, the driver follows behind the horse in a cart called a sulky. The sulky is attached to the horse via a harness.

Skilled individuals known as Harness Horse Race Drivers guide the sulkies. Individuals may also be known as harness drivers, harness race drivers, or harness driver/trainers. Drivers race and train the horses.

Horses in harness racing are called Standardbreds. The two basic types of Standardbreds are pacers and trotters. There are two kinds of harness races: one for trotters and another for pacers. Drivers may work in either type of race.

Most Harness Horse Race Drivers begin their career working at jobs in racetrack stables. They may become grooms and help trainers work with the horses, feeding, brushing, cleaning, and exercising them. After gaining some experience working with horses, aspiring Harness Horse Race Drivers can apply for a license. The first license many Harness Horse Race Drivers earn is called a matinee license. This license is valid only for matinee meets that do not involve wagering or purses.

The next license individuals may apply for is called a qualifying license. These types of licenses are used for extended pari-mutuel (a race in which those who bet on the competitors finishing in the first three places share the total amount bet minus a percentage for the management) meets. In order to obtain this license, Harness Horse Race Drivers are required to take a written exam and a practical test demonstrating their ability to drive. Individuals must demonstrate to those giving the test that they are safe, talented drivers. Individuals must also provide references before they are issued a license.

Drivers will hold their qualifying license for six months and must participate in at least 12 satisfactory drives with a licensed pari-mutuel judge watching. They must then obtain the approval of both the judge and local district track committee in their area.

After these requirements are met, Harness Horse Race Drivers obtain their provisional license. At this point, drivers are like apprentices. Harness Horse Race Drivers who hold a provisional license for a year must then drive either 25 satisfactory drives and obtain the same approvals as noted previously or hold the license for less than a year and drive 50 satisfactory extended pari-mutuel drives.

Those who satisfy these requirements are then granted a full license. Once this license is obtained, individuals can drive in any track in the country.

Harness Horse Race Drivers often travel from track to track to race horses. Some are under contract with a stable or trainer and drive only for those people. Others called catch drivers are not under contract. These individuals drive for hire for any stable or trainer.

Harness Horse Race Drivers who have developed a good reputation are often asked to drive a number of horses in the same race. As Harness Horse Race Drivers are often paid on a percentage of the money (called the purse) earned by the horse, they will likely choose to drive the horse that appears to have the best chance to win. Harness Horse Race Drivers may travel extensively to race horses in tracks across the country.

Harness Horse Race Drivers might prefer to only drive in races, or they might also choose to train the horses. Those who serve as trainers must also have a trainer's license. Trainers spend a great many hours training and driving horses. For most Harness Horse Race Drivers, crossing the finish line as a winner makes all the work worth it.

Salaries

Earnings for Harness Horse Race Drivers vary tremendously. There are some drivers who earn as little as $23,000 a year; others earn $1,500,000 or more. Factors affecting earnings include the driver's experience level and the number of races in which he or she participates.

Other determining factors include the specific tracks the driver races at and the amount of the purse for each horse that the individual drives. Drivers earn a percentage of the purse when the horse places in first through fifth position. If the individual is a driver/trainer, he or she earns 10 percent of the purse. If the driver is not involved with the training, however, he or she earns 5 percent of the purse. In major races with large purses, drivers have the opportunity to earn a great deal of money.

Employment Prospects

Employment prospects for Harness Horse Race Drivers are fair. Individuals must be dedicated and committed to the sport in order to make a living in harness racing. While there is a great deal of competition in this industry, there is always room for skilled drivers.

One of the best ways to obtain work is to find owners who are interested in having their horses trained and raced. If owners are impressed with the skills of a driver, when they purchase other horses, they may ask the individual to work with them.

Depending on the situation, Harness Horse Race Drivers may work full time or part time.

Advancement Prospects

Advancement prospects for Harness Horse Race Drivers are fair. They depend to a great extent on performance. Drivers who consistently do well in races will climb the career ladder by driving horses in more prestigious races that have larger purses. As drivers begin to win races and show that they can drive well, owners and others will seek out their services, resulting in increased earnings.

Education and Training

While there are no formal educational requirements needed to become a Harness Horse Race Driver, individuals do need to have a complete knowledge of maintaining, training, and racing horses. They need to be trained in working with horses as well as driving a sulky in races. These skills usually come from experience working as an apprentice to trainers and/or drivers.

Experience, Skills, and Personality Traits

Harness Horse Race Drivers need experience training and jogging horses. They generally obtain this experience by becoming apprentices to established drivers or driver/trainers.

Harness Horse Race Drivers need to enjoy working around horses. Individuals must have a feel for the way horses think, act, and behave.

Harness Horse Race Drivers need to be confident and have quick reflexes and a natural feel for driving. Driving a sulky is not always as easy as it looks. Individuals must be able to work under pressure without getting flustered. They must also be patient, compassionate, and physically fit.

Harness Horse Race Drivers need to be observant and detail-oriented. The ability to accept constructive criticism and advice without taking it personally is critical.

Special Requirements

Harness Horse Race Drivers must be licensed in the state in which they race. In order to get this licensing, individuals must first pass a written and practical exam given by the United States Trotting Association (USTA). They must additionally be able to demonstrate skills in front of licensed harness racing officials and drivers.

Harness Horse Race Drivers may additionally need a variety of licenses, from matinee to qualifying to provisional. These are usually obtained through the USTA as well.

Unions and Associations

Harness Horse Race Drivers generally belong to the USTA. This organization licenses Harness Horse Race Drivers and provides professional support and career guidance to those in the industry.

Tips for Entry

1. Visit harness racetracks and watch Harness Horse Race Drivers in action.

2. Consider a part-time or summer job in a stable or at a racetrack. This will help give you exposure harness racing. It will also give you the opportunity to get your foot in the door and make important contacts.

3. When you are ready to begin your career, try to find an established trainer or driver whom you like and respect to be your mentor. Learn as much as you can from your mentor. He or she can help you shape your career.

4. Contact the USTA for more information on getting into harness driving as a career.

GROOM

CAREER PROFILE

Duties: Care for horses; feed horses; groom horses; exercise horses; keep stable clean; saddle and unsaddle horses; assist in the training of horses

Alternate Title(s): Stable Hand; Caretaker

Salary Range: $9.00 to $30.00+ per hour

Employment Prospects: Fair

Advancement Prospects: Fair

Best Geographical Locations for Position: Positions located throughout United States in rural areas and areas hosting racetracks, stables, farms, riding schools, racing and showing stables, and stud farms

Prerequisites:

Education or Training—No formal educational requirement; see text

Experience and Qualifications—Experience requirements vary; see text

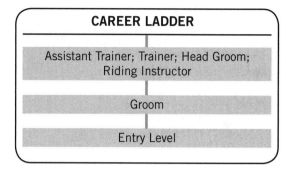

CAREER LADDER

Assistant Trainer; Trainer; Head Groom; Riding Instructor

Groom

Entry Level

Special Skills and Personality Traits—Knowledge of horse care; physical fitness; creativity; love of horses; attention to detail; responsibility

Special Requirements—State licensing may be required; see text

Position Description

Many individuals start their career in the horse industry as Grooms. These individuals are in charge of the day-to-day care of horses. Among other functions, Grooms are responsible for feeding, cleaning, and watering the horses under their care. Responsibilities vary depending on the specific work situation and work environment.

Grooms are expected to brush the horses and comb their manes and tails, detangling them when necessary. They often also plait or braid the horse's manes and tails. Part of the daily activities of a Groom includes washing the horse. This is done from the belly up, generally with a bucket of water and brushes.

Grooming is very important to horse care. In addition to keeping the horses clean, it helps build a bond of trust between horses and humans. This is vital whether horses are racing, in competitions, or just being ridden for recreation.

Another important duty of a Groom is watching to see if there are any signs of injury or disease in the horses under his or her care. If the Groom observes any problems, he or she is expected to report them to the trainer or stable manager so they can be attended to.

It is essential for Grooms to consistently check the horse's hooves to assure its foot health. They make sure, for example, that there are no stones or other debris in

the horse's hooves and that all shoes are intact. They may also oil the animal's hooves.

Grooms are expected to saddle and unsaddle horses, hitch them to sulkies, and get them ready for races and competitions. Grooms exercise the horses, often taking them on rides or walks. They also walk the horses after they have been ridden or raced so they can cool down. Grooms often give them rubdowns as well.

Grooms are responsible for feeding the horses under their care and assuring that they always have enough water. They are expected to follow the feeding schedule, giving any prescribed supplements and medications as directed.

As part of the job, Grooms clean out stalls. They may add new hay or other material for bedding. Individuals are also expected to clean and maintain the tack. Tack includes the horse's harnesses, saddles, and food. They are additionally responsible for keeping the storeroom clean and orderly.

Some Grooms help trainers train horses. Others help with breeding and foaling. The skills learned doing these activities helps many Grooms advance their careers.

In certain situations, Grooms may receive accommodations as part of the job. These individuals may be on call 24 hours a day in case a horse is sick in the middle of the night or needs some other type of care. Many Grooms, especially those who work with racehorses, have the opportunity to travel from track to track around the country with horses under their care.

Salaries

Earnings for Grooms range from approximately $9 to $30 or more per hour, depending on a number of variables. These include the specific employment situation, geographic location, experience, and responsibilities.

Employment Prospects

Employment prospects for Grooms are fair. Individuals may find work throughout the country in a variety of settings. These include racetracks, stables, ranches, stud farms, and boarding facilities, among others. Grooms may also find work with horse owners, veterinarians specializing in horses, and humane societies. Grooms may work full time or part time.

Advancement Prospects

Advancement prospects for Grooms who want to climb the career ladder and establish a career working with horses are fair. Advancement in this field is, to a great extent, based on career aspirations. Some individuals stay in similar positions but find work in larger or more prestigious facilities such as farms, stables, boarding facilities, ranches, riding schools, or racetracks. This generally results in increased responsibilities and earnings.

Some Grooms climb the career ladder by becoming apprentices to trainers, head grooms, foal managers, or riding instructors.

Education and Training

Most employers require or prefer applicants to hold a high school diploma or the equivalent. Individuals do need to have a full knowledge of caring for horses. This may come from on-the-job training, experience as a volunteer caring for horses, or a horse groom apprenticeship program. Apprenticeship programs are often offered through agricultural technical institutes or colleges. This training is a combination of classroom work and hands-on training.

Experience, Skills, and Personality Traits

While experience requirements vary from job to job, Grooms generally need at least some sort of experience working with horses. Grooms must enjoy working with and being around horses. Individuals must have a feel for the way animals think, act, and behave. Grooms should be compassionate and physically fit.

Special Requirements

Depending on the employment situation, Grooms may need to be licensed in the state in which they work. This is usually the case, for example, when Grooms are working with racehorses.

Unions and Associations

There are no trade associations for horse Grooms.

Tips for Entry

1. You can often get your foot in the door by finding a rental stable and a job as a trail guide. While these jobs are very low-paying (sometimes only just tips), you will gain experience working around horses.
2. Go to the stables, racetracks, and farms and ask about job openings.
3. When you are ready to begin your career, try to find an established trainer or driver whom you like and respect. Tell him or her what you want to do. Learn as much as you can from your mentor. He or she can help you shape your career.
4. Visit the library and get some books on horses. The more you know about the industry, the better chance you will have to become successful in it.
5. If you are in an area hosting farms, racetracks, or stables, check out the classifieds section of newspapers for job openings. Look under headings such as "Groom," "Horse Jobs," "Stables," "Racetracks," etc.
6. Check out the bulletin board at a tack shop or feed store. Many people post flyers looking for Grooms. You might also consider putting up your own flyer advertising your expertise.

EQUINE MASSAGE THERAPIST

CAREER PROFILE

Duties: Give horses therapeutic massages; assess horses' conditions; develop courses of treatment

Alternate Title(s): Massage Therapist; Animal Massage Therapist

Salary Range: $50 to $150+ per hour or session

Employment Prospects: Good

Advancement Prospects: Fair

Best Geographical Locations for Position: Positions located throughout the United States in areas hosting horse farms, racetracks, etc.

Prerequisites:

Education or Training—Graduate of certificate program in equine or animal massage therapy

Experience and Qualifications—Experience working with horses

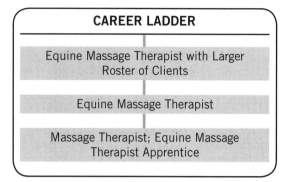

Special Skills and Personality Traits—Strength; physical fitness; calmness; compassion

Special Requirements—Certification and/or state licensing may be required; see text

Position Description

Equine Massage Therapists are responsible for helping improve the health and well-being of horses. Their job is similar to that of massage therapists who work with humans.

Much like people, the behavior of horses is affected by pain, discomfort, anxiety, and stress. When horses receive therapeutic massage, they often loosen up, feel better, and relax.

Equine Massage Therapists are expected to identify any problems the horse may have and find ways to make the animal more comfortable. Through massage, the individual might work to improve the horse's circulation or its range of motion. He or she may work to improve a racehorse's performance or the performance of a horse in another kind of competition. Depending on the specific situation, the Equine Massage Therapist may also perform therapeutic massages on horses to improve their stamina. This is especially important for racehorses or other horses going into competition.

Equine Massage Therapists often massage horses to both loosen scar tissue and stretch the animals' muscle tissue. This is helpful when trying to rehabilitate horses. Horses often experience muscle injuries. The Equine Massage Therapist can provide therapeutic massages to horses to promote healing of these injuries as well. Some-

times the therapist may also provide massages to increase circulation or to increase range of motion in the horse.

One of the important things an Equine Massage Therapist can do with therapeutic massage is improve the overall disposition of a horse. This is useful when horses are acting out because they are distressed in some way.

Equine massage therapy techniques are sometimes called manipulations. These movements affect the horse's muscle tissue and/or nervous system. Equine Massage Therapists start by stroking the horse. They then utilize special massage movements. In order to be effective in doing this, the individual must know a great deal about equine anatomy and physiology.

It is essential that the Equine Massage Therapist take safety measures when giving horses therapeutic massages. Horses are large, strong animals, and without meaning to, they may injure a therapist who is not careful.

Some Equine Massage Therapists also use aromatherapy in helping horses. These individuals may, for example, use various aromatic oils and herbs to help lessen a horse's stress, reduce anxiety, or even strengthen its immune system.

For those who love horses and working with them and are interested in massage therapy, this is the perfect type of career.

Salaries

Earnings for Equine Massage Therapists vary greatly depending on the specific work setting. Self-employed Equine Massage Therapists generally earn between $50 and $150 or more per hour. Factors affecting earnings include the professional reputation and experience of the individual. Other factors include how many clients the Equine Massage Therapist has and how many massages are booked.

Employment Prospects

Employment prospects for talented Equine Massage Therapists are good. Individuals may be self-employed or work as part of an equine massage therapy practice. Opportunities are better in areas hosting horse farms and racetracks. Individuals may find clients in owners of horses of all types.

Advancement Prospects

Advancement prospects for Equine Massage Therapists are fair. Individuals advance their career by becoming more in demand in their field. As an Equine Massage Therapist becomes more in demand, he or she can increase hourly fees, resulting in higher earnings.

Education and Training

The education and training Equine Massage Therapists have varies. Some individuals have a degree in equine science. Others have a degree in human massage therapy. Regardless of other education, Equine Massage Therapists must generally attain a certificate in either equine or animal massage therapy. Courses, programs, and schools in animal massage therapy and equine massage therapy are located throughout the country.

Depending on the specific program, individuals may, for example, become certified in therapeutic massage as an Equine Therapeutic Massage Therapist, an Equine Sports Massage Therapist, or in advanced massage techniques. Some individuals go on to learn animal acupressure as well.

Programs vary in length and content. Equissage, one of the programs approved by the National Certification Board for Therapeutic Massage and Bodywork, offers a five-day certification program that includes both classroom study and practical application.

Most Equine Massage Therapists continue their education throughout their career.

Experience, Skills, and Personality Traits

Equine Massage Therapists need to be strong, physically fit individuals. A love of horses is necessary. Equine Massage Therapists should be kind, compassionate, gentle, and patient. They should not only be calm themselves, but have the ability to exude calmness to horses. Many Equine Massage Therapists start out as human massage therapists.

Special Requirements

In order to become an Equine Massage Therapist, individuals must generally complete a certificate program. Licensing is required in certain states.

Unions and Associations

Equine Massage Therapists may belong to the International Association of Animal Massage and Bodywork. The organization provides professional support and career guidance to those interested in the field of animal massage. Individuals may also be members of the International Association of Animal Massage Therapists or the Equine Sports Massage Association.

Tips for Entry

1. Look for an internship with an Equine Massage Therapist. One-on-one training is always a good idea.
2. Continue taking as many classes, seminars, and workshops as you can. You never can tell when you will learn a new technique or something else that might help your career.
3. Consider working with a business that does equine or animal massage before striking out on your own. This often helps in terms of learning the basics, getting some experience, and making contacts.
4. Look for job openings in the classifieds section of newspapers in areas hosting horse farms and racetracks. Look under key words such as "Equine Massage Therapist," "Massage Therapist," "Equine Jobs," "Animal Massage Therapist," etc.
5. Don't forget to look for job opportunities online. Start with some of the better-known general career sites such as Monster.com. Expand your search from there.
6. If you are working on your own, look into getting liability insurance.

MISCELLANEOUS

ANIMAL BEHAVIORIST

Position Description

People have always been interested in why animals do certain things and why they act the way they do. They might wonder why animals choose certain mates, how they find food, or why they protect their territory. They might wonder how birds know when it is time to fly south, how they find their way, and how they know when it is time to turn around and go back north. They may wonder why some dogs are alpha dogs or why dogs exhibit certain behaviors. They may wonder how animals know how to care for their young and how they determine when it is time to let them go on their own. For individuals who often look at animals and wonder why they are doing something, Animal Behaviorist may be a rewarding career choice.

Animal Behaviorists are scientists who study and observe the way animals behave. This information is then used in a variety of ways, including research and coming up with ways to change or modify animal behaviors.

The job of Animal Behaviorists combines animal physiology, psychology, and the environment. Many feel that behaviorists who work with animals are similar to psychologists who work with people.

Animal Behaviorists may specialize in studying specific types of animals. They may for example, special-ize in the study of the behavior of birds, fish, reptiles, wild animals, livestock, household pets, etc. Individuals observe animals and study their environment. Information gathered can often show causes of behavioral issues. Once those are determined, the Animal Behaviorist may be able to find ways to direct the animal toward a different or more effective behavior.

There are a number of different types of Animal Behaviorists. While each type has its own specialty, they all are interested in studying and analyzing the behavior of animals. One type of Animal Behaviorist is called an applied Animal Behaviorist. These individuals observe and treat behavior problems in animals. Ecologists are Animal Behaviorists who observe and study animals in their natural environments. Biopsychologists or psychobiologists study the physiological and neurological behavior of animals.

Specific duties of Animal Behaviorists depend on their employment situation. Some individuals teach in various departments of colleges or universities, such as wildlife biology, entomology, ecology, anthropology, sociology, and animal sciences. Some teach at medical and veterinary colleges. Some do research. Others are veterinarians who may want to help change the behavior of their patients. Some work in shelters and refuges, helping animals that have been abused, neglected, or abandoned.

Once Animal Behaviorists can identify behaviors, they must try to determine what caused the behaviors. Sometimes this is easy to figure out. Other times it may be more difficult. Are there factors or situations influencing behavior? Is the behavior innate or learned? Does the behavior change over time or is it constant? These are all questions that an Animal Behaviorist must answer at one time or another. Just as many things can influence the way people act, many things can influence the ways animals act. Animal Behaviorists are expected to look at factors that influence animal behaviors. These might include hunger, illness, the weather, or the presence of predators or potential predators, among other things.

Animal Behaviorists specializing in companion animals and pet behavior, as noted previously, are called applied Animal Behaviorists. These individuals often visit pet owners in their home and observe the family's interactions with their pet. They are expected to determine why a pet may be exhibiting certain behaviors. After the Animal Behaviorist sees the interactions, he or she can often make suggestion on how the family can make changes to their behavior so that the pet's behavior changes for the better. One of the best-known Animal Behaviorists of this type is Cesar Millan, better known to many as the Dog Whisperer.

Animal Behaviorists may be called in for any number of reasons. Dogs or cats may exhibit signs of aggression to family members or other animals. Others may exhibit destructive behavior, separation anxiety, or obsessive-compulsive behaviors. Some animals may have fears or phobias that stop them from having a normal, happy life. Some animals are difficult to walk or will bark and jump constantly. Whatever the problem, Animal Behaviorists often use positive training techniques and behavior medication to help change the situation.

Animal Behaviorists investigate the relationships of animals to one another and to their environment. Individuals may, for example, explore ways animals find food and protect that food from other animals. They look at how animals mate, reproduce, and take care of their young. Individuals may also explore how animals avoid predators and choose and find housing.

This information can prove important for many reasons depending on the specific situation. In some cases, it can help save animals from extinction. In others, it can help animals in zoos or other facilities become better adjusted. Animal Behaviorists' work can help ranchers breed better livestock and help hens lay more eggs. It can keep pets from being turned over to shelters

because of behavior problems and help keep animals calm in research labs. It can give researchers important answers to why animals act the way they do and often provide insight into making life better for humans as well.

Salaries
Earnings for Animal Behaviorists range from $35,000 to $100,000 or more annually. Factors affecting earnings include the specific employer as well as its size, prestige, and geographic location. Other factors affecting earnings include the education, experience, and responsibilities of the Animal Behaviorist.

Individuals who are self-employed may charge hourly fees ranging from $50 to $150 or more.

Employment Prospects
Employment prospects for individuals interested in a career as an Animal Behaviorist are good. Depending on an individual's career aspirations, opportunities may be located throughout the United States. Opportunities include teaching in primary schools, secondary schools, colleges, and universities. Research opportunities also exist in universities and government, private research institutions, zoos, aquariums, and museums. Other opportunities include positions as curators or keepers in zoos, aquariums, and museums.

Applied animal behavior training is a growing field and will continue to grow as people continue to look at their pets as members of the family. Some Animal Behaviorists have their own business. Others work for companies, clinics, or veterinarians. Applied animal behavior training is also utilized on farms and in zoos and aquariums.

Advancement Prospects
Advancement prospects for Animal Behaviorists are fair. There are a number of paths for advancement depending on the individual's career aspirations and experience. Those who are teaching may find positions in larger colleges and universities. Individuals performing research may become supervisors or may find similar positions in larger or more prestigious labs or facilities. Applied Animal Behaviorists may find better jobs with larger companies, open their own practice, or expand their practice by acquiring new clients.

Education and Training
Educational requirements vary for Animal Behaviorists depending on the specific job. The minimum education required for any job is a bachelor's degree in biology, microbiology, ecology, psychology, or a related field.

Some positions require a master's degree in wildlife biology or a Ph.D. in zoology.

There are some positions that require a master's degree or doctorate in psychology and a concentration in animal behavior. Others require individuals to hold a doctorate in veterinary medicine.

Those interested in a career in research or working as a curator at a zoo generally must hold a Ph.D. There are some Animal Behaviorists who also have a degree in animal husbandry, comparative psychology, behavioral ecology, sociobiology, ethnology, or another specialized scientific field.

Those interested in careers helping people understand and relate to their pets need a master's degree if they want to become associate applied Animal Behaviorists, or a Ph.D. if they want to become certified applied Animal Behaviorists.

Experience, Skills, and Personality Traits

Experience requirements depend to a great extent on the specific job. Those interested in teaching on a college level, for example, may obtain experience working in a smaller school or community college. Some obtain experience working as research assistants. Still others obtain experience through internships.

Animal Behaviorists should be critical thinkers. They need to be articulate and have excellent communication skills, both verbal and written. There is a great deal of writing necessary in this job, whether it be writing reports or applying for grants. Computer competency is also mandatory.

Individuals must have the ability to work alone and as part of a team. As it is not always easy to get animals to do things in a timely manner, persistence and patience are essential.

Animal Behaviorists should have a great respect for animals and enjoy working with them.

Special Requirements

Voluntary certification is available from the Animal Behavior Society (ABS). The certification of applied Animal Behaviorist requires individuals to have either a Ph.D. or master's degree, five years of experience in the field, and a record of professional accomplishment and contribution to the practice of applied animal behavior.

Unions and Associations

Animal Behaviorists can join the ABS. This organization brings together people interested in the biological study of animal behavior. Individuals may also be members of the National Association of Animal Behaviorists.

Tips for Entry

1. Internships are a great way to get experience. Contact research facilities, colleges, universities, and veterinarians to find opportunities.
2. While certification is voluntary, it illustrates professional expertise and will often give you an edge over other applicants with similar backgrounds.
3. Go to conferences, conventions, and educational seminars to meet industry insiders. They are good sources of education and contacts.
4. Job openings may be advertised in the classifieds section of newspapers under headings including "Animal Behaviorist," "Research," and "Colleges or Universities."
5. Don't forget to look online for job opportunities. Start with some of the better-known career sites such as Monster.com. Jobs may also be listed on government job Web sites.
6. If you are trained as an Animal Behaviorist and want to work with companion animals, contact local veterinarians and dog trainers to discuss your expertise.
7. Contact the local newspaper to gauge interest in a regular column on animal behavior. Once people know about your expertise, they may call you in to help resolve behavior problems with their animals.

PET CLOTHING AND ACCESSORY DESIGNER

Position Description

There is no question that many people today treat their pets like family; some even treat them like children. A large number of pet owners both pamper their pets and dress them in pet clothing. The pampered pet clothing and accessory market has grown by leaps and bounds and promises to keep expanding in the future.

Pet Clothing and Accessory Designers create and design apparel and accessories for pets. There even is a Pet Fashion Week in New York City, similar to the Fashion Week for people, when all the newest fashions are highlighted. While most individuals in the pet fashion industry design clothing and accessories for dogs, there are designers who specialize in apparel and accessories for cats, birds, and other pets.

Pet Clothing and Accessory Designers may design a variety of clothes and accessories. These include coats, sweaters, dresses, shirts, pants, hoodies, scarves, tanks, vests, pajamas, bows, collars, socks, bandanas, and more. They may also design pet carriers, pet beds, leashes, harnesses, and other accessories. Some embroider leashes or collars. Others even create pet jewelry.

Pet Clothing and Accessory Designers started out by creating clothing for smaller dogs, but today many are creating apparel for larger dogs as well. Some Pet Clothing and Accessory Designers specialize in one or more areas of clothing. For example, some create dressy and special-event clothing for animals such as party clothes, wedding attire, and tuxedos. Some create costumes for pets. Others just design accessories. It all depends on the specific designer.

Pet Clothing and Accessory Designers who are just starting out may work from home designing and creating pet fashions. Some have studios. As they build their business, others may have facilities that have the necessary machinery to produce the fashion line. There are some Pet Clothing and Accessory Designers who work for companies that sell directly to retail stores or catalogs.

Pet Clothing and Accessory Designers might just design their line of apparel and accessories, or they might actually create them, or both. Individuals might, for example, come up with the initial designs and then outsource the manufacturing or creation of the products to others.

Pet Clothing and Accessory Designers may sell their products in a number of ways. Some individuals whole-sale, selling their products to stores and boutiques. Others sell them on their own through word of mouth. Still others go to craft shows, dog shows, cat shows, or other specialty events. There are some Pet Clothing and Accessory Designers who set up Web sites or sell online through sites like eBay. Many release catalogs of their apparel and pet accessories. There are also Pet Clothing and Accessory Designers who have their own store or boutique.

Pet Clothing and Accessory Designers are expected to determine the prices they will charge for their merchandise. For some, pricing their work is one of the most difficult areas of the job.

Individuals selling apparel or accessories via Web sites, catalogs, or mail are responsible for packaging the products and mailing or shipping them for delivery. Shipping, like production, may be outsourced.

Personalized clothing and accessories for pets are always in demand. Pet Clothing and Accessory Designers must decide if they want to make an assortment of items or create specific designs for each customer.

Pet Clothing and Accessory Designers have the opportunity to couple their love of design with their love of animals. Some started creating fashions for themselves or others. Many started their career creating fashions and accessories for their own pet.

Self-promotion is essential to success. Individuals may advertise their specialty in the local newspaper or even national magazines. If people don't know that the clothing and accessories are out there, no one can buy or order them. In order to promote their apparel and accessories, individuals may develop press releases, go on radio and television talk and news shows, and take out advertisements. In some cases, individuals retain an outside publicist or public relations specialist to handle these tasks.

Salaries

There are Pet Fashion and Accessory Designers who earn as little as $2,500 a year and others who earn $100,000 or more. However, due to the nature of the job, it is almost impossible to determine the annual earnings of Pet Clothing and Accessory Designers. Earnings are dependent on a number of factors. These include how well the individual and products are known, the professional reputation of the designer or firm, and how many designs are created and sold each year.

Other variables include the price of each piece. Pet Clothing and Accessory Designers need to factor in the cost of materials used to create pieces as well as their time. There are some individuals who charge $5 for an outfit and others who charge $150 or more. There is a fine line between charging too much and too little. A lot of it has to do with what the market will bear.

Employment Prospects

Employment prospects are good for those interested in becoming Pet Clothing and Accessory Designers. This is the type of career that animal lovers who are talented fashion designers can start on a full-time or part-time basis.

Pet Clothing and Accessory Designers may sell their products to big box pet stores, pet boutiques, and other stores featuring pet products. Some individuals sell their designs in their own pet boutique. Others sell their designs at craft shows, pet shows, from their home, or through their own Web site or other sites online.

Individuals may also find employment with companies that design and sell pet clothing and accessories.

Advancement Prospects

Advancement prospects for Pet Clothing and Accessory Designers are fair. Individuals climb the career ladder in a number of ways. Career advancement is based to a great extent on an individual's talent, drive, and career aspirations.

Some develop a private label that they can sell to stores and boutiques. Others develop a large roster of clients who purchase custom-made apparel and accessories. Some individuals become well known for their apparel and accessories and have the ability to increase their business dramatically, resulting in increased earnings. Still others build their business and open up their own pet apparel and accessory boutique.

Education and Training

Education and training varies for Pet Clothing and Accessory Designers. Some individuals are totally self-taught. Others have a college background or degree in fine art or fashion design. Some have gone to art school. Others have taken classes, seminars, and workshops in various aspects of sewing, fashion design, accessory design, working in various mediums, etc. Classes and seminars in business, promotion, and publicity are helpful for learning how to run a successful business.

Experience, Skills, and Personality Traits

As noted previously, Pet Clothing and Accessory Designers often start out their careers creating fashions or accessories for their own pets or those of friends and family. Others create fashions or accessories for themselves. Some individuals design other products and see a need for pet fashions and accessories and decide to go into business.

Successful Pet Clothing and Accessory Designers have a unique blend of sewing and other practical skills and design talent.

Pet Clothing and Accessory Designers should be creative, with a good eye for color and style. Attention to detail is necessary. Business skills are vital. Publicity, promotion, and marketing skills help Pet Clothing and Accessory Designers run a profitable business.

A love of animals is helpful. Keen observation skills are useful. The more designers know about various breeds of animals, the better.

Communication skills are essential in this line of work. It is vital that designers have the ability to hear what pet owners are saying and translate that into what they want when doing custom work. Selling skills are crucial, whether selling apparel and accessories at specialty shows, craft shows, dog shows, cat shows, or other types of pet shows or selling to pet boutiques or larger stores. Customer-service skills are also imperative to success in running this type of business.

Unions and Associations

Pet Clothing and Accessory Designers may belong to the American Pet Products Association. This organization provides professional support and guidance to members. Individuals often also belong to local arts councils and artists' guilds. These groups bring together those with similar interests and often provide networking opportunities.

Tips for Entry

1. Make business cards and give them out to everyone you meet.
2. Donate one or two pieces of your work to a local nonprofit organization for a raffle or door prize for one of their fund-raisers. It will help promote your work.
3. Consider attending an event such as Pet Fashion Week. This event is similar to Fashion Week for people and highlights the newest and best of pet fashions, accessories, and lifestyle products. It will help make contacts and give you some great ideas.
4. A portfolio is essential to your success. Put together a portfolio of photos of some of your best designs to show to prospective buyers. Don't forget to create a digital portfolio that you can display online.
5. Post flyers and business cards on the bulletin boards of pet stores and veterinary offices advertising your specialty.
6. Consider taking out a small advertisement in your local newspaper advertising your pet clothing and accessory design business.
7. Many people look for pet clothing and accessories online. Consider creating a Web site for your business.

PET PHOTOGRAPHER

CAREER PROFILE

Duties: Taking photographs of people's pets; taking photographs of pets for magazines; posing animals; creating calendars, books; manipulating photos with photo software

Alternate Title(s): Animal Photographer; Photographer

Salary Range: $24,000 to $100,000+

Employment Prospects: Good

Advancement Prospects: Fair

Best Geographical Locations for Position: Positions may be located throughout the country

Prerequisites:

Education or Training—Education and training requirements vary; see text

Experience—Experience taking photographs of pets

Special Skills and Personality Traits—Photography skills; creativity; persistence, patience; love of animals; communications skills; detail oriented; ability to multitask; business skills

CAREER LADDER

Pet Photographer with Large Roster of Clients; Pet Photographer with More Prestigious Clients; Owner of Photography Studio Specializing in Pet Photography; Photographer Selling Pet Photographs to Magazines or Books

Pet Photographer

Assistant Photographer; General Photographer

Position Description

There is no question that people love their pets. Many treat their pets as members of the family. Just as people often have professional photographs taken of their children, many want professional photographs taken of their pets.

It is not surprising that today the pet business has turned into a multibillion-dollar industry. Pet photography is a niche business that is growing by leaps and bounds. Pet Photographers specialize in taking photographs of pets. Depending on the situation, they may take portraits, action shots, candid shots, or a combination. Some also offer videotaping services.

Pet Photographers may take pictures of any family pet. Most commonly, these include dogs and cats. However, today pets may also include horses, birds, ferrets, hamsters, lizards, fish, guinea pigs, and potbellied pigs, among others.

Pet Photographers must not only have excellent photography skills but also a connection with animals. Some Pet Photographers have studios where clients can bring their pets. Others go to clients' homes so that pets can be photographed in their own surroundings. Some Pet Photographers even have mobile studios that they bring to clients' homes. Pet Photographers may also go

to special events and functions, such as dog shows, cat shows, horse shows, or even racetracks to photograph animals.

Pet Photographers often have a variety of themed backdrops, settings, costumes, props, and lights. They may photograph animals on chairs, couches, rugs, pet beds, or even their owners' laps. Depending on the situation (and the wishes of the owner), Pet Photographers may dress pets in costumes for pictures. Those photographing pets at shows may take pictures when the animal is competing in the show ring or the winner's circle.

Some Pet Photographers pose pets. They may, for example, pose a puppy with a huge bone or a kitten with a toy mouse or a ball of yarn. Some may also photograph pets for various holidays. They may, for example, take pictures of pets with Santa or the Easter Bunny. Pet Photographers can also take photos of pets with other family pets or their owners.

Photographers are expected to talk to pet owners before the session and determine exactly what they are looking for as a final product. Do the owners want a portrait of their pet? Do they want a photo for holiday cards? Are the owners looking for action shots? Do they want photographs for personal enjoyment or are they using them for other purposes? Once that is determined, the Pet Photographer can proceed.

Most Pet Photographers meet the animals they are photographing and try to form a sort of bond. They may talk to them, play with them, and pet them for a few minutes so that the pet feels comfortable. The Pet Photographer can then set up lighting, props, etc., and get ready to take the photos.

Once photographs are taken, the Pet Photographer's job is not done. He or she may manipulate the photos using various computer software to create a variety of looks. With software, the photographer may, for example, turn color photographs into photos that are black-and-white or sepia-toned. He or she may also take out or reduce red eye. Some Pet Photographers airbrush things that aren't wanted in the picture or use the technique to make the pet look perfect.

Depending on the wishes of the owner, the Pet Photographer may provide anything from a large wall portrait to wallet-sized photographs. Many Pet Photographers offer a variety of photo packages. Some also put the pet's picture on novelty items such as T-shirts, mugs, key rings, calendars, or even stuffed animals.

Some Pet Photographers, such as William Wegman, have parlayed their talent into worldwide fame. Wegman is famous for photographing his pet Weimaraners. Wegman dresses and poses his dogs, creating photographs used in posters, postcards, calendars, and more. His work is featured in exhibits in prestigious museums throughout the country. He also creates videos and short films of his dogs that have been featured on *Sesame Street* and *Saturday Night Live*.

Pet Photographers who do not work for others must also run their own business. They must determine prices, market and publicize their service, send out bills, and collect fees.

Salaries

Earnings for Pet Photographers can vary greatly depending on a number of factors. These include the specific employment situation, as well as the experience, responsibilities, and professional reputation of the individual.

Those who are working for others can have annual earnings ranging from $24,000 to $48,000 or more. Pet Photographers working for themselves can earn between $25,000 and $65,000 or more. Those who photograph celebrity pets can earn $100,000 or more.

Pet Photographers may charge a sitting fee ranging from $25 to $1,000 or more, depending on their professional reputation. They may then charge for copies of photographs. Some individuals instead charge daily rates, ranging from $250 to $1,500 or more.

Employment Prospects

Employment prospects are good for those interested in becoming Pet Photographers. Individuals may find jobs with other photographers or photography studios throughout the country; others freelance.

Some decide to open up their own photography studios or simply advertise their services. There are also some Pet Photographers who specialize in photographing pets at dog, cat, or horse shows, as well as Pet Photographers who work with celebrity pets. One of the great things about this type of career is that people can start part time, working for themselves.

Some get jobs with companies and travel around the country visiting independent pet stores as well as big box stores such as Pet Smart and setting up appointments to photograph pets for owners.

Advancement Prospects

Advancement prospects are fair for Pet Photographers. They are based, to a great extent, on an individual's talent, drive, and career aspirations. Career advancement is also based on where an individual is currently in his or her career.

After obtaining experience and building a reputation, many individuals open up their own studios. Some individuals climb the career ladder by either building a large roster of clients or building a roster of more prestigious clients. This generally results in the ability to charge higher fees. Some individuals sell their photographs to magazines or books.

Education and Training

Education and training requirements vary for Pet Photographers, depending on the specific employment situation. Some Pet Photographers are totally self-taught. Others have a college background or degree in art or photography. Some have gone to art school or photography school. Others have taken classes, seminars, and workshops in various aspects of photography, pet photography, etc. Many individuals also go through internships to hone their skills.

It is essential that whatever type of training Pet Photographers have, they know about lighting, camera angles, camera settings, color, etc. Generally, any education or training requirements will be waived if an individual shows an exceptional portfolio.

Experience, Skills, and Personality Traits

Experience requirements, such as education, often depend on the specific job. Most Pet Photographers will need to show a portfolio of their best work to illustrate what they can do. A portfolio is a compilation of samples of an individual's best work. As noted previously, many Pet Photographers obtain experience in this field with internships.

Successful Pet Photographers have a unique blend of skills and talent. They need both photography skills and the ability to deal well with animals. Pet Photographers should be creative, with good ideas about color, composition, and balance.

Individuals need to be articulate, with excellent communication skills. The ability to find out exactly what a pet owner wants in a photograph is necessary. As it is not always easy to get animals to do things in a timely manner, persistence, patience, and flexibility are essential.

Pet Photographers should like working with animals and understand their behavior. The more they know about various breeds of animals, the better. A working knowledge of digital photography and photography design software is essential.

Unions and Associations

Pet Photographers may belong to a number of associations that provide professional support and networking opportunities. These include the Professional Photographers of America (PPA), the American Dog Owners Association (ADOA), American Association of Cat Enthusiasts (AACE), and Thoroughbred Owners and Breeders Association (TOBA), etc.

Tips for Entry

1. Internships are a great way to get experience. Contact established photographers and photography studios to inquire about opportunities.

2. Another good way to get experience is by offering to take photographs of pets of friends and family.

3. Job openings may be advertised in the classified section of newspapers under headings including "Pet Photographer," "Photographer," "Photography Studio," etc.

4. Don't forget to look online for job opportunities. Start with some of the better known general career sites, such as Monster.com or Hotjobs.com. Then go from there.

5. A portfolio is essential to your success. Put together a portfolio of some of your best work to show to prospective employers and/or clients; contact local veterinarians and dog trainers to discuss your expertise. Don't forget a digital portfolio that you can also show online.

6. Post flyers, cards, etc. on the bulletin boards of pet stores and veterinary offices.

7. Consider taking a small advertisement in your local newspaper advertising your specialty.

PET PORTRAIT ARTIST

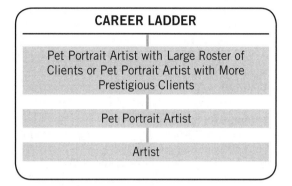
Position Description

Today, many people treat their pets as members of their family. Just as people often have professional photographs taken of their children or portraits painted of various family members, many want portraits of their pets hanging on the wall.

Pet owners often commission a Pet Portrait Artist to paint or draw portraits of their pets. Pet Portrait Artists are artists who specialize in creating portraits of people's pets. They may do them in oils, pastels, acrylics, charcoals, pen-and-ink, colored pencils, or a variety of other media. Depending on the specific medium, Pet Portrait Artists can create portraits of pets on a variety of sizes of papers, canvas, and more.

Pet Portrait Artists have the opportunity to couple their love of art with their love of animals. They may paint or draw portraits of any family pet. Most commonly, these include dogs and cats. However, pets may also include horses, birds, ferrets, hamsters, lizards, fish, guinea pigs, and potbellied pigs. Pet Portrait Artists generally not only have excellent artistic skills, they have a love of animals.

A pet portrait can immortalize and preserve the memories of a favorite family pet. While some individuals have photographs of pets on their wall, many find that an artist's portrait captures more of the special essence, personality, and likeness of an animal.

Talented Pet Portrait Artists can capture a pet's personality and bring it to life. While there are exceptions, as pets don't normally sit in one place for an extended period of time, Pet Portrait Artists generally use one or more photographs. These photographs are used for reference when creating the portrait of the pet. Depending on the situation, they may work from photos that pet owners provide or photographs that they take themselves.

Pet Portrait Artists are expected to determine the prices they will charge for portraits. Individuals might, for example, charge a different amount for a portrait in oils than they do for a portrait in charcoal. They might also charge different amounts for different sizes. For some, pricing their work is one of the most difficult parts of this career.

Part of the job of Pet Portrait Artists is getting clients. Self-promotion is essential to success. Individuals may advertise their specialty in the local newspaper or even national magazines, depending on their experience and professional reputation. Some individuals go to dog or cat shows to make contacts; others get clients through word of mouth. Some put up Web sites. Still others do television or radio interview shows to talk about their specialty.

Pet Portrait Artists must meet with potential clients to discuss exactly what they are looking for in a portrait. Are they looking for a large portrait? Do they want a full-face portrait or a full-body portrait? What type of background do they want? Is there a specific date the portrait needs to be completed by, etc. This meeting may be conducted in person, by phone, or by e-mail.

During the meeting, the individual will discuss the fee for the portrait and how he or she wants to be paid. For example, an artist may ask that he or she receive 50 percent of the fee as a deposit, with the balance paid upon completion and acceptance of the portrait.

The artist may also discuss other details to be sure everything is clear with his or her client. This may include the size of the portrait and whether the price includes just the artwork or matting and/or framing. Other details may include how the portrait will be delivered. For example, whether the client will pick up the portrait in person, or whether the artist will deliver the portrait to the client. Will the artist mail or ship the portrait? If so, what will the costs be? Who will pay for shipping?

People who commission a portrait are usually excited about getting it and don't want to wait forever. It is essential for the Pet Portrait Artist to come up with a realistic time period for creating and finishing the portrait. Knowing approximately how long a portrait might take will be helpful in giving timetables to clients. Every artist works at his or her own pace. Depending on the medium, some artists can do a portrait in a couple of hours. Some need 15 to 20 hours. Others may need days.

Pet Portrait Artists, like all artists, have their own way of creating. Many take the reference photographs they work from and then sketch out and block in the rough draft of what they hope the portrait will turn into. They may take quite a bit of time getting the proportions correct so that everything will look perfect. They may use pencil and then erase the image after they get more into the portrait. Others start working directly in the medium they are using.

As the artist works on the portrait, he or she will begin to see the pet's personality coming out. He or she will see the pet's expression. Bit by bit, the Pet Portrait Artist brings the portrait to life. He or she may need to add detail, such as more color on the muzzle or a shadow on the fur. He or she may need to work on the pet's face or expression. As an artist, the individual needs to look at both the detail and the finished product.

Some artists send photographs of their work to clients as the portrait progresses to see if they have any suggestions or changes. Others wait until the portrait is either completed or near completion to show it to the client. No matter what the time frame, the artist must be ready to make changes or tweaks to make the client happy.

Salaries

Due to the nature of the job, it is almost impossible to determine the annual earnings of Pet Portrait Artists. Earnings are dependent on a number of factors. These include how well known the artist is and his or her professional reputation. Other variables include the fees individuals charge for portraits and the number of portraits they create annually.

Charges for pet portraits can range from $25 to $10,000 or more. In addition to the professional reputation of the artist, charges may depend on the specific medium the portrait is done in, the size of the portrait, whether or not it is framed or matted, etc. Most artists have additional charges for more than one pet in a portrait.

Employment Prospects

Employment prospects are good for those interested in becoming Pet Portrait Artists. This is the type of career that individuals who are talented artists with a love for animals can start up either part time or full time. While there are a number of companies that employ Pet Portrait Artists, most individuals work on their own. With telephones, mail, and e-mail, Pet Portrait Artists can live almost anywhere and have a successful career.

As noted previously, in order to be successful in this line of work, Pet Portrait Artists must do a great deal of self-promotion, advertising their services and networking to get clients. Some Pet Portrait Artists create note cards, stationary, and postcards to augment their income.

Advancement Prospects

Advancement prospects are fair for Pet Portrait Artists. They are based, to a great extent, on an individual's talent, drive, and career aspirations. Career advancement is also based on the level an individual is currently in in his or her career.

Pet Portrait Artists advance their career by obtaining experience, getting their name out and building up either a large roster of clients or more prestigious clients. This generally results in the ability to charge increased fees.

Education and Training

Education and training varies for Pet Portrait Artists. Some individuals are self-taught. Others have a college background or degree in fine art. Some have gone to art school. Others have taken classes, seminars, and workshops in various aspects of art, working in various media, animal anatomy, etc. Classes and seminars in business, promotion, and publicity will also be helpful.

Experience, Skills, and Personality Traits

Pet Portrait Artists commonly have painted or drawn portraits of either their pets or pets of friends and family before embarking on their business. This experience helps hone skills. Individuals may need to show a portfolio of their best work to illustrate to prospective clients what they can do. A portfolio is a compilation of samples of an individual's best work.

Successful Pet Portrait Artists have a unique blend of skills and talent. They need to be skilled in the medium they work in, whether it be oils, acrylics, pen-and-ink, charcoals, colored pencils, etc. A love for animals is helpful in translating a photograph to a portrait. Keen observation skills are useful. The more artists know about various breeds of animals, the better.

Communication skills are essential in this line of work. It is vital that the artist have the ability to hear what pet owners are saying and translate that into what they want in a portrait.

Pet Portrait Artists should be creative, with a good eye for color, composition, and balance. Attention to detail is necessary. Business skills are vital. Publicity, promotion, and marketing skills are also helpful to the success of Pet Portrait Artists in running their business.

Unions and Associations

Pet Portrait Artists often belong to local arts councils and artists guilds. These groups bring together those with similar interests and often provide networking opportunities.

Tips for Entry

1. Donate a portrait to a local not-for-profit organization. It will help get your name out so people think of you when they are looking for someone to paint a portrait of their pet.

2. Get experience by creating portraits of the pets of friends and family. Take photos for your portfolio.

3. A portfolio is essential to your success. Put together a portfolio of some of your best work to show to prospective clients. Don't forget a digital portfolio that you can also show online.

4. Post flyers, cards, etc. on the bulletin boards of pet stores and veterinary offices.

5. Consider taking a small advertisement in your local newspaper advertising your specialty.

6. Many people look for Pet Portrait Artists online. Consider creating a Web site for your business.

ZOOLOGIST

Duties: Study animals and wildlife; develop research projects; conduct experiments; observe animals; analyze data; write grants and proposals; write reports; identify various species of animals

Alternate Title(s): Ornithologist; Mammalogist; Herpetologist; Ichthyologist; Wildlife Biologist; Scientist; Biological Scientist

Salary Range: $33,000 to $120,000+

Employment Prospects: Fair

Advancement Prospects: Fair

Best Geographical Locations for Position: Opportunities located throughout the United States; greatest number of openings exist in areas hosting large numbers of zoos, aquariums, nature centers, refuges, colleges, or universities

Prerequisites:

Education or Training—Minimum of bachelor's degree; advanced degrees required for some positions; see text

Experience and Qualifications—Experience requirements vary; see text

CAREER LADDER

Zoologist at Larger Facility or Institution; Senior or Lead Zoologist; Director of Research Team

↑

Zoologist

↑

Research Associate; Research Assistant; Lab Technician

Special Skills and Personality Traits—Scientific aptitude; analytical mind; inquisitiveness; curiosity; verbal and written communication skills; attention to detail; high energy; articulateness; problem-solving skills; math skills; computer skills; data-management skills; creativity; organization skills; time-management skills

Position Description

Zoologists are biological scientists who study animals and wildlife. In this position, they may study animal origins, behavior, diseases, and life processes. Responsibilities of Zoologists differ depending on their specific employment setting.

Some Zoologists conduct basic research on animals so that information can be learned about their biology. There are a number of applications for this research. It may find solutions to challenges in agriculture or medicine. Research may also help find better answers to dealing with conservation or other environmental issues.

In order to study animals, Zoologists often perform experiments on live animals. These may be done in controlled surroundings such as a laboratory or zoo or in the animal's natural surroundings. Some Zoologists also conduct experiments on dead animals, dissecting them to study their biological structure and looking for reasons for their death or other information.

Zoologists may specialize in a variety of areas. Some specialize in wildlife research and management. These individuals often collect and analyze biological data.

This information is important when determining the environmental effects of current or potential uses of land and water.

Other Zoologists identify the various species of animals. These individuals specialize in studying an area called taxonomy, or the naming and classification of animals. Some study specific groups of animals and are identified by that animal group. For example, individuals who study birds are called ornithologists. Those who study mammals are referred to as mammalogists. Zoologists who study reptiles are called herpetologists. Those who study fish are called ichthyologists.

Some Zoologists study animal physiology. Others study endocrinology. Some study animal behavior or ecology. Still others study genetics or the evolution of animals, which is called phylogeny.

No matter the specialty, Zoologists study the behavior, genetics, life cycle, and health of animals. Some Zoologists study the environmental factors that affect wild animals. Others study their habitats. It all depends on the Zoologist's specialty and the goal of the research.

Zoologists study diseases in various animal populations for a number of reasons. Research may be done to find how diseases develop in animals. Research can also help Zoologists learn how diseases are passed from one generation of animals to the next. This is important to assure that animals don't become extinct.

Depending on their specific job, Zoologists' work can benefit human medical research and development. It may additionally help with wildlife conservation and veterinary medicine. The work of Zoologists also may help with conservation and animal husbandry.

Zoologists often work with other Zoologists and other scientists on their research projects. In addition to actually studying animals, they must develop the actual research projects. Zoologists may also be expected to write grants and proposals for research projects.

Individuals are expected to observe animals and conduct experiments. They may collect specimens of body tissue, bones, or fluids. Zoologists often must physically handle animals to conduct experiments. If they are working in a controlled setting such as a zoo, animals are easier to access. Those who work in the field must often go to the animal's natural habitat. This may include hiking or being in inclement weather for extended periods of time. In some situations, Zoologists must trap animals to observe them. This must be done in a humane manner so as not to hurt animals.

After Zoologists have conducted experiments and observed animals, they must interpret the data they have collected. Once this has been done, Zoologists are responsible for developing reports and papers on their findings. Many individuals have these papers published in scientific and trade journals.

Zoologists may be responsible for caring for animals that have been trapped or are being observed. Those working at zoos or aquariums may also be responsible for public education, giving presentations about animals and helping to maintain and care for animals.

Salaries

Earnings for Zoologists are dependent on a number of factors. These include the individual's specific employment situation, geographic location, education, experience, and responsibilities. There are some Zoologists who earn $33,000 annually, while others earn $120,000 or more.

According to the United States Bureau of Labor Statistics, the median annual wages of Zoologists were $56,500 in 2009. The middle 50 percent earned between $44,830 and $71,990. The lowest 10 percent earned less than $35,280, and the highest 10 percent earned more than $93,140.

Employment Prospects

Employment prospects for Zoologists are fair. Depending on their career aspirations, individuals may work in a variety of settings. Some Zoologists directly care for animals. They may, for example, be zookeepers or veterinarians. Others work as researchers. These individuals may either work in the field or in laboratories. There are also Zoologists who work as educators. These individuals work in a variety of settings, such as wildlife centers, high schools, colleges, and universities.

Some Zoologists find employment in federal, state, and local government. They may, for example, work for the Department of Agriculture, the Department of the Interior (especially its Fish and Wildlife Service), the Department of Defense, or the National Institutes of Health.

Opportunities also exist with nonprofit groups that are interested in conservation. Some Zoologists also work in research laboratories or medical laboratories. Others find employment working in wildlife preserves, fisheries, zoos, zoological gardens, or aquariums.

Advancement Prospects

Advancement prospects for Zoologists are fair. With experience, some climb the career ladder by finding similar jobs in larger or more prestigious facilities, resulting in increased responsibilities and earnings. Others rise through the ranks in their organization. Some become supervisors or senior or lead Zoologists. Those who are associate professors may become full professors.

Many become lead researchers directing a team of scientists and technicians. Some Zoologists decide that they want to work on their own and open up consulting firms.

Some Zoologists make lateral moves to satisfy their career aspirations. Some working in research facilities, for example, may decide that they would rather teach. Others who teach may determine that they would be happier working in zoos. It all depends on the career aspirations of the individuals.

Education and Training

Educational requirements for Zoologists depend to a great extent on career aspirations. The minimum education level for Zoologists is a bachelor of science degree in zoology, biological sciences, or a related field.

Many positions, such as those in research or teaching, require either a master's degree or a Ph.D. in zoology. Those who have advanced degrees will have more opportunities to work in a variety of settings.

Experience, Skills, and Personality Traits

Experience requirements vary from job to job. Generally, the larger and more prestigious the organization for which an individual aspires to work, the more experience will be required. Many Zoologists acquire experience through jobs or internships in veterinary clinics, zoos, aquariums, or on farms while still in school. Some also complete internships with governmental agencies.

Zoologists should be inquisitive individuals with analytical minds and a love and respect for animals. Excellent verbal and written communication skills are necessary. A good command of grammar and the English language will be helpful. Technical writing expertise is useful.

Zoologists should have scientific aptitudes and analytical thinking skills. Problem-solving skills are essential. Math skills are vital in this line of work, as are computer and data-management skills.

Zoologists should also be detail-oriented and organized. The ability to multitask effectively and manage time will also be useful.

Unions and Associations

Zoologists may belong to a number of organizations and trade associations that provide professional support, education, and networking opportunities. Depending on the specific employment situation and the individual's interests, these may include the Society for Marine Mammalogy, the American Society of Mammalogists, the Animal Behavior Society, the American Society of Animal Science, the American Physiological Society, the Society for the Study of Amphibians and Reptiles, the American Society of Ichthyologists and Herpetologists, and the American Association of Zookeepers. Individuals and/or the zoo they work for may also be members of the Association of Zoos and Aquariums.

Tips for Entry

1. If you are still in school, take classes in the biological sciences. This will help you determine what area of zoology would be of most interest to you.
2. Get experience by securing an internship at a zoo, conservation center, aquarium, or animal shelter.
3. Look for a mentor by finding an established Zoologist. Speak to him or her about your career aspirations and the direction in which you want to go.
4. Consider a position as a research assistant with a Zoologist. This will help you obtain experience, hone skills, and make important contacts.
5. Look for openings online. Start with traditional career sites such as Monster.com and go from there.
6. Join trade associations. Read their journals and visit their Web sites. Many list openings.
7. Don't forget to check out federal, state, and local government agency Web sites for general information and listings of job openings.

APPENDIXES

I. Colleges and Universities

II. Directory of Zoos, Aquariums, and Sanctuaries

III. Animal Advocacy Organizations

IV. United States Thoroughbred Racetracks

V. United States Harness Racing Tracks

VI. Career and Job Web Sites

VII. Trade Associations and Other Organizations

APPENDIX I
COLLEGES AND UNIVERSITIES

A. VETERINARY COLLEGES ACCREDITED BY THE AMERICAN VETERINARY MEDICAL ASSOCIATION

The following is a listing of veterinary colleges accredited by the American Veterinary Medical Association (AVMA). As of this writing, there are only 28 colleges accredited by the AVMA in the United States.

Colleges are grouped by state. School names, addresses, phone numbers, Web addresses, and e-mail addresses are included when available.

ALABAMA

Auburn University
College of Veterinary Medicine
104 J.E. Greene Hall
Auburn University, AL 36849-5517
Phone: (334) 844-4546
E-mail: admiss@vetmed.auburn.edu
http://www.vetmed.auburn.edu

Tuskegee University
School of Veterinary Medicine
1200 West Montgomery Road
Tuskegee, AL 36088
Phone: (334) 727-8174
E-mail: cvmnah@tuskegee.edu
http://tuskegee.edu

CALIFORNIA

University of California
School of Veterinary Medicine
One Shields Avenue
Davis, CA 95616
Phone: (530) 752-1360
E-mail: admissions@vmdean.
ucdavis.edu
http://www.vetmed.ucdavis.edu

Western University of Health Sciences
College of Veterinary Medicine

309 East Second Street
College Plaza
Pomona, CA 91766
Phone: (909) 469-5628
E-mail: klopez@westernu.edu
http://www.westernu.edu/xp/edu/
veterinary/about.xml

COLORADO

Colorado State University
College of Veterinary Medicine and
Biomedical Sciences
1601 Campus Delivery
Fort Collins, CO 80523-1601
Phone: (970) 491-7051
E-mail: DVMAdmissions@
colostate.edu
http://www.cvmbs.colostate.edu

FLORIDA

University of Florida
College of Veterinary Medicine
P.O. Box 100125
Gainesville, FL 32610-0125
Phone: (352) 392-2213
E-mail: courtneyc@mail.vetmed.
ufl.edu
http://www.vetmed.ufl.edu

GEORGIA

University of Georgia
College of Veterinary Medicine
501 D.W. Brooks Drive
Athens, GA 30602
Phone: (706) 542-3461
E-mail: kygilmor@uga.edu
http://www.vet.uga.edu

ILLINOIS

University of Illinois
College of Veterinary Medicine
2001 South Lincoln Avenue
Urbana, IL 61802
Phone: (217) 333-2760
E-mail: admissions@cvm.uiuc.edu
http://www.cvm.uiuc.edu

INDIANA

Purdue University
School of Veterinary Medicine
1240 Lynn Hall
West Lafayette, IN 47907-1240
Phone: (765) 494-7607
E-mail: vetadmissions@purdue.edu
http://www.vet.purdue.edu

IOWA

Iowa State University
College of Veterinary Medicine
1600 South 16th Street
Ames, IA 50011
Phone: (515) 294-1242
E-mail: kkuehl@iastate.edu
http://www.vetmed.iastate.edu

KANSAS

Kansas State University
College of Veterinary Medicine
101 Trotter Hall
Manhattan, KS 66506
Phone: (785) 532-5660
E-mail: admit@vet.k-state.edu
http://www.vet.ksu.edu

LOUISIANA

Louisiana State University
School of Veterinary Medicine
Skip Bertman Drive
Baton Rouge, LA 70803-8402
Phone: (225) 578-9900
E-mail: admissions@vetmed.lsu.
edu
http://www.vetmed.lsu.edu

MASSACHUSETTS

Tufts University
School of Veterinary Medicine
200 Westboro Road
North Grafton, MA 01536
Phone: (508) 839-5302
E-mail: vetadmissions@tufts.edu
http://www.tufts.edu/vet

MICHIGAN

Michigan State University
College of Veterinary Medicine
G-100 Veterinary Medical Center
East Lansing, MI 48824-1314
Phone: (517) 355-6509
E-mail: admissions@cvm.msu.edu
http://cvm.msu.edu

MINNESOTA

University of Minnesota
College of Veterinary Medicine
1365 Gortner Avenue
Saint Paul, MN 55108
Phone: (612) 624-9227
http://www.cvm.umn.edu

MISSISSIPPI

Mississippi State University
College of Veterinary Medicine
Mississippi State, MS 39762
Phone: (662) 325-3432
http://www.cvm.msstate.edu

MISSOURI

**University of Missouri–
Columbia**
College of Veterinary Medicine
Columbia, MO 65211
Phone: (573) 882-3877
E-mail: kornegayj@missouri.edu
http://www.cvm.missouri.edu

NEW YORK

Cornell University
College of Veterinary Medicine
Ithaca, NY 14853-6401
Phone: (607) 253-3700
E-mail: vet_admissions@cornell.
edu
http://www.vet.cornell.edu

NORTH CAROLINA

North Carolina State University
College of Veterinary Medicine
4700 Hillsborough Street
Raleigh, NC 27606
Phone: (919) 513-6210
E-mail: mike_davidson@ncsu.edu
http://www.cvm.ncsu.edu

OHIO

Ohio State University
College of Veterinary Medicine
1900 Coffey Road
Columbus, OH 43210-1092
Phone: (614) 292-1171
E-mail: students@cvm.osu.edu
http://www.vet.ohio-state.edu

OKLAHOMA

Oklahoma State University
Center for Veterinary Health
Sciences
110 McElroy Hall
Stillwater, OK 74078
Phone: (405) 744-6595
http://www.cvm.okstate.edu

OREGON

Oregon State University
College of Veterinary Medicine
Corvallis, OR 97331
Phone: (541) 737-2098
E-mail: webmaster.vetmed@
oregonstate.edu
http://oregonstate.edu/vetmed

PENNSYLVANIA

University of Pennsylvania
School of Veterinary Medicine
3800 Spruce Street
Philadelphia, PA 19104-6044
Phone: (215) 898-5438
E-mail: admissions@vet.upenn.
edu
http://www.vet.upenn.edu

TENNESSEE

University of Tennessee
College of Veterinary Medicine
2407 River Drive
Knoxville, TN 37996
Phone: (865) 974-7262
E-mail: gsinfo@utk.edu
http://www.vet.utk.edu

TEXAS

Texas A&M University
College of Veterinary Medicine and
    Biomedical Sciences
Suite 101—VMA
College Station, TX 77843-4461
Phone: (979) 845-5051
http://www.cvm.tamu.edu

VIRGINIA

Virginia Tech
Virginia-Maryland Regional

College of Veterinary Medicine
Duck Pond Drive (0442)
Blacksburg, VA 24061-0442
Phone: (540) 231-7666
E-mail: jpelzer@vt.edu
http://www.vetmed.vt.edu

WASHINGTON

Washington State University
College of Veterinary Medicine
P.O. Box 647010
Pullman, WA 99164-7010

Phone: (509) 335-9515
http://www.vetmed.wsu.edu

WISCONSIN

**University of Wisconsin–
    Madison**
School of Veterinary Medicine
2015 Linden Drive West
Madison, WI 53706-1102
Phone: (608) 263-6716
E-mail: oaa@vetmed.wisc.edu
http://www.vetmed.wisc.edu

B. PROGRAMS ACCREDITED BY THE AVMA COMMITTEE ON VETERINARY TECHNICIANS EDUCATION AND ACTIVITIES

The following is a selected listing of programs for veterinary technicians and technologists that are accredited by the AVMA Committee on Veterinary Technicians Education and Activities.

They are grouped by state. School names, addresses, phone numbers, and Web addresses are included when available. Under each entry are the type(s) of degrees or programs offered as well as the status of the program accreditation as of this writing. For the most current information, visit the educational resources area of the AVMA Web site (http://www.avma.org/education/cvea/vettech_programs/vettech_programs.asp).

ALABAMA

**Jefferson State Community
    College**
Veterinary Technology Distance
    Learning Program
2601 Carson Road
Birmingham, AL 35215-3098
Phone: (205) 856-8519
http://www.jeffstateonline.com/
    VetTech/index.aspx
Associate of Applied Science
Provisional Accreditation

ARIZONA

Anthem College
Veterinary Technology Program
1515 East Indian School Road
Phoenix, AZ 85014
Phone: (866) 502-2627
http://anthem.edu/veterinary-
    technology-school
Associate in Science
Provisional Accreditation

Kaplan College
Veterinary Technology Program
13610 North Black Canyon
    Highway
Suite 104
Phoenix, AZ 85029
Phone: (602) 548-1955
http://getinfo.kaplancollege.com/
    KaplanCollegePortal/Kaplan
    CollegeCampuses/Arizona/
    PhoenixEast
Associate of Occupational Studies
Provisional Accreditation

Mesa Community College
Veterinary Technology/Animal
    Health Program
1833 West Southern Avenue
Mesa, AZ 85202
Phone: (480) 461-7000
E-mail: jill.sheport@mcmail.
    maricopa.edu
http://www.mesacc.edu/programs/
    veterinary-technology

Associate of Applied Science
Provisional Accreditation

Penn Foster College
Veterinary Technician Distance
    Education Program
4300 North Northsight Boulevard
Suite 120
Scottsdale, AZ 85260
Phone: (480) 947-6644
E-mail: infoims@pennfoster.com
http://www.pennfostercollege.edu/
    vettech/ProgramOutline.html
Associate in Science
Provisional Accreditation

**Pima County Community
    College**
Veterinary Technology Program
8181 East Irvington Road
Tucson, AZ 85709
Phone: (520) 206-4500
E-mail: infocenter@pima.edu

http://www.pima.edu/program/
veterinarytech/vet_tech_aas.
shtml
Associate of Applied Science
Full Accreditation

ARKANSAS

Arkansas State University–Beebe

1000 Iowa Street
P.O. Box 1000
Beebe, AR 72012
Phone: (501) 882-6263
http://www.asub.edu
Associate in Applied Science
Provisional Accreditation

CALIFORNIA

California State Polytechnic University–Pomona

College of Agriculture
Animal Health Technology
   Program
3801 West Temple Avenue
Pomona, CA 91768
Phone: (888) 232-9724
Fax: (909) 869-4454
http://www.csupomona.
   edu/~vettech
Bachelor of Science
Full Accreditation

Carrington College California–Citrus Heights Campus

7301 Greenback Lane
Citrus Heights, CA 95621
Phone: (916) 722-8200
http://carrington.edu/ccc/schools/
   citrus-heights/programs/
   veterinary-technology
Associate in Science
Full Accreditation

Carrington College California–Pleasant Hill

Veterinary Technician Program
380 Civic Drive
Suite 300
Pleasant Hill, CA 94523
Phone: (925) 609-6650

http://carrington.edu/ccc/schools/
   pleasant-hill/programs/
   veterinary-technology
Associate in Science
Full Accreditation

Carrington College California–Sacramento

Veterinary Technology Program
8909 Folsom Boulevard
Sacramento, CA 95826
Phone: (916) 361-1660
http://carrington.edu/ccc/schools/
   sacramento/programs/
   veterinary-technology
Associate in Science
Full Accreditation

Carrington College California–San Jose

Veterinary Technician Education
   Program
6201 San Ignacio Avenue
San Jose, CA 95119
Phone: (408) 360-0840
http://carrington.edu/ccc/schools/
   san-jose/programs/veterinary-
   technology
Associate in Science
Provisional Accreditation

Carrington College California–San Leandro

Veterinary Technology Program
170 Bayfair Mall
San Leandro, CA 94578
Phone: (510) 276-3888
http://carrington.edu/ccc/schools/
   san-leonardo/programs/
   veterinary-technology
Associate in Science
Full Accreditation

Carrington College California–Stockton Campus

Veterinary Technician Education
   Program
1313 West Robinhood Drive
Stockton, CA 95207
Phone: (888) 203-9947
http://carrington.edu/ccc/schools/
   stockton/programs/veterinary-
   technology

Associate in Science
Provisional Accreditation

Cosumnes River College

Veterinary Technology Program
8401 Center Parkway
Sacramento, CA 95823
Phone: (916) 691-7344
E-mail: info@crc.losrios.edu
http://www.crc.losrios.edu/College_
   Catalog/Areas_of_Study/
   Veterinary_Techno logy.htm
Associate in Science
Full Accreditation

Foothill College

Veterinary Technology Program
12345 El Monte Road
Los Altos Hills, CA 94022
Phone: (650) 949-7203
Fax: (650) 949-7375
http://www.foothill.edu/bio/
   programs/vettech
Associate in Science
Full Accreditation

Hartnell College

Animal Health Technology
   Program
156 Homestead Avenue
Salinas, CA 93901
Phone: (831) 755-6855
http://www.hartnell.cc.ca.us
Associate in Science
Full Accreditation

Los Angeles Pierce College

Veterinary Technology Program
6201 Winnetka Avenue
Woodland Hills, CA 91371
Phone: (818) 347-0551
http://www.macrohead.com/rvt
Full Accreditation

Mount San Antonio College

Animal Health Technology
   Program
1100 North Grand Avenue
Walnut, CA 91789
Phone: (909) 594-5611
http://www.mtsac.edu
Full Accreditation

Pina Medical Institute–Chula Vista

780 Bay Boulevard
Suite 101
Chula Vista, CA 91910
Phone: (619) 425-3200
http://pmi.edu
Provisional Accreditation

Yuba College

Veterinary Technology Program
2088 North Beale Road
Marysville, CA 95901
Phone: (530) 741-6962
http://www.yccd.edu/yuba/vettech/
index.html
Associate in Science
Full Accreditation

COLORADO

Bel-Rea Institute of Animal Technology

1681 South Dayton Street
Denver, CO 80231
Phone: (800) 950-8001
http://www.bel-rea.com
Associate of Applied Science
Full Accreditation

Colorado Mountain College

Veterinary Technology Program
Spring Valley Campus
3000 County Road 114
Glenwood Springs, CO 81601
Phone: (970) 945-8691
http://www.coloradomtn.edu
Associate of Applied Science
Full Accreditation

Community College of Denver

Veterinary Technology Program
P.O. Box 173363
Campus Box 21
Denver, CO 80217
Phone: (303) 365-8300
http://www.ccd.edu/ccd.nsf/
html/WEBB87SNXF-
Welcome+to+Veterinary+
Technology
Associate of Applied Science
Full Accreditation

Front Range Community College

Veterinary Research Technology
Program
3645 West 112th Avenue
Westminster, CO 80031
Phone: (303) 404-5000
http://www.frontrange.edu/
Academics/Fields-of-Study/
AAS/Veterinary-Technology.
aspx
Associate of Applied Science
Full Accreditation

Pima Medical Institute–Colorado Springs

Christina LeMay, CVT Director
3770 North Citadel Drive
Colorado Springs, CO 80910
Phone: (719) 482-7462
http://pmi.edu/careers/veterinary_
assistant.asp
Associate of Occupational Science
Provisional Accreditation

CONNECTICUT

Northwestern Connecticut Community College

Veterinary Technology Program
Park Place East
Winsted, CT 06098
Phone: (860) 738-6490
http://www.nwctc.commnet.edu/
vettech
Associate in Science
Full Accreditation

DELAWARE

Delaware Technical and Community College

Veterinary Technology Program
P.O. Box 610, Route 18
Georgetown, DE 19947
Phone: (302) 855-5918
Fax: (302) 858-5460
http://www.dtcc.edu
Associate in Science
Full Accreditation

FLORIDA

Brevard Community College

Veterinary Technology Program
1519 Clearlake Road
Cocoa, FL 32922
Phone: (321) 433-7594
Fax: (321) 634-4565
http://www.brevard.cc.fl.us
Associate in Science
Full Accreditation

Hillsborough Community College

Veterinary Technology Program
1206 North Park Road
Plant City, FL 33563
Phone: (813) 757-2157
http://www.hccfl.edu/departments/
vet-tech.aspx
Associate in Science
Provisional Accreditation

Miami-Dade College

Veterinary Technology Program
Medical Center Campus
950 Northwest 20th Street
Miami, FL 33127
Phone: (305) 237-4473
Fax: (305) 237-4278
http://www.mdc.edu/medical/AHT/
Vet/default.asp
Associate in Science
Full Accreditation

Saint Petersburg College

Veterinary Technology Program
Box 13489
Saint Petersburg, FL 33733
Phone: (727) 341-3652
http://www.spcollege.edu/hec/vt/
http://www.spcollege.
edu/bachelors/vtech.
php?program=vtech
Associate in Science
Full Accreditation
Distance Learning Program
Associate in Science
Bachelor of Science
Full Accreditation

GEORGIA

Athens Technical College
Veterinary Technology Program
800 U.S. Highway 29N
Athens, GA 30601
Phone: (706) 355-5107
http://www.athenstech.edu
http://www.athenstech.edu/catalog/
    programs/Veterinary%20
    Technology.pdf
Associate of Applied Science
Full Accreditation

Fort Valley State University
Veterinary Technology Program
1005 State University Drive
Fort Valley, GA 31030
Phone: (478) 825-6424
Fax: (478) 827-3023
E-mail: mobinis@fvsu.edu
    (Dr. Seyedmehdi Mobini,
    Department Head)
http://www.ag.fvsu.edu/VETY/
    academic_overview.cfm
Associate of Applied Science
Bachelor of Science
Full Accreditation

Gwinnett Technical College
Veterinary Technology Program
5150 Sugarloaf Parkway
Lawrenceville, GA 30043
Phone: (770) 962-7580
Fax: (770) 962-7985
http://www.gwinnetttech.edu/vet
Associate of Applied Science
Full Accreditation

Ogeechee Technical College
Veterinary Technology Program
One Joe Kennedy Boulevard
Statesboro, GA 30458
Phone: (912) 681-5500
http://www.ogeecheetech.edu
Associate of Applied Science
Full Accreditation

IDAHO

Brown Mackie College—Boise
9050 West Overland Road, Suite 100
Boise, ID 83709

Phone: (208) 321-8828
http://www.brownmackie.edu/boise
Associate of Applied Science
Provisional Accreditation

College of Southern Idaho
Veterinary Technology Program
315 Falls Avenue
P.O. Box 1238
Twin Falls, ID 83303
Phone: (208) 732-6402
Fax: (208) 736-2136
E-mail: toatterson@csi.edu
http://agriculture.csi.edu/vetTech/
    index.asp
Associate of Applied Science
Full Accreditation

ILLINOIS

Joliet Junior College
Agriculture Sciences Department
1215 Houbolt Road
Joliet, IL 60431
Phone: (815) 280-2746
Fax: (815) 280-2741
http://www.jjc.edu/academics/
    divisions/career-technical/
    agriculture-horticulture/ ag/
    Pages/default.aspx
Associate of Applied Science
Full Accreditation

Parkland College
Veterinary Technology Program
2400 West Bradley Avenue
Champaign, IL 61821
Phone: (217) 351-2224
http://www.parkland.edu/
    academics/departments/health/
    vettech.aspx
Associate of Applied Science
Full Accreditation

Rockford Career College
1130 South Alpine Road
Suite 100
Rockford, IL 61108
Phone: (815) 965-8616
http://www.rockfordcareercollege.
    edu
Associate of Applied Science
Provisional Accreditation

Southern Illinois Collegiate Common Market
Includes schools at John A. Logan
College at Carterville; Kaskaskia College at Centralia; Rend Lake College
at Ina; Shawnee Community College
at Ullin; Southeastern Illinois College at Harrisburg; Southern Illinois
University at Carbondale; Southern
Illinois University at Edwardsville
3213 South Park Avenue
Herrin, IL 62948
Phone: (618) 942-6902
http://www.siccm.com
Associate of Applied Science
Provisional Accreditation

Vet Tech Institute at Fox College
18020 Oak Park Avenue
Tinley Park, IL 60477
Phone: (708) 636-7700
http://www.foxcollege.edu
Associate of Applied Science
Provisional Accreditation

INDIANA

Brown Mackie College–Michigan City
325 East U.S. Highway 20
Michigan City, IN 46360
Phone: (800) 519-2416
http://www.brownmackie.edu
Associate of Science
Provisional Accreditation

Brown Mackie College–South Bend
3454 Douglas Road
South Bend, IN 46635
Phone: (574) 237-0774
http://www.brownmackie.edu
Associate of Science
Provisional Accreditation

Harrison College
School of Veterinary Technology
6300 Technology Center Drive
Indianapolis, IN 46220
Phone: (317) 873-6500

http://www.harrison.edu/courses-and-programs/all-academic-programs/school-of-veterinary-technology.aspx
Associate of Applied Science
Provisional Accreditation

Purdue University
School of Veterinary Medicine
Veterinary Technology Program
625 Harrison Street
West Lafayette, IN 47907
Phone: (765) 494-7607
http://www.vet.purdue.edu/vettech/index.html
On-Campus Program
Associate of Science
Bachelor of Science
Full Accreditation
Distance Learning Program

The Vet Tech Institute at International Business College at Fort Wayne
Veterinary Technology Program
5699 Coventry Lane
Fort Wayne, IN 46804
Phone: (260) 459-4500
http://www.vettechinstitute.edu/ftwayne
Associate of Applied Science
Provisional Accreditation

The Vet Tech Institute at International Business College–Indianapolis
7205 Shadeland Station
Indianapolis, IN 46804
Phone: (317) 813-2300
http://www.ibcindianapolis.edu
Associate of Applied Science
Provisional Accreditation

IOWA

Des Moines Area Community College
Veterinary Technology Program
2006 South Ankeny Boulevard
Ankeny, IA 50023
Phone: (800) 362-2127
Fax: (515) 964-6391

https://go.dmacc.edu/programs/ag/vettech/Pages/welcome.aspx
Associate of Applied Science
Full Accreditation

Iowa Western Community College
Veterinary Technology Program
2700 College Road
Box 4-C
Council Bluffs, IA 51502
Phone: (712) 325-3431
http://www.iwcc.edu/programs/program.asp?id=vettechaas
Associate of Applied Science
Provisional Accreditation

Kirkwood Community College
Animal Health Technology Program
6301 Kirkwood Boulevard, South West
Cedar Rapids, IA 52406
Phone: (319) 398-4978
http://www.kirkwood.edu
Associate of Applied Science
Full Accreditation

KANSAS

Colby Community College
Veterinary Technology Program
1255 South Range Avenue
Colby, KS 67701
Phone: (785) 462-3984
http://www.colbycc.edu/veterinary-technology
Associate of Applied Science
Full Accreditation

KENTUCKY

Brown Mackie College–Louisville
3605 Fern Valley Road
Louisville, KY 40219
Phone: (502) 968-7191
http://www.brownmackie.edu
Associate of Science
Provisional Accreditation

Morehead State University
Veterinary Technology Program

150 University Boulevard
Morehead, KY 40351
Phone: (800) 585-6781
http://www2.moreheadstate.edu/ahs/index.aspx?id=2526
Associate of Applied Science
Full Accreditation

Murray State University
Animal Health Technology Program
Department of Agriculture
102 Curris Center
Murray, KY 42071
Phone: (800) 272-4678
http://www.murraystate.edu/academics/CollegesDepartments/HutsonSchoolOfA griculture/Programs/vetTech.aspx
Bachelor in Science
Full Accreditation

LOUISIANA

Delgado Community College
615 City Park Avenue
Building 4, Room 301
New Orleans, LA 70119
Phone: (504) 671-6234
http://www.dcc.edu/campus/cp/ahealth/vet_tech/
Associate of Applied Science
Provisional Accreditation

Northwestern State University of Louisiana
Veterinary Technology Program
Department of Life Sciences
225 Bienvenu Hall
Natchitoches, LA 71497
Phone: (318) 357-5323
http://www.nsula.edu
Associate in Science
Full Accreditation

MAINE

University College of Bangor
Veterinary Technology Program
1 University Drive
Bangor, ME 04401
Phone: (207) 262-7800

http://www.uma.maine.edu/
college2career-vettech.html
Associate in Science
Full Accreditation

MARYLAND

Essex Campus of the Community College of Baltimore County
Veterinary Technology Program
7201 Rossville Boulevard
Baltimore, MD 21237
Phone: (410) 682-6000
http://www.ccbcmd.edu/allied_
health/vet/index.html
Associate of Applied Science
Probationary Accreditation

MASSACHUSETTS

Becker College
Veterinary Technology Program
61 Sever Street
Leicester, MA 01609
Phone: (508) 791-9241
Fax: (508) 892-8155
http://www.becker.edu/pages/274.asp
Associate in Science
Bachelor of Science
Full Accreditation

Holyoke Community College
Veterinary Technician Program
303 Homestead Avenue
Holyoke, MA 01040
Phone: (413) 538-7000
http://www.hcc.mass.edu
Associate in Science
Full Accreditation

Mount Ida College
Veterinary Technology Program
777 Dedham Street
Newton, MA 02459
Phone: (617) 928-4500
Fax: (617) 928-4072
http://www.mountida.edu/
sp.cfm?pageid=326
Associate in Arts
Bachelor of Animal Science
Full Accreditation

North Shore Community College
Veterinary Technology Program
1 Ferncroft Road
Danvers, MA 01923
Phone: (978) 762-4000
http://www.northshore.edu/
academics/programs/vet
Associate of Applied Science
Full Accreditation

MICHIGAN

Baker College of Cadillac
Veterinary Technology Program
9600 East 13th Street
Cadillac, MI 49601
Phone: (231) 775-8458
http://www.baker.edu/programs/
detail/veterinary-technician
Associate of Applied Science
Full Accreditation

Baker College of Clinton Township
34950 Little Mack Avenue
Clinton Township, MI 48035
Phone: (586) 790-9430
http://www.baker.edu/programs/
detail/veterinary-technician
Associate of Applied Science
Provisional Accreditation

Baker College of Flint
Veterinary Technology Program
1050 West Bristol Road
Flint, MI 48507
Phone: (810) 766-4153
Fax: (810) 766-2055
http://www.baker.edu/programs/
detail/veterinary-technician
Associate of Applied Science
Full Accreditation

Baker College of Jackson
Veterinary Technology Program
2800 Springport Road
Jackson, MI 49202
Phone: (517) 789-6123
http://www.baker.edu/programs/
detail/veterinary-technician
Associate of Applied Science
Provisional Accreditation

Baker College of Muskegon
Veterinary Technology Program
1903 Marquette Avenue
Muskegon, MI 49442
Phone: (231) 777-5275
Fax: (231) 777-5201
http://www.baker.edu/programs/
detail/veterinary-technician
Associate of Applied Science
Full Accreditation

Baker College of Port Huron
Veterinary Technology Program
3403 Lapeer Road
Port Huron, MI 48060
Phone: (810) 985-7000
http://www.baker.edu/programs/
detail/veterinary-technician
Associate of Applied Science
Provisional Accreditation

Macomb Community College
Veterinary Technician Program
Center Campus
44575 Garfield Road
Clinton Township, MI 48044
Phone: (586) 286-2096
Fax: (586) 286-2098
http://www.macomb.
edu/Future+Students/
Educational+Offer
ings/Areas+of+Study/
Veterinary+Technician
Associate of Applied Science
Full Accreditation

Michigan State University
College of Veterinary Medicine
Veterinary Technology Program
A-10 Veterinary Medical Center
East Lansing, MI 48824
Phone: (517) 353-7267
http://www.cvm.msu.edu/vettech
Certificate
Bachelor of Science
Full Accreditation

Wayne County Community College District
Veterinary Technology Program
c/o Wayne State University
Division of Laboratory Animal
Resources

259 Mack Avenue
5th Floor
Detroit, MI 48202
Phone: (313) 577-1156
Fax: (313) 577-5890
http://www.dlar.wayne.edu/vtp
Associate of Applied Science
Full Accreditation

MINNESOTA

Argosy University
Twin Cities
Veterinary Technician Program
1515 Central Parkway
Eagan, MN 55121
Phone: (888) 844-2004
http://www.argosy.edu/colleges/
    ProgramDetail.aspx?id=857
Associate of Applied Science
Full Accreditation

Duluth Business University
Veterinary Technology Program
4724 Mike Colalillo Drive
Duluth, MN 55807
Phone: (800) 777-8406
Fax: (218) 628-2127
http://www.dbumn.edu/pages/vet.
    shtml
Associate of Applied Science
Full Accreditation

Globe University
Veterinary Technology Program
8089 Globe Drive
Woodbury, MN 55125
Phone: (651) 714-7360
Fax: (651) 730-5151
http://www.globeuniversity.
    edu/degree-program/health/
    veterinary-technology.aspx
Associate of Applied Science
Bachelor of Science
Full Accreditation

Minnesota School of Business–Blaine
Veterinary Technology Program
3680 Pheasant Ridge Drive, NE
Blaine, MN 55449
Phone: (763) 225-8000

http://www.msbcollege.edu/degree-
    programs/health-sciences/
    veterinary-technology
Associate of Applied Science
Provisional Accreditation

Minnesota School of Business–Moorhead
2777 34th Street South
Moorhead, MN 56560
Phone: (218) 422-1000
http://www.msbcollege.edu/degree-
    programs/health-sciences/
    veterinary-technology
Associate of Applied Science
Provisional Accreditation

Minnesota School of Business–Plymouth
Veterinary Technology Program
1455 County Road 101 North
Plymouth, MN 55447
Phone: (877) 665-7676
http://plymouth.msbcollege.edu/
    programs/health-sciences/
    veterinary-technology
Associate of Applied Science
Bachelor of Science
Full Accreditation

Minnesota School of Business–Rochester
Veterinary Technology Program
2521 Pennington Drive, NW
Rochester, MN 55901
Phone: (507) 536-9500
http://rochester.msbcollege.edu/
    programs/health-sciences/
    veterinary-technology
Associate of Applied Science
Provisional Accreditation

Minnesota School of Business–St. Cloud
Veterinary Technology Program
1201 2nd Street South
Waite Park, MN 56387
Phone: (320) 257-2000
http://stcloud.msbcollege.edu/
    degree-programs/health-
    science/veterinary-technology
Associate of Applied Science
Probationary Accreditation

Minnesota School of Business–Shakopee
Veterinary Technology Program
1200 Shakopee Town Square
Shakopee, MN 55379
Phone: (952) 345-1200
http://shakopee.msbcollege.edu/
    degree-programs/health-
    sciences/veterinary-tech nology
Associate of Applied Science
Provisional Accreditation

Ridgewater College
Veterinary Technology Department
2101 15th Avenue, NW
Willmar, MN 56201
Phone: (320) 222-5200
Fax: (320) 222-5275
http://www.ridgewater.mnscu.edu
Associate of Applied Science
Full Accreditation

Rochester Community and Technical College
Animal Health Technology
    Program
851 30th Avenue, SE
Rochester, MN 55904
Phone: (507) 285-7210
http://www.rctc.edu/program/vt
Associate of Applied Science
Full Accreditation

MISSISSIPPI

Hinds Community College
Veterinary Technology Program
1100 PMB 11160
Raymond, MS 39154
Phone: (601) 857-3456
Fax: (601) 857-3577
http://www.hindscc.edu/
    Departments/agriculture/
    Veterinary_Technology.aspx
Associate of Applied Science
Full Accreditation

MISSOURI

Crowder College
601 LaClede Avenue
Neosho, MO 64850
Phone: (417) 455-5772

http://www.crowder.edu
Associate of Applied Science
Full Accreditation

Jefferson College
Veterinary Technology Program
1000 Viking Drive
Hillsboro, MO 63050
Phone: (636) 942-3000
Fax: (636) 789-4012
http://www.jeffco.edu
Associate of Applied Science
Full Accreditation

Metropolitan Community College
Veterinary Technology Program
3200 Broadway
Kansas City, MO 64111
Phone: (816) 604-1000
http://www.mcckc.edu/vettech
Associate of Applied Science
Full Accreditation

Sanford-Brown College–Fenton
Veterinary Technology Program
1345 Smizer Mill Road
Fenton, MO 63026
Phone: (888) 769-2433
http://www.sanfordbrown-online.
com/sbc/index.php?Itemid=104
Associate of Applied Science
Probationary Accreditation

Sanford-Brown College–Saint Peters
Veterinary Technology Program
100 Richmond Center Boulevard
Saint Peters, MO 63376
Phone: (888) 769-2433
http://www.sanfordbrown-online.
com/sbc/index.php?Itemid=78
Associate of Applied Science
Provisional Accreditation

The Vet Tech Institute at Hickey College
Veterinary Technology Program
2780 North Lindbergh
Saint Louis, MO 63114
Phone: (314) 434-2212
http://www.hickeycollege.edu

Specialized Associate Degree in
Veterinary Technology
Provisional Accreditation

NEBRASKA

Nebraska College of Technical Agriculture
Veterinary Technology Program
Rural route 3, Box 23A
Curtis, NE 69025
Phone: (308) 367-4124
http://ncta.unl.edu/web/ncta/
VeterinaryTechnology
Associate of Applied Science
Full Accreditation

Northeast Community College
Veterinary Technician Program
801 East Benjamin Avenue
Norfolk, NE 68702-0469
Phone: (402) 371-2020
Fax: (402) 844-7400
http://www.northeast.edu/Degrees-
and-Programs/Veterinary-
Technology
Associate of Applied Science
Full Accreditation

Vatterott College
Veterinary Technician Program
1818 I Street
Omaha, NE 68137
Phone: (402) 392-1300
http://www.vatterott-college.com
Associate of Applied Science
Full Accreditation

NEVADA

The College of Southern Nevada
Veterinary Technology Program
6375 West Charleston Boulevard
Las Vegas, NV 89146-1164
Phone: (702) 651-5852
http://sites.csn.edu/health/
overview-veterinary.html
Associate of Applied Science
Full Accreditation

Pima Medical Institute
Veterinary Technician Program

3333 East Flamingo Road
Las Vegas, NV 89121
Phone: (702) 458-9650
http://pmi.edu/careers/veterinary_
technician.asp
Occupational Associate
Provisional Accreditation

Truckee Meadows Community College
Veterinary Technology Program
18600 Wedge Parkway
Building B, Room 101
Reno, NV 89511
Phone: (775) 850-4004
http://www.tmcc.edu/vettech
Associate of Applied Science
Full Accreditation

NEW HAMPSHIRE

Great Bay Community College
Veterinary Technology Program
320 Corporate Drive
Portsmouth, NH 03801
Phone: (603) 427-7695
Fax: (603) 772-1198
http://www.greatbay.edu
Associate in Science
Full Accreditation

NEW JERSEY

Bergen Community College
School of Veterinary Technology
400 Paramus Road
Paramus, NJ 07652
Phone: (201) 612-5389
Fax: (201) 612-3876
http://www.bergen.edu/pages1/
pages/1091.aspx
Associate of Applied Science
Provisional Accreditation

Camden County College
Animal Science Technology Program
P.O. Box 200
Blackwood, NJ 08012
Phone: (856) 227-7200
http://www.camdencc.edu/
departments/vettech/index.html
Associate in Animal Technology
Full Accreditation

NEW MEXICO

Central New Mexico Community College

Veterinary Technology Program
525 Buena Vista Drive, SE
Albuquerque, NM 87106
Phone: (505) 224-5043
E-mail: bsnyder6@cnm.edu
http://www.cnm.edu/depts/hwps/
    progs/vetsci/vettech/
Associate of Applied Science
Full Accreditation

San Juan College

Veterinary Technology Distance
    Learning Program
4601 College Boulevard
Farmington, NM 87402
Phone: (505) 566-3182
http://www.sanjuancollege.edu/
    vettech
Associate of Applied Science
Full Accreditation

NEW YORK

Alfred State College

Veterinary Technology Program
10 Upper College Drive
Alfred, NY 14802
Phone: (800) 425-3733
Fax: (607) 587-4721
http://www.alfredstate.edu/
    academics/programs/veterinary-
    technology
Associate of Applied Science
Full Accreditation

La Guardia Community College

The City University of New York
Veterinary Technology Program
31-10 Thomson Avenue
Long Island City, NY 11101
Phone: (718) 482-5470
Fax: (718) 609-2051
http://www.lagcc.cuny.edu/vet
Associate of Applied Science
Full Accreditation

Medaille College

Veterinary Technology Program

18 Agassiz Circle
Buffalo, NY 14214
Phone: (716) 884-3281
Fax: (716) 884-0291
http://www.medaille.edu/
    academics/undergraduate/
    vettech
Associate in Science
Bachelor of Science
Full Accreditation

Mercy College

Veterinary Technology Program
555 Broadway
Dobbs Ferry, NY 10522
Phone: (914) 674-7530
https://www.mercy.edu/
    academics/school-of-health-
    and-natural-sciences/depart
    ment-of-natural-sciences/bs-in-
    veterinary-technology
Bachelor of Science
Full Accreditation

State University of New York–Canton

Agricultural and Technical College
Health Sciences and Medical
    Technologies
Veterinary Science Technology
    Program
34 Cornell Drive
Canton, NY 13617
Phone: (315) 386-7011
http://www.canton.edu/sci_health/
    vet_tech
Associate of Applied Science
Bachelor of Science
Full Accreditation

State University of New York–Delhi

College of Technology
Veterinary Science Technology
    Program
2 Main Street
Delhi, NY 13753
Phone: (607) 746-4306
http://www.delhi.edu/academics/
    academic_divisions/applied_
    science_and_recreation/
    veterinary_science_technology
Associate of Applied Science

Bachelor in Business
    Administration
Full Accreditation

State University of New York–Ulster (Ulster County Community College)

Veterinary Technology Program
491 Cottekill Road
Stone Ridge, NY 12484
Phone: (845) 687-5000
E-mail: admissions@sunyulster.edu
http://www.sunyulster.edu/
    programs_courses/credit_
    programs/complete_list/vete
    rinary_technology.jsp
Associate of Applied Science
Full Accreditation

Suffolk Community College

Veterinary Science Technology
    Program
Western Campus
1001 Crooked Hill Road
Brentwood, NY 11717
Phone: (631) 851-6700
http://department.sunysuffolk.
    edu/VeterinaryScience
    Technology_G/index.asp
Associate of Applied Science
Full Accreditation

NORTH CAROLINA

Asheville-Buncombe Technical Community College

Veterinary Medical Technology
    Program
340 Victoria Road
Asheville, NC 28801
Phone: (828) 254-1921
http://www.abtech.edu/ah/vet
Associate of Applied Science
Full Accreditation

Central Carolina Community College

Veterinary Medical Technology
    Program
1105 Kelly Drive
Sanford, NC 27330
Phone: (919) 718-7234
Fax: (919) 775-1221

http://www.cccc.edu/curriculum/
majors/veterinarymedical
Associate of Applied Science
Full Accreditation

Gaston College

Veterinary Medical Technology
Program
201 Highway 321 South
Dallas, NC 28034
Phone: (704) 922-6200
Fax: (704) 922-6440
http://www.gaston.edu/programs/
health_sciences/veterinary_tech.
php
Associate of Applied Science
Full Accreditation

NORTH DAKOTA

North Dakota State University

Veterinary Technology Program
NDSU Department 2230
P.O. Box 6050
Fargo, ND 58108
Phone: (701) 231-7511
Fax: (701) 231-7514
E-mail: teresa.sonsthagen@ndsu.
edu
http://www.ndsu.edu/vettech
Bachelor of Science
Full Accreditation

OHIO

Brown Mackie College–
Cincinnati

Veterinary Technology Program
1011 Glendale-Milford Road
Cincinnati, OH 45215
Phone: (513) 672-1969
http://www.brownmackie.
edu/veterinary/veterinary-
technology-511.aspx
Associate of Science
Provisional Accreditation

Brown Mackie College–
Findlay

1700 Fostoria Avenue
Suite 100
Findlay, OH 45840
Phone: (419) 423-2211

http://www.brownmackie.
edu/veterinary/veterinary-
technology-511.aspx
Associate of Applied Science
Provisional Accreditation

Columbus State Community
College

Veterinary Technology Program
550 East Spring Street
Columbus, OH 43215
Phone: (614) 287-5353
http://cscc.edu/VetTech/index.htm
Associate of Applied Science
Full Accreditation

Cuyahoga Community College

Veterinary Technology Program
700 Carnegie Avenue
Cleveland, OH 44115
Phone: (216) 987-5450
E-mail: Kathy.Corcoran@tri-c.edu
http://www.tri-c.edu/programs/
healthcareers/veterinary/pages/
default.aspx
Associate of Applied Science
Full Accreditation

Kent State University–
Tuscarawas

School of Veterinary Technology
330 University Drive, NE
New Philadelphia, OH 44663
Phone: (330) 339-3391
http://www.tusc.kent.edu/
academics/acprogs_vtec.cfm
Associate of Applied Science
Provisional Accreditation

Stautzenberger College–
Brecksville

Veterinary Technology Program
8001 Katherine Boulevard
Brecksville, OH 44141
Phone: (440) 838-1999
http://www.learnwhatyoulove.
com/Stautzenberger-College-
Programs/veterinary-
technology.aspx
Associate of Applied Science
Full Accreditation

Stautzenberger College–
Maumee

Veterinary Technology Program
1796 Indian Wood Circle
Maumee, OH 43537
Phone: (419) 866-0261
Fax: (419) 866-0261
http://www.sctoday.edu/
content/?page_id=5
Associate of Applied Science
Full Accreditation

University of Cincinnati–
Raymond Walters College

Veterinary Technology Program
9555 Plainfield Road
Blue Ash, OH 45236
Phone: (513) 936-7173
http://www.rwc.uc.edu/vettech/
index.html
Associate of Applied Science
Full Accreditation

Vet Tech Institute at Bradford
School–Columbus

2469 Stelzer Road
Columbus, OH 43219
Phone: (800) 678-7981
http://www.vettechinstitute.edu/
columbus
Associate of Applied Science
Provisional Accreditation

OKLAHOMA

Murray State College

Veterinary Technology Program
One Murray Campus
Tishomingo, OK 73460
Phone: (580) 371-2371
Fax: (580) 371-9844
http://www.mscok.edu/degree/
aasVetTech.html
Associate of Applied Science
Full Accreditation

Oklahoma State University–
Oklahoma City

Veterinary Technology Program
900 North Portland Avenue
Oklahoma City, OK 73107
Phone: (405) 945-9112

http://www.osuokc.edu
Associate of Applied Science
Full Accreditation

Tulsa Community College

Veterinary Technology Program
7505 West 41st Street
Tulsa, OK 74107
Phone: (918) 595-8212
Fax: (918) 918-595-8216
http://www.tulsacc.edu/19569
Associate of Applied Science
Full Accreditation

OREGON

Portland Community College

Veterinary Technology Program
P.O. Box 19000
Portland, OR 97219
Phone: (503) 244-6111
http://www.pcc.edu/programs/
    vet-tech
Associate of Applied Science
Full Accreditation

PENNSYLVANIA

Harcum College

Veterinary Technology Program
750 Montgomery Avenue
Bryn Mawr, PA 19010-3476
Phone: (610) 525-4100
Fax: (610) 526-6031
http://www.harcum.edu/
    PS_ACD_Veterinary_
    Technology_6328398349314062
    50.aspx
Associate in Science
Full Accreditation

Johnson College

Veterinary Science Technology
    Program
3427 North Main Avenue
Scranton, PA 18508
Phone: (570) 342-6404
Fax: (570) 348-2181
http://www.johnson.edu
Associate in Science
Full Accreditation

Lehigh Carbon and Northampton Community Colleges

Veterinary Technology Program
4525 Education Park Drive
Schnecksville, PA 18078
Phone: (610) 799-2121
Fax: (610) 861-4132
http://www.lccc.edu/academics/
    school-healthcare-sciences/
    veterinary-technician-aas
Associate of Applied Science
Full Accreditation

Manor College

Joanna Bassert, VMD-Director
Veterinary Technology Program
700 Fox Chase Road
Jenkintown, PA 19046
Phone: (215) 885-2360
http://www.manorvettech.com
Associate in Science
Full Accreditation

The Vet Tech Institute

Veterinary Technician Program
125 Seventh Street
Pittsburgh, PA 15222
Phone: (412) 391-7021
Fax: (412) 232-4345
http://www.vettechinstitute.edu/
    program
Associate in Specialized Technology
Full Accreditation

Sanford-Brown Institute

Veterinary Technology Program
421 Seventh Avenue
Pittsburgh, PA 15219
Phone: (412) 281-2600
http://www.sanfordbrown.edu/
    Areas-Of-Study/Allied-Health-
    Technicians-And- Therapists/
    Veterinary-Technology
Associate of Specialized Technology
Full Accreditation

Wilson College

Veterinary Medical Technology
    Program
1015 Philadelphia Avenue
Chambersburg, PA 17201
Phone: (717) 264-4141

Fax: (717) 264-1578
http://www.wilson.edu/wilson/asp/
    content.asp?id=249
Bachelor of Science–College for
    Women
Full Accreditation

PUERTO RICO

University of Puerto Rico

Veterinary Technology Program
Medical Sciences Campus
P.O. Box 23341
San Juan, PR 00931-3341
Phone: (787) 758-2525
Fax: (787) 772-1483
http://oeas.uprrp.edu/programas/
    pre-tecnologia-veterinaria
Bachelor of Science
Probationary Accreditation

SOUTH CAROLINA

Piedmont Technical College

Newberry Campus
540 Wilson Road
Newberry, SC 29108
Phone: (803) 276-9000
Fax: (803) 276-9001
http://www.ptc.edu/newberry
Associate in Health Science
Provisional Accreditation

Tri-County Technical College

Veterinary Technology Program
P.O. Box 587
Pendleton, SC 29670
Phone: (864) 646-8361
http://www.tctc.edu/Content/
    Academics/Prepare_for_a_
    Career/Veterinary_Technology.
    xml
Associate in Applied Science
Full Accreditation

Trident Technical College

Veterinary Technology Program
P.O. Box 118067
Charleston, SC 29423
Phone: (843) 574-6111
E-mail: infocenter@tridenttech.
    edu

http://www.tridenttech.edu/3777.htm
Associate in Allied Health Sciences
Full Accreditation

SOUTH DAKOTA

Globe University–Sioux Falls
5101 South Broadband Lane
Sioux Falls, SD 57108-2208
Phone: (715) 855-6600
http://siouxfalls.globeuniversity.edu
Associate of Applied Science
Provisional Accreditation

National American University
Allied Health Division
Veterinary Technology Program
321 Kansas City Street
Rapid City, SD 57701
Phone: (800) 843-8892
http://www.national.edu/Programs/Undergraduate/aas_vettech/Pages/default.aspx
Associate in Applied Science
Full Accreditation

TENNESSEE

Chattanooga State Community College
4501 Amnicola Highway
Chattanooga, TN 37406-1097
Phone: (423) 697-4400
http://www.chattanoogastate.edu/math_science/vet_tech
Associate of Applied Science
Provisional Accreditation

Columbia State Community College
Veterinary Technology Program
1665 Hampshire Pike
Columbia, TN 38401
Phone: (931) 540-2722
http://www.columbiastate.edu/veterinary-technology
Associate of Applied Science
Full Accreditation

Lincoln Memorial University
Veterinary Technology Program
Cumberland Gap Parkway
LMU Box 1659
Harrogate, TN 37752
Phone: (423) 869-6278
Fax: (423) 869-7151
http://www.lmunet.edu/academics/programs/veterinary-admission.shtml
Associate of Applied Science
Bachelor of Science
Full Accreditation

TEXAS

Cedar Valley College
Veterinary Technology Program
3030 North Dallas Avenue
Lancaster, TX 75134
Phone: (972) 860-8201
http://www.cedarvalleycollege.edu/FutureStudents/Degreesand
CertificatePrograms/Technical
Disciplines/Veterinary
Technology/default.aspx
On-Campus Program
Associate of Applied Science
Full Accreditation
Distance Learning Program
Associate of Applied Science
Full Accreditation

Lone Star College
Veterinary Technology Program
5000 Research Forest Drive
The Woodlands, TX 77381-4356
Phone: (832) 813-6500
http://www.lonestar.edu/vet-tech.htm
Associate of Applied Science
Full Accreditation

McLennan Community College
Veterinary Technology Program
1400 College Drive
Waco, TX 76708
Phone: (254) 299-8750
http://www.mclennan.edu/departments/workforce/vtech
Associate of Applied Science
Full Accreditation

Midland College
Veterinary Technology Program
3600 North Garfield Street
Midland, TX 79705
Phone: (432) 685-4619
Fax: (432) 685-6431
http://www.midland.edu/vettech
Associate of Applied Science
Full Accreditation

Palo Alto College
Veterinary Technology Program
1400 West Villaret Boulevard
San Antonio, TX 78224-2499
Phone: (210) 486-3000
http://www.alamo.edu/pac/vettech
Associate of Applied Science
Full Accreditation

Sul Ross State University
School of Agriculture and Natural Resource Sciences
Veterinary Technology Program
P.O. Box C-114
Alpine, TX 79832
Phone: (432) 837-8011
http://www.sulross.edu/pages/3225.asp
Associate Degree
Probationary Accreditation

The Vet Tech Institute of Houston
4669 Southwest Freeway
Houston, TX 77027
Phone: (800) 275-2736
http://www.vettechinstitute.edu/houston
Associate of Applied Science
Provisional Accreditation

UTAH

Broadview University–Layton
869 West Hill Field Road
Layton, UT 84041
Phone: (801) 542-8314
http://www.broadviewuniversity.edu/locations/layton.aspx
Associate of Applied Science
Provisional Accreditation

Broadview University–West Jordan
Veterinary Technician Program
1902 West 7800 South

West Jordan, UT 84088
Phone: (801) 304-4224
Fax: (801) 256-0609
http://www.broadviewuniversity.
edu/programs/health-science/
veterinary-technology.aspx
Associate of Applied Science
Full Accreditation

VERMONT

Vermont Technical College

Veterinary Technology Program
P.O. Box 500
Randolph Center, VT 05061
Phone: (800) 442-8821
E-mail: admissions@vtc.edu
http://www.vtc.edu/interior.php/
pid/4/sid/26/tid/572
Associate of Applied Science
Full Accreditation

VIRGINIA

Blue Ridge Community College

Veterinary Technology Program
P.O. Box 80
Weyers Cave, VA 24486
Phone: (540) 234-9261
Fax: (540) 234-9066
http://community.brcc.edu/vettech
Associate of Applied Science
Distance Learning Initial Accredit-
ation (Virginia residents only)
Full Accreditation

Northern Virginia Community College

Veterinary Technology Program
Loudoun Campus
1000 Harry Flood Byrd Highway
Sterling, VA 20164
Phone: (703) 450-2525
Fax: (703) 404-7322
E-mail: lovettech@nvcc.edu
http://www.nvcc.edu/campuses-
and-centers/loudoun/academic-
divisions/natural/ vettech/index.
html
On Campus Program
Associate of Applied Science
Full Accreditation

Distance Learning Program
Associate of Applied Science
Full Accreditation

WASHINGTON

Bellingham Technical College

3028 Lindbergh Avenue
Bellingham, WA 98225
Phone: (360) 752-8755
http://www.btc.ctc.edu
Associate of Applied Science
Provisional Accreditation

Pierce College Fort Steilacoom

Veterinary Technology Program
9401 Farwest Drive, SW
Lakewood, WA 98498
Phone: (253) 964-6500
http://www.pierce.ctc.edu
Associate in Veterinary Technology
Full Accreditation

Pima Medical Institute–Renton

555 South Renton Village Place
Suite 110
Renton, WA 98057
Phone: (800) 477-7462
http://renton.pmi.edu
Associate of Occupational Science
Provisional Accreditation

Pima Medical Institute–Seattle

Veterinary Technology Program
9709 Third Avenue, NE
Suite 400
Seattle, WA 98115
Phone: (800) 477-7462
http://pmi.edu/locations/seattle.asp
Associate of Occupational Science
Full Accreditation

Yakima Valley Community College

Veterinary Technology Program
P.O. Box 22520
Yakima, WA 98907-1647
Phone: (509) 574-4759
E-mail: swedam@yvcc.edu (Dr. Sue
Wedam, Program Coordinator)
http://www.yvcc.edu/
FutureStudents/

AcademicOptions/Programs/
VeterinaryTec hnology/Pages/
default.aspx
Associate of Applied Science
Full Accreditation

WEST VIRGINIA

Carver Career Center and the Bridgemont Community and Technical College

4799 Midland Drive
Charleston, WV 25306
Phone: (304) 348-1965
Fax: (304) 348-1938
http://www.carvercareercenter.net/
Carver/Vet_Tech.html
Associate of Applied Science
Provisional Accreditation

Pierpont Community and Technical College

Veterinary Technology Program
1201 Locust Avenue
Fairmont, WV 26554
Phone: (304) 367-4892
http://www.pierpont.edu/
schoolofhealthcareers/academics/
veterinary-technology
Associate of Applied Science
Probationary Accreditation

WISCONSIN

Globe University–Eau Claire

4955 Bullis Farm Road
Eau Claire, W 1 54701
Phone: (715) 855-6600
http://www.msbcollege.edu/
campus-locations/eau-claire-wi
Associate of Applied Science
Provisional Accreditation

Madison Area Technical College

Veterinary Technician Program
3550 Anderson Street
Madison, WI 53704
Phone: (608) 246-6800
Fax: (608) 246-6880
http://matcmadison.edu/program-
info/veterinary-technician

Associate of Applied Science
Full Accreditation

Moraine Park Technical College

Veterinary Technology Distance
  Learning Program
235 North National Avenue
Fond du Lac, WI 54936

Phone: (800) 472-4554
http://www.morainepark.edu
Associate of Applied Science
Provisional Accreditation

WYOMING

Eastern Wyoming College

Veterinary Technology Program

3200 West C Street
Torrington, WY 82240
Phone: (866) 327-8996
E-mail: cooper@ewc.wy.edu
http://www.ewc.wy.edu/programs/
  departments/vet_tech.cfm
Associate in Applied Science
Full Accreditation

APPENDIX II
DIRECTORY OF ZOOS, AQUARIUMS, AND SANCTUARIES

The following is a directory of selected zoos, aquariums, and sanctuaries located in the United States. Names, addresses, fax numbers, and phone numbers as well as e-mail addresses and Web sites are included (when available) for each. Use this appendix as a beginning to obtain general information, locate internships, or to send your résumé for job possibilities.

There are many more zoos, aquariums, and sanctuaries located throughout the country. Due to space limitations, every one could not be included. Inclusion or exclusion does not indicate the recommendation or endorsement by the author of any one facility over another.

ALABAMA

Alabama Gulf Coast Zoo
1204 Gulf Shores Parkway
Gulf Shores, AL 36542
Phone: (251) 968-5732
E-mail: info@alabamagulfcoastzoo.
    org
http://www.alabamagulfcoastzoo.
    org

Birmingham Zoo
2630 Cahaba Road
Birmingham, AL 35223
Phone: (205) 879-0409
http://www.birminghamzoo.com

**Limestone Zoological Park and
    Exotic Wildlife Refuge**
30193 Nick Davis Road
Harvest, AL 35749
Phone: (256) 230-0330

The Montgomery Zoo
2301 Coliseum Parkway
Montgomery, AL 36110
Phone: (334) 240-4940
http://montgomeryal.gov/depts/
    zoo.asp

ALASKA

Alaska Zoo
4731 O'Malley Road
Anchorage, AK 99507
Phone: (907) 346-2133
http://www.alaskazoo.org

ARIZONA

Phoenix Zoo
455 North Galvin Parkway
Phoenix, AZ 85008
Phone: (602) 273-1341
Fax: (202) 286-3886
http://www.phoenixzoo.org

Tucson Zoological Society
1030 South Randolph Way
Tucson, AZ 85716
Phone: (520) 881-4753
Fax: (520) 881-1450
http://www.tucsonzoo.org

ARKANSAS

Little Rock Zoo
1 Jonesboro Drive
Little Rock, AR 72205
Phone: (501) 666-2406
http://www.littlerockzoo.com

**Riddle's Elephant and Wildlife
    Sanctuary**
P.O. Box 715
Greenbrier, AR 72058
Phone: (501) 589-3291
Fax: (501) 589-2248

E-mail: info@elephantsanctuary.org
http://www.elephantsanctuary.org

**Wild Wilderness Drive-Through
    Safari**
20923 Safari Road
Gentry, AR 72734
Phone: (479) 736-8383
http://www.wildwildernessdrive
    throughsafari.com

CALIFORNIA

Aquarium of the Pacific
100 Aquarium Way
Long Beach, CA 90802
Phone: (562) 590-3100
E-mail: aquariumofpacific@lbaop.
    org
http://www.aquariumofpacific.org

**Birch Aquarium at Scripps, UC
    San Diego**
9500 Gilman Drive
Mail Code 0207
La Jolla, CA 92093
Phone: (858) 534-3474
Fax: (858) 534-7114
E-mail: aquariuminfo@ucsd.edu
http://www.aquarium.ucsd.edu

Cabrillo Marine Aquarium
3720 Stephen M. White Drive
San Pedro, CA 90731

Phone: (310) 548-7562
http://www.
cabrillomarineaquarium.org

Chaffee Zoological Gardens of Fresno
894 West Belmont Avenue
Fresno, CA 93728
Phone: (559) 498-4692
Fax: (559) 264-9226
http://www.fresnochaffeezoo.org

Charles Paddock Zoo
9305 Pismo Avenue
Atascadero, CA 93422
Phone: (805) 461-5080
Fax: (805) 461-7625
http://www.charlespaddockzoo.org

Emerald Forest Bird Gardens
38420 Dos Cameron Drive
Fallbrook, CA 92028
Phone: (760) 768-2226
http://www.emeraldforestbirds.com

Fear-No-More Zoo
12040 North Seigler Road
Middletown, CA 95461
Phone: (707) 355-0638
http://www.fearnomorezoo.org

Folsom City Zoo
403 Stafford Street
Folsom, CA 95630
Phone: (916) 351-3527
E-mail: information@
folsomzoofriends.org
http://www.folsomzoofriends.org

Happy Hollow Park and Zoo
1300 Senter Road
San Jose, CA 95112
Phone: (408) 794-6400
Fax: (408) 277-4470
E-mail: HHguestservices@
sanjoseca.gov
http://www.
happyhollowparkandzoo.org

Los Angeles Zoo
5333 Zoo Drive
Los Angeles, CA 90027

Phone: (323) 644-4200
Fax: (323) 662-9786
http://www.lazoo.org

Micke Grove Zoo
11793 North Micke Grove Road
Lodi, CA 95240
Phone: (209) 953-8800
Fax: (209) 331-7271
E-mail: info@mgzoo.com
http://www.mgzoo.com

Monterey Bay Aquarium
886 Cannery Row
Monterey, CA 93940
Phone: (831) 648-4800
http://www.montereybayaquarium.
org

Morro Bay Aquarium
595 Embarcadero
Morro Bay, CA 93442
Phone: (805) 772-7647
http://www.morrobay.com

Oakland Zoo
P.O. Box 5238
9777 Golf Links Road
Oakland, CA 94605
Phone: (510) 632-9525
Fax: (510) 635-5719
http://www.oaklandzoo.org

Ocean Institute
24200 Dana Point Harbor Drive
Dana Point, CA 92629
Phone: (949) 496-2274
http://www.ocean-institute.org

Orange County Zoo
1 Irvine Park Road
Orange, CA 92862
Phone: (714) 973-6847
http://www.ocparks.com/oczoo

Project Survival's Cat Haven
38257 East Kings Canyon Road
Dunlap, CA 93621
Phone: (559) 338-3216
http://www.cathaven.com

Sacramento Zoo
3930 West Land Park Drive
Sacramento, CA 95822
Phone: (916) 808-5885
Fax: (916) 264-5887
E-mail: saczooinfo@
cityofsacramento.org
http://www.saczoo.com

San Diego Zoo
P.O. Box 120551
San Diego, CA 92112
Phone: (619) 234-3153
http://www.sandiegozoo.org

San Francisco Bay Bird Observatory
524 Valley Way
Milpitas, CA 95035
Phone: (408) 946-6548
Fax: (408) 946-9279
http://www.sfbbo.org

San Francisco Zoo
1 Zoo Road
San Francisco, CA 94132
Phone: (415) 753-7080
http://www.sfzoo.org

Santa Ana Zoo
1801 East Chestnut Avenue
Santa Ana, CA 92701
Phone: (714) 836-4000
Fax: (714) 953-7401
http://santaanazoo.org

Santa Barbara Zoo
500 Niños Drive
Santa Barbara, CA 93103
Phone: (805) 962-5339
Fax: (805) 962-1673
E-mail: zooinfo@sbzoo.org
http://www.sbzoo.org

Sequoia Park Zoo
3414 W Street
Eureka, CA 95503
Phone: (707) 441-4263
Fax: (707) 441-4237
E-mail: info@sequoiaparkzoo.net
http://www.sequoiaparkzoo.net

COLORADO

Cheyenne Mountain Zoo
4250 Cheyenne Mountain Zoo Road
Colorado Springs, CO 80906
Phone: (719) 633-9925
Fax: (719) 633-2254
E-mail: info@cmzoo.org
http://www.cmzoo.org

Denver Zoo
2300 Steele Street
Denver, CO 80205
Phone: (303) 376-4860
http://www.denverzoo.org

Pueblo Zoo
3455 Nuckolls Avenue
Pueblo, CO 81005
Phone: (719) 561-1452
Fax: (719) 561-8686
http://www.pueblozoo.org

The Wild Animal Sanctuary
1946 County Road 53
Keenesburg, CO 80643
Phone: (303) 536-0118
E-mail: information@wildlife-
sanctuary.org
http://www.wildlife-conservation.
com

CONNECTICUT

Beardsley Zoo
1875 Noble Avenue
Bridgeport, CT 06610
Phone: (203) 394-6565
http://www.beardsleyzoo.org

Maritime Center at Norwalk
10 North Water Street
Norwalk, CT 06854
Phone: (203) 852-0700
http://www.maritimeaquarium.org

Mystic Marinelife Aquarium
Mystic Seaport
55 Coogan Boulevard
Mystic, CT 06355
Phone: (860) 572-5955
Fax: (860) 572-5969

E-mail: info@mysticaquarium.org
http://www.mysticaquarium.org

The Sanctuary
2 Deer Run Road
Farmington, CT 06032
E-mail: kem@ctwaterfowl.org

DELAWARE

Brandywine Zoo
1001 North Park Drive
Wilmington, DE 19802
Phone: (302) 571-7788
Fax: (302) 571-7787
http://www.destateparks.com/
attractions/brandywine-zoo

WASHINGTON, D.C.

National Aquarium
14th and Constitution Avenue, NW
Washington, DC 20230
Phone: (202) 482-2825
http://www.nationalaquarium.com

Smithsonian National Zoological Park
3001 Connecticut Avenue, NW
Washington, DC 20008
Phone: (202) 633-3025
http://nationalzoo.si.edu

FLORIDA

Back to Nature Wildlife
18515 East Colonial Drive
Orlando, FL 32820
Phone: (407) 568-5138
http://www.btn-wildlife.org

Big Cat Rescue
12802 Easy Street
Tampa, FL 33625
Phone: (813) 920-4130
E-mail: info@bigcatrescue.org
http://www.bigcatrescue.org

Brevard Zoo
8225 North Wickham Road
Melbourne, FL 32940
Phone: (321) 254-9453

Fax: (321) 259-5966
http://www.brevardzoo.org

Busch Gardens Zoo Tampa Bay
P.O. Box 9158
Tampa, FL 33674
Phone: (813) 987-5171
http://www.seaworld.org

Central Florida Zoological Park
P.O. Box 470309
Lake Monroe, FL 32747
Phone: (407) 323-4450
Fax: (407) 321-0900
http://www.centralfloridazoo.org

Clearwater Marine Aquarium
249 Windward Passage
Clearwater, FL 33767
Phone: (727) 441-1790
E-mail: info@cmaquarium.org
http://www.seewinter.com

Discovery Cove
6000 Discovery Cove Way
Orlando, FL 32821
Phone: (877) 557-7404
E-mail: DCO-GuestRelations@
DiscoveryCove.com
http://www.discoverycove.com

Disney's Animal Kingdom Park
Disney's Animal Kingdom
P.O. Box 10,000
Lake Buena Vista, FL 32830-1000
Phone: (407) 939-2468
Fax: (407) 939-6386
http://disneyworld.disney.go.com/
parks/animal-kingdom

Dolphin Connection
61 Hawk's Cay Boulevard
Duck Key, FL 33050
Phone: (888) 313-5749
http://www.dolphinconnection.com

Dolphin Research Center
58901 Overseas Highway
Grassy Key, FL 33050
Phone: (305) 289-1121
Fax: (305) 743-7627
http://www.dolphins.org

Florida Keys Wild Bird Rehabilitation Center
93600 Overseas Highway
Tavernier, FL 33070
Phone: (305) 852-4486
http://www.flkinfo.com/wildbird.htm

Green Meadows Farm Petting Zoo
1368 South Poinciana Boulevard
Kissimmee, FL 34746
Phone: (407) 846-0770
E-mail: Info@greenmeadowsfarm.com
http://www.greenmeadowsfarm.com

Gumbo Limbo Nature Center
1801 North Ocean Boulevard
Boca Raton, FL 33432
Phone: (561) 338-1473
http://www.gumbolimbo.org

Jacksonville Zoo
370 Zoo Parkway
Jacksonville, FL 32218
Phone: (904) 757-4463
Fax: (904) 757-2444
E-mail: info@jacksonvillezoo.org
http://www.jacksonvillezoo.org

Key West Municipal Aquarium
1 Whitehead Street
Key West, FL 33040
Phone: (800) 868-7482
http://www.keywestaquarium.com

Loggerhead Marinelife Center
14200 U.S. Highway One
Juno Beach, FL 33408
Phone: (561) 627-8280
Fax: (561) 627-8305
http://www.marinelife.org

Lowry Park Zoo
1101 West Sligh Avenue
Tampa, FL 33604
Phone: (813) 935-8552
Fax: (813) 935-9486
http://www.lowryparkzoo.com

Miami Metro Zoo
One Zoo Boulevard
12400 Southwest 152 Street
Miami, FL 33177
Phone: (305) 251-0400
Fax: (305) 378-6381
http://www.miamimetrozoo.com

Miami Seaquarium
4400 Rickenbacker Causeway
Key Biscayne, FL 33149
Phone: (305) 361-5705
http://www.miamiseaquarium.com

Palm Beach Zoo
1301 Summit Boulevard
West Palm Beach, FL 33405
Phone: (561) 547-9453
Fax: (561) 585-6085
E-mail: info@palmbeachzoo.org
http://www.palmbeachzoo.org

Teaching Zoo (Santa Fe CC)
3000 Northwest 83rd Street
Gainesville, FL 32606
Phone: (352) 395-5000
http://www.sfcollege.edu/zoo

The Zoo of Northwest Florida
5701 Gulf Breeze Parkway
Gulf Breeze, FL 32563
Phone: (850) 932-2229
http://www.thezoonorthwestflorida.org

GEORGIA

Atlanta Zoo
800 Cherokee Avenue, SE
Atlanta, GA 30315
Phone: (404) 624-9453
http://www.zooatlanta.org

Chehaw Wild Animal Park
105 Chehaw Park Road
Albany, GA 31701
Phone: (229) 430-5275
http://www.parksatchehaw.org

Pine Mountain Wild Animal Park
1300 Oak Grove Road

Pine Mountain, GA 31822
Phone: (706) 663-8744
http://www.animalsafari.com/Wild_Animal_Safari.html

HAWAII

The Dolphin Institute
420 Ward Avenue
Honolulu, HI 96814
Phone: (808) 593-2211
E-mail: tdi.hawaii@gmail.com
http://www.dolphin-institute.com

Honolulu Zoo
151 Kapahulu Avenue
Honolulu, HI 96815
Phone: (808) 971-7171
Fax: (808) 971-2622
http://www.honoluluzoo.org

Pacific Primate Sanctuary
500A Haloa Road
Haiku, Maui, HI 96708
Phone: (808) 572-8089
E-mail: info@pacificprimate.org
http://www.pacificprimate.org

Waikiki Aquarium
2777 Kalakaua Avenue
Honolulu, HI 96815
Phone: (808) 923-9741
Fax: (808) 923-1771
http://www.waquarium.org

IDAHO

Tautphaus Park Zoo
2725 Carnival Way
Idaho Falls, ID 83405
Phone: (208) 612-8552
http://www.idahofallsidaho.gov/city/city-departments/parks-recreation/parks-recreation-zoo.html

Zoo Boise in Boise
355 Julia Davis Drive
Boise, ID 83702
Phone: (208) 384-4260
Fax: (208) 384-4059
http://www.zooboise.org/home.asp

ILLINOIS

Brookfield Zoo
3300 Golf Road
Brookfield, IL 60513
Phone: (708) 688-8400
http://www.czs.org/czs/Brookfield/
    Zoo-Home.aspx

Cosley Zoo
1356 North Gary Avenue
Wheaton, IL 60187
Phone: (630) 665-5534
http://www.cosleyzoo.org

Henson Robinson Zoo
1100 East Lake Drive
Springfield, IL 62707
Phone: (217) 753-6217
http://www.hensonrobinsonzoo.org

Lincoln Park Zoo
2001 North Clark Street
Chicago, IL 60614
Phone: (312) 742-2000
http://www.lpzoo.com

Miller Park Zoo
1020 South Morris Avenue
Bloomington, IL 61701
Phone: (309) 434-2250
Fax: (309) 434-2483
E-mail: parks@cityblm.org
http://www.cityblm.org/parks/
    Miller-Park-Zoo/about-the-zoo.
    htm

Niabi Zoological Society
12908 Niabi Zoo Road
Coal Valley, IL 61240
Phone: (309) 799-3482
Fax: (309) 799-5761
http://www.niabizoo.com

Peoria Zoo at Glen Oak Park
2218 North Prospect Road
Peoria, IL 61603
Phone: (309) 686-3365
Fax: (309) 685-6240
E-mail: info@peoriazoo.org
http://www.peoriazoo.org

Phillips Park Zoo
1000 Ray Moses Drive
Aurora, IL 60505
Phone: (630) 978-4774
http://www.phillipsparkaurora.
    com/phillipspark/zoo/
    phillipsparkzoo.html

Scovill Zoo
71 South Country Club Road
Decatur, IL 62521
Phone: (217) 421-7435
http://www.decatur-parks.org/zoo

Wildlife Prarie State Park
3826 North Taylor Road
Hanna City, IL 61536
Phone: (309) 676-0998
E-mail: irequest@
    wildlifeprairiestatepark.org
http://www.wildlifeprairiestatepark.
    com

INDIANA

Black Pine Animal Sanctuary
1426 West 300 North
P.O. Box 02
Albion, IN 46701
Phone: (260) 636-7383
http://www.blackpineanimalpark.
    com

Fort Wayne Children's Zoo
3411 Sherman Boulevard
Fort Wayne, IN 46808
Phone: (260) 427-6800
http://www.kidszoo.org

Indianapolis Zoo
1200 West Washington Street
Indianapolis, IN 46222
Phone: (317) 630-2703
http://www.indyzoo.com

Mesker Park Zoo and Botanic
    Garden
1545 Mesker Park Drive
Evansville, IN 47720
Phone: (812) 435-6143
http://www.meskerparkzoo.com

Potawatomi Zoo
500 South Greenlawn
South Bend, IN 46615
Phone: (574) 288-4639
E-mail: info@potawatomizoo.org
http://www.potawatomizoo.org

Washington Park Zoo
115 Lakeshore Drive
Michigan City, IN 46360
Phone: (219) 873-1510
Fax: (219) 873-1539
http://washingtonparkzoo.com

IOWA

Blank Park Zoo
7401 Southwest 9th Street
Des Moines, IA 50315
Phone: (515) 323-8383
E-mail: info@blankparkzoo.com
http://www.blankparkzoo.com

KANSAS

Brit Spaugh Zoo
2200 Main Street
Great Bend, KS 67530
Phone: (620) 793-4162
http://www.kansastravel.org

Cedar Cove Feline
    Conservatory and Sanctuary
3783 Highway K68
Louisburg, KS 66053
Phone: (913) 837-5515

Clay Center Zoo
4th Street and Pomeroy
Clay Center, KS 67432
Phone: (785) 632-2171
http://www.kansastravel.org

Eagle Valley Raptor Center
927 North 343rd Street
West Cheney, KS 67025
Phone: (316) 393-0710
E-mail: RaptorCare@aol.com
http://www.eaglevalleyraptorcenter.
    org

Emporia Zoo
75 Soden Road
Emporia, KS 66801
Phone: (620) 342-6558
http://www.emporiazoo.org

Riverside Park and Zoo
P.O. Box 9
Independence, KS 67301
http://www.forpaz.com/zoo.htm

Sedgwick County Zoo
5555 Zoo Boulevard
Wichita, KS 67212
Phone: (316) 660-9453
http://www.scz.org

Sunset Zoo
2333 Oak Street
Manhattan, KS 6502
Phone: (785) 587-2737
http://www.ci.manhattan.ks.us

Tanganyika Wildlife Park
1000 South Hawkins Lane
Goddard, KS 67052
http://www.twpark.com

Topeka Zoo
635 Gage Boulevard
Topeka, KS 66606
Phone: (785) 272-7595
http://www.fotz.org

KENTUCKY

Louisville Zoo
1100 Trevilian Way
Louisville, KY 40213
Phone: (502) 459-2181
http://www.louisvillezoo.org

Newport Aquarium
One Aquarium Way
Newport, KY 41071
Phone: (859) 261-7444
Fax: (859) 261-5888
http://www.newportaquarium.com

LOUISIANA

Alexandria Zoological Park
3016 Masonic Drive
Alexandria, LA 71301
Phone: (318) 441-6810
Fax: (318) 473-1149
http://www.thealexandriazoo.com

**Audubon Nature Institute/
New Orleans Zoo**
P.O. Box 4327
New Orleans, LA 70178
Phone: (504) 581-4629
http://www.auduboninstitute.org

BREC's Baton Rouge Zoo
3601 Thomas Road
Baton Rouge, LA 70807
Phone: (225) 775-3877
Fax: (225) 775-3931
http://www.brzoo.org

Chimp Haven Sanctuary
13600 Chimpanzee Place
Keithville, LA 71047
Phone: (318) 925-9575
Fax: (318) 925-9576
http://www.chimphaven.org

Zoo of Acadiana
116 Lakeview Drive
Broussard, LA 70518
Phone: (337) 837-4325
Fax: (337) 837-4253
http://www.zooofacadiana.org

MAINE

Acadia Zoological Park
1201 Bar Harbor Road
Trenton, ME 04605
Phone: (800) 345-4617
Fax: (207) 667-9080
http://www.acadiainfo.com

**Gulf of Maine Aquarium and
Research Institute**
350 Commercial Street
Portland, ME 04101
Phone: (207) 772-2321
Fax: (207) 772-6855

E-mail: info@gmri.org
http://www.gmri.org

York's Wild Kingdom
Route 1
York Beach, ME 03910
Phone: (207) 363-4911
Fax: (207) 363-4299
E-mail: ykingdom@aol.com
http://www.yorkzoo.com

MARYLAND

**The Maryland Zoo in
Baltimore**
Druid Hill Park
Baltimore, MD 21217
Phone: (410) 396-7102
http://www.marylandzoo.org

Plumpton Park Zoo
1416 Telegraph Road
Rising Sun, MD 21911
Phone: (410) 658-6850
http://www.plumptonparkzoo.org

Salisbury Zoo
Salisbury Zoological Park
755 South Park Drive
P.O. Box 2979
Salisbury, MD 21802
Phone: (410) 548-3188
Fax: (410) 860-0919
http://www.salisburyzoo.org

MASSACHUSETTS

Buttonwood Park Zoo
425 Hawthorn Street
New Bedford, MA 00740
Phone: (508) 991-6178
http://www.bpzoo.org

Capron Park Zoo
201 County Street
Attleboro, MA 02703
Phone: (774) 203-1840
Fax: (508) 223-2208
E-mail: zoo@cityofattleboro.us
http://www.capronparkzoo.com

Franklin Park Zoo
Zoo New England
One Franklin Park Road
Boston, MA 02121
Phone: (617) 541-5466
E-mail: info@zoonewengland.com
http://www.franklinparkzoo.org

The New England Aquarium
Central Wharf
Boston, MA 02110
Phone: (617) 973-5200
http://www.neaq.org/index.php

Stone Zoo
149 Pond Street
Stoneham, MA 02180
Phone: (781) 438-5100
http://www.stonezoo.org

MICHIGAN

Belle Isle Nature Zoo
P.O. Box 39
Royal Oak, MI 48068
Phone: (313) 852-4083
Fax: (313) 852-4082
http://www.detroitzoo.org/Visitors/
Nature_Center/Belle_Isle
_Nature_Zoo

Binder Park Zoo
7400 Division Drive
Battle Creek, MI 49014
Phone: (269) 979-1351
Fax: (269) 979-8834
E-mail: info@binderparkzoo.org
http://www.binderparkzoo.org

Detroit Zoo
8540 West 10 Mile Road
Royal Oak, MI 48067
Phone: (248) 541-5717
http://www.detroitzoo.org

Potter Park Zoo
1301 South Pennsylvania Avenue
Lansing, MI 48912
Phone: (517) 483-4222
Fax: (517) 342-2778
http://www.potterparkzoo.org

**Children's Zoo at Celebration
Square**
1730 South Washington Avenue
Saginaw, MI 48601
Phone: (989) 759-1408
E-mail: info@saginawzoo.com
http://www.saginawzoo.com

MINNESOTA

**Como Park Zoo and
Conservatory**
1225 Estabrook Drive
Saint Paul, MN 55103
Phone: (651) 487-8200
http://www.comozooconservatory.
org

Great Lakes Aquarium
353 Harbor Drive
Duluth, MN 55802
Phone: (218) 740-3474
Fax: (218) 740-2020
E-mail: info@glaquarium.org
http://www.glaquarium.org

Lake Superior Zoo–Duluth
7210 Fremont Street
Duluth, MN 55807
Phone: (218) 730-4900
Fax: (218) 723-3750
E-mail: info@lszoo.org
http://www.lszoo.org

Minnesota Zoo
13000 Zoo Boulevard
Apple Valley, MN 55124
Phone: (952) 431-9200
Fax: (952) 431-9300
http://www.mnzoo.com

MISSISSIPPI

Jackson Zoo
2918 West Capitol Street
Jackson, MS 39209
Phone: (601) 352-2580
http://www.jacksonzoo.org

MISSOURI

Dickerson Park Zoo
3043 North Fort
Springfield, MO 65803
Phone: (417) 833-1570
Fax: (417) 833-4459
E-mail: info@dickersonparkzoo.org
http://www.dickersonparkzoo.org

Kansas City Zoo
6800 Zoo Drive
Kansas City, MO 64132
Phone: (816) 513-5800
E-mail: askthezoo@fotzkc.org
http://www.kansascityzoo.org

Saint Louis Zoo
One Government Drive
Saint Louis, MO 63110
Phone: (314) 781-0900
http://www.stlzoo.org

MONTANA

Zoo Montana
2100 South Shiloh Road
Billings, MT 59106
Phone: (406) 652-8100
Fax: (406) 652-9281
E-mail: zoomt@zoomontana.org
http://www.zoomontana.org

NEBRASKA

Omaha's Henry Doorly Zoo
3701 South 10th Street
Omaha, NE 68107
Phone: (402) 733-8401
Fax: (402) 733-7868
http://www.omahazoo.com

Riverside Zoo
1600 South Beltline West
Scottsbluff, NE 69361
Phone: (308) 630-6236
E-mail: tfrench@city.scottsbluff.org
http://www.riversidezoo.org

NEVADA

Southern Nevada Zoo
1775 North Rancho Drive

Las Vegas, NV 89106
Phone: (702) 647-4685
Fax: (702) 648-5955
http://www.lasvegaszoo.org

NEW HAMPSHIRE

New Hampshire Audubon
84 Silk Farm Road
Concord, NH 03301
Phone: (603) 224-9909
Fax: (603) 226-0902
E-mail: nha@nhaudubon.org
http://www.newhampshireaudubon.
    org

NEW JERSEY

Cape May County Park and Zoo
Route 9 and Crest Haven Road
Cape May Court House, NJ 08210
Phone: (609) 465-5271
http://www.beachcomber.com/
    Capemay/zoo.html

Marine Mammal Stranding Center
P.O. Box 773
3625 Brigantine Boulevard
Brigantine, NJ 08203
Phone: (609) 266-0538
Fax: (609) 266-6300
E-mail: mmsc@verizon.net
http://www.mmsc.org

Turtle Back Zoo
560 Northfield Avenue
West Orange, NJ 07052
Phone: (973) 731-5800
http://www.turtlebackzoo.org

NEW MEXICO

Alameda Park Zoo
11th and White Sands Boulevard
Alamogordo, NM 88310
Phone: (505) 439-4290
http://www.zianet.com/hsss/
    webdoc1.htm

Albuquerque Aquarium
2601 Central Avenue, NW
Albuquerque, NM 87104
Phone: (505) 768-2000
Fax: (505) 848-7192
E-mail: biopark@cabq.gov
http://www.cabq.gov/biopark/
    aquarium/index.html

Rio Grand Zoological Park
903 Tenth Street, SW
Albuquerque, NM 87102
Phone: (505) 768-2000
Fax: (505) 764-6281
E-mail: biopark@cabq.gov
http://www.cabq.gov/biopark/zoo

NEW YORK

Binghamton Zoo at Ross Park
60 Morgan Road
Binghamton, NY 13903
Phone: (607) 724-5461
E-mail: info@rossparkzoo.com
http://www.rossparkzoo.com

Bronx Zoo
2300 Southern Boulevard
Bronx, NY 10460
Phone: (718) 220-5100
E-mail: guestrelations@wcs.org
http://www.bronxzoo.com

Central Park Zoo
64th Street and Fifth Avenue
New York, NY 10021
Phone: (212) 439-6500
E-mail: guestrelations@wcs.org
http://www.centralparkzoo.com

New York Aquarium
Surf Avenue and West 8th Street
Brooklyn, NY 11224
Phone: (718) 265-3474
http://www.nyaquarium.com

Rosamond Gifford Zoo at Burnet Park
One Conservation Place
Syracuse, NY 13204
Phone: (315) 435-8511
Fax: (315) 435-8517

E-mail: info@rosamondgiffordzoo.
    org
http://www.rosamondgiffordzoo.org

Staten Island Zoo
614 Broadway
Staten Island, NY 10310-2896
Phone: (718) 442-3101
http://www.statenislandzoo.org

Trevor Zoo
Millbrook School
131 Millbrook School Road
Millbrook, NY 12545
Phone: (845) 677-3704
Fax: (845) 677-3774
E-mail: trevorzoo@millbrook.org
http://www.millbrook.org/podium/
    default.aspx?t=35004

Utica Zoo
99 Steele Hill Road
Utica, NY 13501
Phone: (315) 738-0472
Fax: (315) 738-0475
http://www.uticazoo.org

NORTH CAROLINA

North Carolina Aquarium at Fort Fisher
900 Loggerhead Road
Kure Beach, NC 28449
Phone: (866) 301-3476
Fax: (910) 458-6812
E-mail: ffmail@ncaquariums.com
http://www.ncaquariums.com

North Carolina Aquarium at Pine Knoll Shores
P.O. Box 580
Atlantic Beach, NC 28512
Phone: (866) 294-3477
Fax: (252) 247-0663
E-mail: pksmail@ncaquariums.com
http://www.ncaquariums.com

North Carolina Aquarium on Roanoke Island
P.O. Box 967
Manteo, NC 27954
Phone: (866) 332-3475

E-mail: rimail@ncaquariums.com
http://www.ncaquariums.com

North Carolina Zoo
4401 Zoo Parkway
Asheboro, NC 27205
Phone: (336) 879-7000
http://www.nczoo.org

NORTH DAKOTA

Dakota Zoo
P.O. Box 711
Bismarck, ND 58502
Phone: (701) 223-7543
Fax: (701) 258-835
http://www.dakotazoo.org

Red River Zoo
220 21st Avenue, SW
Fargo, ND 58104
Phone: (701) 277-9240
Fax: (701) 277-9238
http://www.redriverzoo.org

Roosevelt Park Zoo
1219 Burdick Expressway East
P.O. Box 549
Minot, ND 58702
Phone: (701) 857-4166
Fax: (701) 857-4169
http://www.rpzoo.com

OHIO

Akron Zoo
500 Edgewood Avenue
Akron, OH 44307
Phone: (330) 375-2550
Fax: (330) 375-2575
E-mail: info@akronzoo.org
http://www.akronzoo.org

Cincinnati Zoo and Botanical Garden
3400 Vine Street
Cincinnati, OH 45220
Phone: (513) 281-4700
E-mail: info@cincinnatizoo.org
http://www.cincyzoo.org

Cleveland Zoo
Cleveland Metroparks Zoo
3900 Wildlife Way
Cleveland, OH 44109
Phone: (216) 661-6500
http://clemetzoo.com

Columbus Zoo and Aquarium
9990 Riverside Drive
P.O. Box 400
Powell, OH 43065
Phone: (614) 645-3550
http://www.columbuszoo.org

Toledo Zoo
P.O. Box 140130
Toledo, OH 43614
Phone: (419) 385-5721
http://www.toledozoo.org

OKLAHOMA

Little River Zoo
3405 Southeast 120th Avenue
Norman, OK 73026
Phone: (405) 366-7229
E-mail: info@littleriverzoo.com
http://www.littleriverzoo.com

The Oklahoma City Zoo
2101 Northeast 50th Street
Oklahoma City, OK 73111
Phone: (405) 424-3344
http://www.okczoo.com

Tulsa Zoo and Living Museum
6421 East 36th Street North
Tulsa, OK 74115
Phone: (918) 669-6600
E-mail: info@tulsazoo.org
http://www.tulsazoo.org

OREGON

Oregon Coast Aquarium
2820 Southeast Ferry Slip Road
Newport, OR 97365
Phone: (541) 867-3474
E-mail: info@aquarium.org
http://www.aquarium.org

Oregon Zoo
4001 Southwest Canyon Road
Portland, OR 97221
Phone: (503) 226-1561
http://www.oregonzoo.org

PENNSYLVANIA

Elmwood Park Zoo
1661 Harding Boulevard
Norristown PA, 19401
Phone: (610) 277-3825
http://www.elmwoodparkzoo.org

Erie Zoo
423 West 38th Street
Erie, PA 16508
Phone: (814) 864-4091
http://www.eriezoo.org

Lehigh Valley Zoo
5150 Game Preserve Road
P.O. Box 519
Schnecksville, PA 18078
Phone: (610) 799-4171
Fax: (610) 799-4170
http://lvzoo.org

National Aviary
Allegheny Commons West
700 Arch Street
Pittsburgh, PA 15212
Phone: (412) 323-7235
http://www.aviary.org

Philadelphia Zoo
3400 West Girard Avenue
Philadelphia, PA 19104
Phone: (215) 243-1100
Fax: (215) 243-5385
http://www.philadelphiazoo.org

Pittsburgh Zoo
One Wild Place
Pittsburgh, PA 15206
Phone: (412) 665-3640
http://www.pittsburghzoo.org

ZooAmerica
100 West Hersheypark Drive
P.O. Box 866
Hershey, PA 17033

Phone: (717) 534-3900
E-mail: ZooAmerica@HersheyPA.com
http://www.zooamerica.com

Zoological Society of Philadelphia
3400 West Girard Avenue
Philadelphia, PA 19104-1196
Phone: (215) 243-1100
Fax: (215) 243-5385
http://www.philadelphiazoo.org

RHODE ISLAND

Norman Bird Sanctuary
583 Third Beach Road
Middletown, RI 02842
Phone: (401) 846-2577
Fax: (401) 846-2772
http://www.normanbirdsanctuary.org

Roger Williams Park Zoo
1000 Elmwood Avenue
Providence, RI 02907
Phone: (401) 785-3510
E-mail: info@rwpzoo.org
http://www.rwpzoo.org

SOUTH CAROLINA

South Carolina Aquarium
100 Aquarium Wharf
Charleston, SC 29401
Phone: (843) 720-1990
http://www.scaquarium.org

Greenville Zoo
150 Cleveland Park Drive
Greenville, SC 29601
Phone: (864) 467-4300
E-mail: zooinfo@greenvillesc.gov
http://www.greenvillezoo.com

Ripley's Aquarium
1110 Celebrity Circle
Myrtle Beach, SC 29577
http://www.ripleysaquarium.com

Riverbanks Zoo and Garden
500 Wildlife Parkway

Columbia, SC 29210
Phone: (803) 779-8717
Fax: (803) 253-6381
http://www.riverbanks.org

Waccatee Zoo
8500 Enterprise Road
Myrtle Beach, SC 29588
Phone: (843) 650-8500
Fax: (843) 916-0888
E-mail: info@ripleysaquarium.com
http://www.waccateezoo.com

SOUTH DAKOTA

Bramble Park Zoo
Bramble Park
800 10th Street, NW
P.O. Box 910
Watertown, SD 57201
Phone: (605) 882-6269
Fax: (605) 882-5232
http://www.brambleparkzoo.com

Great Plains Zoo
805 South Kiwanis Avenue (16th and Kiwanis Avenue)
Sioux Falls, SD 57104
Phone: (605) 367-8313
Fax: (605) 367-8340
http://www.gpzoo.org

TENNESSEE

Chattanooga Zoo
1254 East 3rd Street
Chattanooga, TN 37404
Phone: (423) 697-1322
Fax: (423) 697-1329
E-mail: info@chattzoo.org
http://www.chattzoo.org

Knoxville Zoo
3500 Knoxville Zoo Drive
P.O. Box 6040
Knoxville, TN 37914
Phone: (865) 637-5331
http://www.knoxville-zoo.org

Memphis Zoo
2000 Prentiss Place
Memphis, TN 38112

Phone: (901) 333-6500
E-mail: zooinfo@memphiszoo.org
http://www.memphiszoo.org

Nashville Zoo
3777 Nolensville Road
Nashville, TN 37211
Phone: (615) 833-1534
E-mail: pr@nashvillezoo.org
http://www.nashvillezoo.org

Tennessee Aquarium
One Broad Street
Chattanooga, TN 37402
Phone: (800) 262-0695
http://www.tennis.org

TEXAS

Abilene Zoo
2070 Zoo Lane
Nelson Park
Abilene, TX 79602
Phone: (325) 676-6200
http://www.abilenetx.com/zoo

Amarillo Zoo
Northeast 24th Avenue and Dumas Highway
Amarillo, TX 79105
Phone: (806) 381-7911
E-mail: zoo@amarilloparks.org
http://www.amarillozoo.org

Austin Zoo
P.O. Box 91808
Austin, TX, 78709
Phone: (512) 288-1490
Fax: (512) 288-3972
E-mail: info@austinzoo.org
http://www.austinzoo.org

Caldwell Zoo
2203 Martin Luther King Boulevard
Tyler, TX 75702
Phone: (903) 593-0121
E-mail: info@caldwellzoo.org
http://www.caldwellzoo.org

Cameron Park Zoo
1701 North 4th Street
Waco, TX 76707

Phone: (254) 750-8400
E-mail: specialevents@
 cameronparkzoo.com
http://www.cameronparkzoo.com

Dallas World Aquarium and Zoo
1801 North Griffin Street
Dallas, TX 75202
Phone: (214) 720-2224
http://www.dwazoo.com

Dallas Zoo
650 South R.L. Thornton Freeway
Dallas, TX 75203
Phone: (214) 670-5656
http://www.dallaszoo.com

El Paso Zoo
4001 East Paisano
El Paso, TX 79905
Phone: (915) 521-1881
E-mail: elpasozoo@elpasotexas.gov
http://www.elpasozoo.org

Fort Worth Zoo
1989 Colonial Parkway
Fort Worth, TX 76110
Phone: (817) 759-7500
Fax: (817) 759-7501
http://www.fortworthzoo.com

Gladys Porter Zoo
500 Ringgold Street
Brownsville, TX 78520
Phone: (956) 546-7187
http://www.gpz.org

Houston Zoo
6200 Hermann Park Drive
Houston, TX 77030
Phone: (713) 533-6500
http://www.houstonzoo.org

San Antonio Zoo and Aquarium
3903 North Saint Mary's Street
San Antonio, TX 78212-3199
Phone: (210) 734-7184
http://www.sazoo-aq.org

Texas Zoo
110 Memorial Drive

Victoria, TX 77901
Phone: (361) 573-7681
Fax: (361) 576-1094
http://www.texaszoo.org

Wild Animal Orphanage
9626 Leslie Road
San Antonio, TX 78254
Phone: (210) 688-2511
Fax: (210) 688-2529
http://www.wildanimalorphanage.
 org

UTAH

Utah's Hogle Zoo
2600 Sunnyside Avenue (840 South)
Salt Lake City, UT 84108
Phone: (801) 582-1631
http://www.hoglezoo.org

Willow Park Zoo
419 West 700 South
P.O. Box 527
Logan, UT 84323
Phone: (435) 716-9265
Fax: (435) 716-9254
E-mail: debbie.harvey@loganutah.
 org
http://www.loganutah.org/parks_
 and_rec/willow_park/index.cfm

VERMONT

Lake Champlain Basin Science Center
54 West Shore Road
Grand Isle, VT 05458
Phone: (802) 372-3213
http://www.lcbp.org

VIRGINIA

Luray Zoo
1087 U.S. Highway 211 West
Luray, VA 22835
Phone: (540) 743-4113
E-mail: reptiles@lurayzoo.com
http://www.lurayzoo.com

Metro Richmond Zoo
8300 Beaver Bridge Road
Moseley, VA 23120

Phone: (804) 739-5666
http://www.metrorichmondzoo.com

Virginia Zoo
Virginia Zoological Society
Norfolk, VA 23504
Phone: (757) 441-2374
http://www.virginiazoo.org

WASHINGTON

Point Defiance Zoo and Aquarium
5400 North Pearl Street
Tacoma, WA 98407
Phone: (253) 591-5337
http://www.pdza.org

The Seattle Aquarium
1483 Alaskan Way
Seattle, WA 98101
Phone: (206) 386-4300
Fax: (206) 386-4328
http://www.seattleaquarium.org

Woodland Park Zoo
601 North 59th Street
Seattle, WA 98103
Phone: (206) 548-2500
E-mail: webkeeper@zoo.org
http://www.zoo.org

WEST VIRGINIA

Oglebay's Good Zoo
465 Lodge Drive
Wheeling, WV 26003
Phone: (304) 243-4000
http://www.oglebay-resort.com/
 goodzoo

WISCONSIN

Henry Vilas Zoo
South Randall Avenue
Madison, WI 53715
Phone: (608) 266-4732
http://www.vilaszoo.org

Lincoln Park Zoo
1215 North 8th Street
Manitowoc, WI 54220
Phone: (920) 683-4530

http://www.manitowoc.org/
parkandrec/Zoo/zoo.htm

Menominee Park Zoo
215 Church Street
Oshkosh, WI 54901
Phone: (920) 236-5082
http://www.ci.oshkosh.wi.us/Zoo/
zoo.htm

Milwaukee County Zoo
10001 West Blue Mound Road
Milwaukee, WI 53226
Phone: (414) 771-3040
http://www.milwaukeezoo.org

Racine Zoo
200 Goold Street
Racine, WI 53402

Phone: (262) 636-9189
http://www.racinezoo.org

Wildwood Park Zoo
608 West 17th Street
Marshfield, WI 54449
Phone: (715) 384-4642
Fax: (715) 384-2799
http://ci.marshfield.wi.us//pr/Zoo

This appendix is a selected listing of animal advocacy organizations in the United States. Use this list to obtain general information, locate internships, or to send your résumé for job possibilities. Names, addresses, phone and fax numbers, e-mail addresses, and Web addresses have been included when available.

There are many more organizations located throughout the country. Due to space limitations, every organization could not be included. Use this list as a starting point. Inclusion or exclusion does not indicate the recommendation or endorsement by the author of any one organization over another.

2nd Chance 4 Pets
1484 Pollard Road
Los Gatos, CA 95032
Phone: (408) 871-1133
E-mail: info@2ndchance4pets.org
http://www.2ndchance4pets.org.

Abundant Wildlife Society of North America
P.O. Box 2
Beresford, SD 57004
Phone: (605) 751-0979
E-mail: research@bmtc.net
http://www.aws.vcn.com

Action for Animals (AFA)
P.O. Box 45843
Seattle, WA 98145
Phone: (206) 227-5752
E-mail: afa@afa-online.org
http://www.afa-online.org

Actors and Others for Animals
11523 Burbank Boulevard
North Hollywood, CA 91601
Phone: (818) 755-6045
Fax: (818) 755-6048
E-mail: webmistress@wom-designs.com
http://actorsandothers.com

Akita Rescue Society of America
237 Venus Street
Thousand Oaks, CA 91360
E-mail: bouyet@roadrunner.com
http://www.akitarescue.com

Alaskan Malamute Assistance League
P.O. Box 6028
Sparta, TN 38583
Phone: (419) 512-2423
E-mail: contact@malamuterescue.org
http://www.malamuterescue.org

Alley Cat Allies
7920 Norfolk Avenue
Bethesda, MD 20814-2525
Phone: (240) 482-1980
Fax: (240) 482-1990
E-mail: alleycat@alleycat.org
http://www.alleycat.org

Alliance for Animals
232 Silver Street
South Boston, MA 02127
Phone: (617) 268-7800
E-mail: allianceforanimals@verizon.net
http://www.afaboston.org

American Anti-Vivisection Society
801 Old York Road
Jenkintown, PA 19046
Phone: (215) 887-0816
E-mail: aavs@aavs
http://www.aavs.org

American Dog Owners Association
P.O. Box 41194
Fredericksburg, VA 22404
Phone: (888) 714-7220
Fax: (540) 786-8337
E-mail: adoamail@yahoo.com
http://www.adoa.org

American German Shepherd Rescue Association
c/o Linda Kury, President
P.O. Box 7113
Clearlake, CA 95422
Phone: (707) 994-5241
E-mail: lindakury@att.net
http://www.agsra.com

American Horse Defense Fund
1718 M Street, NW
Unit 191
Washington, DC 20036
Phone: (202) 609-8198
E-mail: president@ahdf.org
http://www.ahdf.org

American Pet Society
c/o World Wide Pet Industry Association
135 West Lemon Avenue
Monrovia, CA 91016
Phone: (626) 447-2222
Fax: (626) 447-8350
E-mail: info@wwpia.org
http://www.wwpia.org

American Sanctuary Association
2308 Chatfield Drive
Las Vegas, NV 89128
Phone: (702) 804-8562
Fax: (702) 804-8561
E-mail: asarescue@aol.com
http://www.asaanimalsanctuaries.org

American Society for the Prevention of Cruelty to Animals (ASPCA)
424 East 92nd Street
New York, NY 10128
Phone: (212) 876-7700
E-mail: shonalib@aspca.org
http://www.aspca.org

Animal Agents
P.O. Box 555
Kingsburg, CA 93631
Phone: (559) 960-6899
E-mail: animalagents@mac.com
http://www.animalagents.org

Animal Defenders International
953 Mission Street
San Francisco, CA 94103
Phone: (415) 543-2344
Fax: (415) 543-2343
http://www.ad-international.org

Animal House Rescue
P.O. Box 313
Neapolis, OH 43547
Phone: (419) 276-5699
E-mail: doggiesaver@yahoo.com
http://www.ahrescue.org

Animal Kind International
P.O. Box 300
Jemez Springs, NM 87025
E-mail: karen@animal-kind.org
http://www.animal-kind.org

Animal Legal Defense Fund
170 East Cotati Avenue
Cotati, CA 94931
Phone: (707) 795-2533
Fax: (707) 795-7280
E-mail: info@aldf.org
http://www.aldf.org

Animal Liberation Action Group
University of Wisconsin–Oshkosh
Campus Connection, Reeve Memorial Union
748 Algoma Boulevard
Oshkosh, WI 54901-3512
Phone: (920) 424-0265
Fax: (920) 424-7317
E-mail: animallib@uwosh.edu
http://www.uwosh.edu

Animal Place
3448 Laguna Creek Trail
Vacaville, CA 95688
Phone: (707) 449-4814
Fax: (707) 449-8775
E-mail: info@animalplace.org
http://animalplace.org

Animal Protection Institute of America
P.O. Box 22505
Sacramento, CA 95822
Phone: (916) 447-3085
Fax: (916) 447-3070
E-mail: info@api4animals.org

Animal Rights Coalition
2615 East Franklin Avenue
Minneapolis, MN 55406
Phone: (612) 822-6161
E-mail: animalrightscoalition@msn.com
http://www.animalrightscoalition.com

Animal Rights International
P.O. Box 1292
Middlebury, CT 06762
Phone: (203) 598-0554
E-mail: info@ari-online.org
http://www.ari-online.org

Animal Rights Mobilization
P.O. Box 671
Placitas, NM 87043
Phone: (773) 282-8918
E-mail: kayarm@comcast.net
http://www.animalrightsmobilization.org

Animal Rights Network/ Animals and Society Institute
2512 Carpenter Road
Suite 201-A2
Ann Arbor, MI 48108
Phone: (734) 677-9240
Fax: (734) 677-9242
E-mail: info@animalsandsociety.org
http://www.animalsandsociety.org

The Animal Society
723 South Casino Center Boulevard
Second Floor
Las Vegas, NV 89101
Phone: (702) 818-7889
E-mail: support@animalsociety.org

Animals Voice
1354 East Avenue
Number R-252
Chico, CA 95926
Phone: (800) 828-6423
E-mail: 4rights@animalsvoice.com
http://www.animalsvoice.com

Animal Transportation Association
745 Winding Trail
Holly Lake Ranch, TX 75765
Phone: (903) 769-9759
Fax: (903) 704-0970
E-mail: info@aata-animaltransport.org
http://www.aata-animaltransport.org

Animal Welfare Institute
P.O. Box 3650
Washington, DC 20027
Phone: (703) 836-4300
Fax: (703) 836-0400
E-mail: awi@awionline.org
http://www.awionline.org

Anti-Cruelty Society
157 West Grand Avenue
Chicago, IL 60610
Phone: (312) 644-8338
E-mail: info@anticruelty.org
http://www.anticruelty.org

Appalachian Bear Rescue
P.O. Box 364
Townsend, TN 37882
Phone: (865) 448-0143
Fax: (865) 448-0141
E-mail: jcburgin@kramer-rayson.
com
http://www.appalachianbearrescue.
org

Associated Humane Societies
124 Evergreen Avenue
Newark, NJ 07114
Phone: (973) 824-7080
Fax: (973) 824-2720
E-mail: contactus@ahcares.org
http://www.
associatedhumanesocieties.org

**Association of Professional
Humane Educators**
c/o The Latham Foundation
Latham Plaza Building
1826 Clement Avenue
Alameda, CA 94501
E-mail: aphe@aphe.org
http://aphe.org

**Association of Veterinarians
for Animal Rights**
P.O. Box 208
Davis, CA 95617-0208
Phone: (530) 759-8106
Fax: (530) 759-8116
E-mail: info@avar.org
http://avar.org

Avian Welfare Coalition
P.O. Box 40212
Saint Paul, MN 55104
E-mail: denise@avianwelfare.org
http://www.avianwelfare.org

**Back in the Saddle Horse
Adoption**
c/o Joni Fink, Executive Director
1313 Youngs Road
Linden, PA 17744
Phone: (570) 974-1087
Fax: (800) 821-3155
E-mail: bitsinfo@comcast.net
http://www.bitshorseadopt.org

Bide-A-Wee Home Association
410 East 38th Street
New York, NY 10016
Phone: (212) 532-6395
E-mail: bideawee@bideawee.org
http://www.bideawee.org

**Bulldog Club of America
Rescue Network**
c/o Shar Kynaston, Treasurer
P.O. Box 1049
Kaysville, UT 84037
E-mail: resqone@rescuebulldogs.
org
http://www.rescuebulldogs.org

Canine Defense Fund
c/o American Dog Owners
Association
P.O. Box 41194
Fredericksburg, VA 22404
Phone: (888) 714-7220
Fax: (540) 786-8337
E-mail: adoamail@yahoo.com
http://www.adoa.org

Chimp Haven
13600 Chimpanzee Place
Keithville, LA 71047
Phone: (318) 925-9575
Fax: (318) 925-9576
E-mail: information@chimphaven.
org
http://www.chimphaven.org

**Citizens to End Animal
Suffering and Exploitation
(CEASE)**
P.O. Box 440456
Somerville, MA 02144
Phone: (617) 379-0535
E-mail: info@ceaseboston.org
http://www.ceaseboston.org

**Coalition to Protect Animals in
Parks and Refuges**
P.O. Box 26
Swain, NY 14884
E-mail: civitas@linkny.com

**Coast to Coast Dachshund
Rescue**
P.O. Box 1148
Jackson, NJ 08527
E-mail: info@c2cdr.org
http://www.c2cdr.org

**Committee to Abolish Sport
Hunting**
P.O. Box 961
Maywood, NJ 07607
Phone: (201) 937-3721
Fax: (201) 368-7050
E-mail: cash@abolishsporthunting.
com
http://www.all-creatures.org/cash

**Companion Animal Protection
Society**
759 CJC Highway
Number 332
Cohasset, MA 02025
Phone: (781) 210-0938
Fax: (781) 210-0928
E-mail: caps@caps-web.org
http://www.caps-web.org

Defenders of Animals
P.O. Box 5634
Weybosset Hill Station
Providence, RI 02903
Phone: (401) 738-3710
E-mail: dennis@
defendersofanimals.org
http://www.defendersofanimals.org

Dogs Deserve Better
P.O. Box 23
Tipton, PA 16684
Phone: (814) 941-7447
E-mail: info@dogsdeservebetter.
org
http://www.dogsdeservebetter.org

Doing Things for Animals
59 South Bayles Avenue
Port Washington, NY 11050
Phone: (516) 883-7767
Fax: (516) 944-5035
E-mail: dtfafetsvr@aol.com
http://www.dtfa.org

Doris Day Animal League
2100 L Street, NW
Washington, DC 20037
Phone: (202) 452-1100
E-mail: info@ddal.org
http://www.ddal.org

Farm Animal Reform Movement (FARM)
10101 Ashburton Lane
Bethesda, MD 20817
Phone: (301) 530-1737
E-mail: info@farmusa.org
http://www.farmusa.org

Farm Sanctuary
P.O. Box 150
Watkins Glen, NY 14891
Phone: (607) 583-2225
Fax: (607) 583-2041
E-mail: info@farmsanctuary.org
http://www.farmsanctuary.org

Friends of Animals
777 Post Road
Darien, CT 06820
Phone: (203) 656-1522
Fax: (203) 656-0267
E-mail: info@friendsofanimals.org
http://www.friendsofanimals.org

Front Range Equine Rescue
P.O. Box 307
Larkspur, CO 80118
E-mail: info@
frontrangeequinerescue.org
http://www.frontrangeequinerescue.
org

Fund for Animals
200 West 57th Street
New York, NY 10019
Phone: (212) 246-2096
Fax: (212) 246-2633
E-mail: fundforanimals.org
http://www.fundforanimals.org

Global Federation of Animal Sanctuaries
P.O. Box 32294
Washington, DC 20007
Phone: (928) 472-1173

E-mail: patty@sanctuaryfederation.
org
http://www.sanctuaryfederation.org

Greyhound Adoption Center
P.O. Box 2433
La Mesa, CA 91943
Phone: (877) 478-8364
E-mail: info@houndsavers.org
http://www.houndsavers.org

Harmony House for Cats
P.O. Box 18098
Chicago, IL 60618
Phone: (773) 463-6667
E-mail: hhforcats@yahoo.com
http://hhforcats.org

Hearts United for Animals
P.O. Box 286
Auburn, NE 68305
Phone: (402) 274-3679
Fax: (402) 274-3689
E-mail: hua@hua.org
http://www.hua.org

Hooved Animal Humane Society
10804 McConnell Road
Woodstock, IL 60098
Phone: (815) 337-5563
Fax: (815) 337-5569
E-mail: info@hahs.org
http://www.hahs.org

Humane Farm Animal Care
P.O. Box 727
Herndon, VA 20172
Phone: (703) 435-3883
E-mail: info@certifiedhumane.org
http://www.certifiedhumane.org

Humane Farming Association
P.O. Box 3577
San Rafael, CA 94912
Phone: (415) 771-2253
Fax: (415) 485-0106
E-mail: hfa@hfa.org
http://www.hfa.org

Humane Society of the United States
2100 L Street, NW
Washington, DC 20037
Phone: (202) 452-1100
Fax: (301) 258-3078
E-mail: membership@hsus.org
http://www.hsus.org

Humane Society Youth
67 Norwich Essex Turnpike
East Haddam, CT 06423
Phone: (860) 434-8666
E-mail: youth@humanesociety.org
http://www.humanesocietyyouth.
org

In Defense of Animals
3010 Kerner Boulevard
San Rafael, CA 94901
Phone: (415) 448-0048
Fax: (415) 454-1031
E-mail: idainfo@ida.org
http://www.ida.org

International Fund for Animal Welfare
290 Summer Street
Yarmouth Port, MA 02675
Phone: (508) 744-2000
Fax: (508) 744-2009
E-mail: info@ifaw.org
http://www.ifaw.org

International Primate Protection League
P.O. Box 766
Summerville, SC 29484
Phone: (843) 871-2280
Fax: (843) 871-7988
E-mail: info@ippl.org
http://www.ippl.org

International Society for Animal Rights
965 Griffin Pond Road
Clarks Summit, PA 18411
Phone: (570) 586-2200
Fax: (570) 586-9580
E-mail: contact@isaronline.org
http://www.isaronline.org

Johns Hopkins Center for Alternatives to Animal Testing
111 Market Place
Baltimore, MD 21202
Phone: (410) 223-1692
Fax: (410) 223-1603
E-mail: caat@jhsph.edu

National Anti-Vivisection Society
53 West Jackson Boulevard
Chicago, IL 60604
Phone: (312) 427-6065
Fax: (312) 427-6524
E-mail: feedback@navs.org
http://www.navs.org

National Cat Protection Society
6983 West Coast Highway
Newport Beach, CA 92663
Phone: (949) 650-1232
Fax: (949) 650-7367
E-mail: natcatnewport@gmail.com
http://www.natcat.org

National Endowment for the Animals
660 South 40th Street
Boulder, CO 80305
Phone: (720) 252-8449
E-mail: info@neaforever.org
http://www.neaforever.org

National Federation of Humane Societies
800 Cottage Street, NW
Vienna, VA 22180
Phone: (563) 582-6766
E-mail: humanejane@dbqhumane.org
http://www.humanefederation.org

National Greyhound Adoption Program
10901 Dutton Road
Philadelphia, PA 19154
Phone: (215) 331-7918
Fax: (215) 331-1947
E-mail: info@ngap.org
http://www.ngap.org

National Humane Education Society
P.O. Box 340
Charles Town, WV 25414
Phone: (304) 725-0506
Fax: (304) 725-1523
E-mail: nhesinformation@nhes.org
http://www.nhes.org

Noah's Ark Animal Welfare Association
1915 Rowe 46 West
Ledgewood, NJ 07852
Phone: (973) 347-0378
E-mail: info@noahsarknj.org
http://www.noahsarknj.org

People for the Ethical Treatment of Animals (PETA)
501 Front Street
Norfolk, VA 23510
Phone: (757) 622-7382
Fax: (757) 622-0457
E-mail: info@peta.org
http://www.peta.org

People Protecting Animals and Their Habitats
P.O. Box 12022
Fort Pierce, FL 34979
Phone: (617) 354-2826
E-mail: animalpath@aol.com
http://www.ppath.org

Performing Animals Welfare Society (PAWS)
P.O. Box 849
Galt, CA 95632
Phone: (209) 745-2606
Fax: (209) 745-1809
E-mail: info@pawsweb.org
http://www.pawsweb.org

Pets America
P.O. Box 40997
Austin, TX 78704
Phone: (512) 452-4224
Fax: (512) 452-6633
E-mail: info@petsamerica.org
http://www.petsamerica.org

Pet Savers Foundation
750 Port Washington Boulevard
Port Washington, NY 11050
Phone: (516) 883-1461
Fax: (516) 883-1595
E-mail: info@petsavers.org
http://www.petsavers.org

Polar Bears International
P.O. Box 3008
Bozeman, MT 59772
http://www.polarbearsinternational.org

Primarily Primates
26099 Dull Knife Trail
San Antonio, TX 78255
Phone: (830) 755-4616
Fax: (830) 755-4618
E-mail: primarilyprimates@friendsofanimals.org
http://primarilyprimates.org

Sanctuary Workers and Volunteers Association
P.O. Box 637
Boyd, TX 76023
Phone: (940) 433-5091
Fax: (940) 433-5092
E-mail: swava@sbcglobal.net
http://www.swava.org

Save the Chimps
P.O. Box 12220
Fort Pierce, FL 34979
Phone: (772) 429-0403
Fax: (772) 460-0720
E-mail: info@savethechimps.org
http://www.savethechimps.org

Support Our Shelters
c/o Judith White
100 Walsh Road
Lansdowne, PA 19050
Phone: (610) 626-6647
E-mail: sharon@supportourshelters.org
http://www.supportourshelters.org

United Action for Animals
P.O. Box 635

New York, NY 10021
Phone: (212) 249-9178
E-mail: info@ua4a.org
http://www.ua4a.org

United Animal Nations
P.O. Box 188890
Sacramento, CA 95818
Phone: (916) 429-2457

Fax: (916) 429-2456
E-mail: info@uan.org
http://www.uan.org

United Poultry Concerns
P.O. Box 150
Machipongo, VA 23405-0150
Phone: (757) 678-7875
Fax: (757) 678-5070

E-mail: info@upc-online.org
http://www.upc-online.org

Voice for Animals
P.O. Box 120095
San Antonio, TX 78212
Phone: (210) 737-3138
E-mail: voice@voiceforanimals.org
http://www.voiceforanimals.org

APPENDIX IV
UNITED STATES THOROUGHBRED RACETRACKS

The following is a list of Thoroughbred racetracks in the United States.

Some of the more popular Thoroughbred races held annually include the Kentucky Derby at Churchill Downs in Lexington, the Belmont Stakes at Belmont Park in Elmont, New York, the Preakness Stakes at Pimlico in Baltimore, Maryland, and the Travers Stakes at Saratoga in Saratoga Springs, New York.

Some tracks hold racing year-round. Others only have racing dates during specific times of the year.

Tracks are listed by state. Names, addresses, phone numbers, and Web sites are included for each (when available). Use this appendix to obtain general information, locate internships, and/or to send your résumés for job possibilities.

ARIZONA

Apache County Fair at St. John's (Racing dates during fair)
Apache County Fair
825 West 4th Street North
Saint John's, AZ 85936
Phone: (928) 337-2621

Cochise County Fair at Douglas (Racing dates during fair)
Cochise County Fair
P.O. Box 782
Douglas, AZ 85608
Phone: (520) 364-3819
http://www.
cochisecountyfair.50megs.com

Coconino County Horse Races (Racing dates during fair)
Fort Tuthill Downs
Flagstaff, AZ 86001
Phone: (928) 774-5139

Gila County Fair (Racing dates during fair)
P.O. Box 2193
Globe, AZ 88502
Phone: (928) 425-2772
http://gilafair.net

Graham County Fair at Safford (Racing dates during fair)
Graham County Fair
527 East Armory Road
Safford, AZ 85546
Phone: (928) 428-6240

Greenlee County Fair and Racing (Racing dates during fair)
P.O. Box 123
Duncan, AZ 85533
Phone: (928) 359-2032
http://www.co.greenlee.
az.us/FairRacing/
FairRacingHomePage.aspx

Mohave County Fair (Racing dates during fair)
2600 Fairgrounds Boulevard
Kingman, AZ 86401
Phone: (928) 753-2636
http://www.mcfafairgrounds.org

Prescott Downs Racetrack
P.O. Box 26557
Prescott Valley, AZ 86312
Phone: (928) 775-8000
http://www.amdest.com/az/
prescott/pd/prescottdowns.html

Rillito Park
4502 North First Avenue
Tucson, AZ 85718
Phone: (520) 293-5011

Santa Cruz County Horse Races (Racing dates during fair)
Santa Cruz County Fair
P.O. Box 85
Sonoita, AZ 85637
Phone: (520) 455-5553
Fax: (520) 455-5330
http://www.sonoitafairgrounds.com

Turf Paradise
1501 West Bell Road
Phoenix, AZ 85023
Phone: (602) 942-1101
Fax: (602) 942-8659
E-mail: tp@turfparadise.com
http://www.turfparadise.com

Yavapai Downs
P.O. Box 26557
Prescott Valley, AZ 86312
Phone: (928) 775-8000
Fax: (928) 445-0408
E-mail: info@yavapaidownsatpv.
com
http://www.yavapaidownsatpv.com

ARKANSAS

Oaklawn Jockey Club
2705 Central Avenue
Hot Springs, AR 71902
Phone: (501) 623-4411
E-mail: clubinquiries@oaklawn.com
http://www.oaklawn.com

CALIFORNIA

Alameda County Fair (Racing dates during fair)
4501 Pleasanton Avenue
Pleasanton, CA 94566
Phone: (925) 426-7600
E-mail: frontdesk@
  alamedacountyfair.com
http://www.alamedacountyfair.com

Bay Meadows
P.O. Box 5050
San Mateo, CA 94402
Phone: (650) 574-7223
http://www.baymeadows.com

California Exposition
1600 Exposition Boulevard
Sacramento, CA 95815
Phone: (916) 263-3000
E-mail: info@calexpo.com
http://www.calexpo.com

Del Mar Thoroughbred Club
2260 Jimmy Durante Boulevard
Del Mar, CA 92014
Phone: (858) 755-1141
http://www.delmarracing.com

Fairplex Park
P.O. Box 2250
Pomona, CA 91769
Phone: (909) 623-3111
E-mail: info@fairplex.com
http://www.fairplex.com/fp

Ferndale (Racing dates during fair)
P.O. Box 637
Ferndale, CA 95536
Phone: (707) 786-9511

Fresno Fair (Racing dates during fair)
1121 Chance Avenue
Fresno, CA 93702
Phone: (559) 650-3247
http://www.fresnofair.com

Golden Gate Fields
P.O. Box 6027
Albany, CA 94706
Phone: (510) 559-7330
http://www.goldengatefields.com

Hollywood Park
P.O. Box 369
Inglewood, CA 90306
Phone: (310) 419-1500
http://www.hollywoodpark.com

Los Alamitos
4961 East Katella Avenue
Los Alamitos, CA 90720
Phone: (714) 820-2800
http://www.losalamitos.com/laqhr

Santa Anita Park
P.O. Box 60014
Arcadia, CA 91066
Phone: (626) 574-7223
http://www.santaanita.com

Santa Rosa (Racing dates during fair)
Sonoma County Fairgrounds
P.O. Box 1536
Santa Rosa, CA 95402
Phone: (707) 545-4200

Solano County Fair (Racing dates during fair)
900 Fairgrounds Drive
Vallejo, CA 94589
Phone: (707) 551-2000
Fax: (707) 642-7947
http://www.scfair.com

Stockton (Racing dates during fair)
San Joaquin County Fair
1658 South Airport Way
Stockton, CA 95205

Phone: (209) 466-5041
http://www.sanjoaquinfair.com

COLORADO

Arapahoe Park
26000 East Quincy Avenue
Aurora, CO 80016
Phone: (303) 690-2400
http://www.mihiracing.com/
  mihi/index.php?get=
  showpage&catid=2

FLORIDA

Calder Race Course
P.O. Box 1808
Miami, FL 33055
Phone: (954) 523-4324
http://www.calderracecourse.com

Gulfstream Park
901 South Federal Highway
Hallandale, FL 33009
Phone: (954) 454-7000
Fax: (954) 457-6510
http://www.gulfstreampark.com

Hialeah Park
2200 East 4th Avenue
Hialeah, FL 33010
Phone: (954) 305-8000
E-mail: info@hialeahparkracing.
  com
http://www.hialeahparkracing.com

Tampa Bay Downs
11225 Racetrack Road
Tampa, FL 33626
Phone: (813) 855-4401
http://www.tampabaydowns.com

IDAHO

Blackfoot (Racing dates during fair)
97 Park Street
Blackfoot, ID 83221
Phone: (208) 785-2480
Fax: (208) 785-2483
http://www.funatthefair.com

Burley (Racing dates during fair)
Cassia County Fair
P.O. Box 1222
Burley, ID 83318
Phone: (208) 678-8610
http://www.cassiacounty.org/fair/index.htm

Emmett (Racing dates during fair)
Gem County Fairboard
Box 443
Emmett, ID 83617
Phone: (208) 365-6828
Fax: (208) 365-0932
E-mail: gemcofair@co.gem.id.us
http://www.gemcountyfairgrounds.com

Jerome (Racing dates during fair)
Jerome County Fair
200 North Fir Street
Jerome, ID 83338
Phone: (208) 324-7209
Fax: (208) 324-7057
E-mail: jcf@bridgemail.com
http://www.jeromecountyfair.com

Les Bois Park
5610 Glenwood Road
Boise, ID 83714
Phone: (208) 321-0222
http://www.lesboispark.org

Malad (Racing dates during fair)
Oneida County Fair
P.O. Box 13
Malad City, ID 83252
Phone: (208) 766-4706

Pocatello Downs
P.O. Box 0248
Pocatello, ID 83204
Phone: (208) 238-1721
Fax: (208) 238-1763

Rupert Downs
P.O. Box 263
Rupert, ID 83350
Phone: (208) 436-3109

Sandy Downs
3665 North 15th East
Idaho Falls, ID 83401
Phone: (208) 529-0671

ILLINOIS

Arlington Park
2200 West Euclid
Arlington Heights, IL 60006
Phone: (847) 255-7500
http://www.arlingtonpark.com

Fairmont Park
9301 Collinsville Road
Collinsville, IL 62234
Phone: (618) 345-4300
http://www.fairmountpark.com

Hawthorne Race Course
3501 South Laramie Avenue
Cicero, IL 60804
Phone: (708) 780-3700
http://www.hawthorneracecourse.com

Sportsman's Park
3301 Laramie Avenue
Cicero, IL 60804
Phone: (708) 780-3700
http://www.sportsmanspark.com

KENTUCKY

Churchill Downs
700 Central Avenue
Louisville, KY 40208
Phone: (502) 636-4400
http://www.churchilldowns.com

Ellis Park
3300 U.S. Highway 41 North
Henderson, KY 42420
Phone: (800) 333-8110
E-mail: info@ellisparkracing.com
http://www.ellisparkracing.com

Keeneland
P.O. Box 1690
Lexington, KY 40588
Phone: (859) 254-3412
Fax: (859) 255-2484
http://www.keeneland.com

Kentucky Downs
P.O. Box 405
Franklin, KY 42135
Phone: (270) 586-7778
Fax: (270) 586-8080
E-mail: jongoodman@kentuckydowns.com
http://www.kentuckydowns.com

Kentucky Harness Racing Track
The Red Mile
1200 Red Mile Road
Lexington, KY 40504
Phone: (859) 255-0752
Fax: (859) 231-0217
E-mail: info@theredmile.com
http://www.theredmile.com

Turfway Park
P.O. Box 8
Florence, KY 41022
Phone: (859) 371-0200
Fax: (859) 647-4730
http://www.turfway.com

LOUISIANA

Delta Downs
2717 Delta Downs Drive
Vinton, LA 70668
Phone: (800) 589-7441
http://www.deltadowns.com

Evangeline Downs
2235 Creswell Lane Extension
Opelousas, LA 70570
Phone: (866) 472-2466
http://www.evangelinedowns.com

Fairgrounds Racecourse
1751 Gentilly Boulevard
New Orleans, LA 70119
Phone: (504) 944-5515

Fax: (504) 948-1160
E-mail: info@fgno.com
http://www.fairgroundsracecourse. com

Louisiana Downs
8000 East Texas Street
Bossier City, LA 71111
Phone: (318) 742-5555
http://www.harrahslouisianadowns. com

MARYLAND

Laurel Park
P.O. Box 130
Laurel, MD 20725
Phone: (301) 725-0400
E-mail: racing@marylandracing. com
http://www.laurelpark.com

Pimlico
5201 Park Heights Avenue
Baltimore, MD 21215
Phone: (410) 542-9400
E-mail: racing@marylandracing. com
http://www.pimlico.com

Timonium Race Track (Racing dates during fair)
Maryland State Fair
2200 Block York Road
Timonium, MD 21094
Phone: (410) 252-0200
Fax: (410) 561-5610
E-mail: msfair@msn.com
http://www.marylandstatefair.com

MASSACHUSETTS

Northampton (Racing dates during fair)
P.O. Box 305
Northampton, MA 01061
Phone: (413) 584-2237

Suffolk Downs
111 Waldemar Avenue
East Boston, MA 02128

Phone: (617) 567-3900
http://www.suffolkdowns.com

MICHIGAN

Detroit Race Course
28001 Schoolcraft
Livonia, MI 48150
Phone: (734) 525-7300

Mount Pleasant Meadows
P.O. Box 220
Mount Pleasant, MI 48858
Phone: (989) 773-0012
Fax: (989) 773-4632
http://www.michigan.org/Property/ Detail.aspx?p=G5143

Pinnacle Racetrack
18000 Vining Road
New Boston, MI 48164
Phone: (734) 543-3200
http://www.pinnacleracecourse.com

MINNESOTA

Canterbury Park
1100 Canterbury Road
Shakopee, MN 55379
Phone: (612) 445-7223
E-mail: cbypark@canterburypark. com
http://www.canterburypark.com

MONTANA

Great Falls (Racing dates during fair)
Montana State Fair
P.O. Box 1524
Great Falls, MT 59403
Phone: (406) 727-8900
http://www.montanastatefair.com/ index.php

Kalispell (Racing dates during fair)
Northwest Montana Fair
256 North Meridian Road
Kalispell, MT 59801
Phone: (406) 758-5810
http://www.nwmtfair.com

Missoula (Racing dates during fair)
Western Montana Fair
1101 South Avenue West
Missoula, MT 59801
Phone: (406) 721-3247
http://www.westernmontanafair. com

Yellowstone Downs
Yellowstone Downs Horseracing Alliance, Inc.
P.O. Box 1138
Billings, MT 59103
Phone: (406) 869-5251
Fax: (406) 869-5253
E-mail: racing@yellowstonedowns. com
http://www.yellowstonedowns.com

NEBRASKA

Columbus Races
Platte County Agricultural Society
822 15th Street
Columbus, NE 68601
Phone: (402) 564-0133
http://www.agpark.com

Fonner Park
P.O. Box 490
Grant Island, NE 68802
Phone: (308) 382-4515
Fax: (308) 384-2753
E-mail: fonnerpark@aol.com
http://www.fonnerpark.com

Horseman's Park
6303 Q Street
Omaha, NE 68117
Phone: (402) 731-2900
http://www.horsemenspark.com

Lincoln State Fair
P.O. Box 81233
Lincoln, NE 68501
Phone: (402) 474-5371
http://www.statefair.org/ statefairpark

NEVADA

Elko County Fair (Racing dates during fair)
P.O. Box 2067
Elko, NV 89803
Phone: (775) 738-3616
Fax: (775) 778-3648
E-mail: elkcountyfair@hotmail.com
http://www.elkocountyfair.com

Winnemucca
Tri-County Fair and Stampede
50 West Winnemucca Boulevard
Winnemucca, NV 89445
Phone: (775) 623-5071
Fax: (775) 623-5087
E-mail: information@winnemucca.
   com
http://www.winnemucca.nv.us

NEW JERSEY

Atlantic City Race Course
4501 Black Horse Pike
Mays Landing, NJ 08330
Phone: (609) 641-2190
http://www.acracecourse.com

Garden State Park
P.O. Box 4274
Cherry Hill, NJ 08034
Phone: (856) 488-8400
http://www.gardenstatepark.net

Meadowlands Racetrack
50 State Route 120
East Rutherford, NJ 07073
Phone: (201) 843-2446
E-mail: media@njsea.com
http://www.thebigm.com

Monmouth Park
175 Oceanport Avenue
Oceanport, NJ 07757
Phone: (732) 222-5100
E-mail: monmouthinfor@njsea.
   com
http://www.monmouthpark.com

NEW MEXICO

Downs at Albuquerque
P.O. Box 8510
Albuquerque, NM 87198
Phone: (505) 266-5555
Fax: (505) 268-1970
http://www.abqdowns.com

Ruidoso Downs
P.O. Box 449
Ruidoso Downs, NM 88346
Phone: (505) 378-4431
E-mail: info@raceruidoso.com
http://www.ruidownsracing.com

Sun Ray Park
9 Road 5568
Farmington, NM 87401
Phone: (505) 566-1200
http://www.sunraygaming.com

Sunland Park
1200 Futurity Drive
Sunland Park, NM 88063
Phone: (505) 874-5200
http://www.sunland-park.com

Zia Park
3901 West Millen Drive
Hobbs, NM 88240
Phone: (888) 942-7275
Fax: (575) 492-7098
E-mail: zia.contact@pngaming.com
http://www.blackgoldcasino.net

NEW YORK

Aqueduct Raceway
110-00 Rockaway Boulevard
Jamaica, NY 11417
Phone: (718) 641-4700
E-mail: suggestions@nyrainc.com
http://nyra.com/index_aqueduct.
   html

Belmont Park
2150 Hempstead Turnpike
Elmont, NY 11003
Phone: (718) 641-4700
http://www.nyra.com/index_
   belmont.html

Finger Lakes
P.O. Box 25250
Farmington, NY 14425
Phone: (585) 924-3232
http://www.fingerlakesracetrack.
   com

Saratoga
267 Union Avenue
Saratoga Springs, NY 12866
Phone: (518) 584-6200
http://www.nyra.com/index_
   saratoga.html

NORTH DAKOTA

Belcourt
Sky Dancer Hotel and Casino
P.O. Box 900
Highway 5 West
Belcourt, ND 58316
Phone: (701) 244-2400
http://www.skydancercasino.com

North Dakota Horse Park
5180 19th Avenue North
Fargo, ND 58102
Phone: (701) 277-8027
http://www.hrnd.org

OHIO

Beulah Park
P.O. Box 850
Grove City, OH 43123
Phone: (614) 871-9600
Fax: (614) 871-0433
http://www.beulahpark.com

River Downs
6301 Kellogg Avenue
Cincinnati, OH 45230
Phone: (513) 232-8000
http://www.riverdowns.com

Thistledown
21501 Emery Road
North Randall, OH 44128
Phone: (216) 662-8600
http://www.thistledown.com

OKLAHOMA

Blue Ribbon Downs
P.O. Box 489
Sallisaw, OK 74955
Phone: (918) 775-7771
http://www.blueribbondowns.net

Fair Meadows
P.O. Box 4735
Tulsa, OK 74159
Phone: (918) 743-7223
Fax: (918) 743-8053
http://www.exposquare.com

Remington Park
One Remington Place
Oklahoma City, OK 73111
Phone: (405) 424-1000
E-mail: contact@remingtonpark.com
http://www.remingtonpark.com

Will Rogers Downs
20900 South 4200 Road
Claremore, OK 74919
Phone: (918) 283-8800
http://www.cherokeestarrewards.com/casinos/willrogersdowns/Pages/default.aspx

OREGON

Crook County Fairground
P.O. Box 507
Prineville, OR 97754
Phone: (541) 447-6575
Fax: (541) 447-3225
E-mail: ccfg@clearwire.net
http://www.crookcountyfairgrounds.com

Grants Pass
P.O. Box 282
Grants Pass, OR 97526
Phone: (541) 476-3215

Portland Meadows
1001 North Schmeer Road
Portland, OR 97217
Phone: (503) 285-9144
Fax: (503) 286-9763

E-mail: info@portlandmeadows.com
http://www.portlandmeadows.com

Tillamook (Racing dates during fair)
Tillamook County Fair
P.O. Box 455
Tillamook, OR 97141
Phone: (503) 842-2272
Fax: (503) 842-3314
E-mail: tillamookfair@wcn.net
http://www.tillamookfair.com

Union (Racing dates during fair)
P.O. Box 4092
Union, OR 97883
Phone: (541) 562-5768

PENNSYLVANIA

Penn National
777 Hollywood Boulevard
Grantville, PA 17028
Phone: (717) 469-2211
http://www.pennnational.com

Philadelphia Park
P.O. Box 1000
Bensalem, PA 19020
Phone: (215) 639-9000
http://www.philadelphiapark.com

Presque Isle Downs
8199 Perry Highway
Erie, PA 16509
Phone: (866) 374-3386
E-mail: pidinfo@pidowns.com
http://www.casinoinerie.com

SOUTH DAKOTA

Brown County
25 Market Street
Aberdeen, SD 57401
Phone: (605) 626-7116
http://www.thebrowncountyfair.com

South Dakota Horse Racing
P.O. Box 426
Fort Pierre, SD 57532

Phone: (605) 223-2178
E-mail: sdqhra@sdhorseracing.com
http://www.sdhorseracing.com

TEXAS

Gillespie County Fair (Racing dates during fair)
P.O. Box 526
Fredericksburg, TX 78624
Phone: (830) 997-2359
Fax: (830) 997-4923
E-mail: info@gillespiefair.com
http://www.gillespiefair.com

Lone Star
1000 Lone Star Parkway
Grand Prairie, TX 75050
Phone: (972) 263-7223
http://www.lonestarpark.com

Manor Downs
P.O. Box 141309
Austin, TX 78714
Phone: (512) 272-5581
E-mail: manordowns@manordowns.com
http://www.manordowns.com

Retama Park
P.O. Box 47535
San Antonio, TX 78265
Phone: (210) 651-7000
E-mail: run@retamapark.com
http://www.retamapark.com

Sam Houston Race Park
7575 North Sam Houston Parkway West
Houston, TX 77064
Phone: (281) 807-8700
http://www.shrp.com

UTAH

Dixie Downs
P.O. Box 444
Washington, UT 84780
Phone: (435) 673-4932

VIRGINIA

Colonial Downs

10515 Colonial Downs Parkway
New Kent, VA 23124
Phone: (804) 966-7223
http://www.colonialdowns.com

WASHINGTON

Dayton (Racing dates during fair)

Columbia County Fairgrounds
P.O. Box 264
Dayton, WA 99328
Phone: (509) 382-2370

Emerald Downs

P.O. Box 617
Auburn, WA 98071
Phone: (253) 288-7000
http://www.emdowns.com

Sun Downs

P.O. Box 6662
Kennewick, WA 99336
Phone: (509) 582-5434

Waitsburg (Racing dates during fair)

Waitsburg Fairgrounds
P.O. Box 391
Waitsburg, WA 99361
Phone: (509) 337-6241

Walla Walla (Race dates during fair)

Walla Walla County Fairgrounds
P.O. Box G
Walla Walla, WA 99362
Phone: (509) 527-3247
Fax: (509) 527-3259
E-mail: wwfair@hscis.net
http://www.wallawallafairgrounds.com

WEST VIRGINIA

Charles Town Races

750 Hollywood Drive
Charles Town, WV 25414
Phone: (800) 795-7001
http://www.ctownraces.com

Mountaineer Racetrack

Route 2
Chester, WV 26034
Phone: (800) 804-0468
E-mail: info@mtrgaming.com
http://www.mtrgaming.com/index.php

WYOMING

Wyoming Downs

P.O. Box 1607
Evanston, WY 82930
Phone: (307) 789-0511
http://www.wyomingdowns.com

APPENDIX V
UNITED STATES
HARNESS RACING TRACKS

The following is a list of harness racing tracks in the United States. Harness racing utilizes a specific breed of horse called Standardbreds. Instead of saddling and riding the horse as in Thoroughbred racing, in harness racing a driver follows behind the horse in a two-wheeled cart called a sulky. The sulky is attached to a horse via a harness.

Some tracks have racing year-round. Others only have racing dates during specific times of the year. Some of the most well-known harness races held annually include the Hambletonian in the Meadowlands, New Jersey, the Kentucky Futurity in Lexington, and the Yonkers Trot in Yonkers, New York.

Tracks are listed by state. Names, addresses, phone and fax numbers, e-mail addresses, and Web sites are included for each when available. Use this list to obtain general information, locate internships, and/or to send your résumés for job possibilities.

CALIFORNIA

Cal Expo Horse Racing
1600 Exposition Way
Sacramento, CA 95852
Phone: (916) 263-3000
http://www.calexpoharness.com

Los Alamitos Race Course
4961 East Katella Avenue
Los Alamitos, CA 90720
Phone: (714) 820-2800
E-mail: larace@losalamitos.com
http://www.losalamitos.com/laqhr

DELAWARE

Dover Downs
1131 North DuPont Highway
Dover, DE 90720
Phone: (302) 674-4600
http://www.doverdowns.com

Harrington Raceway
15 West Rider Road
Harrington, DE 19952
Phone: (302) 398-5970
http://www.harringtonraceway.com

FLORIDA

Pompano Park
777 Isle of Capri Circle
Pompano Beach, FL 33069
Phone: (800) 843-4753
http://pompano-park.
    isleofcapricasinos.com/racing.
    aspx

ILLINOIS

Balmoral Park
26435 South Dixie Highway
Crete, IL 60417
Phone: (708) 672-1414
Fax: (708) 672-5932
http://www.balmoralpark.com

DuQuoin State Fair (Racing dates during fair)
P.O. Box 19281
Springfield, IL 62794
Phone: (217) 782-2172
http://www.agr.state.il.us/dq

Fairmont Park
9301 Collinsville Road
Collinsville, IL 62234
Phone: (618) 345-4300
http://www.fairmountpark.com

Hawthorne Race Course
3501 South Laramie Avenue
Cicero, IL 60804
Phone: (708) 780-3700
http://www.hawthorneracecourse.
    com

Marywood Park Raceway
8600 West North Avenue
Marywood, IL 60153
Phone: (708) 343-4800
http://www.maywoodpark.com

Springfield (Racing dates during Illinois State Fair)
P.O. Box 19281
Springfield, IL 62794
Phone: (217) 782-4321
http://www.illinoisstatefair.info

INDIANA

Hoosier Park
4500 Dan Patch Circle
Anderson, IN 46013
Phone: (765) 642-7223
Fax: (765) 608-2754
E-mail: info@hoosierpark.com
http://www.hoosierpark.com

Indiana Downs
4200 North Michigan Road
Shelbyville, IN 46176
Phone: (317) 421-0000
http://www.indianadowns.com

Indiana State Fair (Racing dates during fair)
1202 East 38th Street
Indianapolis, IN 46205
Phone: (317) 927-7500
http://www.in.gov/statefair

IOWA

Prairie Meadows Racetrack
One Prairie Meadows Drive
Altoona, IA 50009
Phone: (800) 325-9015
http://www.prairiemeadows.com

KENTUCKY

The Red Mile
1200 Red Mile Road
Lexington, KY 40504
Phone: (859) 255-0752
Fax: (859) 231-0217
E-mail: info@theredmile.com
http://www.theredmile.com

Thunder Ridge
164 Thunder Road
Prestonburg, KY 41653
Phone: (606) 886-7223

MAINE

Bangor Raceway
500 Main Street
Bangor, ME 04401
Phone: (877) 779-7771
http://www.bangorraceway.net

Cumberland Fair (Racing dates during fair)
6 Crossing Brook Road
Cumberland, ME 04021
Phone: (207) 829-6647
http://www.cumberlandfair.com

Oxford County Fair (Racing dates during fair)
P.O. Box 223
Norway, ME 04268
Phone: (207) 743-9594
http://www.oxfordcountyfair.com

Scarborough Downs
P.O. Box 468
Scarborough, ME 04070
Phone: (207) 883-4331
http://www.scarboroughdowns.com

Skowhegan Fair (Racing dates during fair)
P.O. Box 39
Skowhegan, ME 04976
Phone: (207) 474-2947
Fax: (207) 474-6257
E-mail: office@skowheganstatefair. com
http://www.skowheganstatefair.com

MARYLAND

Ocean Downs
P.O. Box 11
Berlin, MD 21811
Phone: (410) 641-0600
E-mail: info@oceandowns.com
http://www.oceandowns.com

Rosecroft Raceway
6336 Rosecroft Drive
Fort Washington, MD 20744
Phone: (301) 567-4000
http://www.rosecroft.com

MASSACHUSETTS

Plainridge Racecourse
301 Washington Street
Plainville, MA 02762
Phone: (508) 643-2500
http://www.prcharness.com

MICHIGAN

Hazel Park Harness Raceway
1650 East Ten Mile Road
Hazel Park, MI 48030
Phone: (248) 398-1000
Fax: (248) 398-5236

E-mail: info@hazelparkraceway. com
http://hazelparkraceway.com

Northville Downs
301 South Center Street
Northville, MI 48167
Phone: (248) 349-1000
http://www.northvilledowns.com

Saginaw Harness Raceway
2701 East Genesee Street
Saginaw, MI 48601
Phone: (987) 755-3451

Sports Creek Raceway
4920 Morrish Road
Swartz Creek, MI 48473
Phone: (810) 653-3333
E-mail: info@sportscreek.com
http://sportscreek.com

MINNESOTA

Running Acres
15201 Zurich Street, NE
Forest Lake, MN 55025
Phone: (651) 925-4600
http://www.runningacesharness. com

NEW HAMPSHIRE

Rockingham Park
P.O. Box 47
Salem, NH 03079
Phone: (603) 898-2311
E-mail: askquestion@ rockinghampark.com
http://www.rockinghampark.com

NEW JERSEY

Freehold Raceway
P.O. Box 6249
Freehold, NJ 07728
Phone: (732) 462-3800
Fax: (732) 462-2920
http://www.freeholdraceway.com

Meadowlands Racetrack
50 State Route 120
East Rutherford, NJ 07073

Phone: (201) 935-8500
http://www.thebigm.com

NEW YORK

Batavia Downs
8315 Park Road
Batavia, NY 14020
Phone: (585) 343-3750
http://www.batavia-downs.com

Buffalo Raceway
5600 McKinley Parkway
Hamburg, NY 14075
Phone: (716) 649-1280
Fax: (716) 649-0033
http://www.buffaloraceway.com

Goshen Historic Track
44 Park Place
Goshen, NY 10924
Phone: (845) 294-5333
Fax: (845) 294-3998
http://www.goshenhistorictrack.
   com

Monticello Raceway
Route 17B
Raceway Road
Monticello, NY 12701
Phone: (845) 794-4100
http://www.monticelloraceway.com

Saratoga Raceway
P.O. Box 356
Saratoga Springs, NY 12866
Phone: (518) 584-2110
Fax: (518) 580-0126
E-mail: info@saratogagaming.com
http://www.saratogaraceway.com

Syracuse Mile (Racing dates during State Fair)
P.O. Box 860
Vernon, NY 13476

Phone: (315) 829-2201
http://nysfair.org

Tioga Downs
2384 West River Road
Nichols, NY 13812
Phone: (888) 946-8464
http://www.tiogadowns.com

Vernon Downs
P.O. Box 860
Vernon, NY 13476
Phone: (315) 829-2201
http://www.vernondowns.com

Yonkers Raceway
810 Yonkers Avenue
Yonkers, NY 10704
Phone: (914) 968-4200
E-mail: info@yonkersraceway.com
http://www.yonkersraceway.com

OHIO

Delaware Ohio Fair (Racing dates during fair)
236 Pennsylvania Avenue
Delaware, OH 43015
Phone: (740) 362-3851
Fax: (740) 363-4132
E-mail: fair@delawarecountyfair.
   com
http://www.littlebrownjug.com

Lebanon Raceway
P.O. Box 58
Lebanon, OH 45036
Phone: (513) 932-4936
Fax: (513) 932-7894
E-mail: trotter@your-net.com
http://www.lebanonraceway.com

Northfield Park
P.O. Box 374
Northfield, OH 44067

Phone: (330) 467-4101
Fax: (330) 468-2628
E-mail: info@northfieldpark.com
http://www.northfieldpark.com

Raceway Park
5700 Telegraph Road
Toledo, OH 43612
Phone: (419) 476-7751
Fax: (419) 476-7979
E-mail: racewayparkinfo@
   pngaming.com
http://www.racewayparktoledo.com

Scioto Downs
6000 South High Street
Columbus, OH 43207
Phone: (614) 491-2515
Fax: (614) 491-4626
http://www.sciotodowns.com

PENNSYLVANIA

The Meadows
210 Racetrack Road
Washington, PA 15301
Phone: (724) 225-9300
http://www.themeadowsracing.com

Pocono Downs
1280 Highway 315
Wilkes-Barre, PA 18702
Phone: (570) 831-2100
Fax: (570) 823-9407
http://www.poconodowns.com

VIRGINIA

Colonial Downs
10515 Colonial Downs Parkway
New Kent, VA 23124
Phone: (804) 966-7223
http://www.colonialdowns.com

APPENDIX VI
CAREER AND JOB WEB SITES

The following is a list of career and job Web sites. Some are general in nature. Others are designed for those interested in working with animals in some capacity. Use this list to help you start your job search. There are many other sites on the Internet. This list is provided for informational purposes. The author does not endorse or recommend any one site over another.

American Association of Zookeepers Job Site
http://www.aazk.org/job_listings.php

ASPCA Jobs
http://www.aspca.org/about-us/jobs

Association of Zoos and Aquariums Job Listings
http://www.aza.org/JobListings

AVMA (American Veterinary Medical Association) Career Center
http://www.avma.org/vcc/default.asp

Biology Jobs.com
http://www.biologyjobs.com

CareerBuilder.com
http://www.carerbuilder.com

Department of Wildlife and Fisheries Science–Texas A&M University Job Board
http://wfsc.tamu.edu/jobboard

EcoEmploy.com
http://www.ecoemploy.com

Environmental Jobs and Careers
http://www.ejobs.org

Horse and Equine Industry Jobs
http://www.horsehats.com/horse-jobs.html

Houston Zoo Jobs
http://www.houstonzoo.org/careers

Humane Society of the United States Employment Opportunities
http://www.humanesociety.org/about/contact/employment/employment.html

Job Bank USA
http://www.jobbank.com

Jobs.com
http://www.jobs.com

JUJU.com
http://www.job-search-engine.com

Marine Biology Employment Opportunities
http://www.biosci.ohiou.edu/faculty/currie/ocean/MEJobs/index.htm

Maritime Aquarium
http://www.maritimeaquarium.org/about_career_ops.html

Monster.com
http://www.monster.com

National Park Service
http://www.nps.gov/index.htm

National Wildlife Refuge System
http://www.nwrawildlife.org/jobsearch.asp

Oregon Zoo Jobs
http://www.oregonzoo.org/Involved/jobs.htm

PetSmart Careers
http://careers.petsmart.com/store-careers

Sam Houston Racing Park Careers
http://shrp.teamworkonline.com/teamwork/jobs/default.cfm

San Diego Zoo Jobs
http://www.sandiegozoo.org/jobs

Saratoga Race Course Jobs
http://www.saratoga.com/news/racetrack-jobs.cfm

SimplyHired.com
http://www.simplyhired.com

TopUSAJobs.com
http://www.topusajobs.com

USAjobs.com
http://www.usajobs.com

USDA Career Site

http://www.aphis.usda.gov/career_
opportunities

Veterinary Crossing

http://www.veterinarycrossing.com

Wetlands Institute
http://www.wetlandsinstitute.org

Zoological Park Careers
http://www.seaworld.org/career-
resources/info-books/zoo-
careers/training.htm

APPENDIX VII
TRADE ASSOCIATIONS AND OTHER ORGANIZATIONS

The following is a list of trade associations and other organizations discussed in this book. There are also numerous other associations listed here that may also be useful to you in your career. The names, addresses, phone numbers, fax numbers, e-mail addresses, and Web sites (when available) are included to help you get in touch with any of the organizations for information.

Use this list to help you find internships, explore job opportunities, and to obtain other useful information.

Abundant Wildlife Society of North America
P.O. Box 2
Beresford, SD 57004
Phone: (605) 751-0979
E-mail: research@bmtc.net
http://www.aws.vcn.com

Academy of Veterinary Homeopathy
P.O. Box 232282
Leucadia, CA 92023
Phone: (866) 652-1590
E-mail: office@theavh.org
http://www.theavh.org

Actors and Others for Animals
11523 Burbank Boulevard
North Hollywood, CA 91601
Phone: (818) 755-6045
Fax: (818) 755-6048
E-mail: webmistress@wom-designs.com
http://actorsandothers.com

American Alliance of Paralegals
4001 Kennett Pike
Wilmington, DE 19807
E-mail: info@aapipara.org
http://www.aapipara.org

American Animal Hospital Association (AAHA)
12575 West Bayaud Avenue
Lakewood, CO 80228
Phone: (303) 986-2800
Fax: (303) 986-1700
E-mail: info@aahanet.org
http://www.aahanet.org

American Anti-Vivisection Society
801 Old York Road
Suite 204
Jenkintown, PA 19046
Phone: (215) 887-0816
E-mail: aavs@aavs.org
http://www.aavs.org

American Association of Bovine Practitioners
P.O. Box 3610
Auburn, AL 36831
Phone: (334) 821-0442
Fax: (334) 821-9532
E-mail: aabphq@aabp.org
http://www.aabp.org

American Association of Equine Practitioners
4075 Iron Works Parkway
Lexington, KY 40511
Phone: (859) 233-0147
Fax: (859) 233-1968
E-mail: aaepoffice@aaep.org
http://www.aaep.org

American Association of Wildlife Veterinarians
c/o Dr. Colin Gillin, Secretary
Oregon Department of Fish and Wildlife
7118 Northeast Vandenberg Avenue
Corvallis, OR 97330
E-mail: colin.m.gillin@state.or.us

http://www.aawv.net

American Association of Zoo Veterinarians
581705 White Oak Road
Yulee, FL 32097
Phone: (904) 225-3275
Fax: (904) 225-3289
E-mail: aazvorg@aol.com
http://www.aazv.org

American Bar Association
321 North Clark Street
Chicago, IL 60654
Phone: (312) 988-5000
E-mail: service@americanbar.org
http://www.abanet.org

American College of Zoological Medicine
3930 West Landpark Drive
Sacramento, CA 95822
Phone: (530) 979-0704
Fax: (916) 264-7602
http://www.aczm.org

American Collegiate Retailing Association
c/o Scarlett Wesley
University of Kentucky
Erikson Hall
Lexington, KY 40506
Phone: (859) 257-7778
Fax: (859) 257-1275
E-mail: scarlett.wesley@uky.edu
http://www.acraretail.org

American Dog Show Judges
c/o Carl G. Liepmann, Secretary
144 West Mt. Morris Road
Flushing, MI 48433
Phone: (810) 639-7075
Fax: (810) 639-7075
E-mail: cen06886@centurytel.net
http://www.adsj.org

American Fisheries Society
5410 Grosvenor Lane
Bethesda, MD 20814
Phone: (301) 897-8616
Fax: (301) 897-8096
E-mail: grassam@fisheries.org
http://www.fisheries.org

American Grant Writers'
Association
P.O. Box 8481
Seminole, FL 33775
Phone: (727) 366-9334
E-mail: customerservice@agwa.us
http://www.agwa.us

American Holistic Veterinary
Medical Association
P.O. Box 630
Abington, MD 21009-0630
Phone: (410) 569-0795
Fax: (410) 569-2346
E-mail: office@ahvma.org
http://www.ahvma.org

American Humane Association
63 Inverness Drive East
Englewood, CO 80112
Phone: (303) 792-9900
Fax: (303) 792-5333
E-mail: info@americanhumane.org
http://www.americanhumane.org

American Institute of
Biological Sciences
1900 Campus Commons Drive
Suite 200
Reston, VA 20191
Phone: (703) 674-2500
Fax: (703) 674-2509
E-mail: rogrady@aibs.org
http://www.aibs.org

American Kennel Club
260 Madison Avenue
New York, NY 10016
Phone: (212) 696-8200
Fax: (212) 696-8299
E-mail: info@akc.org
http://www.akc.org

American Pet Products
Association
255 Glenville Road
Greenwich, CT 06831
Phone: (203) 532-0000
Fax: (203) 532-0551
E-mail: bob@americanpetproducts.
    org
http://www.appma.org

American Pet Society
c/o World Wide Pet Industry
    Association
135 West Lemon Avenue
Monrovia, CA 91016
Phone: (626) 447-2222
Fax: (626) 447-8350
E-mail: info@wwpia.org
http://www.wpamail.org

American Riding Instructors
Association
28801 Trenton Court
Bonita Springs, FL 34134
Phone: (239) 948-3232
Fax: (239) 948-5053
E-mail: aria@riding-instructor.com
http://www.riding-instructor.com

American Sanctuary
Association
2308 Chatfield Drive
Las Vegas, NV 89128
Phone: (702) 804-8562
Fax: (702) 804-8561
E-mail: asarescue@aol.com
http://www.asaanimalsanctuaries.
    org

American Society for the
Prevention of Cruelty to
Animals (ASPCA)
424 East 92nd Street
New York, NY 10128

Phone: (212) 876-7700
E-mail: shonalib@aspca.org
http://www.aspca.org

American Veterinary
Chiropractic Association
442154 East 140 Road
Bluejacket, OK 74333
Phone: (918) 784-2231
Fax: (918) 784-2675
E-mail: avcainfo@junct.com
http://www.animalchiropractic.org

American Veterinary Medical
Association
1931 North Meacham Road
Suite 100
Schaumburg, IL 60173
Phone: (847) 925-8070
Fax: (847) 925-1329
E-mail: avmainfo@avma.org
http://www.avma.org

American Veterinary Medical
Law Association
1666 K Street, NW
Washington, DC 20006
Phone: (202) 449-3818
Fax: (202) 449-8560
E-mail: admin@avmla.org
http://www.avmla.org

American Working Dog
Federation
c/o Al Govednik, President
4282 Illinois Highway 17
Alpha, IL 61413
Phone: (309) 334-3403
E-mail: algovfh@yahoo.com
http://www.awdf.net

Animal Agents
P.O. Box 555
Kingsburg, CA 93631
Phone: (559) 960-6899
E-mail: animalagents@mac.com
http://www.animalagents.org

Animal Legal Defense Fund
170 East Cotati Avenue
Cotati, CA 94931
Phone: (707) 795-2533

Fax: (707) 795-7280
E-mail: info@aldf.org
http://www.aldf.org

Animal Medical Center

510 East 62nd Street
New York, NY 10065
Phone: (212) 838-8100
E-mail: info@amcny.org
http://www.amcny.org

Animal Protection Committee of the American Bar Association

321 North Clark Street
Chicago, IL 60654
Phone: (312) 988-5522
E-mail: service@americanbar.org
http://www.americanbar.org/aba.html

Animals and Society Institute

2512 Carpenter Road
Suite 202-A
Ann Arbor, MI 48108-1188
Phone: (734) 677-9240
Fax: (734) 677-9242
E-mail: info@animalsandsociety.org
http://www.animalsandsociety.org

Aquarium and Zoo Facilities Association

3900 Wildlife Way
Cleveland, OH 44109
E-mail: support@azfa.org
http://www.azfa.org

Association of American Veterinary Medical Colleges

1101 Vermont Avenue, NW
Suite 301
Washington, DC 20005
Phone: (202) 371-9195
Fax: (202) 842-0773
http://www.aavmc.org

Association of Avian Veterinarians–USA

P.O. Box 811720
Boca Raton, FL 33481

Phone: (561) 393-8901
Fax: (561) 393-8902
E-mail: aavcentraloffice@gmail.com
http://www.aav.org

Association of Companion Animal Behavior Counselors

P.O. Box 104
Seville, FL 32190
Phone: (866) 224-2728
E-mail: ed@animalbehaviorcounselors.org
http://animalbehaviorcounselors.org

Association of Fish and Wildlife Agencies

444 North Capitol Street, NW
Suite 725
Washington, DC 20001
Phone: (202) 624-7890
Fax: (202) 624-7891
E-mail: info@fishwildlife.org
http://www.fishwildlife.org

Association of Fundraising Professionals

4300 Wilson Boulevard
Suite 300
Arlington, VA 22203
Phone: (703) 684-0410
Fax: (703) 684-0540
E-mail: afp@afpnet.org
http://www.afpnet.org

The Association of Pet Dog Trainers

101 North Main Street
Suite 610
Greenville, SC 29601
Phone: (800) 738-3647
Fax: (864) 331-0767
E-mail: information@apdt.com
http://www.apdt.com

Association of Professional Humane Educators

c/o The Latham Foundation
Latham Plaza Building
1826 Clement Avenue

Alameda, CA 94501
E-mail: aphe@aphe.org
http://aphe.org

Association of Zoos and Aquariums

8403 Colesville Road
Suite 710
Silver Spring, MD 20910
Phone: (301) 562-0777
Fax: (301) 562-0888
E-mail: membership@aza.org
http://www.aza.org

Born Free USA

1222 S Street
Sacramento, CA 95811
Phone: (916) 447-3085
Fax: (916) 447-3070
E-mail: info@bornfreeusa.org
http://www.bornfreeusa.org

Companion Animal Protection Society

759 CJC Highway
Number 332
Cohasset, MA 02025
Phone: (339) 309-0272
Fax: (886) 884-0452
E-mail: caps@caps-web.org
http://www.caps-web.org

Consortium for Ocean Leadership

1201 New York Avenue, NW
Washington, DC 20005
Phone: (202) 232-3900
Fax: (202) 332-8887
E-mail: rgagosian@oceanleadership.org
http://www.oceanleadership.org

Council for the Advancement and Support of Education

1307 New York Avenue, NW
Washington, DC 20005
Phone: (202) 328-2273
Fax: (202) 387-4973
E-mail: memberservicecenter@case.org
http://www.case.org

Defenders of Wildlife
1130 17th Street, NW
Washington, DC 20036
Phone: (202) 682-9400
E-mail: defenders@mail.defenders.
org
http://www.defenders.org

Dogs for the Deaf
10175 Wheeler Road
Central Point, OR 97502
Phone: (541) 826-9220
Fax: (541) 826-6696
E-mail: info@dogsforthedeaf.org
http://www.dogsforthedeaf.org

Elephant Managers Association
c/o Daryl Hoffman, Executive
Director
Buffalo Zoo
300 Parkside Avenue
Buffalo, NY 14214
Phone: (407) 938-1988
E-mail: emaboard@elephant-
managers.com
http://www.elephant-managers.com

**Federation of American
Aquarium Societies**
c/o Pat Smith, Membership
Chairman
109 Bucknell Road
West Sayville, NY 11796
Phone: (217) 359-6707
http://www.faas.info

**Global Federation of Animal
Sanctuaries**
P.O. Box 32294
Washington, DC 20007
Phone: (928) 472-1173
E-mail: patty@sanctuaryfederation.
org
http://www.sanctuaryfederation.
org/gfas/home

**Guide Dog Foundation for the
Blind**
371 East Jericho Turnpike
Smithtown, NY 11787
Phone: (800) 548-4337

E-mail: info@guidedog.org
http://www.guidedog.org

Humane Farming Association
P.O. Box 3577
San Rafael, CA 94912
Phone: (415) 485-1495
Fax: (415) 485-0106
E-mail: hfa@hfa.org
http://www.hfa.org

**Humane Society of the United
States**
2100 L Street, NW
Washington, DC 20037
Phone: (202) 452-1100
Fax: (202) 778-6132
E-mail: membership@hsus.org
http://www.humanesociety.org

Humane Society Youth
67 Norwich Essex Turnpike
East Haddam, CT 06423
Phone: (860) 434-8666
Fax: (860) 434-6282
E-mail: youth@humanesociety.org
http://www.nahee.org/aboutus

**Institute for Marine Mammal
Studies**
P.O. Box 207
Gulfport, MS 39502
Phone: (228) 896-9182
Fax: (228) 896-9183
E-mail: contactus@imms.org
http://www.imms.org

**International Alliance of
Theatrical State Employees,
Moving Picture Technicians,
Artists and Allied Crafts
of the United States and
Canada**
1430 Broadway
20th Floor
New York, NY 10018
Phone: (212) 730-1770
http://www.iatse-intl.org

**International Association for
Aquatic Animal Medicine**
c/o Cindy P. Driscoll, DVM,
Membership Chair
Maryland Department of Natural
Resources
904 South Morris Street
Oxford, MD 21654
Phone: (410) 226-5193
E-mail: cdriscoll@dnr.state.md.us
http://iaaam.org

**International Association of
Bomb Technicians and
Investigators**
P.O. Box 160
Goldvein, VA 22720
Phone: (540) 752-4533
Fax: (540) 752-2796
E-mail: admin@iabti.org
http://www.iabti.org

**International Association of
Canine Professionals**
P.O. Box 560156
Montverde, FL 34756
Phone: (407) 469-2008
E-mail: iacpadmin@mindspring.
net
http://canineprofessionals.com

**The International Cat
Association**
P.O. Box 2684
Harlingen, TX 78551
Phone: (956) 428-8046
Fax: (956) 428-8047
E-mail: information@tica.org
https://online.tica.org

**International Marine Animal
Trainers Association**
1200 South Lake Shore Drive
Chicago, IL 60605
Phone: (312) 692-3193
Fax: (312) 939-2216
E-mail: info@imata.org
http://www.imata.org

**International Wildlife
Rehabilitation Council**
P.O. Box 3197
Eugene, OR 97403
Phone: (866) 871-1869
Fax: (408) 876-6153
E-mail: director@theiwrc.org
http://www.iwrc-online.org

Jockey's Guild
103 Wind Haven Drive
Suite 200
Nicholasville, KY 40356
Phone: (859) 305-0606
Fax: (859) 219-9892
E-mail: info@jockeysguild.com
http://www.jockeysguild.com

Marine Aquarium Council
P.O. Box 90370
Los Angeles, CA 90009
Phone: (808) 550-8217
Fax: (310) 846-4040
E-mail: certifiedfish@
aquariumcouncil.org
http://www.aquariumcouncil.org

**Marine Aquarium Societies of
North America**
P.O. Box 105603
Atlanta, GA 30348
E-mail: join@masna.org
http://www.masna.org

**National Animal Control
Association**
P.O. Box 480851
Kansas City, MO 64148
Phone: (913) 768-1319
Fax: (913) 768-1378
E-mail: naca@nacanet.org
http://www.nacanet.org

National Aquarium Society
U.S. Department of Commerce
Building
Room B-077
14th Street and Constitution
Avenue, NW
Washington, DC 20230
Phone: (202) 482-2825

Fax: (202) 482-4946
E-mail: info@nationalaquarium.
com
http://www.nationalaquarium.com

**National Association for Search
and Rescue**
P.O. Box 232020
Centreville, VA 20120
Phone: (703) 222-6277
Fax: (703) 222-6277
E-mail: info@nasar.org
http://www.nasar.org

**National Association of Dog
Obedience Instructors**
PMB 369
729 Grapevine Highway
Hurst, TX 76054
E-mail: corrsec2@nadoi.org
http://www.nadoi.org

**National Association of Legal
Assistants**
1516 South Boston Avenue
Suite 200
Tulsa, OK 74119
Phone: (918) 587-6828
Fax: (918) 582-6772
E-mail: nalanet@nala.org
http://nala.org

**National Association of Marine
Laboratories**
Phone: (912) 598-2400
Fax: (912) 598-2310
E-mail: web@naml.org
http://www.naml.org

**National Association of
Professional Pet Sitters**
15000 Commerce Parkway
Suite C
Mount Laurel, NJ 08054
Phone: (856) 439-0324
Fax: (856) 439-0525
E-mail: napps@ahint.com
http://www.petsitters.org

**National Association of
Veterinary Technicians in
America**
1666 K Street, NW
Suite 260
Washington, DC 20006
Phone: (703) 740-8737
Fax: (202) 449-8560
E-mail: navta@navta.net
http://www.navta.net

National Audubon Society
225 Varick Street
New York, NY 10014
Phone: (212) 979-3000
http://www.audubon.org

**National Cattlemen's Beef
Association**
9110 East Nichols Avenue
Suite 300
Centennial, CO 80112
Phone: (303) 694-0305
Fax: (303) 694-2851
E-mail: membership@beef.org
http://www.beefusa.org

**National Dog Groomers
Association of America**
P.O. Box 101
Clark, PA 16113
Phone: (724) 962-2711
Fax: (724) 962-1919
E-mail: ndga@
nationaldoggroomers.com
http://www.nationaldoggroomers.
com

**National Federation of
Paralegal Associations**
P.O. Box 2016
Edmonds, WA 98020
Phone: (425) 967-0045
Fax: (425) 771-9588
E-mail: info@paralegals.org
http://www.paralegals.org

**National Narcotic Detector
Dog Association**
379 County Road 105
Carthage, TX 75633

Phone: (888) 289-0070
E-mail: thennndda@yahoo.com
http://www.nndda.org

National Retail Federation
325 7th Street, NW
Washington, DC 20004
Phone: (202) 783-7971
Fax: (202) 737-2849
http://www.nrf.com

National Wildlife Rehabilitators Association
2625 Clearwater Road
Suite 110
Saint Cloud, MN 56301
Phone: (320) 230-9920
Fax: (320) 230-3077
E-mail: nwra@nwrawildlife.org
http://www.nwrawildlife.org

New York State Marine Education Association
146 Suffolk Hall
Stony Brook, NY 11794
Phone: (631) 632-9216
E-mail: joinnysmea@nysmea.org
http://www.nysmea.org

North American Fish Breeders Guild
Rural Route 2, Box 67-L
Orangeville, PA 17859
Phone: (717) 683-6126
E-mail: nafbg-mem@rocketmail.com

North American Police Work Dog Association
4222 Manchester Avenue
Perry, OH 44081
Phone: (440) 259-3169
Fax: (440) 259-3170
E-mail: napwda@napwda.com
http://www.napwda.com

North American Wildlife Enforcement Officers Association
c/o Steve Kleiner, Secretary
P.O. Box 22

Hollidaysburg, PA 16648
Phone: (801) 942-9432
Fax: (206) 201-6953
E-mail: naweoa@ureach.com
http://www.naweoa.org

Pet Care Services
4100 North Michigan Avenue
Suite 2200
Chicago, IL 60611
Phone: (312) 321-5128
Fax: (312) 673-6881
E-mail: webmaster@petcareservices.org
http://www.petcareservices.org

Pet Sitters International
201 East King Street
King, NC 27021
Phone: (336) 983-9222
E-mail: info@petsit.com
http://www.petsit.com

Professional Handlers' Association
17017 Norbrook Drive
Olney, MD 20832
Phone: (301) 924-0089
E-mail: kathy@phadoghandlers.com
http://www.phadoghandlers.com

Public Relations Society of America
33 Maiden Lane
11th Floor
New York, NY 10038-5150
Phone: (212) 460-1400
Fax: (212) 995-0757
E-mail: membership@prsa.org
http://www.prsa.org

Sanctuary Workers and Volunteers Association
P.O. Box 637
Boyd, TX 76023
Phone: (940) 433-5091
Fax: (940) 433-5092
E-mail: swava@sbcglobal.net
http://www.swava.org

Society of Internet Professionals
120 Carlton Street
Suite 305
Toronto, ON M5A 4K2
Canada
Phone: (416) 891-4937
E-mail: info@sipgroup.org
http://www.sipgroup.org

Student American Veterinary Medical Association
1931 North Meacham Road
Suite 100
Schaumburg, IL 60173
Phone: (800) 248-2862
Fax: (847) 925-1329
E-mail: savma@cvm.tamu.edu
http://www.avma.org/savma/default.asp

Student Conservation Association
SCA President
P.O. Box 550
689 River Road
Charlestown, NH 03603
Phone: (603) 543-1700
Fax: (603) 543-1828
E-mail: ask-us@thesca.org
http://www.thesca.org

Therapy Dogs International
88 Bartley Road
Flanders, NJ 07836
Phone: (973) 252-9800
Fax: (973) 252-7171
E-mail: tdi@gti.net
http://www.tdi-dog.org

United States Equestrian Federation
4047 Iron Works Parkway
Lexington, KY 40511
Phone: (859) 258-2472
Fax: (859) 231-6662
http://www.usef.org

United States Fish and Wildlife Service–Gavins Point National Fish Hatchery and Aquarium
31227 436th Avenue
Yankton, SD 57078
Phone: (605) 665-3352
E-mail: gavinspoint@fws.gov
http://www.fws.gov/gavinspoint

United States Police Canine Association
P.O. Box 80
Springboro, OH 45066
Phone: (937) 751-6469
http://www.uspcak9.com

United States Trotting Association
750 Michigan Avenue
Columbus, OH 43215
Phone: (877) 800-8782
http://www.ustrotting.com

Wildlife Disease Association
P.O. Box 7065
Lawrence, KS 66044
Phone: (800) 627-0326
E-mail: wildlifedisease@gmail.com
http://www.wildlifedisease.org

Wildlife Management Institute
Steven A. Williams, President
1440 Upper Bermudian Road
Gardners, PA 17324
Phone: (717) 677-4480
E-mail: swilliams@wildlifemgt.org
http://www.
    wildlifemanagementinstitute.org

Wildlife Society
5410 Grosvenor Lane
Bethesda, MD 20814
Phone: (301) 897-9770
Fax: (301) 530-2471
E-mail: tws@wildlife.org
http://www.wildlife.org

World Wide Kennel Club
P.O. Box 62
Mount Vernon, NY 10552
Phone: (914) 654-8574
Fax: (914) 654-0364
E-mail: wwkc1com@aol.com
http://www.worldwidekennel.qpg.
    com

World Wide Pet Industry Association
135 West Lemon Avenue
Monrovia, CA 91016
Phone: (626) 447-2222
Fax: (626) 447-8350
E-mail: info@wwpia.org
http://www.wwpia.org

World Wildlife Fund
P.O. Box 97180
Washington, DC 20090
Phone: (202) 293-4800
E-mail: plannedgiving@wwfus.org
http://www.worldwildlife.org

BIBLIOGRAPHY

A. BOOKS

There are thousands of books written on all aspects of working with animals. The books listed below are separated into general categories. The subject matter of many of the books overlaps.

These books can be found in bookstores and libraries. If your local library does not have the one you want, ask your librarian to order it through the intralibrary loan system.

This list should be used as a starting point. For other books that might interest you, look in the animals section of bookstores and libraries. You can also check *Books in Print* for other books. *Books in Print* may be located in your local library or online.

ANIMAL CRUELTY

Arluke, Arnold. *Brute Force: Policing Animal Cruelty.* West Lafayette, Ind.: Purdue University Press, 2004.

Arluke, Arnold. *Just a Dog: Understanding Animal Cruelty and Ourselves.* Philadelphia: Temple University Press, 2006.

Ascione, Frank R. *Child Abuse, Domestic Violence and Animal Abuse: Linking the Circles of Compassion for Prevention and Intervention.* West Lafayette, Ind.: Purdue University Press, 1999.

Ascione, Frank R. *Children and Animals: Exploring the Roots of Kindness and Cruelty.* West Lafayette, Ind.: Purdue University Press, 2005.

Ascione, Frank R., ed. *The International Handbook of Animal Abuse and Cruelty: Theory, Research, and Application.* West Lafayette, Ind.: Purdue University Press, 2007.

Karlekar, Hiranmay. *Savage Humans and Stray Dogs: A Study in Aggression.* New Delphi, Ind.: SAGE Publications India, 2008.

Merck, Melinda D. *Veterinary Forensics: Animal Cruelty Investigations.* Hoboken, N.J.: John Wiley and Sons, 2008.

ANIMAL EXPERIMENTATION

Arluke, Arnold. *The Sacrifice: How Scientific Experiments Transform Animals and People.* West Lafayette, Ind.: Purdue University Press, 2006.

ANIMAL HOARDING

Arluke, Arnold, and Celeste Killeen. *Inside Animal Hoarding: The Case of Barbara Erickson and Her 552 Dogs.* West Lafayette, Ind.: Purdue University Press, 2009.

ANIMAL RIGHTS

Beirne, Piers. *Confronting Animal Abuse: Law, Criminology, and Human-Animal Relationships.* Lanham, Md.: Rowman & Littlefield, 2009.

Donald, Rhonda Lucas. *Animal Rights: How You Can Make a Difference.* Bloomington, Minn.: Capstone Press, 2009.

Kistler, John M. *People Promoting and People Opposing Animal Rights: In Their Own Words.* Portsmouth, N.H.: Greenwood, 2002.

Morrison, Adrian R. *An Odyssey with Animals: A Veterinarian's Reflections on the Animal Rights and Welfare Debate.* New York: Oxford University Press, 2009.

Newkirk, Ingrid. *The PETA Practical Guide to Animal Rights: Simple Acts of Kindness to Help Animals in Trouble.* New York: St. Martin's Press, 2009.

Pash, Chris. *The Last Whale.* North Fremantle, W.A. Australia: Fremantle Press, 2008.

ANIMALS, GENERAL

Allen, Judy, and Simon Mendez. *Animal Homes.* New York: Roaring Brook Press, 2009.

Campbell, Sam A. *The Seven Secrets of Somewhere Lake: Animal Ways that Inspire and Amaze.* Brushton, N.Y.: TEACH Services, 2001.

Kays, Roland. *Mammals of North America.* Princeton, N.J.: Princeton University Press, 2009.

Johnson, Jinny. *Animal Tracks and Signs: Track over 400 Animals from Big Cats to Backyard Birds.* Washington, D.C.: National Geographic Society, 2008.

ANIMAL SHELTERS

Lee, Joy. *Rover's Rescues: True Stories of Shelter Dogs and Second Chances.* Bloomington, Ind.: Xlibris, 2009.

McDonnell, Patrick. *Shelter Stories: Love, Guaranteed.* Kansas City, Mo.: Andrews McMeel, 2008.

ANIMAL WELFARE

Williams, Jane. *The Complete Textbook of Animal Health and Welfare.* Philadelphia: Elsevier–Health Sciences Division, 2009.

AQUARIUMS

Birch, E. *Life Beneath the Waves: And a Description of the Brighton Aquarium.* Whitefish, Mont.: Kessinger, 2008.

Edwards, Arthur Mead. *Life Beneath the Waters: Or the Aquarium in America.* Whitefish, Mont.: Kessinger, 2009.

Gosse, Philip Henry. *A Handbook to the Marine Aquarium.* San Francisco: Books LLC, 2009.

Hargreaves, Vincent. *The Complete Book of the Freshwater Aquarium: A Comprehensive Reference Guide to More than 600 Freshwater Fish and Plants.* San Diego: Advantage, 2007.

BOARDING KENNELS

Cavill, David. *Running Your Own Boarding Kennels: The Complete Guide to Kennel and Cattery Management.* Boulder, Colo.: NetLibrary, 2008.

Rowley, Bonnie. *Tails of a Boarding Kennel: P.S. This Is a Really Cheap Motel!* Bloomington, Ind.: Authorhouse, 2008.

DAIRY FARM

Gurler, Henry Benjamin. *The Farm Dairy.* Charleston, S.C.: BiblioBazaar, 2008.

DOG GROOMING

Blackburn, Sandy. *Dog Grooming: All You Need to Help Your Pet Look and Feel Great!* Avon, Mass.: Adams Media, 2009.

Kohl, Sam. *The Business Guide to Pet Grooming.* Hicksville, N.Y.: Aaronco, 2005.

Stone, Ben. *The Stone Guide to Dog Grooming for All Breeds.* Hoboken, N.J.: John Wiley and Sons, 2009.

Young, Peter. *Groom Your Dog Like a Professional: Step-by-Step Techniques and Tips for a Great-Looking Dog.* Neptune, N.J.: TFH Publications, 2009.

ENDANGERED ANIMALS

Goodall, Jane. *Hope for Animals and Their World: How Endangered Species Are Being Rescued from the Brink.* New York: Grand Central, 2009.

GRANT-WRITING

Carlson, Mim. *Winning Grants Step by Step.* Hoboken, N.J.: John Wiley and Sons, 2008.

Helweg, Richard. *How to Get Your Share of the $30-Plus Billion Being Offered by U.S. Foundations: A Complete Guide for Locating, Preparing, and Presenting Your Proposals.* Ocala, Fla.: Atlantic, 2009.

Karsh, Ellen. *The Only Grant-Writing Book You'll Ever Need: Top Grant Writers and Grant Givers Share Their Secrets.* New York: Basic Books, 2009.

Koch, Deborah S. *How to Say It—Grantwriting: Write Proposals that Grantmakers Want to Fund.* Paramus, N.J.: Prentice Hall, 2009.

Stanton, Sally. *Grant Writing Made Simple: 87 Tips for Great Grants.* Milwaukee: Great Lakes Literary, 2009.

Walters, Mary W. *Write an Effective Funding Application: A Guide for Researchers and Scholars.* Baltimore: Johns Hopkins University Press, 2009.

HOLISTIC AND ALTERNATIVE HEALING

Drakeford, Jackie. *Essential Care for Dogs: A Holistic Way of Life.* Shrewsbury, U.K.: Swan Hill Press, 2004.

Goldstein, Martin, DVM. *The Nature of Animal Healing: The Definitive Holistic Medicine Guide to Caring For Your Dog and Cat.* New York: Random House, 2001.

Khalsa, Deva. *Dr. Khalsa's Natural Dog: A Holistic Feeding Guide for Healthier Dogs.* Freehold, N.J.: Kennel Club Books, 2009.

Knueven, Doug. *The Holistic Health Guide: Natural Care for the Whole Dog.* Neptune, N.J.: TFH Publications, 2008.

Wynn, Raquel. *Stretch Your Dog Healthy: A Hands-On Approach to Natural Canine Care.* New York: Penguin Group, 2008.

HORSES AND HORSE RACING

Ball, Liz. *A Standardbred Star: Learn about Harness Racing with Star and Friends.* Columbus, Ohio: United States Trotting Association, 2007.

Brodowsky, Pamela K. *Two Minutes to Glory: The Official History of the Kentucky Derby.* New York: HarperCollins, 2009.

Brower, Dave. *Harnessing Winners: The Modern Guide to Harness Racing Handicapping.* New York: Daily Racing Form Press, 2009.

Brown, Randy W. *Harness the Winning: The Definitive Book on How to Make a Living Wagering on Nothing but Harness Racing.* North Charleston, S.C.: CreateSpace, 2008.

Christgau, John. *Kokomo Joe: The Story of the First Japanese American Jockey in the United States.* Lincoln: University of Nebraska, 2009.

Conley, Kevin. *Stud: Adventures in Breeding.* New York: Bloomsbury, 2008.

Davis, John H. *The American Turf: History of the Thoroughbred, Together with Personal Reminiscences by the Author, Who Has Been Jockey, Trainer and Owner.* Whitefish, Mont.: Kessinger, 2007.

Estep, Maggie. *Bloodlines: A Horse Racing Anthology.* New York: Knopf Doubleday, 2009.

Gruender, Scott A. *Jockey: The Rider's Life in American Thoroughbred Racing.* Jefferson, N.C.: McFarland, 2006.

Jung, Claudia. *Caring for the Older Horse: How to Keep Your Veteran Fit and Healthy.* Richmond, U.K.: Cadmos, 2009.

Lyons, Jane. *Skipingo Home: A Thoroughbred's Second Chance.* Lexington, Ky.: Blood-Horse, 2009.

McLellan, Charles Arthur. *The Art of Shoeing and Balancing the Trotter.* Brookfield, Wisc.: Lessiter, 2001.

Prado, Edgar, and John Eisenberg. *My Guy Barbaro: A Jockey's Journey Through Love, Triumph, and Heartbreak.* New York: HarperCollins, 2009.

Simpson, Joseph Cairn. *Horse Portraiture: Embracing Breeding, Rearing and Training Trotters, with Their Management in the Stable and on the Track, and Preparation for Races.* Whitefish, Mont.: Kessinger, 2008.

Splan, John. *Life with the Trotters.* Whitefish, Mont.: Kessinger, 2008.

HUMANE EDUCATION

Krause, Flora Helm. *Manual of Moral and Humane Education: June to September Inclusive.* Charleston, S.C.: BiblioBazaar, 2009.

Krueger, May. *Humane Education.* Charleston, S.C.: BiblioBazaar, 2009.

ILLUSTRATORS

Silvers, William L. *Painting Realistic Wildlife in Acrylic: 30 Step-by-Step Demonstrations.* Cincinnati: F&W Media, 2009.

INVESTIGATION AND ANIMAL ABUSE INVESTIGATORS

Estes, Allison, and Tina Salaks. *Paw and Order: Dramatic Investigations by an Animal Cop on the Beat.* Irvine, Calif.: Bowtie Press, 2008.

Neme, Laurel A. *Animal Investigators: How the World's First Wildlife Forensics Lab Is Solving Crimes and Saving Endangered Species.* New York: Simon & Schuster, 2009.

PET BUSINESSES

Bev, Jennie. *Breaking into and Succeeding in Pet Care Services.* Mountain House, Calif.: Afton Institute, 2007.

Niemeyer, Darlene. *Doggy Business 101: A Practical Guide to Starting and Running Your Own Business.* Neptune, N.J.: TFH Publications, 2009.

Nigro, Joseph. *101 Best Businesses for Pet Lovers.* Naperville, Ill.: Sourcebooks, 2007.

PETS

Berger, Randi. *My Recycled Pets: Diary of A Dog Addict.* Bothell, Wash.: Book Publishers Network, 2007.

Dratfield, Jim. *Best Friend for Life: 75 Simple Ways to Make Me a Happy, Healthy and Well-Behaved Dog.* New York: Black Dog & Leventhal, 2008.

Foster, Ken. *The Dogs Who Found Me: What I've Learned from Pets Who Were Left Behind.* Guilford, Conn.: Globe Pequot Press, 2006.

Hoyt, Peggy R. *All My Children Wear Fur Coats.* Oviedo, Fla.: Legacy Planning Partners, 2009.

Jarolim, Edie. *Am I Boring My Dog? And 99 Other Things Your Dog Wishes You Knew.* New York: Penguin Group, 2009.

Swanbeck, Steve. *Disposable Dogs.* Chester, N.J.: White Swan, 2004.

PET SITTING

Duea, Anglea Williams. *How to Open and Operate a Financially Successful Pet Sitting Business.* Ocala, Fla.: Atlantic, 2008.

Edmonds, Lynette, and Mike Edmonds. *Endless Holidays: A Guide to House and Pet Sitting Around the World.* Pittsburgh: Dorrance, 2008.

Moran, Patti J. *Pet Sitting for Profit.* Hoboken, N.J.: John Wiley and Sons, 2006.

Primm, Steven. *Pet Sitting Company.* North Charleston, S.C.: CreateSpace, 2009.

Roncevich, Tim. *Doggie Day Care Company.* North Charleston, S.C.: CreateSpace, 2009.

PUBLIC RELATIONS, PUBLICITY, PROMOTION, AND MARKETING

Basic Books Staff. *Stylebook and Briefing on Media Law.* New York: Basic Books, 2007.

Field, Shelly. *Career Opportunities in Advertising and Public Relations.* New York: Ferguson, 2005.

Yudkin, Marcia. *Six Steps to Free Publicity.* Franklin Lakes, N.J.: Career Press, 2008.

RELATIONSHIPS BETWEEN ANIMALS AND HUMANS

Arluke, Arnold. *Between the Species: Readings in Human-Animal Relationships.* Toronto: Pearson Education Canada, 2008.

Grandin, Temple. *Animals Make Us Human: Creating the Best Life for Animals.* Boston: Houghton Mifflin Harcourt, 2010.

Niven, David. *100 Simple Secrets Why Dogs Make Us Happy: The Science Behind What Dog Lovers Already Know.* New York: HarperCollins, 2007.

SANCTUARIES AND RESCUES

Aufhauser, Michael. *Paradise for Rescued Animals.* New York: teNeues, 2008.

Aufhauser, Michael. *A Happy Ending for Rescued Horses.* New York: teNeues, 2008.

Banish, Roslyn. *Just Gus: A Rescued Dog and the Woman He Loved.* New York: McWitty Press, 2006.

Best Friends Animal Society. *Not Left Behind: Rescuing the Pets of New Orleans.* New York: Yorkville Press, 2006.

Bowyer, Christine. *A Life for Lucy: The Touching True Story of a Wild Dog's Journey to Happiness.* Bloomington, Ind.: iUniverse, 2009.

Glen, Samantha. *Best Friends: The True Story of the World's Most Beloved Animal Sanctuary.* New York: Kensington, 2001.

Harper, Rex. *An Eagle in the Airing Cupboard: More True Tales from an Animal Sanctuary.* London: Headline Book Publishing, 2009.

O'Hara, Shelley. *Hopeful Tales: Stories of Rescued Pets and Their Forever Families.* Hoboken, N.J.: John Wiley and Sons, 2007.

Rescue Training Association Staff. *Rescue Ink: How Ten Guys Saved Countless Dogs and Cats, Twelve Horses, Five Pigs, One Duck and a Few Turtles.* New York: Penguin Group, 2009.

Scott, Cathy. *Pawprints of Katrina: Pets Saved and Lessons Learned.* Hoboken, N.J.: John Wiley and Sons, 2008.

Stevens, Kathy. *Where the Blind Horse Sings: Love and Healing at an Animal Sanctuary.* New York: Skyhorse, 2009.

Sullivan, Christine. *Saving Cinnamon: The Amazing True Story of a Missing Military Puppy and the Desperate Mission to Bring Her Home.* New York: St. Martin's Press, 2009.

Vassallo, Russell A. *Tears and Tales: Stories of Animal and Human Rescue.* Danville, Ky.: Krazy Duck Productions, 2006.

Weller, Frank. *Equine Angels: Stories of Rescue, Love, and Hope.* Guilford, Conn.: Globe Pequot Press, 2008.

SHELTERS

Harbolt, Tami L. *Bridging the Bond: The Cultural Construction of the Shelter Pet.* West Lafayette, Ind.: Purdue University Press, 2007.

Scott, Traer. *Shelter Dogs.* London: Merrell, 2009.

STRESS AND DOGS

Lawson, Patti. *The Dog Diet: What My Dog Taught Me about Shedding Pounds, Licking Stress and Getting a New Leash on Life.* Deerfield Beach, Fla.: Health Communications, 2006.

Scholz, Martina. *Stress in Dogs: Learn How Dogs Show Stress and What You Can Do to Help.* Wentachee, Wash.: Dogwise, 2006.

THERAPY DOGS

Hugo, Lynne. *Where the Trail Grows Faint: A Year in the Life of a Therapy Dog Team.* Lincoln: University of Nebraska Press, 2009.

Long, Lorie. *A Dog Who's Always Welcome: Assistance and Therapy Dog Trainers Teach You How to Socialize and Train Your Companion Dog.* Hoboken, N.J.: John Wiley and Sons, 2008.

Pichot, Teri. *Transformation of the Heart: Tales of the Profound Impact Therapy Dogs Have on Their Humans.* Bloomington, Ind.: iUniverse, 2009.

Woo, Candace Y. *Ralphie, the Therapy Dog.* Bloomington, Ind.: Authorhouse, 2008.

TRAINING ANIMALS

Davey, Pete. *A Dolphin in Front of You.* Finger Beach, Fla.: Ocean, 2005.

Davey, Pete. *Whales with Fur: How to Train Any Animal Using Dolphin Training Techniques.* Finger Beach, Fla.: Ocean, 2004.

Fisher, Gail Tamases. *The Thinking Dog: Crossover to Clicker Training.* Wentachee, Wash.: Dogwise, 2009.

Hart, Ben. *The Art and Science of Clicker Training for Horses: A Positive Approach to Training Equines and Understanding Them.* London: Souvenir Press, 2008.

Millan, Cesar. *Be the Pack Leader: Use Cesar's Way to Transform Your Dog . . . and Your Life.* New York: Crown, 2008.

Millan, Cesar. *Cesar's Way Deck: 50 Tips for Training and Understanding Your Dog.* New York: Crown, 2008.

Millan, Cesar. *A Member of the Family: The Ultimate Guide to Living with a Happy, Healthy Dog.* New York: Crown, 2009.

Ray, Mary. *Click and Train Your Dog: Using Clicker Training to Transform Your Common Canine into a Superdog.* Neptune, N.J.: TFH Publications, 2008.

VETERINARIANS

Burkett, Charles William. *The Farmer's Veterinarian: A Practical Treatise on the Diseases of Farm Stock.* Whitefish, Mont.: Kessinger, 2009.

Freyburger, Peter J. *Vetting: The Making of a Veterinarian.* North Tonawanda, N.Y.: PJF Publications, 2009.

WILDLIFE

Dennis, Nigel. *Ultimate African Wildlife.* 4th ed. Capetown, South Africa: Sunbird, 2009.

Garshelis, Judy Swain. *The Otter Spotters: A Wildlife Adventure in Alaska.* Bloomington, Ind.: iUniverse, 2009.

Hentz, Peggy Sue. *Rescuing Wildlife: A Guide to Helping Injured and Orphaned Animals.* Mechanicsburg, Pa.: Stackpole Books, 2009.

Humane Society of the United States Staff. *Wild Neighbors: The Humane Approach to Living with Wildlife.* Washington, D.C.: Humane Society of the United States, 2007.

Ireland, Kenneth. *Big Cats.* New York: Oxford University Press, 2009.

ZOOS

Hosey, Geoff, Vicky Melfi, and Sheila Pankhurst. *Zoo Animals: Behaviour, Management and Welfare.* New York: Oxford University Press, 2009.

Lee, Keekok. *Zoos: A Philosophical Tour.* New York: Palgrave Macmillan, 2006.

Mee, Benjamin. *We Bought a Zoo: The Amazing True Story of a Young Family, a Broken Down Zoo, and the 200 Wild Animals that Changed Their Lives Forever.* New York: Perseus Books, 2009.

Zoehfeld, Kathleen Weidner. *Wild Lives: A History of People and Animals of the Bronx Zoo.* New York: Random House, 2006.

B. PERIODICALS

Magazines, newspapers, membership bulletins, and newsletters may be helpful for finding information about a specific job category, locating a job in a specific field, or gaining insight into what certain jobs entail.

As with the books in the previous section, this list should serve as a starting point. Due to space limitations, there are many periodicals that are not listed. Periodicals also tend to come and go. Look in your local library, on the Internet, and in newspaper and magazine shops for other periodicals of interest. Don't forget to check out relevant trade associations as they generally have their own publications as well.

ANIMALS IN THE MEDIA

Animal Agents Newsletter
Animal Agents
P.O. Box 555
Kingsburg, CA 93631
Phone: (559) 960-6899
http://www.animalagents.org

ANIMAL RIGHTS AND ANIMAL ADVOCACY

Action Line
Friends of Animals
777 Post Road
Suite 205
Darien, CT 06820
Phone: (203) 656-1522
Fax: (203) 656-0267

E-mail: info@friendsofanimals.org
http://www.friendsofanimals.org

Activate for Animals
American Anti-Vivisection Society
801 Old York Road
Suite 204
Jenkintown, PA 19046
Phone: (215) 887-0816
E-mail: aavs@aavs.org
http://www.aavs.org

Alley Cat Action
Alley Cat Allies
7920 Norfolk Avenue
Suite 600
Bethesda, MD 20814
Phone: (240) 482-1980
Fax: (240) 482-1990
E-mail: alleycat@alleycat.org
http://www.alleycat.org

AnimaLessons
American Society for the Prevention of Cruelty to
    Animals
424 East 92nd Street
New York, NY 10128
Phone: (212) 876-7700
E-mail: shonalib@aspca.org
http://www.aspca.org

The Animals' Advocate
Animal Legal Defense Fund
170 East Cotati Avenue
Cotati, CA 94931
Phone: (707) 795-2533
Fax: (707) 795-7280
E-mail: info@aldf.org
http://www.aldf.org

Animal Rights Coalition Newsletter
Animal Rights Coalition
317 West 48th Street
Minneapolis, MN 55419
Phone: (612) 822-6161
E-mail: animalrightscoalition@msn.com
http://www.animalrightscoalition.com

Animal Times Magazine
People for the Ethical Treatment of Animals
501 Front Street
Norfolk, VA 23510

Phone: (757) 622-7382
Fax: (757) 622-0457
E-mail: info@peta.org
http://www.peta.org

The Animals Voice Magazine
1354 East Avenue
#R-252
Chico, CA 95926
Phone: (800) 828-6423
E-mail: 4rights@animalsvoice.com
http://www.animalsvoice.com

Anti-Cruelty Magazine
Anti-Cruelty Society
157 West Grand Avenue
Chicago, IL 60610
Phone: (312) 644-8338
Fax: (312) 644-3878
E-mail: info@anticruelty.org
http://www.anticruelty.org

ASPCA Action
American Society for the Prevention of Cruelty to
    Animals
424 East 92nd Street
New York, NY 10128
Phone: (212) 876-7700
E-mail: shonalib@aspca.org
http://www.aspca.org

ASPCA News Alert
American Society for the Prevention of Cruelty to
    Animals
424 East 92nd Street
New York, NY 10128
Phone: (212) 876-7700
E-mail: shonalib@aspca.org
http://www.aspca.org

AWI Quarterly
Animal Welfare Institute
900 Pennsylvania Avenue, SE
Washington, DC 20003
Phone: (202) 337-2332
Fax: (202) 446-2131
E-mail: awi@awionline.org
http://www.awionline.org

The CASH Courier
Committee To Abolish Sport Hunting (CASH)
P.O. Box 13815

Las Cruces, NM 88013
Phone: (575) 640-7372
E-mail: cash@abolishsporthunting.com
http://www.all-creatures.org/cash

Feral Cat Activist
Alley Cat Allies
7920 Norfolk Avenue
Suite 600
Bethesda, MD 20814
Phone: (240) 482-1980
Fax: (240) 482-1990
E-mail: alleycat@alleycat.org
http://www.alleycat

For the Animals
People for Animal Rights
P.O. Box 8707
Kansas City, MO 64114
Phone: (816) 767-1199
E-mail: parinfo@parkc.org
http://www.parkc.org

HSUS News
Humane Society of the United States
2100 L Street, NW
Washington, DC 20037
Phone: (202) 452-1100
http://www.hsus.org

International Society for Animal Rights—Report
International Society For Animal Rights
965 Griffin Pond Road
Clarks Summit, PA 18411
Phone: (570) 586-2200
Fax: (570) 586-9580
E-mail: contact@isaronline.org
http://www.isaronline

Sanctuary: Farm Sanctuary's Compassionate Quarterly
Farm Sanctuary
P.O. Box 150
Watkins Glen, NY 14891
Phone: (607) 583-2225
Fax: (607) 583-2041
E-mail: info@farmsanctuary.org
http://www.farmsanctuary.org

The True Nature Network Newsletters
The True Nature Network
P.O. Box 20672

Colombus Circle Station
New York, NY 10023
E-mail: info@truenaturenetwork.org
http://www.truenaturenetwork.org/newsletters.html

ANTI-VIVISECTION

AV
American Anti-Vivisection Society
801 Old York Road
Suite 201
Jenkintown, PA 19046
Phone: (215) 887-0816
E-mail: aavs@aavs
http://www.aavs.org

AQUARIUMS

Aquarium Fish International
FishChannel.com
P.O. Box 6050
Mission Viejo, CA 92690
Phone: (949) 855-8822
Fax: (949) 855-3045
http://www.fishchannel.com/affc_portal.aspx

EDUCATION

The Packrat
Association of Professional Humane Educators
c/o The Latham Foundation
Latham Plaza Building
1826 Clement Avenue
Alameda, CA 94501
E-mail: aphe@aphe.org
http://aphe.org

EXOTIC PETS

Journal of Exotic Pet Medicine
Elsevier Inc.
1600 John F. Kennedy Boulevard
Philadelphia, PA 19103
Phone: (215) 239-3733
Fax: (215) 239-3734
E-mail: healthpermissions@elsevier.com
http://www.exoticpetmedicine.com

GROOMERS

Groomer to Groomer
American Mobile Groomers Association

c/o Barkleigh Management Group
970 West Trindle Road
Mechanicsburg, PA 17055
Phone: (717) 691-3388
E-mail: info@amgroomers.com
http://www.amgroomers.com

HORSE RACING

Daily Racing Form
Daily Racing Form LLC
708 Third Avenue
12th Floor
New York, NY 10017
Phone: (212) 366-7600
http://www.drf.com

Hoof Beats
United States Trotting Association
750 Michigan Avenue
Columbus, OH 43215
Phone: (614) 224-2291
Fax: (614) 222-6791
http://www.ustrotting.com

Horse Illustrated
Bowtie, Inc.
2401 Beverly Boulevard
P.O. Box 57900
Los Angeles, CA 90057
Phone: (213) 385-2222
Fax: (213) 385-8565
E-mail: adtraffic@bowtieinc.com
http://www.bowtieinc.com

The National Horseman
16101 North 82nd Street
Suite 10
Scottsdale, AZ 85260
Phone: (480) 922-5202
Fax: (480) 922-5212
E-mail: info@tnh1865.com
http://www.tnh1865.com

Thoroughbred Times
Thoroughbred Times Company
2008 Mercer Road
Lexington, KY 40511
Phone: (859) 260-9800
Fax: (859) 260-9812
E-mail: letters@thoroughbredtimes.com
http://www.thoroughbredtimes.com

MARKETING

Direct Marketing
Hoke Communications
224 Seventh Street
Garden City, NY 11530
Phone: (516) 746-6700
Fax: (516) 294-8141
http://directmarketingmag.com

Journal of Marketing
American Marketing Association
311 South Wacker Drive
Suite 5800
Chicago, IL 60606
Phone: (312) 542-9000
Fax: (312) 542-9001
E-mail: info@ama.org
http://www.marketingpower.com

MEDIA

Bacon's Media Directories
Cision US
332 South Michigan Avenue
Chicago, IL 60604
Phone: (866) 639-5087
E-mail: info.us@cision.com
http://www.us.cision.com

Broadcasting and Cable
Reed Business Information
360 Park Avenue South
New York, NY 10010
Phone: (646) 746-6400
Fax: (646) 746-7131
http://www.reedbusiness.com

PartyLine: The Weekly Roundup of Media Placement Opportunities
PartyLine Publishing
35 Sutton Place
New York, NY 10022
Phone: (212) 755-3487
Fax: (212) 755-4859
E-mail: byarmon@ix.netcom.com
http://www.partylinepublishing.com

PETS

Cat Fancy
BowTie, Inc.
P.O. Box 6050

Mission Viejo, CA 92690
Phone: (949) 855-8822
Fax: (949) 855-3045
E-mail: letters@catfancy.com
http://www.catchannel.com/cfcc_portal.aspx

Colleen Paige's Pet Home Magazine
Colleen Paige, LLC
P.O. Box 2061
Kingston, WA 98346
E-mail: editor@pethomemagazine.com
http://www.pethomemagazine.com

Dog Fancy
BowTie, Inc.
P.O. Box 6050
Mission Viejo, CA 92690
Phone: (949) 855-8822
Fax: (949) 855-3045
E-mail: barkback@dogfancy.com
http://www.dogchannel.com

Dog World
BowTie, Inc.
P.O. Box 6050
Mission Viejo, CA 92690
Phone: (949) 855-8822
Fax: (949) 855-3045
E-mail: letters@dogworld.com
http://www.dogchannel.com

Healthy Pet Magazine
7777 Center Avenue
Suite 350
Huntington Beach, CA 92647
Phone: (877) 596-1919
http://thinkpets.com

Modern Dog
Modern Dog Inc.
343 Railway Street
Suite 202
Vancouver, BC V6A 1A4
Canada
Phone: (604) 734-3131
Fax: (604) 734-3031
E-mail: info@moderndogmagazine.com
http://www.moderndogmagazine.com

Tame Pet
Hudson-Bryce, LLC
219 West Commercial Street
Springfield, MO 65803

Phone: (417) 830-8121
E-mail: editor@tamepetmag.com
http://tamepetmag.com

Whole Dog Journal
Belvoir Publications
P.O. Box 1349
Oroville, CA 95965
http://www.whole-dog-journal.com

PUBLIC RELATIONS AND PUBLICITY

Bulldog Reporter
Infocom Group
124 Linden Street
Oakland, CA 94607
Phone: (510) 596-9300
E-mail: bulldog@infocomgroup.com
http://www.bulldogreporter.com

Community Relations Report
Joe Williams Communications
P.O. Box 924
Bartlesville, OK 74005
Phone: (918) 336-2267

Lifestyle Media Relations Reporter
Infocom Group
124 Linden Street
Oakland, CA 94607
Phone: (510) 596-9300
E-mail: bulldog@infocomgroup.com
http://www.bulldogreporter.com

PR Daily
Lawrence Ragan Communications
111 East Wacker Drive
Chicago, IL 60601
Phone: (312) 861-3592
http://www.ragan.com/Main/Home.aspx

PR Week
Haymarket Media
114 West 26th Street
New York, NY 10001
Phone: (646) 638-6000
Fax: (646) 638-6114
http://www.haymarket.com

SANCTUARIES

American Sanctuary Association Newsletter
American Sanctuary Association

2308 Chatfield Drive
Las Vegas, NV 89128
Phone: (702) 804-8562
Fax: (702) 804-8561
E-mail: asarescue@aol.com
http://www.asaanimalsanctuaries.org

VETERINARIANS

American Journal of Veterinary Research
American Veterinary Medical Association
1931 North Meacham Road
Suite 100
Schaumburg, IL 60173
Phone: (800) 248-2862
Fax: (847) 925-1329
E-mail: avmainfo@avma.org
http://www.avma.org

California Veterinarian
California Veterinary Medical Association
1400 River Park Drive
Sacramento, CA 95815
Phone: (916) 649-0599
Fax: (916) 646-9156
E-mail: staff@cvma.net
http://www.cvma.net/doc.asp?id=3233

Journal of the American Veterinary Medical Association
American Veterinary Medical Association
1931 North Meacham Road
Suite 100
Schaumburg, IL 60173
Phone: (847) 925-8070
Fax: (847) 925-1329
E-mail: avmainfo@avma.org
http://www.avma.org

Texas Veterinarian
Texas Veterinary Medical Association
8104 Exchange Drive
Austin, TX 78754
Phone: (512) 452-4224
Fax: (512) 452-6633
E-mail: info@tvma.org
http://www.tvma.org

VETERINARY TECHNICIANS AND TECHNOLOGISTS

The NAVTA Journal
National Association of Veterinary Technicians in America
1666 K Street, NW
Suite 260
Washington, DC 20006
Phone: (703) 740-8737
Fax: (202) 449-8560
E-mail: navta@navta.net
http://www.navta.net

ZOOS

Animal Keeper's Forum
American Association of Zoo Keepers
3601 Southwest 29th Street
Suite 133
Topeka, KS 66614
Phone: (785) 273-9149
http://aazk.org

AZA Communique
Association of Zoos and Aquariums
8403 Colesville Road
Suite 710
Silver Spring, MD 20910
Phone: (301) 562-0777
Fax: (301) 562-0888
E-mail: g.e.n.e.r.a.l.i.n.q.u.i.r.y@aza.org
http://www.aza.org

Journal of Zoo and Wildlife Medicine
American Association of Zoo Veterinarians
581705 White Oak Road
Yulee, FL 32097
Phone: (904) 225-3275
Fax: (904) 225-3289
E-mail: aazvorg@aol.com
http://zoowildlifejournal.com

Smithsonian ZooGoer
Friends of the National Zoo
P.O. Box 37012
Washington, DC 20013
Phone: (202) 633-4470
E-mail: nationalzoo@nzp.si.edu
http://nationalzoo.si.edu/Publications/ZooGoer

Zoo Biology
John Wiley and Sons
111 River Street
Hoboken, NJ 07030
Phone: (201) 748-6000
Fax: (201) 748-6088
E-mail: info@wiley.com
http://www3.interscience.wiley.com/cgi-bin/jhome/35728

Zoo Guide
Greater Los Angeles Zoo Association
5333 Zoo Drive
Los Angeles, CA 90027
Phone: (323) 644-4200
Fax: (323) 644-4720
E-mail: webmaster@lazoo.org
http://www.lazoo.org/glaza

INDEX

ABOUT THE AUTHOR

Shelly Field is a nationally recognized motivational speaker, career expert, stress management specialist, personal career and life coach, and author of more than 35 best-selling books in the business and career fields.

Her books help people find careers in a wide variety of areas, including the hospitality, music, sports, and communications industries, casinos and casino hotels, advertising and public relations, theater, the performing arts and entertainment, animal rights, heath care, writing, and art. She is a frequent guest on local, regional, and national radio, cable, and television talk, information, and news shows and has been the subject of numerous print interviews for articles and news stories.

Field is a featured speaker at conferences, conventions, expos, corporate functions, spouse programs, employee training and development sessions, career fairs, casinos, and events nationwide. A former comedienne, she adds a humorous spin whether speaking on empowerment; motivation; stress management; staying positive; the power of laughter; careers; attracting, retaining, and motivating employees; or customer service. Her popular presentations, "STRESS BUSTERS: Beating the Stress in your Work and Your Life" and The De-Stress Express," are favorites around the country.

A career consultant to businesses, educational institutions, employment agencies, women's groups and individuals, Field is sought out by executives, celebrities, and sports figures for personal and career coaching and stress management.

In her role as a corporate consultant to businesses throughout the country, she provides assistance with human resources issues, such as attracting, retaining, and motivating employees, customer-service training, and stress management in the workplace

President and CEO of the Shelly Field Organization, a public relations, marketing, and management firm handling national clients, Shelly has represented celebrities in the sports, music, and entertainment industries, as well as authors, businesses, and corporations.

For media inquiries, information about personal appearances, seminars, workshops, stress management, or personal coaching, please contact the **Shelly Field Organization** at P.O. Box 437, Syracuse, NY 13214 or visit Shelly on the Web at www.shellyfield.com.